D1521107

Living and Value

Toward a Constructive Postmodern Ethics

Frederick Ferré

State University of New York Press

Published by
State University of New York Press, Albany

For information, address State University of New York Press,
90 State Street, Suite 700, Albany, NY 12207

Production by Michael Haggett
Marketing by Fran Keneston

Library of Congress Cataloging-in-Publication Data

Ferré, Frederick.
    Living and value : toward a constructive postmodern ethics / Frederick Ferré.
        p. cm. — (SUNY series in constructive postmodern thought)
    Includes bibliographical references and index.
    ISBN 0-7914-5059-1 (alk. paper) — ISBN 0-7914-5060-0 (pbk. : alk. paper)
    1. Ethics. 2. Postmodernism. I. Title. II. Series.

BJ1012.F47 2001
170—dc21

                                                            00-066069

10   9   8   7   6   5   4   3   2   1

To my teachers, who helped show me how
values can be criticized and helped to grow

CONTENTS

PART TWO
ETHICS AND RELIGION

PART THREE
ETHICS AND SOCIETY

PREFACE

Completion of a book like this is for any author a great satisfaction, the outcome (in A. N. Whitehead's language) of a prolonged "concrescence." That is, from an indefinite range of possibilities begging to be considered, compared, evaluated—many eliminated—some propositions have been woven together in the author's best effort for harmony, and, by application of physical and mental energy, have been actualized on paper. What once was ideal and infinite is now real and limited. The limitations are obvious, but finitude is always the price paid for actuality. The satisfaction rises from the fact that what once did not exist now does.

For me, the satisfaction of completing this book feels like no other I have finished. Because it is the final book of a trilogy, the equation has obviously changed. But the multiplier is somehow far more than merely three. So much interacting complexity makes for a geometrical, rather than an arithmetic, outcome. Can we speak of "joy cubed"? Probably not. But the inclination is strong.

The trilogy project defines my decade of the 1990s. My appointment as Research Professor in 1988 allowed me the time to dream big dreams. The larger framework was dreamt by 1991. Contracts for all three volumes were signed in 1992. This was the period of what (continuing the Whiteheadian metaphor) could be considered "reversion" while I sorted out and chose my ideal goals. Then came the challenge to maintain the "subjective aim," harnessing the energy needed to make the goals actual. *Being and Value* appeared in 1996; *Knowing and Value* was published in 1998; now, with the present volume, metaphysics and epistemology have been made concrete in ethics.

Ethics was not absent from the first two volumes, but here it takes center stage. After the first chapter, which sets the problem of ethics in general, comes part one, "Ethics," which I begin with a survey of the history of ethics and ethical theory from their very beginnings in biological advantage and social expectation. Then come two chapters dealing with the epistemology and metaphysics, respectively, behind ethics. Chapter 3, "Ethics and Knowing," applies the conclusions on epistemology reached in the second volume of this trilogy, showing that ethical skepticism is not required on the richer, ecological understanding of knowing I proposed there. And chapter 4, "Ethics and Being," addresses the question of ethical realism in the context of the metaphysical overview presented in volume one.

Mentioning these earlier books should not, I hope, put anyone off. One of my main aims, while writing the present volume, has been to welcome and include any reader who may be starting with me here. I have worked hard to make sure that the first two volumes are not necessary for understanding this one. But for those who come with those books in mind, the context for this book will already be set. Any newcomer who feels the need for more richness of connection, historical or systematic, is invited to take a more leisurely trip through the underlying metaphysics and epistemology in *Being and Value* and *Knowing and Value*, respectively.

In view of those earlier volumes, one aspect of my organization of part one may strike some readers as a bit odd. After my narrative chapter on the history of ethics, I turn immediately in chapter 3 to epistemology, only afterward in chapter 4 engaging metaphysics directly. But the trilogy as a whole begins with metaphysics and only later turns to epistemology! Substantively, in those two volumes, I make it clear that I believe issues of Being come first, and that what we can claim to know depends on what kind of knowers we are and what there is to be known. As a consequence of these beliefs, I contemplated reversing the sequence of these chapters, starting once more with metaphysics. But I decided to take on the challenge of the present order of exposition for two main reasons: first, in order to tie my alternative more naturally to most readers' questions, given the dominance of epistemology in modern philosophy; and second, even more important for me, to give myself a chance to shape a positive ethical construct in chapter 3 by which to illustrate in chapter 4 the many points at which ethics depends on metaphysical assumptions, explicit or implicit.

Part two, "Ethics and Religion," shows how ethics depends on a religious context, too, at least on my proffered definition of "religion" as primarily a value phenomenon. I resist any dissolution of ethics into religion, or any reduction of religion to ethics. Even though both are essentially practical phenomena, they are distinguishable and sometimes even in tension with one another. Still, ethical meaning depends on prior context supplied by value-drenched images providing (*a*) conceptual definiteness for what is basically so, and (*b*) guidance as to what is ultimately important. These images, discussed in chapter 5, need not be "holy" or "spiritual." They can be austerely materialist and still, in my sense, provide a functioning religious world model. In chapter 6, I take up the question of God in this connection, as central to a major type of religious world model long fascinating in our culture and beyond. Also vital to the context of ethics is an understanding of the fundamental status of ugliness and evil, and what attitudes and actions are appropriate to take towards instances when we encounter them. This is the role of chapter 7.

Part three, "Ethics and Society," applies maxims from the ethics of personalistic organicism to three major domains. First, in chapter 8, I portray nature and culture in a continuous way, intending to avoid both Scylla, the reduction usually associated with forms of social Darwinism, and Charybdis, the sharp breaks often introduced between "human" and "environmental" ethics. Second, in chapter 9, I explore technological ethics, considering several technological examples (drawn from each of the major domains of human practical interests) for their suitability in a postmodern world—a world that could be embraced on the principles of personalistic organicism. Finally, in chapter 10, I apply these principles to economics and governance, that is, to "politics" broadly conceived. I end not with easy optimism, which is ruled out by the inevitability of ugliness and evil in the nature of things, but on a note of hope, which is permitted by the worldview I have advanced.

It is hard to know just whom to single out as inspirers of that worldview and therefore for the very idea of the trilogy through which I have tried to express it. Although the 1990s were defined for me as the decade of this work, the trilogy's roots go much further back into childhood influences from my theologian father and my literary mother. And, of course, they go back to Alfred North Whitehead, introduced to me through his *Science and the Modern World*, a gift from my father while I was still in high school. My teachers in college and graduate school, to whom this volume is dedicated, deserve major thanks for requiring me to grow in judgment as well as learning. They were also the ones who led me to Ludwig Wittgenstein, whose later views on language and its role in life are central both to my epistemology and to my understanding of norms. There are other favorites, like William James, who reminds us always to remember the "cash value" in experience of what we are thinking. Some friendly philosophical contemporaries also played a strong role in the formation of my thinking, through their writings or in personal conversations, or both. Some of these—only a sample but a significant cadre—are: George Allan, John B. Cobb, Jr., Joseph Grange, David Ray Griffin, Jay McDaniel, Robert Neville, Larry L. Rasmussen, Nicolas Rescher, and Stephen Toulmin. As I write these names, I am reminded of many more. It is impossible to list them all. My whole life and career are implicit in the gradual concrescence of the project as a whole.

Much easier is expressing specific thanks to the various helpful individuals who have contributed to improving this volume. David Orr, at Oberlin College, generously answered my request for details on the Adam Joseph Lewis Center for Environmental Studies, which has a place of honor in my pantheon of wise technologies. Donald Sherburne, noted Whitehead scholar, kindly helped trace a quotation I could not find on my own. Frank Golley, of the Institute of Ecology at the University of Georgia, gave chapter 8 the benefit of his expert scientific eye. And in this connection I wish to acknowledge the *Grolier Multimedia Encyclopedia* (through various annual editions culminating in the Year 2000 edition), whose articles guided me on many factual details. Where other references are not explicitly given in such cases, I used the faithful *Grolier*.

Two University of Georgia colleagues from the Department of Philosophy, Clark Wolf and John Granrose (the latter now emeritus), read Part One and gave it the benefit of their gracious, understanding critiques. I am thankful for their expertise and even more for their friendship and generous support. A group of students who were members of the last seminar I taught before retirement have also contributed suggestions, all of which I have welcomed, considered, and in most cases accepted. These former students are: Derek Bowman, Joseph Council, Jesse Griffin, Christina Hart, Clay Hawkins, Nathan Segars, and Mark Taormina. They carefully read chapters for no reward in academic credit and on three occasions came to my home for nights of "dinner and discussion" that turned out to be shining examples of what philosophy seminars should be. Another former student, Dr. Bethe Segars McRae, who read and helpfully commented on the first two volumes of this trilogy, also read much of this one, despite the distractions of a newly arrived daughter, a postdoctoral program, and many other obligations. To all these generous persons, my heartfelt thanks.

Not exactly a "person" but still an important factor in the creation of this and the previous books is my curly-haired, black and tan, mixed-breed dog, Weibi, whose regular need for outings provided me with quiet times for reflection on what the next day's "phase of concrescence" needed to include. Readers of earlier volumes will recognize in her the source of examples, too. Thank you, Weibi. I can hardly picture the process of writing these books without our walks.

"Weibi" is Bavarian slang for "little woman," which brings me to "Big Weibi," my wife. Barbara is not Bavarian but is very German. She has been a huge support, not just of this book but of the whole trilogy project from its inception to its completion. This was not a small matter. For years we have had to bend vacation schedules and other practical matters to the demands of this seemingly endless effort. She has also cheerfully maintained two households, facilitating a writing schedule divided between Athens, Georgia, where books abound, and Highlands, North Carolina, where cool summer breezes fan an author's fevered brow. And every morning, in either setting, she has accepted the job of defending my writing time from the infinite supply of distractions that life offers. She also has lent a willing ear to passages that worried me and needed to be read aloud to an intelligent companion. Whenever she stopped me, it was to my benefit. When she was content, I could be too.

Finally, my thanks go again to my gifted editorial assistant, Mona Freer. She can read both for the larger meaning of a passage and at the same time spot minute flaws in diction or typography. Many can do one or the other; Mona does both exceedingly well. She has seen me through all three books and has left her stamp (and her indexes) on each. I realize, now that the project is over, that I am going to miss our editorial conferences. I have learned much from them.

"Now that the project is over," the once subjective concrescent process becomes, in Whiteheadian language, "superjective." That is, it becomes an actuality in the physical-cultural environment, available as an ingredient for other, future concrescences. The baby is born and eventually toddles off to make new adventures. May those future adventures of ideas—whether undertaken in agreement or in vigorous dissent—bring experiences of satisfaction for those who engage in them! The creative process certainly brought joy to this author.

Frederick Ferré
Highlands, North Carolina

INTRODUCTION TO SUNY SERIES IN CONSTRUCTIVE POSTMODERN THOUGHT*

The rapid spread of the term *postmodern* in recent years witnesses to a growing dissatisfaction with modernity and to an increasing sense that the modern age not only had a beginning but can have an end as well. Whereas the word *modern* was almost always used until quite recently as a word of praise and as a synonym for *contemporary*, a growing sense is now evidenced that we can and should leave modernity behind—in fact, that we must if we are to avoid destroying ourselves and most of the life on our planet.

Modernity, rather than being regarded as the norm for human society toward which all history has been aiming and into which all societies should be ushered—forcibly if necessary—is instead increasingly seen as an aberration. A new respect for the wisdom of traditional societies is growing as we realize that they have endured for thousands of years and that, by contrast, the existence of modern civilization for even another century seems doubtful. Likewise, *modernism* as a worldview is less and less seen as the Final Truth, in comparison with which all divergent worldviews are automatically regarded as "superstitious." The modern worldview is increasingly relativized to the status of one among many, useful for some pur-poses, inadequate for others.

Although there have been antimodern movements before, beginning perhaps near the outset of the nineteenth century with the Romanticists and the Luddites, the rapidity with which the term *postmodern* has become widespread in our time suggests that the antimodern sentiment is more extensive and intense than before, and also that it includes the sense that modernity can be successfully overcome only by going beyond it, not by attempting to return to a premodern form of existence. Insofar as a common element is found in the various ways in which the term is used, *postmodernism* refers to a diffuse

---

*The present version of this introduction is slightly different from the first version, which was contained in the volumes that appeared prior to 2000. My thanks to Catherine Keller and Edward Carlos Munn for helpful suggestions.

sentiment rather than to any common set of doctrines—the sentiment that humanity can and must go beyond the modern.

Beyond connoting this sentiment, the term *postmodern* is used in a confusing variety of ways, some of them contradictory to others. In artistic and literary circles, for example, postmodernism shares in this general sentiment but also involves a specific reaction against "modernism" in the narrow sense of a movement in artistic-literary circles in the late nineteenth and early twentieth centuries. Postmodern architecture is very different from postmodern literary criticism. In some circles, the term *postmodern* is used in reference to that potpourri of ideas and systems sometimes called *new age metaphysics*, although many of these ideas and systems are more premodern than postmodern. Even in philosophical and theological circles, the term *postmodern* refers to two quite different positions, one of which is reflected in this series. Each position seeks to transcend both *modernism*, in the sense of the worldview that has developed out of the seventeenth-century Galilean-Cartesian-Baconian-Newtonian science, and *modernity*, in the sense of the world order that both conditioned and was conditioned by this worldview. But the two positions seek to transcend the modern in different ways.

Closely related to literary-artistic postmodernism is a philosophical postmodernism inspired variously by physicalism, Ludwig Wittgenstein, Martin Heidegger, a cluster of French thinkers—including Jacques Derrida, Michel Foucault, Gilles Deleuze, and Julia Kristeva—and certain features of American pragmatism.* By the use of terms that arise out of particular segments of this movement, it can be called *deconstructive, relativistic,* or *eliminative* postmodernism. It overcomes the modern worldview through an anti-worldview, deconstructing or even entirely eliminating various concepts that have generally been thought necessary for a worldview, such as self, purpose, meaning, a real world, givenness, reason, truth as correspondence, universally valid norms, and divinity. While motivated by ethical and emancipatory concerns, this type of postmodern thought tends to issue in relativism. Indeed, it

---

*The fact that the thinkers and movements named here are said to have inspired the deconstructive type of postmodernism should not be taken, of course, to imply that they have nothing in common with constructive postmodernists. For example, Wittgenstein, Heidegger, Derrida, and Deleuze share many points and concerns with Alfred North Whitehead, the chief inspiration behind the present series. Furthermore, the actual positions of the founders of pragmatism, especially William James and Charles Peirce, are much closer to Whitehead's philosophical position—see the volume in this series entitled *The Founders of Constructive Postmodern Philosophy: Peirce, James, Bergson, Whitehead, and Hartshorne*—than they are to Richard Rorty's so-called neopragmatism, which reflects many ideas from Rorty's explicitly physicalistic period.

seems to many thinkers to imply nihilism.* It could, paradoxically, also be called *ultramodernism*, in that its eliminations result from carrying certain modern premises—such as the sensationist doctrine of perception, the mechanistic doctrine of nature, and the resulting de-nial of divine presence in the world—to their logical conclusions. Some critics see its deconstructions or eliminations as leading to self-referential inconsistencies, such as "performative self-contradictions" between what is said and what is presupposed in the saying.

The postmodernism of this series can, by contrast, be called *revisionary, constructive*, or—perhaps best—*reconstructive*. It seeks to overcome the modern worldview not by eliminating the possibility of worldviews (or "metanarratives") as such, but by constructing a postmodern worldview through a revision of modern premises and traditional concepts in the light of inescapable presuppositions of our various modes of practice. That is, it agrees with deconstructive postmodernists that a massive deconstruction of many received concepts is needed. But its deconstructive moment, carried out for the sake of the presuppositions of practice, does not result in self-referential inconsistency. It also is not so totalizing as to prevent reconstruction. The reconstruction carried out by this type of postmodernism involves a new unity of scientific, ethical, aesthetic, and religious intuitions (whereas post-structuralists tend to reject all such unitive projects as "totalizing modern metanarratives"). While critical of many ideas often associated with modern science, it rejects not science as such but only that *scientism* in which the data of the modern natural sciences alone are allowed to contribute to the construction of our public worldview.

The reconstructive activity of this type of postmodern thought is not limited to a revised worldview. It is equally concerned with a postmodern *world* that will both support and be supported by the new worldview. A postmodern world will involve postmodern persons, with a postmodern spirituality, on the one hand, and a postmodern society, ultimately a postmodern global order, on the other. Going beyond the modern world will involve transcending its individualism, anthropocentrism, patriarchy, economism, consumerism, nationalism, and

---

*Peter Dews says that although Derrida's early work was "driven by profound ethical impulses," its insistence that no concepts were immune to deconstruction "drove its own ethical presuppositions into a penumbra of inarticulacy" (*The Limits of Disenchantment: Essays on Contemporary European Culture* [London, New York: Verso, 1995], 5). In his more recent thought, Derrida has declared an "emancipatory promise" and an "idea of justice" to be "irreducible to any deconstruction." Although this "ethical turn" in deconstruction implies its pulling back from a completely disenchanted universe, it also, Dews points out (6–7), implies the need to renounce "the unconditionality of its own earlier dismantling of the unconditional."

militarism. Reconstructive postmodern thought provides support for the ethnic, ecological, feminist, peace, and other emancipatory movements of our time, while stressing that the inclusive emancipation must be from the destructive features of modernity itself. However, the term *postmodern*, by contrast with *premodern*, is here meant to emphasize that the modern world has produced unparalleled advances, as Critical Theorists have emphasized, which must not be devalued in a general revulsion against modernity's negative features.

From the point of view of deconstructive postmodernists, this reconstructive postmodernism will seem hopelessly wedded to outdated concepts, because it wishes to salvage a positive meaning not only for the notions of selfhood, historical meaning, reason, and truth as correspondence, which were central to modernity, but also for notions of divinity, cosmic meaning, and an enchanted nature, which were central to premodern modes of thought. From the point of view of its advocates, however, this revisionary postmodernism is not only more adequate to our experience but also more genuinely postmodern. It does not simply carry the premises of modernity through to their logical conclusions, but criticizes and revises those premises. By virtue of its return to organicism and its acceptance of nonsensory perception, it opens itself to the recovery of truths and values from various forms of premodern thought and practice that had been dogmatically rejected, or at least restricted to "practice," by modern thought. This reconstructive postmodernism involves a creative synthesis of modern and premodern truths and values.

This series does not seek to create a movement so much as to help shape and support an already existing movement convinced that modernity can and must be transcended. But in light of the fact that those antimodern movements that arose in the past failed to deflect or even retard the onslaught of modernity, what reasons are there for expecting the current movement to be more successful? First, the previous antimodern movements were primarily calls to return to a premodern form of life and thought rather than calls to advance, and the human spirit does not rally to calls to turn back. Second, the previous antimodern movements either rejected modern science, reduced it to a description of mere appearances, or assumed its adequacy in principle. They could, therefore, base their calls only on the negative social and spiritual effects of modernity. The current movement draws on natural science itself as a witness against the adequacy of the modern worldview. In the third place, the present movement has even more evidence than did previous movements of the ways in which modernity and its worldview *are* socially and spiritually destructive. The fourth and probably most decisive difference is that the present movement is based on the awareness that *the continuation of modernity threatens the very survival of life on our planet*. This awareness, combined with the growing knowledge of the interdependence of the modern worldview with modernity's militarism, nuclearism, patriarchy, global apartheid, and ecological devastation, is providing an unprecedented impetus for people to see the evidence for a postmodern worldview and to envisage postmodern ways of relating to each other, the rest of nature, and the cosmos as a whole. For these reasons, the failure of the previous antimodern movements says little about the possible success of the current movement.

Advocates of this movement do not hold the naively utopian belief that the success of this movement would bring about a global society of universal and lasting peace, harmony and happiness, in which all spiritual problems, social conflicts, ecological destruction, and hard choices would vanish. There is, after all, surely a deep truth in the testimony of the world's religions to the presence of a transcultural proclivity to evil deep within the human heart, which no new paradigm, combined with a new economic order, new child-rearing practices, or any other social arrangements, will suddenly eliminate. Furthermore, it has correctly been said that "life is robbery": a strong element of competition is inherent within finite existence, which no social-political-economic-ecological order can overcome. These two truths, especially when contemplated together, should caution us against unrealistic hopes.

No such appeal to "universal constants," however, should reconcile us to the present order, as if it were thereby uniquely legitimated. The human proclivity to evil in general, and to conflictual competition and ecological destruction in particular, can be greatly exacerbated or greatly mitigated by a world order and its worldview. Modernity exacerbates it about as much as imaginable. We can therefore envision, without being naively utopian, a far better world order, with a far less dangerous trajectory, than the one we now have.

This series, making no pretense of neutrality, is dedicated to the success of this movement toward a postmodern world.

David Ray Griffin
Series Editor

1

How Should We Approach Ethics?

One of several strange things one notices on approaching ethics is the paradox of expertise. There are no universally recognized experts, but everyone acts as an expert. Some public figures, like the Pope, are revered by large numbers who suppose him to have special expertise in ethical matters, but at least equally large numbers (including even many among those who sincerely acknowledge the Pope as supreme leader of their church) disregard what he most earnestly says, for example, about birth control and female clergy. Obviously, they place their own ethical judgment over his, to his evident chagrin. How can this be, if he is the expert? We do not display this sort of behavior toward brain surgeons, aircraft captains, or bomb detonation crews.

If ethical questions could be dismissed as trivial, it would be easy to understand why people might not take them seriously enough to heed those who claim expertise. But this is far from the case. Ethical opinions have a felt importance that makes it doubly odd that people seem prepared to go against distinguished advice in favor of their own leadings. If the captain of an aircraft orders us to fasten our seat belts, we quickly fasten them. Among the jobs of aircraft captains is expertly judging likely levels of turbulence. If we know what is good for us, we follow instructions. This is only prudent. But do we really know "what is good" for us, or anyone, in a broader, ethical sense? How is it that we so often find people declining to defer to ethical authorities on the subject of what is ethically good and bad? The answer must be that ethical matters are too important to be left to experts. But this means that there are no experts in the sense that counts. If I follow you only if I first judge that it is right to follow, that makes *me* the expert of last resort. If I go along with you even when I sense I am wrong in so doing, I earn my uneasy conscience.

Still, it seems odd that ordinary individuals can sit confidently in the ethical judgment seat when they have omitted all the usual preparatory work to qualify as judge between purported experts. Experts in the usual sense are people who have earned credentials of some sort. Is there no way we can at least *improve* our ethical judgments, even if we decline the role of expert over others?

Another strange point to notice on approaching ethics is how ethical beliefs tend to function. All of our beliefs are invested with some degree of value to us (or we would take no notice of them), but ethical beliefs behave in strikingly different ways from most. They are far more resistant to challenge or change than other kinds. Take for an example an ordinary nonethical belief. If you believe that Moscow and Mombasa are in the same time zone, and I believe that Mombasa lies in the same time zone as Cairo but not in the same zone as Moscow, I may be convinced otherwise by consulting appropriate maps. Once I brush up on my geography, I shall acknowledge that all three are in the same zone, though I had been "just sure" that Moscow was one zone farther to the east. Ethical differences are different. There are no convenient ethical maps to consult; if authoritative texts are presented in lieu of maps, we still need to be prepared to accept the ethical authority of such purportedly authoritative texts. It is up to us, somehow, to authorize the authorities. This makes settling differences a qualitatively different matter from usual differences, even though we might not have been indifferent about those nonethical differences.

Moreover, with ethical differences we do not find it merely *harder* to come to agreement, it is also *riskier*. We often find that there is a flavor of *disapproval* underlying the discussion. If you believe that Mombasa is in the same time zone as Moscow and I do not, the difference of opinion may have some felt importance for me, but I do not disapprove of you personally for holding your view. Later, when I learn that I was wrong, I may be a little crestfallen at my previous ignorance, but I do not need to feel moral shame. I never felt personally threatened in my status as a "good person" by the disagreement while it lasted. Ethical disputes, however, are more likely to be laced with blame, even if unspoken. If you maintain, for example, that it should be your right to smoke in my company and I disagree, citing my right to lungs free from secondhand smoke, the discussion may remain polite, even jovial, but there is more involved than the airing of different opinions. The atmosphere may become heavy, even in the absence of lit cigarettes.

Perhaps what is hanging in the air belongs to the third area of strangeness in approaching ethics. It is the prospect of action. Ethical beliefs are not unique, of course, in having a behavioral component. A disposition to act under appropriate circumstances is an important part of the definition of normal belief. Often this may be expressed in a disposition to linguistic behavior, saying or affirming something when the context calls for it. In the case of my newfound belief that Mombasa is in the same time zone as Moscow, this is likely under most circumstances to be a verbal matter, but not entirely. If I plan to telephone someone in Mombasa, I may time my call differently if I believe that the other party is eight, not seven, hours ahead of me. And, if I should fly to Kenya from the capital of Russia, I shall then not be disposed to reset my watch at all.

Ethical matters are different, not merely in involving dispositions for action but in disposing us to organize actions at many interconnected levels. My disposition to object to the presence of your used smoke in my lungs ties into a web of many other beliefs and dispositions to behavior, ranging from etiquette and courtesy to deepest concerns about the value of life and the dignity of persons. Ethical beliefs engage individuals more centrally than most beliefs and also bear essentially on how our neighbors are expected to behave toward us and each other. These expectations are not merely *predictions*, as in more ordinary issues of life, but are also *norms* of expectation and cooperation which, when violated can justify moral blame. Further, this blame is directed against others—and (significantly) ourselves—when ethical expectations are disappointed.

This leads to the question of sincerity. In ordinary matters of belief we may judge whether a person sincerely believes something by observing the person's behavior under normally "triggering" conditions. If someone claims to believe that the stock market is about to crash but steadily buys new investments and passes up chances to sell, then questions of sincerity (or rationality) are appropriate. These questions appear also in ethics, but here there is added the further question of hypocrisy, an especially nasty flavor of insincerity. Action is always expected to be coordinated with words, but in ethics (and, significantly, religion) we find special accusations of hypocrisy reserved for discrepancies between profession and action.

Approaching ethics, therefore, is to be done with care and trepidation. In the following sections of this chapter, I shall try to sort out three sorts of key considerations, all interrelated. The first section looks at the extent to which we can improve ourselves as ethical thinkers. Though never "expert," in the sense of directing others with authority, we might at least aim at being responsible in handling ethical concepts and the facts that matter ethically. The second section explores the depth and relevance of emotion in ethical judgments. Thoughts are never isolated from feelings (Ferré 1998), but here, with due warning, I shall take them up sequentially. The final section will fold in the active dimension of ethics. Since we find ourselves to be living organisms, set in vast networks of relationships to others, human and nonhuman, action is never far from thought and feeling.

AS A WAY OF THINKING

To some it could come as a surprise that there might be such a thing as ethical *thinking* at all. They see the domain of ethics as a great shouting match between the deaf. There are, alas, too many examples of such hyperventilating contests in the contemporary world to dismiss the suggestion altogether. If ethical thinking—real *thinking*, not simply venting—is possible, what is it like?

It will come as no surprise to the readers of the previous two volumes of this trilogy that I see ethical thinking as properly assessed under exactly the same standards as good thinking in general. Thinking is thinking, whether the subject matter is metaphysics, epistemology, or the good. I have tried also to show the continuities between philosophical theorizing on such all-comprehensive topics, at one end of the spectrum, and theory making in other more limited topics, such as are found in the sciences or police detective work or even in ordinary daily problems, at the other end.

One of the two great maxims of good thinking in any domain is to make sure our logic is not flawed. This is not, as some complain, an external imposition on our freedom of thought; it is an internal empowerment for effective thought of any kind. It allows us our freedoms of thought. Logic is nothing other than methods we have learned that keep thinking on the rails. Jumping the tracks does not enhance a journey; it defeats it.

Ethical thinking, if it is not to defeat itself from the start, needs first to make sure that it is *consistent*. Self-contradiction radically confuses meaning. It can creep in, unawares, in several ways. One common route to self-confusion is to use a single word to express incompatible concepts, or concepts different enough to be capable of clashing. For example, the word "natural" is often found in ethical discourse, but it does not always function to express the same thought. Sometimes we may want to say that a practice is "unnatural" because it seems to us to go against the proper *natures* of the agents involved. Homosexuality is sometimes condemned because it "goes against our natures" as gender-differentiated creatures whose sex organs are adjusted quite obviously to accommodate one another. But there is another sense of "natural" in which the concept simply refers to whatever is found outside human culture, in *nature*. Then, when it is discovered that homosexual activity occurs outside human culture (among chimpanzees, birds, and rats, for example), in this second sense of the word, it must be classed as "natural." If the thinker unwarily had adopted as a premise the common view that "What is natural is *good* and what is unnatural is *evil* (i.e., not-good)," then such a thinker is in conceptual trouble. Homosexuality turns out to be both natural and unnatural, therefore both good and not-good. Thinking has jumped the rails. Both *A* and not-*A* seem necessary to assert, but they cannot both be asserted without destroying each other's claims to truth. No single judgment on homosexuality—or anything else—is possible, since from a set of propositions containing a contradiction, any and every conclusion can be drawn. Paradox has its place as goad and stimulus to thinking, but it affords no resting place.

We need to be consistent in our use of words, therefore, and careful in our delimiting of concepts, if we are to be effective ethical thinkers. But there is another kind of consistency that is especially key to ethical thinking. That is the kind of consistency that applies the same classification to an act or practice or character trait wherever it is found under like circumstances. The issue of "like circumstances" is a tangled one and will require some historical attention in the next chapter, but as a logical point it is fairly obvious. If stealing from a blind person's cup to pay for a pack of cigarettes is ethically disgusting when done by Jack, it makes no sense (all other things being equal) not to apply the same classification when done by Jill. To some extent the famous even-handedness of the "ethical point of view" is a function of conceptual consistency. There may, of course, be ethically extenuating circumstances even here. But unless these are convincingly brought forward, the stability of the meaning of the phrase "ethically disgusting" will be undermined and the path to clear thinking blocked.

I have not been discussing matters of high theory. Consistency is even more obviously a concern when gossamer strands of thought are flung far from ordinary activities and intuitions. But consistency is vital not only there; we must remember to keep our logic clear at all levels of abstraction. Using words always involves us in some degree of abstraction. As I showed in the previous volume, abstraction is inherently dangerous, since the fissure it opens between immediate actuality and ideal possibility lets error creep in. Dangerous or not, it is the soul of thinking and cannot be avoided (Ferré 1998, chaps. 9–10). The moral is to be extra careful. Concept formation and language use must constantly be subject to conscious scrutiny in ethical thinking—as everywhere else.

The internal requirement of consistency is just the beginning of respect for logic in ethical thinking. Much can be thought without contradiction but also without clear sense. Consistency, though vital, is only an entrance ticket to a theater of thought that must also *hang together*, internally, if it is to have any distinct shape or character. If I think "Today is Tuesday," and also "There are mice in the basement," there is no obvious contradiction between these two thoughts. They do not cancel each other out in the manner of contradictions; but, since completely out of relation to one another, they go nowhere, make no theory.

To do its work, then, ethical thinking will need to seek *coherence*. Coherence is the measure of how well thoughts hang together. It allows the thinker to pass from one idea to another and thereby to grasp a subject as a unity. Perfect wholeness or integrity of thinking is an ideal unreachable by human beings, but coherence provides a goal against which our actual efforts at conceptual connection can be measured. Coherence often operates by enrichment. Filling in, by either conceptual or causal connections, the logical spaces between previously unrelated thoughts can allow a whole picture gradually to appear, just as developing a photographic print, at first just scattered blotches, lets it, little by little, show a unified scene. If, for example, I add to the previously unrelated thoughts about Tuesday and mice the following: "Every Monday the Cheese Connoisseur Club dinner is held in the basement," and "On Sunday the clubhouse cat died," then something comprehensible starts to take shape. Ethical thinking, too, sometimes develops gradually by hitherto unconnected elements being linked. Cuts of veal, neatly packaged in cellophane, may at first seem to have no unpleasant associations, just conceptual relations with happy thoughts of schnitzel or scallopini, or the like. But, enriched by the fuller context of thoughts on how veal calves are currently constrained from birth and undernourished to keep their meat light-colored and tender, ethical considerations of various sorts—ideas about deliberate, systematic infliction of suffering on entities capable of feeling frustration and pain—may well arise. This is only a first pass, of course, and still more enrichment of the topic from the perspective of the meat industry and from animal welfare organizations will be needed before acceptable levels of coherence are reached.

Coherence does not rise from enrichment alone. Sometimes it is achieved through rearrangement. The pattern as a whole may be revolutionized, and a new pattern of connections may make for a more compelling unity than the partial one it replaces. Some mystery writers make entertaining use of this way of weaving and replacing coherences. All along, the evidence has seemed to be building against the parlor maid, but suddenly the brilliant detective rearranges everything to reveal the duchess as culprit. There need not be new evidence in order to achieve this rearrangement, though often there may be; and when there is, the method of enrichment and rearrangement work together. In ethical thinking, religious conversion can provide spectacular examples of rearranged coherences. At one moment Saul of Tarsus was breathing fire and brimstone against the young Christian churches, considering it his duty to root them out. At the next, everything was different. The conceptual unity framed by his new arrangement of thought was so strikingly incompatible with the old that he took a new name, Paul, and spent the rest of his life furthering the Christian cause.

Conceptual rearrangement need not be so complete or so dramatic, of course. But it is an important source of ethical change. For some years I smoked several packs of cigarettes daily and thought of myself as a smoker. Even on those scattered occasions when I genuinely tried to stop, the world seemed conceptually obvious as one in which I was essentially a smoker, just one currently (and uncomfortably) not at the moment indulging the habit. In the early 1960s, there came a crucial period when the conceptual pattern changed. Shocked by the publication of British medical findings even before the appearance of the first American Surgeon General's report, I found myself thinking of myself as "essentially a nonsmoker," just one still hooked on the weed. Once that rearranged coherence took place, the new picture greatly changed my sense of what I should do and so helped me overcome the physical addiction and keep me free from it ever since.

Consistency and coherence are immensely important internal standards for ethical thinking, but taken alone they are hollow. The second great maxim of good thinking, to balance the assurance that our logic is not flawed, is to make sure that our facts are accurate and complete. When I mentioned "enrichment" as one of the ways in which coherences are formed and reformed, I was already referring to something beyond good conceptual housekeeping. "Enrichment" is the introduction of data, evidence, the *applicability* of concepts to subject matter. Good thinking requires more than simple applicability. It requires as many relevant data as possible to be introduced concerning the subject matter. If one is to think well about a topic, the *whole* topic needs to be available for thought. Leaving relevant evidence aside can skew the whole picture. Therefore, in addition to consistency and coherence, there remains the demanding standard of *adequacy*.

Adequacy, like coherence, is an ideal. Human cognizers are limited by our organisms as to the ranges of information we can detect and recognize, thus limited in the domains for which we can construct concepts. Modern instrumentation has thrillingly extended our species' reach, but we have (and can have) literally no idea how much relevant information remains undetectable. This means that our judgments of "relevance" always need to be tentative, since what seems relevant evidence under one patterning of thought may seem quite otherwise under another. Contrariwise, what was dismissed as irrelevant under one picture of things can be of utmost relevance under another. Relevance, that is, is theory dependent; but theories are based on, and tested by, relevant evidence. This is circular, inevitably. For this reason, as well as the sheer impossibility of having access to all the information there is on any subject matter, perfect adequacy is out of reach.

It is still a most important built-in requirement of theorizing *about* anything, that our intellectual practice should come as close as possible to acknowledging and respecting all the data that might be concerned. Closing our minds to possibly important features of a situation, or (even worse) systematically downplaying or denying the significance of whole ranges of experience, such as moral intuition, feelings of obligation, stirrings of conscience, or the like, truncate ethical thought before it begins.

Naturally, not all items need to be taken at face value. As theoretical coherences form, some information will become more prominent, while some will be subordinated and understood in ways that might not be immediately apparent. But experience needs first to be allowed to resonate. If not, any coherences reached by thinking released from having to deal with all the evidence will be too easy. Verdicts, if reached by juries from whom relevant evidence has been kept, are suspect. Theories, when built on carefully sifted data, are no better.

In ethical thinking, as in all thinking, the two key ideals of coherence and adequacy pull against each other, further complicating the task of thinking well. The more strongly one leans toward adequacy—giving fair hearing to all data that may prove relevant—the heavier the task of forming a pattern showing coherence. Tight little coherences can thrive as long as adequacy is slighted. The hardest job for thinking is to remain open to the evidence while seeking to integrate it in a pattern that does it no violence. It is hard, but it is nonetheless our obligation as would-be thinkers—an obligation set by the goals of effective thinking itself, which to do its job needs acceptable levels of clarity in meaning (consistency), internal integrity (coherence), subject matter reference (applicability), and appropriate scope (adequacy).

Since the best we can do will never be perfect, and since our key standards pull us in opposite directions, it should be expected that a number of coherences will rise to "acceptable levels" in all these qualities, and that they will vie with one another. Pluralism of this sort is a consequence of the finite human condition. But pluralism is not to be equated with lazy relativism, according to which there is no better, no worse, in thinking. On the contrary, a position accepted within the context of principled pluralism needs to work hard to establish its credentials and defend, in respectful dialogue with other responsible thinkers, its unique blend of adequacy and coherence.

Approaching ethics as a way of thinking is open to judgments of better and worse, therefore. And inasmuch as the internal standards of thinking can be taught, there are ways to improve ourselves as ethical thinkers. We can learn to be careful with our concepts, concerned about factual accuracy and completeness, slow to shut off conversation with others who are in their way attempting to cover the same ground with different patterns in mind. We know we are not epistemologically perfect. Our thinking is always capable of improvement, and others may see what we have missed, whether regarding consistency in our use of concepts, coherence in our reasoning, or our theory's adequacy to the facts. Likewise, we may be able to help others see what they are missing, either by enriching their coherences with additional relevant material or by offering them a radically different way of turning idea fragments into whole vision.

These, as I have treated them for the most part, are *epistemological* obligations to the theoretical enterprise in general. But there is yet another important peculiarity of ethical thinking: that we find ourselves under distinctly *ethical* obligation to good epistemological practice when we take up ethical subject matter. There is something distinctly blameworthy about sloppy, uncaring intellectual conduct, especially when it purports to determine standards of right and wrong behavior, good and bad goals for life. Just as, in law, there is such a thing as "culpable ignorance," so, in approaching ethics as a way of thinking, we find such a thing as "culpable rationalization." Someone guilty of culpable ignorance should have known better, should have taken the trouble to gain the pertinent information. Someone guilty of culpable rationalization should have thought better, should have resisted the blandishment of inconsistent, incoherent, or inadequate patterns in ethical thought. Careless thinking in ethics, then, is not only an epistemological flaw; it is also a moral failure. We are, after all, the final authorizers of our authorities. This is a domain of personal responsibility we cannot duck. Under the limited epistemic circumstances it should now be clear why, indeed, we can never aspire to be ethical "experts" who may order others about, or do their thinking for them. But we can be judged ethically lacking if we fail to do all we can to keep our ethical thinking clear, comprehensive, and well-informed.

As a Way of Judging

It should be obvious already that the transition from thinking to judging in general is neither long nor difficult. They are intertwined from the start. There can be no thinking without judging. Not ethical (yet) but epistemological judgments are at the root of all concept construction and language use. In order to form and refine our concepts, we need continually to judge for ourselves whether something we seem to recognize as familiar is really a "good enough case" of the "same type of thing" so as to be classed with the others. Further, as we use words, we need to judge for ourselves whether the terms we hear and speak are managing to fall within the normal range of usage for public intelligibility. We need to certify our own conceptual performances, that is, even to reach the stage where dialogue, criticism, and improvement of such performances become possible (Ferré 1998, chap. 9).

The same holds for ethical concept construction and language use. We learn what "bad" means in the same general way we learn to understand "green." But, of course, there is a distinctive affective tone—a feeling or emotion—that goes with "bad," not found with "green."

Repeated associations and countless corrections go into acquiring normal conceptual/linguistic competence, across the entire range of human interests, shared in one's community, that have led to noticing and naming the regularly repeating aspects of experience. Judging that something is a certain color (e.g., green) requires a discriminating eye for recognizing distinct visual perceptions, as well as a sense of where, in the continuum of color experiences, one's language community on the average classifies perceptions of a certain recognizable quality. Judging that something has a certain ethical status (e.g., bad) requires similar, but higher-order, skills of recognizing characteristic social situations and a sense of how one's language community applies (again within a normal range lacking sharp boundaries) ethically evaluative terms to these situations.

As mentioned earlier, judging that a color term should be used gives quite a different feeling from judging that an ethical term applies. Both are truly *judgments*, inescapably personal when made, though in principle open to eventual public review, but the second is far more *judgmental*. It is in this second sense, in which ethics coordinates and expresses powerful feelings, that we can proceed to consider it a way of judging.

When I wrote at the end of the previous section that we could be "judged ethically lacking" for failure to think well about ethical matters, I meant that we could appropriately *blame* ourselves and others for doing *wrong* if we or they were to neglect key intellectual responsibilities. One important motive, indeed, for thinking carefully in ethics is to gain a surer sense of when to blame or praise. Moral praise and blame are strongly linked to emotion, even when there is nothing to be done. We can heap praise on Albert Schweitzer's selfless doctoring efforts at Lambaréné, though Schweitzer is in his grave and his medical methods are long since outmoded. Contrariwise, we can blame Adolph Hitler for the horrors of the Holocaust, even though such blaming fails to bring back a single Jew or Gypsy.

Emotion is intensely important in ethics. All the key words in the ethical vocabulary are loaded with affect. Feelings of "shame," "remorse," or "guilt" are, for better or for worse, part of most people's daily lives, causing discomfort ranging from nagging distraction to full incapacitation. Feelings of "indignation," "outrage," or "blame" may cause ulcers. *Should* one feel morally indignant at what seemed like unwarranted cruelty perpetrated by the boss on an innocent underling? This depends on whether it was properly judged to be cruelty, and rightly judged to be unwarranted. Sometimes feelings of outrage can be misdirected, as can feelings of guilt or shame. Ethics as a way of judging needs to be tied to ethics as a way of thinking if feelings are to be appropriately directed. Feelings of moral admiration or approval, after all, can transform a life. Chafings from injustice, strongly and widely enough felt, can overturn a society.

Thus far I have avoided the hackneyed question of "good," which has sparked endless philosophical debate. It will be enough here simply to point to the obvious, strong, positive feelings attached to whatever we judge to be worthy of being classified as good. We will see at a later time that it is interesting (and appropriate) that "good" is not exclusively an ethical term.

A distinctly ethical concept with powerful emotional force is "moral obligation." This phenomenon is inseparable from judgment—one must judge (or not) that one is under obligation—but sometimes, paradoxically, it may feel that one is more judged than judging. The character of this affect is such that one may feel not so much agent as patient, with moral obligation bearing down from outside. This may be linked to the felt conflict, often, between one's feelings of moral obligation and other feelings and preferences, making it painful and difficult to acknowledge one's obligations. It may also be linked to the profoundly social rooting of ethical life. At the start, at least, we learn the meaning of obligation, and some of its basic features, in the same way we learn to recognize the key characters and habits of the external world.

Moral obligation can be intensely felt, so much so that great sacrifices of personal well-being can be made on its behalf. Most of us are not moral heroes, but there is such a thing as heroism, going well beyond what could be considered normal duties. Concepts of moral obligations, like all concepts, are matters of averages on a normal curve without clear boundaries. Most people judge somewhere in the middle of the curve (which, of course, is what *makes* it the middle); however, we also recognize where the curve shades downward toward moral sleaze, and where it shades upward toward a point where most would find obligation unbearable, though certainly to be admired. Not everyone in a squad needs to feel obliged to jump on the live hand grenade that rolls into the midst of them. It would make no sense, anyway, for all the squad to pile on in a futile gesture of solidarity. All their individual lives are precious. Perhaps no one in the squad has a moral obligation to die for the others. There may be no strict duty here, for anyone present, to commit benevolent suicide. But if one member of the squad, in the moment of danger, acts so as to absorb the explosion and save the others, we judge that person as deserving extreme ethical approval. The others, who lived, need not feel guilt, since they did not fail in any normal obligation. They may feel guilt anyway (that would be a normal human reaction), but they can be shown—if they approach ethics as a way of thinking—that they need not, and probably should not if they are to make the most of the lives for which their friend sacrificed everything.

The intensity of felt moral obligation may be great, as in such cases of heroism, but it is possible to go even further, as it were, off the scale. Rarely, but sometimes, religious commandments can be felt so strongly as to overwhelm considerations of ethics. The classical case, meditated on at length by Søren Kierkegaard (Kierkegaard 1954), is that of Abraham, who was willing to violate every accepted ethical standard by luring to a deserted place, then preparing to murder, his innocent and dependent son, Isaac, in the conviction that this act would be a sacrifice commanded by and acceptable to his God. The fact that something intervened, that the ritual murder did not take place, is irrelevant to the frame of mind: Abraham felt his religious commitment so intensely that accepted fundamentals of morality could be swept aside in ecstatic devotion to what he judged to be the ultimate. We must not forget that his was, indeed, a judgment. Even the Knight of Faith—especially the Knight of Faith—must take the risk of personally judging that the ultimate is truly at stake, though it may feel less like a personal judgment than a cosmic commandment. Had Abraham not judged, as a responsible person, that he should hear and obey this commandment as coming from God, rather than as a temptation coming from Satan, then Abraham would have been merely an automaton, a puppet deserving neither ethical nor religious attention. No, he definitely made a judgment; that is what some admire and some deplore.

If we are to approach ethics as a way of judging, we can hardly avert attention from this sort of "teleological suspension of the ethical" (Kierkegaard 1954, 70–77). The world is increasingly encountering people who judge with approval such acts as suicide bombing of buses containing peaceful shoppers or blowing up buildings full of innocent children—while fully recognizing that such acts are entirely contrary to normal ethical fundamentals. It is not wise to dismiss these people as mere religious fanatics or political "crazies." They have an intensely held ethics by which they judge events, though it is not (by definition) the majority ethics. I consider such persons, whether conventionally religious or not, *functionally* religious, inasmuch as their judgments reflect their most intense and comprehensive valuations. At its deepest, that is just what I believe religion is: our way of valuing most intensely and comprehensively (Ferré 1967, chap. 2). This issue need not delay us now. The point here is to recognize, within any approach to ethics as a way of judging, the presence of judgments not only *expressing* widely shared ethical intuitions but also profoundly *challenging* them.

Two brief comments, before we go on. First, the challenges from intensely committed minorities (or "loners") to widely held intuitions need not be deranged or malevolent, as my examples might suggest. Great reforms come this way, too, as witness the influence of Socrates and Jesus. Still, even benevolent challengers of the status quo stir deadly opposition. The moral may be that to challenge widely shared intuitions is likely to be perceived as destructive, however rational or loving the motivation. One of the great problems for ethical thinking and judging, therefore, is to determine whether there is a way of distinguishing moral genius from immoral fakery. Are there *grounds*, accessible through thought or feeling, to support one and expose the other, or must we choose blindly and without grounds? This will be one of the key questions with which we need to wrestle as this book proceeds. Second, there will be a great difference, on this account, between the "true believer," who violates widely shared ethical intuitions in the name of something above common morality, and the careless gangster who shreds ethical restraints without a second thought. It should be possible, as we proceed, to give an account of the range from saint to psychopath. We are likely to find that only a tiny minority of those who "overthrow . . . boundary stones" (Nietzsche 1954, 93) are moral reformers or geniuses.

What, though, *are* these widely shared "ethical intuitions" that saints and sinners variously may challenge but most ordinary people do their best to respect? Sometimes they seem to function like deep beliefs. If, for example, I intuit that taking a human life in exchange for a pack of chewing gum would be wrong, many functions of belief can be found associated with this intuition. For example, the rules of logic will apply, so that I will likely agree that if taking a human life for a pack of chewing gum is wrong, then taking a human life for a stick of chewing gum is *a fortiori* wrong as well. Again, I am likely to exhibit dispositions to language, feeling, and action that would be appropriate to belief; that is, I will be disposed consistently to answer questions in ways classifying this type of action as forbidden, I will be disposed to feel and perhaps express revulsion at the very thought, and I will be disposed to do whatever I reasonably can to prevent or punish behavior of this kind.

At the same time, intuitions seem sometimes to be prior to formulation into words and sentences. An intuition is first of all directly felt, with the unmediated character we associate with perception. Sensory intuition must come before we formulate our various experiences and tag them with the further sounds and marks we call words. Somehow words need to be grounded in something prelinguistic, namely, in differentiated perceived regularities that can account for the distinctions we make and for the linguistic regularities we agree on. If *mathematical intuition* is direct inspection of the formal necessities before, or apart from, the proofs (all the steps of which themselves need to be intuited as valid to escape from an infinite regress of proofs), and if *sensory intuition* is direct perception of the empirical given before, or apart from, the language in which we discuss those intuitions, then might not *ethical intuition* be direct grasp, somehow, of the ethical values involved in situations, possibilities, or persons? That would establish intuition as prior to beliefs, giving ethical beliefs their basis. Just as a sensory (visual) intuition gives one ground for believing that a certain ripe apple is red, so an ethical intuition might give one ground for moral revulsion at the experience of (or thinking about) killing a human being for a pack of gum.

The great problem is that there seems to be no obvious faculty for performing ethical intuitions in the way one might argue that "eye and brain" team to perform visual intuitions and "pure reason" performs mathematical and logical intuitions. Ethical intuitions are not like logical intuitions, since ethical judgments, unlike logical or mathematical ones, purport to inform us of something important that is not simply implicit in the meanings of abstractions. But ethical intuitions are not like perceptual intuitions, since they offer alleged "grounds" that are not able to be smelled, tasted, touched, heard, or seen, and are often open to more doubt and dispute than perceptual ones normally allow.

"The conscience" is sometimes proposed as a faculty for performing ethical intuitions, but conscience is notoriously unreliable, is always personal, is sometimes idiosyncratic. Conscience can be corrupted, trained, retrained, and even converted. Despite this, the demands of conscience are not optional. Listening to and heeding conscience are somehow matters of basic personal integrity. The stirrings of conscience lie somewhere between belief and perception. They are (or can be) felt as direct warnings, scoldings, or permissions, but in all these ways they seem to express deeply felt *beliefs*. Contrariwise, they can be thought of as beliefs, through which persons, acts, or situations are justified or condemned, yet these are beliefs that are deeply *felt*.

Readers who have come to this point via *Being and Value* (1996) and *Knowing and Value* (1998) will realize that, from my point of view, such interwoven complexity of belief with valuation is not exceptional. It is only an exceptionally clear case of what is everywhere more or less so. All beliefs, that is, including those in the sciences, and even in abstract metaphysical theories of highest generality, are steeped in likes and dislikes, adversions and aversions, commitments, preferences, and—in a word—values. Likewise, all cognitive processes, from childhood hunches to brilliant feats of established knowledge, rest on judgments deeply grounded in feeling. It is no surprise, then, that ethical judgments share characteristics of belief, and that ethical beliefs are full of affective power to express and coordinate attitudes toward their subject matter, as well as to shape and reflect dispositions to action.

Action has thus far been the missing element in my discussion. This may seem odd to some, since it might well be argued that action is the "bottom line" of ethics, the dimension most revealing what ethics is *for*. I do not disagree, as will be clear in the next section of this chapter, but I resist the easy slide toward reducing ethics to behavior. To prevent such reduction, I have saved action until last, giving other dimensions their due. Ethics is not just for acting but also for thinking—the best thinking possible—even when no particular context for action is presented. Likewise, ethics is not only for action but also for judging: adopting and correcting attitudes, coordinating feelings, classifying persons, situations, or events (actual or possible), even when overt behavior is inappropriate or impossible.

Crucial among such intellectually contemplated or affectively judged "events," of course, are human actions; crucial among such "situations" are those created by, or calling for, human actions; and crucial to ethical judgments about "persons" are their voluntary actions, which evoke moral praise or blame in multifarious, nuanced ways, and which even more deeply reveal moral character. It is time, therefore, to move from *thinking* and *judging*, however legitimately respected they should be for their own sakes, to the "bottom line" of *action*.

AS A WAY OF ACTING

On reflection, we should realize that we have never been far away from acting. Judging and thinking are both modes of acting that may or may not be overt, that is, expressed in speech or other public behavior. If one's act happens to be that of judging some overt action (one's own or another's), then this act of judging can be classified as a *meta*-action, an action with another action as its object. The meta-levels have no obvious limit. An example of *meta-meta*-action might be *thinking* about *judging* some overt action. And one could, in principle, judge one's thinking about judging an action . . . and so on. There is a practical but no logical limit to this regression.

One of the things we *do* with our judgments, as mentioned above, is to co-ordinate our attitudes toward matters of ethical significance. In the same way that we learn to judge and classify qualities of our visual experience in a way that allows us to coordinate color talk within our language community (e.g., this is "pink" and that is "orange"), we also learn to judge and classify actions, characters, and situations as expressible in publicly intelligible terms (e.g., this is "generous" and that is "noble"). Just as similar but discriminable visual ex-periences are associated with "pink" and "orange," similar but discriminable attitudes of approval are associated with "generous" and "noble" deeds. Each pair is close on its relevant spectrum, but normal speakers can judge exemplary cases of each and can coordinate judgments about which cases will count as borderline as well.

These judgments will have an emotional component, of course, but the judgments themselves are not made merely on the basis of feelings. Judgments on the right concept to use are made, rather, on the basis of recognizable char-acteristics, facts of the matter, which influence how one comes to feel. Feelings of moral outrage, for example, may quickly fade when one comes upon facts which offer extenuating circumstances. Likewise, feelings of ap-proval may give way to contempt when a supposedly "noble" action turns out to be a charade done for ignoble purposes. Then one's judgment about this ac-tion's appropriate classification—naming the kind of action it was—and one's feelings toward it change in tandem.

The coordination of feelingful judgments makes possible not only pub-lic praise or blame, but also coordinated action. We act only when we care about something. Emotion serves to motivate. If I feel deeply that some situ-ation is properly to be judged "unjust," and I feel strongly that unjust situ-ations should be changed, then my judgment can lead to the formation of a personal disposition to engage in actions (under appropriate circumstances) aimed variously at achieving that result. I might write checks to reform-minded organizations, vote for political candidates promising to change the situation, or take direct actions of many kinds. My feelingful judgment has the effect of harmonizing a coherent moral purpose in my personal behavior.

More than this, when my judgment is a matter of public discourse, and others in my community make the same affectively rich judgment, individual behavior can be coordinated in common efforts by many individuals. Reform-minded organizations can be created and supported; political causes can be articulated and champions recruited; the social world can be reshaped.

The coherence and coordination derived from shared intuitions on the appropriate ethical classification of actions, situations, and persons, can be impressive. As W. D. Ross pointed out, there are widespread dispositions to moral approval of what is judged to be *honest* (including truth telling, promise keeping); of what is judged to be *just*; of what is judged worthy of *gratitude*; of activities judged to be *beneficent*; of what is judged to be *self-improving*, without rendering harm to others; and of what is judged generally *noninjurious* (Ross 1988, 16–39). Ross interpreted these widely shared positive evaluations as revealing a set of what he called "prima facie duties" to coordinate our actions in ways furthering these qualities. But widespread intuitive agreement on these judgments can never, according to Ross, decide what should be done when, in a concrete case, a course of action may be judged to satisfy one classification but to violate one or more others. Keeping a promise (to have lunch with a friend) may be in conflict with rushing a pregnant wife to the delivery room. In this particular case, promise keeping, while still having moral weight—all other things being equal—must bend to the emergency provision of benevolent aid to one who justly may expect it and who, without it, could be severely injured. Sometimes the principles of beneficence and fidelity may have different weightings. For example, a panhandler's request (carrying genuine ethical weight because of the beneficence it would represent) might be refused if all one's cash had been encumbered to fulfill a solemn promise. In the abstract, there is no settling the issue of preeminence among our basic ethical concepts (or "duties," in Ross's language), since the facts of the matter—on the basis of which actual judgments need to be made—are not yet at hand.

Approaching ethical action in this way leaves pluralism, not relativism (if by relativism is meant the position that "anything goes" in a context of no established standards of "better" or "worse"), since a large amount of ethical guidance is provided by these widespread agreements on the basic structures of ethical discourse. What is *not* available on this approach is any tidy way of settling conflicts between powerful ethical concepts in the abstract, and no way—other than by self-certified, personally responsible judgments—to determine what ought to be done in specific cases where "facts of the matter" are available to give traction for decision making. The informal, "judgmental" logic of ethical concept making, as I have described it, establishes many concepts as important in many contexts. It does not establish a single, unique "ruling" concept for all occasions.

Approaching ethical action through the more formal logic of rational thought, however, may yet attempt to winnow out a dominant rule or principle for arranging our judgments and consequent ethical behavior in a definite, hierarchical order. For many philosophers, pluralism is not orderly enough. It allows rationally unresolved—unresolvable—conflicts, and thus leaves important matters open to fallible human judgments: thereby requiring nonexperts, as we have seen, to take on the role of experts, at least for the disposition of their own lives. The same quest for unity that one finds in metaphysical speculation and epistemological theorizing reveals itself again in ethics when pluralism is rejected in favor of forms of ethical monism.

The path to unification, as we saw earlier in this chapter, has long run through the medium of thought. Coherence and consistency are built-in requirements of effective theorizing. Approaching ethics as a way of acting via these criteria of good thinking, therefore, is attractive to those who place the demand for unity high on their priorities list.

Thinking, after all, has never been absent from the scene. Judgments are not thoughtless. To *recognize* the characteristics of the facts of the matter, to sort out the appropriate *ethical concepts* involved, and to make a feelingful, self-certified *classification* of these particulars under general categories, is at every stage a thoughtful process. Recognizing and classifying is always—in science and well as ethics—theory-laden. Equally, thinking (as the two earlier books of this trilogy have shown) is always judgment-laden. Human actions are shot through with ideational elements; ideational elements are shot through with intuitions of value. Hence, action is no stranger to thought, or thought to action.

Understandably, many philosophers have attempted to bring all ethical action under a single, supreme theoretical principle that would serve to unify what intuitive judgments left unsatisfyingly pluralistic and unresolved. John Stuart Mill offered the principle of "Greatest Happiness for the Greatest Number"; Immanuel Kant offered the "Categorical Imperative."

Kant's Categorical Imperative illustrates the turn to logical consistency as the grand unifier of ethical actions. Kant claims that his great principle derives from reason itself. For *theoretical* reason, only what is logically consistent is capable of being intelligibly thought; for *practical* reason, only what is logically consistent is capable of being morally willed. To violate the principle of consistency in the speculative domain is to undermine one's status as a rational thinker; to violate the principle of consistency in the domain of action is to undermine one's status as a moral agent. Inconsistent behavior would not be blameworthy in unthinking creatures, but to recognize ourselves—willy-nilly—as rational agents is to find ourselves under norms of thinking and living consistently. Out of rational respect for the fundamental law of Reason that animates us, the obligation *to will our actions* always in accordance with logical consistency (so that the essential character, the "maxim," of our action could without contradiction be made a universal law for every rational agent under essentially like circumstances) is simply laid upon us. This is the "categorical" quality of moral respect for consistency in action. There is no "if"-clause that qualifies, or makes merely hypothetical, the demand to respect pure rational lawfulness for its own sake.

Kant's attempt to unify ethics under the requirement of pure consistency or "lawfulness in general" (his universalizability test—i.e., can this maxim be willed in all like circumstances?—being in its service) marks an all-time high in the quest for a completely unitary ethics, though it is not the only example of its kind. It seeks complete rational system for normative human behavior. At sufficiently high levels of abstraction, it succeeds in offering the absolutes, and the unwavering clarities, that Ross's intuitive pluralism is unable to provide. For example, Kant proves that it is always immoral to lie, no matter what the circumstances. To will a lie, he points out, would be in effect to will the destruction of truthfulness in general, since the maxim of this behavior must in all consistency be taken as a universal rule for all agents, but it would be logically inconsistent—unintelligible—to will the destruction of all truthfulness, since this would make lying (which is parasitic on the presumption of truthfulness) itself impossible. Any maxim prescribing a lie would literally destroy itself. Therefore here is one absolute. Other absolutes, Kant believed, can also be derived: on suicide, slavery, monogamy, and the like. Thus, we escape the perceived sloppiness of conflicting fundamental intuitions, or "judgment calls," required by shifting circumstances.

The question for some remains: is this admirable unity worth the distance it inserts between theory and the concrete facts of human life? "Consistency," or "lawfulness in general," remains exceedingly high on an abstraction ladder that rests, at bottom, on the recognized regularities of preconceptual experience, then climbs through concept formation, language making, symbolic freedom from the immediately given, creative speculation, and comprehensive system construction (Ferré 1998, chap. 9). Coordinating ethical action while giving preferential attention to the needs of theory for *consistency* and *coherence*, as Kant's deductive monism does, may provide satisfying absolutes and unities at high levels of abstraction, but the no less legitimate needs for *applicability* and *adequacy*, noted earlier, thereby suffer.

Ross's intuitive pluralism, in contrast, is much more attentive to the requirements of applicability and adequacy. Coordinating ethical action with studious concern for widely shared judgments about basic ethical concepts, together with close attention to particular facts of the matter, as Ross does, may provide a rich sense of the concrete moral life as lived, but at the cost of contradictions and ambiguities. Coherence pulls against adequacy; adequacy threatens consistency and makes coherence more difficult. The same bipolarity is found at the heart of metaphysics and epistemology, as well. I do not believe the tension can be overcome; however, I have argued that it can be harnessed creatively in the quest for truth (Ferré 1998, chap. 10). As we shall see, similar creative opportunity awaits in ethics.

Action coordinated by abstract theory, action coordinated by personal judgments of "conceptual fit" within widely shared normative categories, the common denominator in approaching ethics as a way of acting seems to be *co-ordination*. This topic in itself deserves a final reflection before we plunge into the argument of the book as a whole.

Every individual organism, if it is to endure through time, depends on internal coordination for survival. One might in fact identify living organisms in terms of the highly coordinated processes that take place within them. There need be no sharp lines drawn between the living and the nonliving, since we have reason to believe that the universe as a whole is characterized by nested societies of coordinated entities "all the way down" (Ferré 1996, chaps. 10–12). Regarding some apparent entities, like clods of earth, internal coordination may be so loose that terming it "an entity" seems more an artifact of human noticing and naming than something belonging to nature (Ferré 1996, 324–38). But living entities, like the microbes or beetles within the clod of earth — or the farmer who breaks it up—are characterized by immensely complex systems such as nutrition, waste disposal, and (as in the cases of beetles and farmers) gross behaviors, such as locomotion, performed by the organism as a whole.

It does not *reduce* ethics to mere behavior to recognize its ancestry in biological advantage. Rather, it *grounds* ethics in the larger continuities of nature to understand it, in its biological context, as the ideational means (in living beings for whom mentality commands significant influence over action) for normative coordination of voluntary behavior.

Human beings are the best (not necessarily the only) examples of living systems which have reached levels of complexity and central organization sufficient to allow mentality an obvious role in coordinating individual behavior—guiding and controlling impulses by ideally entertained goals. These coordinating goals are made possible by the symbolic freedoms of human thinking, cut loose by language from the immediate perceptible environment (Ferré 1998, chap. 9). Without this capacity to take account of ideal goals, glimmering possibilities, likely consequences, and general characters (of persons, actions, or situations), there could be no ethics. Ethics is embedded in the thoughtful, feelingful character of living organisms which must internally coordinate activity or perish.

But it is impossible to consider individual organisms alone in this context. There is such a thing as *personal* ethics (what one does in private may be of a sort, or may have consequences, deserving of moral praise or blame); and, in the end, all ethics must be personal, since persons—inexpert though they may be—must actually make the judgments and perform the actions that shape their world. But, equally, there is no such thing as ethics that is not also *social.* Without other noticers and namers of regularities in nature, there would be no language at all, much less ethical concepts. Without other interactive human agents, there would be no basis for the special quality of personal empathy that underlies and empowers felt obligations of community.

Community depends on coordination of the actions of its many members. In order to achieve any common goals, sufficiently many numbers of a society must be prepared to limit and redirect their individual behavior in ways that will bring about some shared ideal possibility. For example, some must subordinate their contrasting inclinations (e.g., fear, laziness) to endure the dangers of the hunt, others must control impulses to accept the fatigue of gathering berries and tending the fire, if there is to be feasting for all at the end of the day. The "common good" requires meta-coordination, that is, general coordination of the particular coordinations, the private ideals and purposes, of many individuals. These common goals need to be made part of—often enlarging, sometimes reorganizing—many private goals.

More, living in community requires that members of a given society be reasonably capable of anticipating most of the actions of other members most of the time. Societies do not flourish on erratic and unpredictable behavior. Meeting someone on the path should not be cause, each time, for debilitating uncertainty. If the larger goals of a society are to be met, social lawfulness needs to be created through nurturing structures of habitual normative behavior. Societies that fail in large measure to achieve this will be selected against, under the pressures of survival, no less surely than will be individuals who are unable to achieve coordination of personal behavior.

Felt obligation to act in normative ways, once learned socially, continues to be felt in private. Moral character is personal but also deeply social. Just as individuals become part of society, so also society becomes part of individuals.

In light of this, how then should we approach ethics? Above all, I believe, we should approach ethics as a domain full of continuities and interactions. There is no ethical action without thought and feeling, no ethical thought without feeling and potential action, no ethical feeling without conceptual recognition and implications for behavior. Without society there can be no ethics; an ethic is inescapably personal. In ethics we are the boss, but we can learn how to boss ourselves better. Ethical thinking, indispensable in ethical action, is connected by links of logic to all the rest of our thinking, scientific and religious. Therefore, as our thinking changes, our ethical categorizations may change, and with them our feelings and our deeds. As in ecology, so ethics: everything is connected to everything else.

In the following chapters, I shall show how the story leading to modern ethics has led to a breakdown, and to the need for fresh thinking, feeling, and acting under the guidance of a postmodern, ecological worldview. This will involve reflecting not only on ethics *per se*, but also on religion, nature, technology, and the social environment, all interconnected through the need for a more adequate and coherent ethics for the future. With one eye on the past, measuring our resources and noticing our mistakes, and with another on the future, assessing our needs and clarifying fresh possibilities—this is how I recommend we approach ethics.

PART ONE

Ethics

2

HOW DID WE GET HERE?

This chapter outlines the sweep of Western ethical theory from its fresh beginnings in awakening Greek city-states down to the last, cynical decades of the twentieth century. With two-and-a-half millennia to "cover" in one chapter, this story will be highly selective, shaped to make a point. The point will be that modern ethical theory lost its way, wandering into a maze of self-doubt both untypical of our main heritage and historically avoidable. Although unforced, certain epistemological and metaphysical choices made by early modern leaders brought their followers to a troubled place.

I plan to focus on two main developments: one leads toward modern ethical *skepticism*, the other to modern ethical *irrealism*. A modern cliché holds that no one can rightly claim *knowledge* of what is right or wrong. All ethics are just opinions, beliefs, preferences, many clashing much of the time. And just as "beauty is in the eye of the beholder," on the modern outlook, so "it may be right for you, but that doesn't make it right for me." There is no basis in *reality* for ethics. Facts are just facts, without value in themselves, valuable only to the extent we subjectively attribute value to them. Values are grounded in our minds, runs the modern refrain, not in the particles of matter whose collisions make up the modern universe.

The point of tracing, in bold strokes, the path by which we came to accept these items as received wisdom is to show a better way in the two chapters following. But first, before we worry about where we may be going, we need to have a sense of where we have come from. For this we need to go back roughly ninety generations, to the time when ethical theory was gaining its start. And even before.

EARLY PRETHEORETICAL DAYS

It would be arrogant and wrong to suppose that early *Homo sapiens* had no ethics. Abundant evidence from paleontology and anthropology makes it clear that our ancestors lived in communities; the survival of communities in general presupposes regular, predictable, cooperative behavior. It might be too much to infer "codes" of behavior, since codification requires a level of abstraction that might not yet be thinkable in the conceptual development of those just inventing the marvelous freedoms of human language. But habits, expectations, and regularities in the daily affairs of life are necessary for social existence. Habits develop a hold on people and could, under some circumstances, feel akin to obligation. Likewise, expectations of regularity in others, when disappointed, are disturbing, quite possibly giving rise to feelings of justified outrage akin to blame.

The notion of lawfulness, in nature as well as in society, is the offspring of regularities that are noticed and named. It is not surprising, therefore, that among the earliest deposits of human civilization are codes of laws, naming in tablets of clay or stone such regularities of behavior as were judged important enough to value, prescribe, and enforce. By four thousand years ago, and probably much earlier, codes of normative regularity for social behavior were developed in Sumer and Akkad, in the triangle of land between the Tigris and Euphrates rivers. These Mesopotamian codes were compiled by the Babylonian king, Hammurabi, eighteen centuries before the Common Era. The 282 items in Hammurabi's Code were grouped under the main categories of social importance: business, family, trade, labor, and property. Already abstract regularities like sale, lease, gift, barter, loan, and usury (forbidden) were fully recognized and named. Crime and punishment were fully conceptualized, as was the symbolic appropriateness of proportioning sanctions to outrage ("an eye for an eye" comes from this code). The vocabulary for disappointed social expectation included adultery, theft, false witness, political corruption, and the like. Even divorce and alimony were recognized. Behind this compilation of the norms of social life was the combined authority of the state and of religion. There was as yet no sorting out of obligations into moral, religious, and purely civic. All were bound together in a normative blend of anticipated regularity in behavior.

The same unity of obligation was incorporated five hundred years later in the Mosaic Code, the Ten Commandments. This Code is much briefer than Hammurabi's, but it formulates what was taken as the most important obligations on those who would try to perpetuate a society under the commandments. The first part of the Code prescribes behavior regarding religious obligations: limiting reverence to one God, refraining from making images of this God, avoiding vain speech about God, and honoring a special Sabbath day.

The second part prescribes social behavior: requiring honorable treatment of parents, forbidding murder, adultery, theft, false witness, and covetousness. This great Code of general principles became fundamental to the ethics of Judaism, Christianity, and Islam. Many more laws—some quite detailed and closely linked to the circumstances of daily life in ancient Israel—rose out of priestly decisions over the years and were attributed to Moses. Ever since, these laws, found in the first five books of the Bible, have been revered by Jews as Torah, though Christianity took a different attitude toward detailed codes of conduct, stressing norms dictated by love more than adherence to specific prescriptions.

A dramatically different, though functionally similar, means of establishing social norms of attitude and behavior developed in Greece during roughly the same time period in which the Hebrews were establishing their codes. Instead of using codes of law, the Greeks expressed their ideals of human behavior through epic poetry—story telling with an authority that gave the Greek poets a status similar to the priests of Jewish culture. Homer's epics, the *Iliad* and the *Odyssey*, showed what to admire, what to abhor. Misbehavior, even among the gods, was all the more readily recognized because of its shocking character. Ideal heroes, though greatly admirable for their courage and nobility, were also shown lapsing into unacceptable anger and overweening pride—faults punished by the moral order of the *kosmos*. These poems, offering innumerable themes for tragic literature as well as upholding standards of better and worse, had come to be considered divinely inspired by the time of the rise to consciousness of ethical theory itself.

Ethical theory presupposes readiness to *reflect* on one's norms of attitude and action. This is not easy, even today, after centuries of critical thinking. Any teacher of freshman or sophomore classes in ethics can testify to students' initial difficulty—even with faculty encouragement—in gaining mental distance from the often unspoken norms of attitude and action that function in families, religions, and peer groups. How much more difficult it must have been before the development of philosophy! Without considerable shaking up, it probably would not have happened at all.

CLASSICAL PREMODERN ETHICAL THEORY

Aristotle said that philosophy begins in wonder, and, of course, he was right. But how does wonder itself begin? Without some jolt—from something unfamiliar, threatening, or strikingly attractive—wonder, in the sense of reflective questioning, could hardly be expected to take place. A crack needs to open between the taken-for-granted, causing no wonder, and new wonder-full, possibilities. For those not practiced in dealing abstractly with pure possibilities, the most effective way of forcing attention to an alternative possibility is by clothing it in startling actuality. That something is *actual* proves its *possibility*, like it or not; thus, hitherto unimagined alternatives intrude into mental spaces unaccustomed to making room for such "otherness." The mere presence of homosexual men and women—the fact of their "queerness"—is often enough to disturb the mental and emotional status quo among "normal" heterosexuals and start an argument or a fight. Such conflict is not yet philosophy, but without mental disturbance there will be no wonder, and without wonder, no critical questioning.

It was no coincidence, then, that philosophy was born at the point of contact between two great spheres of civilization, where merchants, seamen, and soldiers rubbed shoulders with concrete "otherness" incarnated in people of different religions, politics, manners, and ethics. Miletus, the city in Ionia where Thales founded philosophy in the seventh century B.C., lay on the western coast of what is now western Turkey, a port on the Aegean Sea where Asia meets Europe. In Thales' century, the burst of arts and sciences and trade that bubbled in Miletus led (for a time) to the Hellenizing of a swath of territory reaching to the Black Sea and thus, inevitably, to a great deal of cultural conflict, creativity, and wonder.

Two centuries later, amid huge power struggles—Europe and Asia both hungering to dominate the strategic interface between their civilizations—the Europeans had defeated the Oriental potentate Xerxes in 479 B.C., and the triumphant Athenians held sway. In this context of optimism and self-confidence, the Athenian statesman, Pericles (495–429 B.C.), built many buildings (including the Parthenon), instituted democracy, and strengthened the Athenian Empire. This empire, made up of the Aegean islands and much of the coast, contained many diverse local cultures. That was no problem. Their primary role within the empire was to provide military support in time of need and to remit regular tribute to Athens.

A close friend of Pericles was the professional teacher, Protagoras (490–420 B.C.), who travelled to various cities of the empire with skilled instruction in rhetoric and law. He taught his students how to argue so as to win their cases in court, whichever side they were assigned. He seems to have been completely flexible in his approach to the different belief systems and established cultural norms he encountered in the different cities of the empire. The point of his instruction was instrumental: how to function successfully within any set of norms. They were taken as primary. He was a perfect relativist, and his ethical theory, the abstract formulation of his thinking about the behavioral norms he encountered, was simple: "Man is the measure." In this he seems to have included both cultures and individuals. His relativism did not stop at measuring norms, it also applied to what is real or true. "Man is the measure of all things, of those that are that they are, of those that are not that they are not" (Burnet 1961, frag. 1; Plato 1937b, 152a). Such explicit relativism, based on experience of a diverse world with many jarring viewpoints and mutually inconsistent customs, intruded itself as "other" in the minds of some who listened and started wondering. Among these, most importantly, was Socrates.

Socrates inherited two centuries of philosophical tradition, some of it involving prescriptions for behavior (notably the cult-like Pythagoreans and their followers), but it was Socrates who more than any other gave *ethical theory* its first significant exponent and its martyr. Others had proclaimed what they thought was good; Socrates wondered why such proclamations should be accepted as binding or true, and further wondered what "good" might *mean*, not just in particular contexts but in general, in all contexts. Protagoras had declared, in effect, that there can be no such general context, since everyone "measures" uniquely, always in particular circumstances. Itinerant Sophists like Protagoras took their clue, that is, exclusively from the local norms, laws, and codes of the societies into which they travelled. But Socrates wondered. The doctrine of "man as measure" would mean, if taken as a general theory, that something might be measured by me as good and measured by you as not-good, thus turning out both good and not-good, with no further appeal or resolution allowed. This consequence Socrates found deeply troubling, theoretically no less than practically. There must be something in common between instances of things named by the same word or there would be no point in naming them one way rather than another. Language between isolated measurers would become unintelligible, and teaching impossible. Since Protagoras lived by purporting to teach virtue, there had better be some general sense behind his words. Otherwise "virtue," if measured entirely without reference to some common intelligible core of meaning, would be completely unteachable.

"Measuring" remains of vital importance in ethics, Socrates agrees, but not the helter-skelter, private measurements Protagoras seems to have had in mind. Instead, there must be a *science* of measuring, so as to correct for distortions introduced by limited viewpoints. If happiness depends on our aiming for what is *really* more greatly satisfying, then we need such a science of moral measurement to help us avoid being deceived when lesser goods appear momentarily greater than in the long run they really are. Such a knowledge-based form of measurement, "would do away with the effect of appearances, and, showing the truth, would fain teach the soul at last to find rest in the truth, and would thus save our life" (Plato 1937b, 356c).

The line between Socrates' views and Plato's is unclear, but Socrates undoubtedly lived his life, and met his death, for the cause of knowledge based ethics, for the "examined life" (Plato 1937a, 38). Socrates' divinely felt mission in pursuit of universal, core meanings of great ethical concepts like courage, piety, justice, and the like, was an expression of this cause. And his refusal to grasp the opportunity for escape from his imminent execution—

"measuring" the urgently attractive lesser good of living a few more years (Plato 1985a) against the greater meaning of his life—was his ultimate affirmation of reason's power to "teach the soul at last to find rest in the truth." Afterward Plato, an admiring witness to this commitment and eager to vindicate his master, drove further into ethical theory.

"Resting in the truth," as we have seen, was far from Protagoras' goal. For him, ethics was not so much a matter of truth as of technique, a flexible tool for gaining practical successes in life. But for Plato, even more than Socrates, ethics was first of all a matter of successes of the mind and spirit. Ethical truth was for him born of conceptual vision into the universal and eternal.

After a long, rigorous educational process (described in the *Republic* [Plato 1954]), the properly prepared learner will move up from general truths about visible things, such as natural scientists pursue, and then further up, even beyond the universal truths of pure mathematics, to a realm of pure formal truths that cannot be interpreted by the sensuous imagination. This is the highest realm of the forms, for Plato, but as long as we think about forms and truths (plural), we are not at the "got it!" point. Unity and necessity have not yet prevailed. A Form of Forms still needs to unite all the rest into the vision of a perfect unity of Being, Truth, and Goodness. Grasping—and being grasped by—such a vision is the ultimate success of the soul's quest for the transcendent Wisdom beloved by true philosophers. Plato called this the "Form of the Good," and acknowledged that ultimate knowledge of it would be ineffable, since language breaks ideas apart into words, while the Good is beyond all such fragmentation. Still, rising to contemplate the Form of the Good was the goal that Plato set for those who would establish and enforce the norms of behavior for the truly good society. There would be nothing arbitrary about social and personal ethics derived from such a source—the universal Good itself. Philosopher Kings (and Philosopher Queens, too, since Plato was not at all sexist in his educational admissions policy) would, he thought, see the same necessary reality and legislate particular norms of behavior appropriate to the norms of the universe. Socrates' dream of a science of ethics would be vindicated in Plato's wisely governed state.

From Protagoras, for whom ethics was a tool, the pendulum had swung very far, via Socrates and Plato, to the vision of ethics as an exact science. This extreme, though it left a legacy and attracted followers for centuries to come, was immediately tempered by the last of the great early premodern philosophers, Aristotle. Once a student and then a colleague of Plato, Aristotle was firm in his rejection of Protagoras' extreme relativism. The "man as measure" doctrine would make ethical discourse unintelligible. But demanding an exact science of the good life is reaching too far. There are indeed general ethical principles, Aristotle held, but they are neither open to quasi-mathematical formulation, as Plato seemed to think, nor capable of perfectly precise application to concrete circumstances. In this, ethics resembles more some great field of art—whose rules are shot through with connoisseurship—than any deductive science.

For example, Aristotle saw no great difficulty in demonstrating that happiness is the one supreme good, sought always for itself and never as a mere means to something else. But such a principle is just the start of ethical inquiry, since "happiness" itself needs clarification and definition. It is not mere pleasure, since we sometimes subject ourselves to considerable pains for the sake of activities, like rock climbing or long-distance running, that make us happy. Happiness seems rather to be a satisfaction that rises from functioning well, fulfilling of our capacities. But what are our distinctive capacities? The well-functioning of a racehorse is manifested in its healthy capacity for running fast. Is there a way of working out the well-functioning of human beings? We are *bodies* in need of good nourishment; we are centers of *sensation*, of appetites and passions, in need of good experience; and we are *minds* in need of good thinking. When all of these dimensions are functioning well, then we are functioning well as humans.

But what does "good nourishment" mean, when it comes to concrete application of such a general principle? Clearly, it does not mean the same thing relative to a child as to a man, or to a sedentary scholar as to a wrestler. In each case, there is a normative amount and a normative kind of food, but these norms can only be understood by the normative exercise of our mental capacities. Hitting the right amount and kind, neither too much nor too little, whether in connection with nourishment or with the sorts of experiences we should seek out for ourselves, will always be a matter of judgment.

This holds especially true when it comes to hitting the mark with major life policies and character traits. It is fine to agree that one should be courageous, neither rash (an excess of the spirit needed for courage) nor cowardly (a deficiency of such spirit). But how does one judge in a particular case that a given specific decision would be over the line toward rashness while another might be under the line toward cowardice? Clear thinking is required to sort out the extremes in this and all such cases, but there is no way mathematical algorithms can solve such questions. They must be approached expecting no more precision than is appropriate to the topic, "for it is the mark of an educated mind to seek only so much exactness in each type of inquiry as may be allowed by the nature of the subject-matter" (Aristotle 1946: Book I, 1094B).

Aristotle differed with Plato over the epistemological level of assurance that should be expected in ethical thinking, but they both agreed on the availability of genuine ethical knowledge. They stood together, as well, on the solid grounding of ethics in realities transcending the "measure" of human preferences or cultural habits. Plato's realities were eternal Ideas, absolute archetypes in which particular virtuous actions participated more or less well—all ultimately unified in the Form of the Good itself. Aristotle's ethical realities were closer to Earth. He rejected as unnecessary any such transcendent realm of Forms, especially any separate Form of the Good, somehow imagined over and above the world of substantial things which are, he argued, capable of carrying their own characters. Given the existence of individual substances with specific natures, the virtue of any of those substances would be the full realization of its nature, the complete performance of its ideal function. If the ideal nature of a knife is to cut, then the virtue of an actual knife lies in its cutting well. If the ideal nature of racehorses is to run fast, then the virtue of actual racehorses is shown in the speed of their running. Knives and horses are not ethical agents, since they lack the mental powers that allow humans to foresee, deliberate, and choose courses of action. But we human beings are like all other substances in that our virtue is measured by actual fulfillment of the potentials in our nature. Those potentials are real, grounded in the formal aspect of our complex hylomorphic union. And they are demanding, since if we neglect to cultivate them—particularly the potentials for exercising rationality, both for its own sake and for shaping our lives and characters according to the rules of moderation—we fail a standard of human virtue that is prior to and larger than ourselves.

After Aristotle, early premodern ethical thinking remained on the course set by the pioneers. The primary alternatives during Hellenistic times before the advent of Christianity, were Epicureanism and Stoicism. Though they differed sharply on the ethics they prescribed—and differed, too, on the realities to which they appealed—they agreed that ethical knowledge is available and that ethics is firmly grounded in reality.

For Epicureanism, reality was held to be radically dissimilar from the universe either of Plato or of Aristotle. Both Plato and Aristotle believed that there are universal realities, despite disputing whether these could exist apart from substances incorporating them. From this belief Epicureans entirely dissented. Adopting the atomism of Democritus (c. 460–c. 370 B.C.), the Epicureans acknowledged as real only two types of things: either tiny bits of *matter* in constant motion, or total *void*, empty space, in which these atoms could move, collide, and aggregate. There was no room for real universal *qualities* in this vision of the universe, or for values of any sort outside valuers who might establish them. But given the fact that some atoms have clumped into complex structures, specifically ourselves, with strong preferences and the desire for happiness, Epicureans believed that reasoning could prescribe what any such human clump should do to achieve the best sort of life.

First, the best and most lasting happiness needs to be defined negatively, as absence of pain, on the analogy of the glow of a good digestion which at its best is hardly noticed. With this sort of pleasure as one's goal, one should choose to avoid "spicy foods," that is, pleasures that lead to upset. The "natural" pleasures of life—simple eating and drinking, conversation with friends, avoidance of the tumult of political involvement—are to be chosen, the "unnatural" avoided. The symbol of Epicurean ethics is the walled garden, where women and men gently converse without anxiety or stress. Epicurean beliefs about reality could foster this peace of mind, by staving off the "philosophical" anxieties that might otherwise invade the garden walls: fear of death, fear of fate, and fear of arbitrary treatment by the gods. *Death* need not be feared by atomists, since the dissolution of our complex living structure leaves no residue. When we live, *death* is nothing; when we die, *we* are nothing. *Fate*, too, need not be feared on Epicurean atomism, since built into the world picture was an element of randomness, a capacity of atoms to "swerve" into one another. We need not consider ourselves trapped in an inexorable universe. *The gods*, finally, are negligible on an atomist ontology, since even if real (as Epicureans accepted) they are made from the flimsiest of all atoms and are barred from intervening in our lives. Best, then, to enjoy moderate pleasures in the garden of life, undisturbed and at peace.

Stoicism took a very different attitude toward ethics. If Epicureanism can be roughly characterized as breathing the earthy, moderate air of Aristotle, Stoicism soared to the rarified altitudes of Plato and Socrates. Socrates, as hero and martyr, was especially dear to Stoic thinking, since it was he who emphasized that no one could do real harm to a virtuous person and that purity of soul was the one truly important goal of life. The Stoics were fond of pointing out to rival Epicureans that life is not much like a walled garden, that real life is full of vulnerabilities, and that happiness, defined as avoidance of pain, is hardly within the reach of anyone. Wars, illness, economic collapse, personal betrayal—hurtful events of all sorts—are neither caused by us nor avoidable by retreat from the world. Pain happens. One's own living, sensitive body is not guaranteed safe. Others can capture it, torture it, kill it. But in all this, the Stoics insisted, there is one domain that is wholly under one's control: the inner self's thought and volition. If one maintains personal virtue, as Socrates declared, nothing else matters. No one can really "harm" a righteous person.

For this rigorous call to virtue, only an exact science of ethics would suffice. The control of thought by the demands of reason alone is the supreme goal. Then it will be evident that what is not under our control does not really matter. Once the rationality of the universe is acknowledged, whatever happens can be accepted in the virtuous spirit that controls and overwhelms the merely emotional rejection of painful happenings. The goal was calm feelinglessness, *apatheia*, in place of mental tumult. Like the Epicureans, Stoics rejected the doctrine of Forms, but they also rejected atomism and randomness in favor of a vision of universal Logos, ruling every detail and present in every rational soul.

CHRISTIAN PREMODERN ETHICAL THEORY

Christian ethical thought flourished in the soil prepared by all this. Indeed, pervasive Hellenistic ideas of a universal Logos—ideas at home both in both Stoicism and Platonism—helped to shape the new religion from its early days. The New Testament's fourth Gospel, attributed to the disciple known as John, begins by identifying the human Jesus with the eternal Word informing everything "from the beginning." "And the Word was made flesh and dwelt among us . . ." (John 1:14), puts the central mystery of Incarnation in what, for Platonism, is sheer paradox: the Absolute became relative, the Eternal entered time, the Universal became particular in a man who was also God. These Platonic (and Stoic) subtexts, thus incorporated into the Christian canon itself, were prepared for by similar Logos thinking emerging in Jewish thought of the time, developed by Philo of Alexandria (20 B.C.–A.D. 50). Philo's allegorizing of the Hebrew scriptures attempted to reconcile the historical stories of Torah with the eternal Forms. Plato's Demiurge became the creative Logos, ordering all things; the Form of the Good became God.

St. Augustine (354–430), a once-pagan philosopher converted to Christianity through the power of Christian Platonism to unite his head with his heart, becomes the next great shaper of ethical thought (Ferré 1996, 78–84). Augustine stressed an ethic of love, but not of sentimental or disorganized love. He knew, all too well and at first hand, the temptations of promiscuity. Loving the wrong things, or loving with the wrong priorities, was for him the bane of human existence. The Original Sin of Adam and Eve, he believed, was grounded in willfully misplaced love: succumbing to love of self over love of God, love of the finite over the Infinite, the created over the Creator. Getting one's loves straight is the key to ethical life. "Love God and do what you will."

Augustine's metaphysics, epistemology, and ethics all come together at this point. God is the most Real. Just as for Plato the Form of the Good is the principle of Being for whatever is, so for Augustine God's infinite reality anchors and upholds the Great Chain of Being in which every grade of reality is linked. God is also the most True. Just as for Plato the Form of the Good is the unifying principle of Intelligibility for whatever can be known, so for Augustine God provides the intellectual illumination that alone allows knowledge of any kind, secular or spiritual. And, of course, God is the most Worthy. Just as for Plato the Form of the Good is the principle of Excellence for whatever has merit (and everything that has any degree of reality has some degree of intelligibility and merit), so for Augustine God's Goodness and Beauty constitute the perfection of all value.

God, as our maker, is our only ultimate satisfaction. "Thou hast made us for Thyself, and our hearts find rest in Thee." But this will not be obvious to us as long as we have centered our deepest love on ourselves and other finite things, distracting our attention and distorting our priorities. Alas, it is our human condition to live with twisted love and clouded vision. This is why we cannot, as the stern Pelagians preached, simply will ourselves into righteousness. Such an ethical theory, by exaggerating the human possibility of attaining virtue, would make God's intervention for our salvation unnecessary. God's Incarnation in history would then become pointless. The suffering of Jesus, and his victory over sin and death, would be redundant.

Augustine, despite holding that the human will is free (so that we are fully responsible for our sins), fiercely battled the self-help Pelagians to defend the centrality of God's grace in the dynamics of human salvation. In this, as in our creation, he argued, the initiative remains with our Maker. We do not have the power of being; we do not make ourselves. We do not have the power of knowing; we know nothing without God's subtle illumination of our minds. We do not have the power of saving; we are lost without God's redeeming interventions, through the incarnation of Jesus in history and through the operation of Christ in our lives. Our role in this is simply personal faith, which precedes (and unleashes) understanding and allows our love to be reordered as it must be for our ultimate beatitude.

Once that love is focused on what is truly ultimate and best, we shall organize our lives in accordance with this central devotion. Ethics is no problem. We shall do the right out of love for the Good. Our will, once it is in the loving service of the Best, can be counted on to choose rightly. "Love God and do what you will" sounds laissez-faire, even antinomian, but it is hardly anarchistic. Given (metaphysically) that there is a central reality which shines (epistemologically) the same intelligible light to all faithful minds on what is (ethically) best, Christians in love with God will live in harmony in the same way that Plato's properly educated philosopher kings were expected to guide the ideal Republic with objectively right policies.

The Augustinian visionary, semimystical approach to ethical matters dominated the many years between Augustine and Europe's rediscovery of Aristotle. This rediscovery, made possible by the labors of Arabian scholars and followed by the geographical spread of Islam into Spain, occurred during the twelfth century and spread rapidly. By the middle of the thirteenth century, Thomas Aquinas (1224–1274) was engaged in crafting one of the towering intellectual works of all time: the synthesis of Aristotelian philosophy with Christian theology.

The empirical, earthy spirit of Aristotle was not at first a promising vehicle for a Christianity that had been associated with the far more ethereal Plato for a thousand years. Aristotle, we recall, provided no conceptual foothold for immaterial Forms wholly detached from matter, and rejected the "Form of the

Good" as a confused, unhelpful notion. Epistemologically, Aristotle shunned dependence on direct mental illumination in favor of accounts of sensory, then mental abstractions from the world of sense perception. Despite these differences, Thomas Aquinas and others were so impressed with the power of Aristotle's science and logic—and, in general, with the systematic coherence of his grand theory—that they could not in conscience settle for less than a Christian understanding of all things through Aristotle's conceptual framework. Especially if Aristotle's massive works were to force honest thinkers to acknowledge them as *true*, then Christians, committed to the truths of the Gospel (and to the fundamental unity of all truth), would be obliged to reexamine their beliefs, despite the alien feel of new categories.

For Thomas, many elements of Christianity underwent deep metamorphosis (Ferré 1996, 94–99; Ferré 1998, 77–86). The soul began to be understood not as a separate immaterial substance but, in this life, as the form of the living, thinking body, and, after the Resurrection, the form of the "spiritual body." God began to be envisioned more as Prime Mover than as Form of the Good. Knowledge of God's existence was based not on direct intellectual illumination through the awareness of conceptual necessities (e.g., Anselm's Ontological Argument) but, rather, on inferences from widely shared perceptual experiences (e.g., the observed dependence of artifacts on intelligent designers).

It is important to notice that the ethical theory of Thomas and his successors was no less grounded in metaphysics and epistemology than was the ethical theory of Platonist Christians. But the theory is significantly different. Rather than recoiling from matter in favor of things purely spiritual, as the Platonists tended to do, the Aristotelians accepted the inextricable interweaving of matter with form in substances. The matter gives substances individual existence, distinguishing each one from other entities sharing the same general characteristics. Thomas went to some lengths to defend the appropriateness of bodily functions, even within the uniquely human capacities of cognition. Knowing by means of physical perception, from which universal elements are abstracted, is *normative* for humans, he insisted. It is nothing to be ashamed of; even in the life to come, he argued, the same general epistemic structures would appropriately persist through the resurrection body.

Ethical knowledge, thus grounded, could not pretend to be so absolutely certain as the Platonists claimed. But precision comes in degrees, depending on the subject matter, as Aristotle himself declared. Knowledge remains knowledge, even if inductively based. Observation often gives strong grounds, especially when dealing with practical affairs.

What, then, needs to be observed for specific ethical knowledge to be obtained? Here Thomas' metaphysics gives the clue: we need to observe the development of substances according to their own natures. Every particular substance, we remember, is the hylomorphic unity of its matter and its formal structure. The forms do not exist independently, but they do powerfully characterize whatever they inform. All other things being equal, every substance strives for the fulfillment of its formal nature. It is in the nature of every acorn to be a lofty oak—the form of the oak is the "final cause," or aim, built into and guiding the acorn's growth. Not all other things are equal, however. The world could hardly hold all the oaks potentially in all the acorns that fall. Other things get in the way. Accidents happen. Squirrels divert acorns to perform other entirely natural functions, such as nourishing squirrel tissues; but this is "natural" according to the squirrel's nature. It is external to the acorn's own inner trajectory. Left to itself, the acorn had a different agenda. Thus, we observe and from such empirical data we draw important ethical consequences.

Everything has a nature, and the virtue of everything is the fulfillment of its nature. "Natural law" in ethics is based on a generalization from the observable fact that things unfold lawfully. There is an inner propensity toward ideal end-states, and these can be distinguished by reason from the mere "endings" that happen when this propensity is interrupted or deflected by external events. To this add Thomas' Christian conviction that the world of things is the expression of divine Reason, and the prescriptive force of natural law, based on this metaphysics and associated epistemology, becomes quite clear. Besides the sacred virtues, revealed in Holy Scripture, of faith, hope, and love, there is a huge domain in which the natural order can be consulted directly and duties discovered without need of special revelation. If we are attentive observers, nature will show us the internal ideals that need to be respected by all, Christian and pagan alike. It is in this tradition that some modern Roman Catholics, following Thomas, consider it legitimate to urge secular governments to legislate against such "unnatural" acts as contraception and abortion. On this ethical theory, such mandates do not depend on a special religious perspective. They are not thought by their advocates to be sectarian in the least, but, rather, public truths capable of being understood by rational observers of nature. Every entity seeks its own preservation, every living entity seeks its own propagation. Human intervention in such fundamental natural processes, to thwart what nature and nature's God have ordained, should be seen, they argue, as obviously and universally wrong, not merely the preference of a particular community of faith. Even without faith—namely, without the conviction that nature manifests the intentions of nature's God—reason can, on Thomas' ethical theory, provide much firm ethical guidance in the secular domains of life.

This concession to reason, however, was anathema to Thomas' successors in the later years of premodern ethical theory. John Duns Scotus (1265–1308) and William of Ockham (1285?–1349), though differing in other respects, were both enthralled with the Divine Omnipotence. Nothing at all could limit the freedom of the infinite God they worshipped. This religious commitment had huge consequences not only for metaphysics and epistemology but also for ethical theory.

Scotus broke radically with the centuries-long "tilt" toward universals (the Forms of Plato and Aristotle) and declared instead in favor of particularity (Ferré 1998, 84). The "thatness" of the unique entity we encounter is important, too, over and above its general "whatness." Admittedly, knowledge of this particularity is not clear and distinct (here Scotus blamed Original Sin for dimming our perceptions), but it is real and vital, especially when we are dealing with an object of our love (Ferré 1998, 85).

In keeping with this shift to the particular, Scotus emphasized intuition over deduction, and held that salvation is through the *love* of God, not the *knowledge* of God (as Thomas and his followers had maintained). Indeed, theology itself is not a theoretical science, Scotus held. It is not based on general principles at all, but on a particular revelation given freely by God. This interpretation of theology later freed the Scotists from dependence on the dubitable arguments of natural theology, which they were quick to criticize severely.

Most important for ethics, Scotus stressed that God's infinite freedom requires us to reject any suggestion that God is captive of general principles of any kind. If there can be no limits on God, then God is not legislated to by prior universals, even of morality. Thomas had suggested that God's will is guided in conformity to eternal virtues; Scotus found this religiously intolerable. God rules! What is good is good only because God wills it so. There can be nothing intrinsic in the virtues approved by God that forces divine approval. If we suppose we can use our human reason to deduce the necessity of moral truths independent of revelation, we are faithlessly putting ourselves above God and seeking to guide our behavior by our own intellects rather than by obedience to God's will.

Theology, for Scotus and his followers, is ultimately a *practical science*, rooted in revelation by an absolutely omnipotent God and aimed at guiding human conduct and affection. The speculative intellect may, if it likes, travel on the parallel track of metaphysics and other theoretical sciences, but Scotism requires the radical uncoupling of ethics from reason. On religious grounds, we are to consider our ethical precepts to be arbitrary, ultimately indefensible by thinking. If God had willed otherwise, what we now revile as vices would have been virtues. The practical science of theology, Scotus concluded, can be fully adequate even in the absence of theoretical understanding.

William of Ockham went further. For Ockham, theology is no science at all. It is simply the avenue to salvation. It is authoritative in its own domain, but it does not run on tracks that can be usefully considered to parallel those of reason. Theology's tracks can cross, and conflict with, the tracks laid down by reason. When this happens, the Church, Scripture, and Tradition rule; reason must bow, but only at those isolated points.

The total independence of reason and religion, as Ockham saw it, could assure logicians and other scholars freedom to pursue their studies, but also could preserve the precious doctrine of the absolute freedom of God. To realize (deeply) that God can do *anything meaningfully conceivable* is to realize how utterly contingent the world is. Whatever we find happening might have been caused by God to have happened otherwise. Nothing factual can be deduced from first principles, since God (as Scotus also insisted) can never be enslaved to principles. The contingency of the world shifts attention to observation of *how* the world is and undercuts the question *why* the world is as it is.

Exactly the same can be concluded about ethical principles, namely, that they are simply given by God's inscrutable will. To live a righteous life is to bow before the authority of God's revealed will. There are no "natural" or "logical" reasons in ethics.

EARLY MODERN ETHICAL THEORY

Traditionally, the story of modern philosophy begins with René Descartes (1596–1650), the universally acknowledged "Father of Modern Philosophy." I shall happily adhere to this tradition, but rather than dwell on the sharp differences between Descartes and his premodern predecessors (as Descartes himself chose to do), I prefer to note—for our present topic—the continuities. Regarding ethics, Descartes simply continues what late medieval thinkers like Scotus and Ockham had begun. They had severed the link between morality and reason. Their motives had been pious. God's infinite freedom, they thought, was best defended by insisting on the complete arbitrariness of any prescription about right or wrong. Omnipotence must not be ruled by prior rules. Nothing *in* acts of kindness, for example, as contrasted with cruelty, justifies them apart from God's untrammeled choice. Probe as we wish, our minds will not be able to come up with universal, self-luminous reasons to account for God's inscrutable will. If they could, then God would have been under obligation to choose one way rather than another. But since that is intolerable, our minds must instead defer to unarguable revelation as the guide for life.

Descartes loved nothing more than universal, self-luminous reasons for justifying his metaphysical and epistemological views. In this he was, indeed, a radical opponent of late premodern attitudes, more a throwback to Plato's visionary absolutism. But, significantly, for him this whole approach to thinking ended abruptly at ethics. Unlike Socrates, who sought a science of ethics, and Plato, who offered one, Descartes limited his "scientific" quest to questions of being, not acting.

In fact, Descartes adopts as his first moral rule simply the readiness to "obey the local laws" (Descartes 1960, 19)—*whatever* they are. Here is no determination to deduce the eternal good from first principles, just a resolution to get along within the given moral framework. The framework is not revealed by God, in this case, but revealed in practice. It might have been different. In different localities it *is* different. Descartes refrains from even pretending that any "local" prescriptions are intrinsically justifiable. But some sort of framework is needed for life, and within this framework Descartes resolves, as his second moral rule, to live "resolutely." This rule he defends not in terms of some sort of rational insight into the moral appropriateness of a life lived resolutely by found standards arbitrarily accepted, but instead in terms of the practical benefit. Even an arbitrary course, followed straight ahead, works better (he asserts) than mere wandering, "now turning this way, now that" (Descartes 1960, 19).

The arbitrariness of Ockham's ethics is here reexpressed at the dawn of the modern period in a way that embraces both Protagoras and William James. Protagoras, the Sophist, is the patron of social "revelation" as the measure of right and wrong; James, the Pragmatist, is the patron of resoluteness as a self-justifying prudential practice (Ferré 1998, 251–8). The unbinding of ethics from any metaphysical tapestry, accomplished in the name of God's omnipotence, foreshadowed this portentous theme in the thinking of the Father of Modern Philosophy.

As I have argued elsewhere (Ferré 1998, 93–120), modern philosophy really had two Fathers (impossible though this may be for biology). The other Father was Thomas Hobbes (1588–1679). These were personally timid men, each with grand ideas and each with self esteem to match. Their zones of agreement largely marked out the playing fields for modern philosophy. Both demanded absolute certainty as the essential mark of knowledge. This included for both a stress on clarity and distinctness of basic ideas and on indubitability of conclusions. Both employed an analytical method in reducing ideas and problems to their smallest parts. Both relied on deduction, making mathematics, geometry in particular, their model for thinking. Both dismissed as fictions the nonmathematical, unquantifiable qualities of experience, the so-called secondary qualities of the familiar sensed world of colors, tastes, and sounds. Descartes even accused Hobbes of plagiarizing his views here, but that was unfair; on this, both were actually followers of Galileo.

In one basic respect, however, they were at daggers drawn. Hobbes was content with atomism, remaining (like Epicurus and the ancient Atomists) a monist, admitting only matter as nonvacuous reality. Descartes, in contrast, was a dualist, insisting on two irreducible domains: one of unthinking matter and one of immaterial mind. From this great difference flowed consequences on several fronts. Hobbes' materialism ruled out the possibility of immaterial ideas; all ideas, he held, *must* be particular vibrations of very fine material things, since atoms alone must account for all that is.

Ethically, this atomism led to straightforward deductions that Hobbes delighted in drawing. First, if material atoms are all that is, then the only properties that are ultimately genuine are the properties of material atoms. Atoms do not have color, and so forth, and therefore color qualities are not ultimately genuine but, rather, are dependent on being produced, somehow, in subjective experience as a by-product of the motion of atoms. Atoms do not have any sort of value in themselves. They are merely inert, impenetrable, and massive. Therefore human valuing does not reflect anything in the objective structure of things but, rather—like seeing colors—is also the by-product of each person's internal material makeup.

Just as all this could be deduced with certainty from the clear axioms and postulates of atomistic materialism, so likewise, Hobbes believed, ethical theory could be deduced as well, with equally coercive force. In this he went far beyond Descartes' mild social relativism to construct an ethic of atomism. Each human subjective center is for itself central in its own universe, in which there is one great Right of Nature:

> The RIGHT OF NATURE . . . is the liberty each man hath, to use his own power, as he will himself, for the preservation of his own nature; that is to say, of his own life; and consequently, of doing any thing, which in his own judgment, and reason, he shall conceive to be the aptest means thereunto (Hobbes 1993, 40).

This right, if exercised by each personal atom, would lead to the worst possible outcome imaginable, the "war of all against all," reminiscent of the constant, random banging against one another of unfeeling material particles. But human beings feel—and fear—this terrible State of Nature and would rightly exercise their Right of Nature to seek peace and protection, if possible. This, indeed, is the First Law of Nature, "*that every man, ought to endeavour peace, as far as he has hope of obtaining it*" (Hobbes 1993, 41 [emphasis original]). And the Second Law of Nature stands also to reason: "*that a man be willing, when others are so too, as far-forth, as for peace, and defence of himself he shall think it necessary, to lay down this right to all things; and be contented with so much liberty against other men, as he would allow other men against himself*" (Hobbes 1993, 41 [emphasis original]).

From these premises it follows, Hobbes maintained, that to obtain the protections of peace requires an absolute sovereign who will enforce on the unruly, self-interested atoms of society a firm external structure to keep the peace in everyone's best interest. In Hobbes' long lifetime, he lived contentedly both under kings (for whose rights Hobbes argued with passion) and under a Lord

Protector, after Oliver Cromwell's revolution succeeded. By any name or title, the controlling presence of a sovereign will was the key for Hobbes. What the sovereign wills is the law and the *law is just*, by definition, since there is no justice or injustice prior to, or outside, the covenant that the sovereign enforces. Hobbes' sovereign, we may note, echoes the omnipotence of Ockham's God in human terms. The *content* of what is willed is completely arbitrary. It is right because it is willed, not vice versa. Hobbes, of course, had a completely different idea of what was being achieved by the life of obedience to the law giver. For Ockham, it was eternal salvation. For Hobbes, it was worldly security. But for both, ethics was an instrument, a tool to achieve an end wholly distinct from the means.

The *arbitrariness* of ethics has been a recurrent theme since the breakdown of the medieval synthesis in late premodern and early modern thinking. The notion of the "arbitrary" itself has double-edged associations. On the negative side, heard most often in ordinary discourse, it means "unreasonable," "despotic," or "imposed." What is arbitrary does not reflect rules, but is a matter of someone's mere decision. On the more positive side, however, the Latin *arbitrium* (will or judgment) is at the root of "arbiter," one chosen to end deadlock by making a decision, and "arbitration," a process in which wise judgment is called for.

The relation between reason and judgment is key. At one extreme, Plato can be read as stressing universal truth in moral qualities so strongly that judgment is unnecessary. One's rational soul is illuminated, overwhelmed, by the eternal Good. Even God would have no choice, no judgment to make. The temporal notion of "making a choice" or "exercising will" is entirely out of place in this framework. It is even hard to square the dynamic images befitting a personal God (as was felt by Ockham) with the unchanging perfection of the Forms. At the other extreme, therefore, judgment can be stressed to the exclusion of reason. Scotus and Ockham came to this point in defense of the unlimited freedom of the will of God. Omnipotence suffers no rules. Arbitration, in the positive sense, is God's prerogative. Laying down the moral law is not a matter of *following* rules but *determining* them. Descartes and Hobbes, as we have seen, emphasized the primacy of decision over reason in ethics on other grounds. But no one brought this matter—the utter disconnect between reasons and ethical judgments—to such a pitch of clarity as David Hume.

Hume (1711–1776) came to his views as a young man, perhaps as early as eighteen years of age, in the context of wider doctrines expounded in his great *Treatise of Human Nature* (1739). I have dealt with this context in some detail in an earlier volume (Ferré 1998, 146–56). In this chapter, narrating ethical theory, we need only recall the immense power of Hume's capacity for making mutually exclusive distinctions, especially the distinction between ideas and impressions. Ideas are copies of impressions, marked by faded force and vivacity as second hand. We use ideas to think about matters near or far—sometimes we simply construct new topics by the imagination, with the materials afforded by ideas. Impressions, in contrast, are the original, first-hand encounter in experience on which ideas later depend for their meaningful content, if such there be. Sometimes, Hume shows, we may be grossly mistaken in supposing that an idea (such as "causal connection") has any meaning of the sort we suppose. To find out, we need to check for the impression behind the questionable idea. There are only two kinds of impressions, Hume says: those that enter experience through the five senses and those that are experienced internally, by "reflexion." If, in taking careful inventory, we find that there are no impressions of either sort to support a supposed idea, we need to conclude that the idea is, to that extent, empty of content, just a word without clear sense. In the case of "causal connection," for example, the only impression Hume can find to give content to this phrase is the experience of expecting (based only on subjective habit) that similar events will be followed by other familiar events. If this exposes science as only a tissue of hunches and habits, rather than a domain of reason or certainty, so much the worse for science.

The same methodological threshing machine, separating what is distinguishable, is at work when young Hume turns his attention to ethics. To the question whether ethics is a matter of reasoning or not, Hume is able to give a firm negative, drawing on the same distinctions made in the earlier, epistemological part of the *Treatise*. Reason works by means of ideas, he reminds us. We think in words and concepts, not in the original impressions they faintly copy. Ideas passively represent subject matters. Reason takes up these limp markers and manipulates them. But moral sentiments, blame or praise, for example, do not *represent* anything. They *are* direct experiences of condemnation or approval. They are impressions (of "reflexion") that we feel directly, when they are present. They are "hot" while ideas are "cool." Admittedly, there can be "calm passions," Hume recognizes, but these are themselves directly felt as among the most agreeable and pleasurable of impressions, in a distinctive moral way capable of motivating us toward justice and generosity.

Ideas alone, then, cannot possibly motivate. This means that reason, our capacity for considering rules and principles, is entirely disqualified from playing a motivational role in life. Preferences and aversions are what drive us, and reason is necessarily powerless to oppose or deflect these motivating forces.

> Since reason alone can never produce any action, or give rise to volition, I infer, that the same faculty is as incapable of preventing volition, or of disputing the preference with any passion or emotion. This consequence is necessary (Hume 1955, 414–15).

Not only is it necessary, Hume continues, it is appropriate. Reason should focus on what it can do well: calculating the means of achieving our preferences and evading our perceived dangers. It brings only confusion to speak of "the combat of passion and of reason. Reason is, and ought only to be the slave of the passions, and can never pretend to any other office than to serve and obey them" (Hume 1955, 414).

Much depends on exactly how the moral "passions" are to be understood. Are they—as in some conceptions of conscience—feelings that reflect or detect some authoritative moral reality? Hume's favored phrase, "moral sentiment," might be compatible with an interpretation of "sentiment" which (like its cousin, "presentiment") involves a referent to something (in the latter case, a dreaded objective event) beyond itself. Hume insists that moral passions are impressions, not ideas; occasionally he applies to them the term "moral *sense*" (Hume 1955, 470). Are moral sentiments "passions" in this cognitively informative sense, for Hume?

His answer is emphatically negative. The feelings by which we distinguish moral good and evil are particular kinds of agreeable or disagreeable feelings in ourselves, and nothing more.

> An action, or sentiment, or character is virtuous or vicious; why? because its view causes a pleasure or uneasiness of a particular kind. In giving a reason, therefore, for the pleasure of uneasiness, we sufficiently explain the vice or virtue. To have the sense of virtue, is nothing but to *feel* a satisfaction of a particular kind from the contemplation of a character. The very *feeling* constitutes our praise or admiration. We go no farther; nor do we enquire into the cause of the satisfaction. We do not infer a character to be virtuous, because it pleases: But in feeling that it pleases after such a particular manner, we in effect feel that it is virtuous. The case is the same as in our judgments concerning all kinds of beauty, and tastes, and sensations (Hume 1955, 471).

The feeling *constitutes* the virtue; the sense of virtue is *nothing but* the feeling. It may indeed be possible to compare "moral sentiments" with "impressions of sensation," but only with the sort of sensations that reflect nothing objectively real. Here Hume's classically modern doctrine of secondary qualities (accepted from Galileo through Newton) comes to the aid of his ethical theory. Just as modern epistemic orthodoxy excludes the crackling sound of a tree falling in the forest from what is objectively in the forest, in just the same way Hume urges that the moral sense is generated entirely within the observer and has reference to nothing beyond. Do you feel moral disapprobation toward some action or other matter of fact?

It lies in yourself, not in the object. So that when you pronounce any action or character to be vicious, you mean nothing, but that from the constitution of your nature you have a feeling or sentiment of blame from the contemplation of it. Vice and virtue, therefore, may be compar'd to sounds, colours, heat and cold, which, according to modern philosophy, are not qualities in objects, but perceptions in the mind (Hume 1955, 469).

In the immediate context of this invocation of the mind-dependent status of secondary qualities by "modern philosophy," Hume draws his famous conclusion that "ought" can never be derived from "is." Matters of fact are questions of "is" and "is-not," containing no trace of "ought." No matter how closely we observe facts, there are only more facts, not values or obligations, which are "entirely different" (Hume 1955, 469). Since completely different, moral terms can never be the subject of valid deduction from descriptive terms. Hume puts his case against traditional ethical theory as follows:

> In every system of morality, which I have hitherto met with, I have always remark'd, that the author proceeds for some time in the ordinary way of reasoning, and establishes the being of a God, or makes observations concerning human affairs; when of a sudden I am surpriz'd to find, that instead of the usual copulations of propositions, *is* and *is not*, I meet with no proposition that is not connected with an *ought*, or an *ought not*. This change is imperceptible; but is, however, of the last consequence. For as this *ought*, or *ought not*, expresses some new relation or affirmation, 'tis necessary that it shou'd be observ'd and explain'd; and at the same time that a reason should be given, for what seems altogether inconceivable, how this new relation can be a deduction from the others, which are entirely different from it (Hume 1955, 469).

Hume's special place in the narrative of ethical theory would have been secure had he made only one such major argument for the utter arbitrariness of ethical "aversions" and "attractions." But it was his genius to make three equally momentous arguments, approaching the same conclusion from epistemology, metaphysics, and logic. From *epistemology*, he showed that reason has no authority in ethics since, on his understanding of "ideas," ethical ideas cannot possibly motivate or even contradict moral motivations. Ideas—with which reason is alone concerned—are faint, passive copies; moral motivators are something else entirely. Directly experienced impressions, sentiments—the moral passions—are what rightly rule. From *metaphysics*, he linked these impressions (at best) to the sort of mind-dependent sensations that "modern philosophy" had strongly concluded were not rooted in reality. Just as there is nothing like the quality "redness" in the material order constituting nature, so there is nothing like "goodness" in the world of fact. From *logic*, similarly, drawing on the axiom that nothing can appear in the conclusion of a deduction that is not present in the premises, he warned against attempting to derive "ought" from "is." Put more sweepingly, no assertions of value can be legitimately deduced from assertions of fact, or vice versa. Hume's incomparably incisive mind managed in these ways to block, with utmost clarity, all possible legitimization of morality by reason.

Immanuel Kant (1724–1804), once "awakened from his dogmatic slumbers" by Hume's brilliant but outrageous doubts about the power and dignity of reason, whether in science or morals, devoted his philosophical life to giving conclusive answers to these unsettling challenges. One of the deepest ironies in the history of philosophy is reflected in Kant's epoch-making successes. In metaphysics (see Ferré 1996, 197–205), Kant stoutly defended, for example, the necessity of causality in science, but only at the cost of absolutizing the mystery of how the free mind and reason, causality's guarantor, can possibly live in the deterministically closed world studied by science. Kant's revolutionary response to Hume made the modern agenda of finding a place for mind and value in nature even more intractable. Again, in epistemology (see Ferré 1998, 156–62), it was Kant's impassable epistemic gap between the knowable (phenomenal) world and the utterly unknowable (noumenal) world of things in themselves—things as they really are—that snapped and sealed shut the trap set by Hume on modern theory of knowledge. Now we see that Kant's epic struggle to rebut Hume's aspersions on the peripheral role of reason in morality simply intensifies the sense of how much was lost in winning these ultimately Pyrrhic victories.

Significantly, Kant began his campaign against Hume on ethics by surrendering to his opponent's seemingly clear but fatal distinction between facts and values. Nothing at all in the merely factual empirical world is good in itself, Kant declared.

> Intelligence, wit, judgment, and the other *talents* of the mind, however they may be named, or courage, resolution, perseverance, as qualities of temperament, are undoubtedly good and desirable in many respects; but these gifts of nature may also become extremely bad and mischievous if the will which is to make use of them, and which, therefore, constitutes what is called *character*, is not good (Kant 1949, 11).

Wealth and power, riches and health—even happiness itself—all these merely factual "gifts of fortune," too, are bad things if enjoyed by a scoundrel. Ethics therefore must remain clear of anything that smacks of empirical fact. Anthropological or sociological information about human beings in general must be ruled irrelevant to ethical values. Obviously, ethics may be allowed no grounding in such merely psychological facts as preferences or inclinations (or moral sentiments of aversion or attraction). Even facts about the consequences of actions or policies of action need to be dismissed from consideration.

The strongly anti-consequentialist character of Kant's ethics is a matter of perplexity for many who come unprepared by history to this viewpoint. It should not astonish anyone who first has felt the force of Hume's powerful arguments against deriving "ought" from "is." The consequences of our actions are mere matters of fact. They may please or displease us, may occasion approval or disapproval, but such feelings, as matters of psychology or social conditioning, are morally irrelevant. Further, the empirical facts following our actions are not under our control. Nature's mechanism follows its own causal laws, often surprising us with sad outcomes from the best intentions (and sometimes with happy results to frustrate even the most malicious). What, in any case, counts as "the outcome" of an action in nature's unbroken causal flow? Time, the a priori form of every intuition, necessarily goes on, making every judgment based on empirical consequences merely a temporary subtotal of outcomes so far. Moral judgments, were they to be based on matters of fact, would always have to be postponed, since the facts are never complete. What is needed instead is an understanding of morality independent of empirical fact but open to rigorous immediate assessment by a universal standard.

This need is answered, Kant argued, by concentrating on the *principles of our intentions* as the sole standard for moral judgment. The first sentence of his *Fundamental Principles of the Metaphysics of Morals* declares: "Nothing can possibly be conceived in the world, or even out of it, which can be called good without qualification, except a *good will*" (Kant 1949, 11). What we mentally intend when we will an action can be judged quite apart from the action's factual outcome. This way we do not need to wait for the never-ending cascade of consequences. Intentions are measured instead by the principles on the basis of which we will our actions. Principles are universal, not particular empirical derivatives of my contingent psychological makeup or your social setting. Principles allow recognition by reason and assessment by the rigors of logic. The morally good will in fact is defined by its readiness to respect universal lawfulness in general. The moral imperative behind all imperatives, the *categorical* imperative, is to will in each case so that the principle reflected in that intention could be consistently willed by anyone. In other words, that one should make sure that the principle involved in any action could logically be willed as a universal law. Duty in general, as Kant concludes, "*is the necessity of acting from respect for the law*" (Kant 1949, 18). Specific duties can be derived by holding relevant principles to one rigorous logical test: "can this principle be universalized?"

Kant's most famous application of logic to a specific moral question deals with telling lies. Is it ever morally permissible to deceive? The answer, once subjected to logical analysis, is necessarily no. A case of lying would require willing the principle that language be used to create belief in what is false. But this principle cannot possibly be universalized. If language were always used to attempt deceit, no one would believe anything asserted. It would be logically impossible to universalize the principle contained in any lie. Lies are only possible because language is normally used to state what is true. Willing as a universal law the principle contained in a lie is logically impossible. It is therefore always contrary to duty to lie. Morally, we must always tell the truth, no matter what the empirical consequences.

Kant realized that this conclusion is in many ways deeply counter-intuitive, but he defended it, even against critics who asked whether one has a duty to tell the truth even when one is harboring a friend against a murderous maniac who demands to know whether the friend is in the house. If told the truth, the maniac is likely to break in and kill the friend. This is a possible consequence, Kant agreed, but beyond our control. What we can control is our respect for duty. What if we *had* lied to the maniac, but meanwhile the friend, fearing that we would tell the truth, had slipped out of the window, right into the path of the one whom we had deceptively turned away? Then we would have been responsible (morally) for violating our duty to the truth and (causally) for the friend's falling into murderous hands despite our lie.

Such thought experiments, although ingeniously defended, expose the grave weakness of Kant's readiness to insulate moral value from considerations of fact. Principles, derived by logical deduction and defended by appeal to the necessities of logic, tend either (*a*) to become so enmeshed with factual circumstances that they lose their generality, or (*b*) to become so general as to lose relevancy to life. At the first extreme, the maxims defining the issues in a given case can be made so specific (e.g., "*If* I knew that the maniac would turn away *and* I knew that my friend would slip out the window," etc.) that all the circumstances taken together would define a unique case. But at the other extreme, maxims can be stated so generally (e.g., "One cannot consistently will the general rule both to deceive and to be believed," and "One cannot consistently will the general rule both to care for and to allow harm to befall one's friend," etc.) that the application of such principles—and even settling which principles are more relevant to the circumstances—is made impossible.

The abstract air of Kant's ethical theory not only gives it the feel of unreality, but also opens the door to fanaticism. Where absolute principle bears down with unblinking focus on one issue, although many factors are tangled in the complexities of real life, the nuances of wise judgment are likely to be lost.

To be sure, Kant at one point tried to qualify his absolutism, even about lying, in extremis:

> If force is used to extort a confession from me, if my confession is improperly used against me, and if I cannot save myself by maintaining silence, then my lie is a weapon of defence. The misuse of a declaration extorted by force justifies me in defending myself. . . . The forcing of a statement from me under conditions which convince me that improper use would be made of it is the only case in which I can be justified in telling a white lie (Kant 1963, 228).

But if the threat of torture in an immoral cause is the "only case" in which Kant can imagine lying justified, our sense of unreality is, if anything, intensified.

Still more serious in principle is Kant's metaphysically awkward stance toward the whole enterprise of morality. He insisted that the whole domain of nature is under the rule of causal necessity (Ferré 1996, 200–202), but morality requires freedom. If I am determined by prior causes to perform a certain act, then it makes no sense to blame me for doing as I must. "Ought implies can." If I *cannot* do otherwise, then to say I *ought* to do otherwise is absurd. This is a valid argument *modus tollens*: If O_{ught}, then C_{an}; but not C_{an}, therefore not-O_{ught}. If mechanistic nature implies "heteronomy of the will," then morality is impossible.

Kant responded by attempting to turn the tables. From *modus tollens* (denying the consequent) he boldly moved to the equally valid *modus ponens* (affirming the antecedent): If O_{ught}, then C_{an}; but O_{ught}, therefore C_{an}. In other words, since ought implies can and I find conclusively that *I am indeed under obligation*, then I must conclude that *I can make moral choices*—that somehow "autonomy of will" holds for moral agents, despite the deterministic laws of Nature.

For Kant, the "somehow" was solved by appeal to the noumenal realm of things in themselves, unfettered by the a priori categories through which we necessarily think the phenomenal world of experience. The freedom essential to morality is not part of the empirical order open to scientific scrutiny. Where science looks, it inevitably finds nothing but causality. But the agency of moral choice is not part of that domain. "For the law of pure will, which is free, puts the will in a sphere entirely different from the empirical, and the necessity which it expresses, not being a natural necessity, can consist only in the formal conditions of the possibility of a law in general" (Kant 1956, 34).

The noumenal realm, however, is literally unknowable (Ferré 1998, 160–62). All the conceptual tools that allow us to understand the world of experience are useless where, by definition, they cannot apply. Kant's "solution," therefore, is not a theoretical one, as he acknowledges. It is purely practical. But this means that the crucially needed answers for ethical theory are forever out of reach, on the far side of the epistemological gap. From a theoretical perspective, the assertion of moral obligation and the postulation of freedom are purely arbitrary. In winning his victory over Hume's empirical challenge to reason in ethics, Kant cemented the foundations of ethics in the unthinkable.

LATE MODERN ETHICAL THEORY

John Stuart Mill (1806–1873), whose life spanned the middle of the nineteenth century and whose values reflected the very center of maturing modernity, rejected Kant's highly inferential approach to ethics. In place of the model of logical deduction, Mill offered the model of quantitative calculation. In nearly all respects Mill was the antithesis of Kant. For Kant, consequences could count not at all; for Mill, consequences were all that counted. For Kant, happiness was a mere fact of psychology, not morally relevant (or even a potentially dangerous temptation); for Mill, happiness, or "utility," as he called it, was the only ultimately relevant measure of the good. For Kant, the good in itself was identified with the will's respect for the right, or duty; for Mill, the right was defined by maximizing the good in itself, or happiness. But for all their obvious differences, Mill and Kant were both intent on removing the taint of mere arbitrariness from ethics. Kant's failure in this enterprise came from his excessive abstraction in the mode of general principles. Mill's analogous failure, though he was far more attentive to the roots of ethics in particular emotion-drenched human actions, came from another sort of abstraction long present at the core of modern sensibility, the cult of quantification.

Utilitarianism, since its founding by Jeremy Bentham (1748–1842) and until the present, requires a quasi-mathematical approach. Bentham invented the famous "hedonic calculus," in which the pleasure and pain of all concerned is to be calculated and the action maximizing net pleasure is to be chosen. The "bottom line" must show *more* of what is ultimately valued in the morally favored outcome. Mill softened the strictly countinghouse atmosphere created by Bentham's refusal to make qualitative distinctions among types of happiness, but in so doing (as adequacy to the phenomena of moral experience indeed requires) he raised problems of coherence within his own position. That is, this introduced a second, independent standard, not explicable in terms of the first, for the measurement of utility.

Quantification, however, was the primary standard for Mill, and the aim of his quintessentially modern ethical theory was for the *greatest happiness for the greatest number*. His own definition of what he calls the "ultimate end" reads as follows:

According to the "greatest happiness principle," as above explained, the ultimate end, with reference to and for the sake of which all other things are desirable (whether we are considering our own good or that of other people), is an existence exempt as far as possible from pain, and as rich as possible in enjoyments, both in point of quantity and quality; the test of quality, and the rule for measuring it against quantity, being the preference felt by those who in their opportunities of experience, to which must be added their habits of self-consciousness and self-observation, are best furnished with the means of comparison (Mill 1993, 55).

Since it is impossible to quantify who is "best furnished," or expert, to judge the quality of enjoyments, adding this proviso invites suspicion of arbitrariness (or snobbery). But in application, the proviso is in any case mainly ignored. The dream of modern utilitarianism is to reduce ethical decision as much as possible to a calculation. Like the ubiquitous cost-benefit analysis of more recent days (itself an institutional device largely rooted in utilitarian ways of thinking), Mill's theory, no less than Bentham's, requires that in making an ethical decision the probable utilities (the enjoyments, benefits) be quantified and aggregated in one column, then the disutilities (the pains, costs) be likewise added up in another column. The total gross disutilities of the second column are then subtracted from the total gross utilities of the first, showing the net consequence of a decision as either positive or negative in quantity of utility. If the "bottom line" is positive, then the act is morally right; if negative, then it is wrong.

Making happiness the "ultimate end" centers Mill's ethical theory in personal satisfaction, but this must not be confused with egoism. Mill is careful to insist that each center of pleasures and pains must count equally in the moral calculation. Each one counts as one. My personal utility must be weighted no more heavily than my neighbor's, or than a stranger's in a foreign land. Modern democratic spirit breathes through Mill's theory no less prominently than does modern confidence in mathematics.

Despite the many admirable features of this mature modern approach to ethics, it cannot possibly survive scrutiny. Assigning units of utility or disutility to pleasures and pains is an exercise in absurdity. How many units of utility should go to eating an ice cream cone? When? Under what circumstances? How many to holding one's baby? How many to successfully reconciling one's checking account? Or, conversely, how many units of disutility should be assigned to hearing one's baby cry for an hour? How many to undergoing a blood test? How many to preparing one's income tax? A hedonic pricing system, even if such a system were attempted, would quickly be wrecked by the introduction of differently "furnished" individuals with different qualitative perspectives on the pleasures of an evening with a good book versus an evening watching professional wrestling.

Without a standard pricing system, adding and subtracting utilities is not merely difficult; it is without meaning. Even my own pleasures and pains seem to a large extent incommensurable. How many ice cream cones would balance hearing my baby cry for an hour? What if the cause for the crying is an open diaper pin? Does this require my eating more ice cream to compensate? Such a question makes it obvious that the pains and pleasures of others are even more hopelessly incommensurable. Suppose that on some proposed pricing system I can receive more units of utility from a steak dinner (with excellent wine) than my baby receives units of disutility from (say) being left with soggy diapers (all pins secured, this time) while I am gone. Is it meaningfully possible to subtract someone else's discomfort from my pleasure, in order to calculate the net worth of the resulting situation? If such quasi-mathematical moves are hard even in the limited context of my own often incommensurable utilities and disutilities, it is much harder to do among the many centers of suffering and satisfaction involved in serious ethical decision making.

I should say not merely "harder," but worse, repulsive. Modern utilitarianism *defines* the "right" by calculating the net utility (the residual quantity of intrinsic good) in an outcome. But *is* it really right, we want to know, to maximize the "ultimate end" if the cost to some individuals is unfairly high? If a million distant consumers of cheap electricity enjoy a marginal increase of utility (multiplied vastly by their large numbers), does this compensate for severe disutilities inflicted on the health and aesthetic enjoyments of the few who live near the generating plant? In aggregating the totals, if attention is paid only to the "bottom line," the sharp sufferings of a handful, subtracted from the mildly enhanced but hugely multiplied enjoyments of the many, may leave a large remainder of net utility that, for utilitarianism, will justify the policy as "right." But the question *who* suffers and *who* benefits has been ignored. The sense of fairness has been violated. No matter how meticulously the ethical books are kept, something vital has escaped. Perhaps the spirit of ethics, itself, has evaporated. Mill's younger contemporary, Friedrich Nietzsche (1844–1900), expressed his disdain for such theory by dismissing utilitarianism as an ethic "fit only for a nation of shopkeepers."

George Edward Moore (1873–1958) was no less critical of utilitarianism, but for different reasons and in quite a different spirit. His great concern in ethics (as in the rest of his philosophy) was to avoid mixing up different things, confusing them with one another. The epigraph Moore placed on the title page of his major book, *Principia Ethica* (1903) is an apt quotation from Bishop Joseph Butler (1692–1752): "Everything is what it is, and not another thing."

Moore was convinced that Bentham and Mill had mixed up the concept of "good" with something that it is not. They had identified good with happiness, and the greatest good with the greatest happiness for the greatest number. Mill, as we saw, had termed this the "ultimate end." But in this identification, *equating* good with some empirical (what Moore called a "natural") matter of fact like the happiness of people, he found a deep mistake, amounting to a logical fallacy. Similar to Hume's logical point (that a syllogism containing only factual terms in its premises cannot suddenly sprout value expressions in its conclusion), Moore's argument declared it a fallacy to define "good" in terms drawn wholly from natural matters of fact.

Several reasons are given by Moore for rejecting any definition of good offered in such terms. In one argument, Moore points out that definitions always combine elements, at least a genus term linked to a differentiating term or terms, for example, "triangle" can be defined as a "closed plane figure" (genus) composed of "three straight lines" (differentia). But "good" is itself elementary; that is, it is a simple quality not made up of parts.

> It is in this sense that I deny good to be definable. I say that it is not composed of parts, which we can substitute for it in our minds when we are thinking of it. We might think just as clearly and correctly about a horse, if we thought of all its parts and their arrangement instead of thinking of the whole; . . . but there is nothing whatsoever which we could so substitute for good; and that is what I mean, when I say that good is indefinable (Moore 1956, 8).

To drive home the elementary and unanalyzable character of good, Moore compares it with a simple natural quality, yellow. Yellow is indefinable in exactly the same way. Without a sensory intuition of the quality, no amount of defining in other terms will do. Talk about light wavelengths may be relevant to scientific explanations of our visual experience, but electromagnetic vibrations are not what we mean by yellow.

> *They* are not what we perceive. Indeed we should never have been able to discover their existence, unless we had been struck by the patent differences of quality between the different colours. The most we can be entitled to say of those vibrations is that they are what corresponds in space to the yellow which we actually perceive.
>
> Yet a mistake of this simple kind has commonly been made about 'good.' It may be true that all things which are good are *also* something else, just as it is true that all things which are yellow produce a certain kind of vibration in the light. And it is a fact, that Ethics aims at discovering what are those other properties belonging to all things which are good. But far too many philosophers have thought that when they name those other properties they were actually defining good; that these properties, in fact were simply not 'other,' but absolutely and entirely the

same with goodness. This view I propose to call the 'naturalistic fallacy'
... (Moore 1956, 10).

Mill, we saw, thought that happiness was absolutely and entirely the same
with goodness. That this was a fallacy is shown in two ways by Moore. First, if
happiness were simply *the same thing* as good, then to say "happiness is good"
would be the same as saying "happiness is happiness"—nothing would have
been added. Second, if happiness were logically identical with good, it would
be meaningless to ask the obvious question: "But *is* happiness *really* good?" It
is always open to critics, however, to raise this issue, when goodness is defined
in terms of some natural state or property. As Kant pointed out (following the
Psalmist long before), the happiness of the wicked is morally troubling.
Happiness is not always or necessarily good. Honor may also be good, but
honor and happiness are not always identical. Because of the availability of the
open question—"But is *X* really good?"—by which one may challenge whatever matters of natural fact might be defined as exhausting the meaning of
good, no natural fact or quality can satisfy.

Moore's quest for making distinctions carries him one more step. He offers a dilemma to those who may still doubt that good is something simple, a
"non-natural" quality, sui generis, that needs no definition but serves as the
basis for any meaningful talk in ethics. "In fact," he writes, "if it is not the case
the "good" denotes something simple and indefinable, only two alternatives
are possible: either it is a complex, a given whole, about the correct analysis of
which there may be disagreement; or else it means nothing at all, and there is
no such subject as Ethics" (Moore 1956, 15). That it is not the former, a complex to be analyzed, has been shown, especially by the Open Question argument, which can be brought to bear on any alleged natural complex. This
would leave only the latter alternative, that good "means nothing at all" and
that "there is no such subject" as ethics. Moore finds the latter alternative even
more patently absurd than the former. In his hands, the Naturalistic Fallacy
was a weapon used in defense of ethics rooted in the meaning-bestowing intuition of a completely simple and unique nonnatural quality: *goodness itself*,
which is "what it is, and not another thing."

What seemed absurd to Moore—that good "means nothing at all"—struck
A. J. Ayer (1910–1989), instead, as the obvious consequence of his theory of
meaning. In a culmination of key modern trends toward (1) the total elimination of values from nature, and (2) the radical reliance on sensory perception as
the only route to knowledge, Ayer's promulgation of Logical Positivism (Ferré
1998, 179–87) announced the futility of ethical theory as it had been attempted
over the ages. Deep unease at the looming threat of this futility remains a dominant mood suffusing ethical theory to this day.

Ayer struck at the very heart of all discussion of value, aesthetic as well as ethical, when he pushed Moore's argument just one step further. Moore had succeeded, Ayer agreed, in showing the logical impossibility of reducing value terms ("good" or "right" or even "beautiful") to anything empirically definable. There is always the logical possibility of meaningfully asking the open question for any such terms. "Certainly, X is *approved by all*, but does that make it really good?" Or, "Agreed, Y will bring about *greatest net happiness*, but is it really right?" Or, "Yes, Z is *pleasingly harmonious*, but is it really beautiful?" Moore was sure that this empirical elusiveness, this indefinability by anything natural, proved that value terms must be grounded in a nonnatural, indefinable, intuition—an absolute contact with value required on pain of the utter collapse of the ethical enterprise. Ayer, however, grasped the nettle shunned by Moore and concluded that in the traditional sense, there is indeed "no such subject" as ethics.

Ethical talk abounds, of course. But behind that talk, except for the (purely formal) lexicographical work of establishing or clarifying syntactical connections among the words we use when we make ethical utterances, there is no foothold for reasonable discussion. The fact that value terms are not finally definable in terms of any natural, empirically observable equivalent shows, Ayer declared, that they are empty of factual significance. They are empirically unverifiable in principle. Moore may be certain that he absolutely intuits the good, but this certainty is merely one more fact.

> For it is notorious that what seems intuitively certain to one person may seem doubtful, or even false, to another. So that unless it is possible to provide some criterion by which one may decide between conflicting intuitions, a mere appeal to intuition is worthless as a test of a proposition's validity. But in the case of moral judgements, no such criterion can be given. Some moralists claim to settle the matter by saying that they "know" that their own moral judgements are correct. But such an assertion is of purely psychological interest, and has not the slightest tendency to prove the validity of any moral judgement. For dissentient moralists may equally well "know" that their ethical views are correct. And, as far as subjective certainty goes, there will be nothing to choose between them (Ayer 1946, 106).

Clearly, these disputing intuitionists do not mean to acknowledge that the "good" means merely that they strongly feel certain of something. They would see this as objectionably reductionist, and, besides, it would fall prey to the Open Question: "Yes, you are absolutely certain that X is good, but is it *really good?*" They intend, rather, to make an informative claim that goes beyond anyone's subjective feelings. They want to assert a nonnatural fact. But this seems ruled out by the very insulation from empirical test that they have demanded.

A factual assertion, as Ayer argues, is simply equivalent to the set of simpler empirical assertions that we would be able to make if the first assertion is true. "It is raining" is simply equivalent to "I see water drops falling from the sky" (together with all the other confirming sensory assertions that could be made). Hence, the informative content (the meaning) of a factual assertion can be equated with the empirical observations that would tend to verify it. But, as we have seen, if we are to avoid the Naturalistic Fallacy, no such observations can be allowed for ethical (or other value) utterances. Therefore *ethical utterances* are empty of factual significance.

> We begin by admitting that the fundamental ethical concepts are unanalysable, inasmuch as there is no criterion by which one can test the validity of the judgements in which they occur. So far we are in agreement with the absolutists. But, unlike the absolutists, we are able to give an explanation of this fact about ethical concepts. We say that the reason why they are unanalysable is that they are mere pseudo-concepts. The presence of an ethical symbol in a proposition adds nothing to its factual content (Ayer 1946, 107).

Still, if ethical symbols do not express genuine concepts, then some account is needed showing what *is* going on when we utter ethical symbols. Ayer's account, still widely influential (in various forms) among ethical theorists, is that ethical terms are used simply and exclusively to express emotion. We show how we feel when we add "good" or "bad" to our sentences. We are not *asserting anything* thereby, not even that we feel in a certain way (though this psychological report could meaningfully be made in a different context)—rather, we are *evincing* our feeling, *manifesting* that we feel in a certain way when we use such language. Since we are not asserting anything, our utterance is not of the sort that could be true or false. Nor can others appropriately argue with me.

> For in saying that a certain type of action is right or wrong, I am not making any factual statement, not even a statement about my own state of mind. I am merely expressing certain moral sentiments. And the man who is ostensibly contradicting me is merely expressing his moral sentiments. So that there is plainly no sense in asking which of us is in the right. For neither of us is asserting a genuine proposition (Ayer 1946, 107–108).

We have come a long way, from the confident days of Socrates and Plato in search of an ethical science to anguished contemporary wonderment whether in ethics we can argue reasonably—or even say anything meaningful at all. A great deal of wrestling with these matters has occurred since Ayer brought to clarity the implicit consequences for ethics of modern irrealism regarding natural value and modern skepticism about supra- and infrasensory modes of knowing. But I shall end my narrative here. The next two chapters represent my attempt to address constructively the issues of ethical skepticism and ethical irrealism bequeathed to us at the start of a new millennium.

Despite much churning, I do not believe that philosophers have made much real advance from Ayer in recent years. The problem, I think, has been that most ethical theorists have attempted to answer these quintessential modern dilemmas from within either premodern or essentially unreformed modern frameworks of epistemology and metaphysics. My hope is that constructive postmodern thought, specifically the epistemology of continuity suggested by the ecological metaphysics of personalistic organicism—by offering ground cleared both of premodern overconfidence and modern despair—will allow the seeds of a more satisfying ethical theory to germinate. Providing explicit grounds for this hope is the main task of the next two chapters.

3

ETHICS AND KNOWING

After the previous review of Western philosophy's long slide toward ethical arbitrariness, it is clear that rebuilding confidence in the possibility of reasonable
ethical judgments—the aim of this chapter—is no small task. The main trouble, I believe, comes from presumed disconnections. In the late Middle Ages,
God's goodness was (piously) uncoupled from God's omnipotence, with the
latter valued above all else. God must be free (argued Scotus, Ockham, and
their followers) to choose anything, literally *anything*, as "good." There must
be no strings on divine freedom. In this case, human thinking should never expect to find independent, intrinsic "qualities of goodness" (which would bind
God's choices) in what we are commanded to do or to approve.

Similar sorts of disconnection, now justified on secular rather than sacred
grounds, were advanced by the shapers of modern ethical theory. Descartes
quietly uncoupled his ethical commitments from rational principle. Hobbes
defended the arbitrary legislation of any sovereign over the horrors of anarchy.
Hume separated moral sentiments from ideas, in principle, leaving reason
"slave of the passions." Kant, in trying to rescue reason, made consequences
irrelevant and the application of abstract principle to daily life endlessly elusive. Moore forced an either/or choice between ethical intuition and every natural state of affairs. Ayer emphatically chose empirical fact, concluding that
ethical intuition, if empirically unverifiable, must be something entirely bereft
of cognitive meaning.

My proposal is that we step back from the categorizations and dichotomies that have dominated modern discussion, taking a fresh look at ethical *experience*, ethical *thinking*, and ethical *knowing*, but now with an eye to

the continuities and connections underlying overemphasized modern distinctions. If we do this, we may find that ethics is not so far removed from other domains of experience, thought, and knowledge. We may—though continuing to recognize that we must live in a world without ethical "experts"—find grounds for renewed confidence in the possibility of developing socially responsible, reasonable ethical judgments of our own.

ETHICAL EXPERIENCING

Attending to direct experience is something philosophers need to do often and carefully. Frequently even the "empiricist" tradition has fallen into traps because it has not been empirical enough. The prestige of David Hume, for example, has been such that generations of "empiricist" followers have followed his dictum that we have no experience of real causality (Ferré 1998, 154–56), even though every experience of a bodily reflex, every struggle against an ingrained habit, and every deliberate act of mental reorientation would—if really noticed—falsify that dogma (Ferré 1998, 295–99). Another unfortunate legacy of modern empiricism has been to concentrate only on the clear and distinct aspects of experience, those that can easily be noticed and named. This has left much, perhaps most, experience unremarked, thus undermining the adequacy of positions built on such highly selected aspects of awareness. Likewise, the clear and distinct portions of experience, though easier to talk about, are also easier to chop apart from one another and thus to present as either/or dichotomies. This encourages philosophers to miss or dismiss dimmer connections and ignore murkier relationships, thereby seriously undermining the coherence of any theories they may base on such bright *fragments* of experience misidentified as *all* experience (Ferré 1998, 276–303).

Fortunately, discussions of experience need not be taken on faith, or on someone else's prestige. My own claims are made in full confidence that every reader will test whatever I say against the touchstone of first-hand subjectivity. For this reason, I shall not decorate my account with learned citations from scholars in philosophy or psychology. They are in the end redundant. Discussing the general character of human experience is not supposed to be providing new information. It is simply drawing attention to features that should be familiar, but are sometimes overlooked. It is a reminding. It is emphasizing the importance of what might be underrated because of ingrained habits of thinking. It is, finally, letting a pattern show that each one will see— or not see. In that spirit, let me offer a few reminders about experiencing value in general and then, more specifically, experiencing ethical value.

The first and most important reminder I can offer is that the celebrated (supposed) isolation of facts from values is utterly unsupported by genuine experience. The exact opposite is found. There is no experience without some affective tone containing at least vague (but sometimes very sharp) feelings of approval or disapproval, contentment or discontentment, preference or revulsion. Our world, our inner bodily states, our mental condition, are constantly colored with evaluations. Through our waking hours, we move immersed in an ocean of values, positive and negative; when we sleep, our never-ending swim through the value sea becomes even more prominent in our dreams.

This does not mean, of course, that our experience of facts and our experience of values, even though they come together, are indistinguishable. If we are confronted on the beach with a magnificent specimen of the opposite sex, we can, on reflection, distinguish the elements of height, weight, hair color, contours, and so forth, present in our experience from the delight, attraction, approval, and so forth, we experience at the same time. But to distinguish in thought (despite popular dogma with roots in Hume) is not to separate in reality. I am not addressing "thought" at this point, in any case. I am simply offering reminders about experience. In experience, the facts and the values are intertwined. In this example, if it were not for the facts we would not have these stimuli to evoke our positive evaluations, but if it were not for our positive evaluations, we would not be experiencing the factual world as we do—we might indeed find something else for our sensory organs to dwell on. The relation is mutual: we do not experience facts without a context of preferences, and we do not experience preferences without a context of facts.

In special cases it may seem otherwise. I may find myself in a powerfully good mood, an evaluative condition, not focused on any specific set of facts. But even then there is a factual context to which my generalized valuations are responding, at least as necessary conditions; for example, my body's state of health and digestive contentment (least noticed, as Epicurus remarked, when functioning well), and generally supportive environmental circumstances, such as enough moderately clean air to breathe, temperatures within the range suitable for human comfort, and the like. Although below the level of conscious awareness, there is an array of chemical facts, as well, that sometimes buoy, sometimes depress resultant experience. But with this remark, I am straying too far from the simple description of experience and touching on theory about what experiencing human organisms are. To this we must return in the next chapter. But there is nothing untoward about noticing that our valuational experience is intimately entwined with our bodily condition. Hunger makes me grouchy. The world looks much better after a meal. That is not too theoretical to be mentioned here. The important point is that valuational experience is constantly surrounded by and influenced through factual contexts. There are no entirely free-floating value experiences.

Conversely, there are no entirely value free factual experiences. In some exceptional circumstances, one may deliberately suppress one's usual value responses to factual data. Scientists learn to do this in their laboratories;

medical staff must do this in their emergency rooms. Soldiers anticipating battle, and police officers facing dangerous situations, train to stay "cool," and to remain competent despite normal negative judgments and urges to flee. But none of these examples offers an exception to the main rule: There is no value free experience. Scientists and medical staff *value* the composure that allows meticulous observation and trained response to occur. Soldiers and police are trained to *commit* their lives to squadmates and partners, and are likewise trained to give intense *approval* to their larger causes, defense of country or enforcement of law. Within these strong valuational contexts, other more normal (but counterproductive) "civilian" value judgments may be overwhelmed for the sake of important work that must be done. Pilots, too, need to remain cool in case of emergency. I can report from first-hand experience that when one's single engine quits during the takeoff climb, there is no time to dither with judgments like, "Oh, isn't this dreadful!" One must immediately push the nose forward to avoid a stall. One must search the terrain for suitable emergency landing places. One must "Fly the plane!" as every instructor drums into every student pilot. But this does not mean that the pilot who keeps command is making no value judgments under such circumstances. On the contrary, affect levels are high. They are simply more focused than normal on tasks that will allow the valuer to continue valuing into another day.

In this profoundly value filled urge for survival—and, beyond simple survival, for well-being and ever-greater flourishing—human subjectivity takes its place in what on its face looks like a great continuum of adversions and aversions, preferences and fears, attractions and repulsions, throughout nature. Still minimizing theoretical matters, it *seems*, at least, that dogs are interested, both positively and negatively, in other dogs (and in squirrels, rabbits, people, old shoes, and folded newspapers), and that hummingbirds are positively interested in flowers as well as negatively in other hummingbirds (if only to drive them away from the territory), and that robins are positively interested in earthworms and negatively interested in hawks and owls. And so on. At first blush we experience a biosphere pulsing with tropisms. We find chemotropism, hydrotropism, thigmotropism, traumatropism, rheotropism, geotropism, electrotropism, phototropism, and thermotropism, to name but a few. Turning toward or away from a stimulus, advancing or retreating, are behaviors shared by plant and animal kingdoms alike. Experience places us among myriads of interrelated centers of attractions and repulsions. Raw experience does not speak to the question of whether some of these other centers are conscious of their adversions and aversions in any faint way resembling our own values and disvalues. This must be discussed in terms of theory of reality in the next chapter, but whether they are wholly unconscious or preconscious or dimly aware, we experience preferential behaviors in organic nature wherever we look. How far down in the fine structure of reality the phenomenon of attraction and repulsion extends remains a matter for theoretical debate, not experiential witness.

What we do witness directly is our own preferential experience of a world that also behaves preferentially. Ecology is the study of the dynamic interactions among a vast variety of entities related valuingly and disvaluingly, both within species and among species, and the interactions between these organic entities and the physical habitats that sometimes nurture and sometimes destroy them. Seen from the perspective of the ecological worldview from which this trilogy of books is written, the universe is abuzz with centers of value, of which the experience of human value centers is distinguished as more complex, probably more vivid, and certainly more richly stocked with normative alternative possibilities.

Nothing in my discussion so far has dealt with *ethical* value-experience. Most of the valuing in the universe is not ethical valuing. And most human experience of valuing is not particularly ethical, either. True, wanting something or fearing something involves valuing and disvaluing, respectively; but the "wanting" (as Hobbes reminded us) could be for unlimited rape and pillage, and the "fearing" might be about falling into the hands of justice. Experiencing ethically is, indeed, a type of value experience, but it is a much more limited, more specialized experience than the simple preferences, aversions, and appreciations that pervade our living and (apparently) our world.

Delineating the distinctive features of ethical experience requires me to mix more theory with my descriptions. This demands no apology, since all descriptions involve some theoretical element (if only through the public concepts used to communicate meaning from mind to mind), but it does deserve notice. I shall try to remain focused on the qualities of ethical experience in what follows, but inevitably a general stance on what ethics *is* will emerge from my treatment of how ethics *rises* from pre-ethical valuational roots.

These roots, I believe, lie deep in human social experience. The primal social relation is between the expectant woman and her fetus, which turns into the relation between mother and child. Just as woman and fetus are both identifiably distinct entities and yet not separate ones, so the neonate, though physically separated from the mother's tissues, remains related in deep ways to its giver of life and its source of continued nourishment, protection, and care. Mother and child offer a paradigm for intimate human sociality, defined partly by internal, partly by external relations (Ferré 1996, 316–24), and involving the deepest emotions on both sides, including, perhaps, vague but powerful telepathic feelings (Ferré 1998, 299–303). In this social microcosm there is both independence and interdependence. It is a complex of powerful valuations, sometimes in tension, sometimes in harmony, but always strong. It con-

stitutes a primitive community of two individuals who are not wholly individual without the other, and who are shaped by each other's inescapable preferences, aversions, pleasures, and pains.

Such various valuings are experienced, not merely inferred. The mood or
affect of the other is directly felt. Mothers need not argue by analogy to convince themselves that the sobbing child is unhappy, disvaluing the wet diaper
or the empty stomach. The relationship itself—begun before birth—is
grounded in skeins of sympathy and empathy: "feeling with" and "feeling
into" the other. The child feels the comforting warmth of the love emanating
from the mother (as well as her anger, disapproval, fatigue), and the mother
feels the child's unhappiness or contentment.

Bonds of feeling also tie families together, with strong attractions (and
sometimes equally strong repulsions), creating the dynamic interplay that is
found between parent and parent, between parents and children, and among
offspring. These manifest in various cultural expressions, worldwide, for
human beings generally. Some other species produce young capable of fending for themselves immediately upon hatching or being born. But since that is
not at all the case for human infants, who are totally dependent upon adult care
givers for an extended period, after which the young remain largely in need of
assistance and protection for years, the institution of some sort of family is a
universal characteristic of Homo sapiens. Families are cauldrons of feeling.
Members identify with one another, feel sympathy and rage toward one another, love and hate one another, defend and murder each other. Through it
all—sacrificing for each other, tormenting each other—there throbs the sense
of connection, for better or for worse.

Families, as they grow, shade into tribes, depending on such cultural variables as the number of wives and husbands and children living in close proximity, the continuing presence or absence of older generations, and the mobility of subgroups. Once again, in the tribe (or extended family) there are the
bonds of feeling, the experience of being part of each other. Sorrows are
shared; joys are occasions for group rejoicing. Notoriously, families and tribes
often band together against outsiders, who are felt as alien, out of relationship.
Such repulsion against nonmembers may enhance feelings of solidarity among
members. In any case, within the functioning group, members sympathize
with each other, share with each other, count on each other for help. The very
identity of members—who it is they feel themselves to be—is shaped by these
affectively powerful relationships.

I have been offering reminders about the natural origins of felt sympathy,
fellow feeling, community spirit. Were it not for such experiences, we would
be reduced to emotional atoms, bouncing off one another in a social void.
Without sympathy, without the capacity to feel for and with another, to take
another's pain seriously, to put oneself in another's place, to share another's

joys and fears and value them as important—ethics could never take root. There are, perhaps, in empirical fact, some individuals who are incapable of such experience. For them, cut off in a barren social desert from normal empathetic access to others, the meaning of consideration for the feelings of others is empty. Those close to them need to be protected from harm by external measures, not by appeals to conscience. Fortunately, such individuals are exceptions, not the rule.

There is an interesting parallel here between egoism and solipsism. Solipsism is the denial of the existence of other centers of subjectivity. It is a position that cannot be refuted by clear bits of evidence, since every distinct bit of evidence must be presented in, and can be devoured by, the all-encompassing subjectivity of the solipsist. But I have argued that it is a deranged, absurd position (Ferré 1996, 351). The answer to solipsism, if the question arises in abstract debate, is in a richer account of experience, pointing not to clear bits of evidence but to vague direct awareness of a looming, causally effective objective world containing other minds (Ferré 1998, 276–84). The answer to solipsism, if its specter is raised by psychological disturbance, is therapy.

Like theoretical solipsism, egoism, taken as the abstract possibility of systematically discounting the importance of the pains and satisfactions of other people, affirming instead the importance solely of one's own, is not open to theoretical refutation. But a fuller examination of ethical experience may help change minds if they are open. Perhaps a theoretical egoist will draw the line somewhere on utter disregard for others, given reminders of social bonds of sympathy with some other important self (e.g., a mother, a spouse), evoking ties of fellow feeling that normally can be counted on to raise doubts in the mind even of the most stubborn theoretical egoist. If, however, egoism comes as sociopathic deficiency in normal capacities for sympathy, the appropriate answer is caution and a good police force.

Mention of the police and enforcement reminds us that in dealing with the roots of moral sentiment we are dealing with practical matters, heavy with importance for life and limb. Feelings have consequences. Attitudes can bring peril or assistance. We experience the connection between values and concrete results every day.

In these platitudes, universally applicable to human arrangements for living, whatever the specific arrangements may be, we find the practical grounds for norms in human behavior. To live as a tribe, or as a family, or even as a dyadic society of mother and child, there must be some regularities of behavior. Without regularities there can be no recognized types of situation, no anticipation of what is coming next, no orderly responses. Pure chaos provides no foothold for cooperation. Without cooperation, we lose the possibility of planning, mutual endeavors, shared tasks, division of labor—all that constitutes the advantages of human society.

Normative behavior, at the most primitive level, is simply what is "normal," what meets expectations for what is regular in a recognizable type of situation. Most situations allow a good deal of leeway, of course, for what might be judged "regular" by the society. Some situations are less relaxed. The clothing worn by the justices and attorneys at the United States Supreme Court, for example, admits little latitude. Bathing trunks or even blue jeans would be highly irregular, outside the norm. What is worn to backyard barbecue parties, in contrast, falls under a much broader norm, though there are still some expectations. Nakedness, in most circumstances, would be outside the norm, as would white tie and tails.

I am not yet discussing ethical norms, but even at this level of social practice, norms regularly guide behavior and tend to engage strong feelings. It would evoke feelings of outrage at a formal dinner party if one were to lick food off the plate like a dog. Even eating peas with one's knife might create an affective storm (perhaps involving some amusement, some disdain). In linguistic behavior, the shape of the bell curve guiding the range of acceptable pronunciation and choice of words is no less stimulative of strong feelings. Let one Englishman disappoint regularities of expectation and we will soon see "another Englishman despise him."

Norms are found everywhere in human life. Not only as we talk and dress and eat, but also as we drive and work and play, go to the toilet, make love, pray, meet on the street—the list is endless—we live and laugh and die in an enormous invisible network of normative expectations. Most of the time we take these so much for granted (with others in our community) that we simply do not notice. It is when we go to an alien context, perhaps one where slurping one's tea is a normative regularity, or belching loudly after a meal, that we are acutely aware of our own set of norms and how they are not shared. Feelings of disapproval are deeply ingrained and hard to shake, even when circumstances do not call for them. Feelings of disapproval, furthermore, are in most cases more easily noticed when norms are disappointed than are feelings of approval when expectations are fulfilled, since most normative behavior is (by definition) the normal—the most frequent—experience, a matter of routine. I do not actively approve the many other drivers staying on their side of the road and not passing on hills and curves. I take that for granted. But I feel outrage at drivers who weave across the solid yellow line, risking their lives (and mine) by speeding past me up hills and around blind curves.

Now we are edging toward ethics. The norms of driving involve manners, questions of politeness that seem not to rise to the ethical level; they involve legal expectations, questions of enforcement and penalty through available social institutions; but, in addition, they involve a normative residue that seems none of the above. Driving impolitely may occasionally stir road rage and lead to serious ethical and legal violations, but mere lack of manners, in itself, gives rise more to feelings of contempt or pity than moral blame. "Where was that idiot brought up?" we may ask ourselves, and promptly forget the matter. Driving illegally often endangers others and then is both a legal and an ethical issue, but simple illegality may not endanger anything and still be punishable. A well-maintained automobile on a dry, empty highway might safely attain speeds far in excess of local speed limits. This may be true, but the law is the law, and if the regularities prescribed by society are not heeded, punishment could be warranted. Where does the distinctively ethical arise? Suppose a driver is speeding on that empty highway in that well-maintained car in order to bring a woman in labor to a hospital. All other things being equal, and assuming no one else is endangered, high speed (though illegal) need not be reckless and may not be morally blameworthy. Even minions of the law might provide escort service under these circumstances. The ethical norm of doing what one can for the well-being of another seems to trump the legal norm of obeying the speed limit. Why?

The why question will be addressed in the following section on ethical thinking. What is important here, as we draw this section to a close, is that we attend to our ethical feelings of approval and disapproval, valuing and disvaluing, within the context of the fuller range of normative human behavior. Generic approval and disapproval occur much more widely. There is a special flavor to *ethical* approval—commendation, admiration, sometimes even veneration. Likewise there is a special edge to *ethical* disapproval—blame, condemnation, outrage. And as in virtually all normative circumstances, we are capable of judging our own performance by the norms we have come to recognize and expect. Just as we can judge that we made a poor swing in tennis, once we have come to recognize the norms, so we can and do judge ourselves as well as others in terms of the ethical norms we recognize. Social norms are not just for others. True, others have normative expectations of what our behavior should be (in table manners, in dress, in speech, as well as in the ethical we are attempting to define), but we often—usually—*share* those expectations. Their expectations combined with our own expectations gives rise to feelings of legitimate obligations: obligations to fulfill acceptable table manners, acceptable driving practices, and morally acceptable ways of life. When we fail, and judge that we have failed, we feel something. We experience embarrassment, shame, self-blame, and, when it involves ethics, the pangs of moral guilt.

This is about as far as we should go on the topic of ethical experiencing before we try to gain a grip on the pressing topic of ethical thinking. I have at this level not defined the ethical (this requires more work on concepts in general), but I have tried to describe its context in human feelings of the normative. I have especially avoided any suggestion that any specific ethical experience, for example, of obligation or guilt, might be more appropriate than any other. I think these judgments can be made. I am not driving toward relativism. But judgments are a form of thinking. Judgments require concepts and an apparatus for the evaluation of better and worse ethical reasoning, more or less appropriate ethical attitudes. Given the experiential ground I have described—in living, questing, subjective centers, deeply related to one another, and to nature, in societies shaped everywhere by norms—how then shall we understand ethical thinking?

ETHICAL THINKING

The first, most important thing to note about ethical thinking is that it is a species of genuine thinking. This thesis has been vigorously doubted in recent times (as illustrated by A. J. Ayer's emotivist reduction at the end of the previous chapter), but the purpose of this section is to set such doubts to rest. That there is a huge emotional component in ethical thinking will not be disputed. The whole domain of ethical thinking is loaded with feeling. But attitudes, feelings, and judgments are decisively present in *all* human thinking, without making it "nonsense" or irrational. That is what the first part of this section will seek to show. It should remove the sting from the emotivist attack on ethical language as somehow disqualified simply by its inevitable association with feelings and judgments.

All thinking is normative. To back that bold assertion, I need to take a short excursion into concept formation and language use. I am restricting the topic of "thinking" here to *conceptual* mentation. Mental activity goes on preconceptually, of course, or concepts could never rise out of the raw material of experience. Still, it is useful to limit the range designated by thinking to the sorts of mental activity involved in the making, using, and reforming of concepts, normally in adult humans by the use of words. Preconceptual mental activities, like grasping the immediate world in its vague physical intrusiveness and responding positively or negatively to its felt characters, is even more obviously awash in affect. But so is conceptual thinking. Too often, we overlook the feelingful and normative character of conceptual thought from bottom to top.

At the bottom of concept formation is the preconceptual mental power of recognition, across time, of similarities in experience. If we could not remember and recognize features within the flux of mental passage from moment to moment, we would not be able to sort out a cosmos from the chaos of pure present happening. Only thanks to the "hello again!" experience of significant repetition can we notice structure in our world. This implies that some feature or set of features impresses us as being vivid enough to notice and important enough to recognize. "Vivid" is an aesthetic term on a qualitative judgment scale; "important" is a value term equally dependent on qualitative judgment.

Conceptual formation from the start depends on aesthetic responses and judgments of significance.

Once primitive concepts form as recognized, providing stable features of experience across time, they begin to develop relationships. A bright flash (though still unnamed in any language) may offer an initial "hello again!" experience; a loud, rumbling sound may offer a second. But these two prelinguistic concepts, each selected for its vividness and importance, soon develop symbolic connections if the recognition of one leads to the mental expectation of the other. I use the term "symbolic" in the broad sense defined by Alfred North Whitehead as follows: "The human mind is functioning symbolically when some components of its experience elicit consciousness, beliefs, emotions, and usages, respecting other components of its experience" (Whitehead 1927, 8). All the components may either be present simultaneously in experience or not. In the case of the wordless flash and the loud rumble, the symbolic connection of reference is gradually established from the present former (the symbol) to the absent latter (the symbolized) by means of expectation (quite possibly laden with feelings of uneasiness or fear). Animal minds make these connections all the time. Pavlov showed that by ringing a bell he could condition dogs to take account (by salivating) of not-yet-experienced-but-expected food. Far more subtle and impressive feats of animal mentation have been demonstrated in more recent decades.

Noticing and recognizing a feature (or bundle of features) in experience is enough to form a working concept even prior to the emergence of language, and nonlinguistic conceptual activity (as we are increasingly learning) can be highly impressive. But *naming* a noticed feature—forming a word as a symbolic referent to a remembered concept—vastly enlarges the powers of conceptual mentation. The biggest difference between a nonlinguistic symbol (e.g., a bright flash) and a linguistic symbol (e.g., the word lightning) is that the nonlinguistic symbol cannot be produced easily (or at all) by which to "think about" its referent, "thunder," whereas the linguistic symbol can be readily realized, either by producing a sequence of phonemes suited to the human larynx, teeth, and tongue, or by producing a set of visual patterns (letters, ideograms, etc.) equally open to reproduction at will. At first these sounds and shapes are simply additional recognizable features of experience, but as linguisticality develops and the web of symbolic references increases, the felt importance of these features rises steadily, and language learners become sensitized to ever-greater feats of noticing significant similarities and differences between humanly produced sounds and shapes. Eventually, capacities for vividness in discrimination within these domains of experience are honed to achieve really remarkable feats of subtlety. Unaccustomed accents, dialectical variations, quirks of penmanship, gross differences among fonts, misspellings, mispronunciations, odd choices of words—all are recognized and usually coped with successfully.

Given words like "lightning" and "thunder," we no longer need to wait for flashes of lightning in order to take symbolic account of peals of thunder. We are freed by the availability of these easily producible symbols to take clear and specific mental account of thunder on a sunny day, or to bring up the subject to a friend who shares in our speech community. We can think of snow in the midst of summer, and can direct our efforts to chopping wood or otherwise coping with snow long in advance of its arrival. Through language we are permitted to work and play to our heart's content in the realms of symbolic thought and action.

But at all levels, from initial recognition of regularities in experience to sophisticated manipulations of verbal symbols, we must depend on normative judgments and certify our own performances. I have already mentioned the primitive judgments of importance and vividness that underlie the ability to notice and recognize regularities in the otherwise chaotic flow of experience. At this basic level of recognition, one must simply judge that this is a genuine "hello again!" experience, sufficiently similar to earlier cases to count as another instance. Sometimes one might be wrong, but one must be right enough of the time, or no reliable concept will be able to form (and unreliable concepts at the practical level may be dangerous to one's health). How much is "enough"? There is no a priori standard. It is a judgment call with consequences.

In the same way, when we reach the level of language and attempt to name what we have noticed and recognized, we must certify that we have gotten the word right. Since concepts are always general, the words we use to name them must cover a variety of specific cases (this follows from the Law of Poverty in language [Ferré 1998, 318]), but, if so, we may always wonder whether we have chosen the best word. Is this a good occasion for use of the word, "pink"? There will be a normal curve of acceptable usage, in the center of which there is hardly any doubt. At the boundaries, however, other words might have been used instead, perhaps to better effect. Connoisseurship in language, as in other domains, is shown by the capacity to make subtle discriminations.

To the extent language is public (and it is virtually all public), there will be plenty of room for discussion. "Don't you mean 'mauve' in this case?" "I think 'fuchsia' would be better." And since language is so largely public, other users may serve as helpful critics of one's conceptual performance, which may indeed be in need of improvement. It was from others that we learned the normal usage of general terms in the first place.

The words of a natural language belong to no one in particular. Misusing a word, departing too far from the norms involved, defeats the function of language to communicate reliably within the speech community, whose norms they are. Therefore, while a person's eccentric use of a word, if the person insists on it, cannot be *disproved* as a factual matter might be, it can be *reasonably argued against* as unhelpful, inappropriate, confusing, or self-defeating (Ferré 1998, 328–34). Language has many functions, but high on the list is communication, which can occur only when grammar and word choice are "sufficiently" within normal curves so as to be intelligible. Without respecting these public norms of intelligibility, common enterprises cannot be planned and executed; common attitudes cannot be formed, strengthened, or revised; common dangers cannot be identified and defended against. "Communication" is necessary for "community," and what threatens community may lead to evolutionary unfitness.

No less than surviving and thriving may be at stake in achieving at least average levels of connoisseurship in normative linguistic judgments. These judgments, to summarize, include the use of memory and recognitional capacities (identifying the regularities of experience *well enough*), as well as interpretation and production capacities (attaching the *best* choice of words to the recognized concept and pronouncing or inscribing these words acceptably well within the bounds of *good* grammar). In each case the norms can be represented by the statistician's familiar bell-shaped curve, in which there is a spread of central, relatively uncontroversial ways of satisfying the norm, shading off on one side to the poetic, on the other side to the merely perverse. Conceptual thinking of a sort can be accomplished despite poor grammar, barbaric spelling, and weird choice of words, as every philosophy professor is well aware from reading student papers. But clarity and precision increases as the relevant norms are better and better met. One major goal of teaching is to help students become aware of these norms and to become capable of critical assessments of their own performance, responsibly certifying their own successes and shortcomings in meeting them. Then evaluating the performances of others, when one's own performance is also under self-surveillance, becomes far more fruitful and fair.

"Fair" is an ethical term. This is a reminder that so far my discussion has dwelt generally on the norms behind language and thought, but has not dealt specifically with ethical thinking. Perhaps the reader is now ready to venture into this distinctive area.

What do ethical words allow us to do, or, to put it the other way, what do we accomplish with ethical concepts? Among other things, we describe, positively and negatively, human actions and policies of action; we distinguish, sort out, and take up attitudes towards whole ways of human life and patterns of human existence, individually and socially; we discriminate and evaluate the actions and characters of others; and, through all this, we judge ourselves, our actions, our motives, and our virtue.

This may be true, but it is not yet enough. There are many kinds of evaluations; and normative judgments, as we now realize, are ubiquitous in thinking. How shall we isolate the distinctive "flavor" of moral evaluation, the "feel" of ethical judgment? If someone tries to empty the ocean with a teaspoon, we may characterize the action as hopeless (and judge it merely foolish), without adding moral condemnation. When does the condemnation come in? Or, contrariwise, if someone rushes into the sea in a desperate effort to save a distant, drowning swimmer, we may judge the action morally praiseworthy despite its hopelessness. Why does the commendation come in?

In these two examples, it seems clear that the crucial ingredient has to do with helping or hurting someone. In the first hopeless case, the action was merely foolish, doing no good but harming no one. We may judge the action "silly" or even "stupid" without getting into morality (though if the "stupid" behavior could be shown to have come at the expense of other uses of time that might have helped someone or might even have bettered the "silly" agent, ethical judgments might, on reflection, be triggered). In the second case, the desperate effort was aimed at helping someone in urgent need. Even if hopeless, it reflected a motive and a personal character inclined toward helping others, and so might be subject to moral approval, even aside from the futility of the specific action.

In this otherwise trivial example, we find some hints we were looking for. Distinctively ethical thinking has two major elements: first, *material* norms prescribing concrete helps and harms; and, second, *formal* norms prescribing patterns for realizing those material norms. This sounds forbiddingly theoretical when I state it so succinctly, but nothing could be more down to earth and familiar. The ethical is born in the nursery, where children learn that it is *wrong to hurt* one another and *right to share*.

Pain is a concrete harm, suffered by a subject whose normal preference is to avoid pain for its own sake, that is, for no other reason than not to have it. This is a factual matter with major normative implications, but at this first, lowest level, it is a nonmoral fact about subjects capable of pain, and even the norms of aversion and avoidance are themselves nonmoral. Where the moral enters is with the prescription against randomly, wantonly inflicting nonmoral bad on those capable of suffering it. Pain for Harry is *bad*, no matter how caused; but all other things being equal, it is *wrong* for you to cause Harry's pain. In the nursery this ethical prescription is seldom explained or justified. It is repeated, usually in loud, attention-getting tones. It could be justified, of course, if the teacher were challenged for a reason. If we are to avoid social chaos, we must somehow learn to live without the radical defensiveness that would be required if every other person might randomly inflict pain at any time on any other person. We need to learn how to classify some *types* of acts—some experienced social regularities felt important enough to be noticed, recognized, and named—as not to be done. You must not do this type of act to me; I must not do this type of act to you. Hitting Harry hurts him; therefore hitting Harry is "bad," "forbidden," "disapproved," "shameful," "wrong." But at the nursery level, such justifications are out of place. The teacher or parent is transmitting ethical concepts, using words available in the local language community, in the same way all other concepts are taught. Thus: "Please notice these significant regularities, these situations. Here is how they are named: First, this building block is 'square'. Second, this flower is 'red'. Third, this act of hitting Harry is 'wrong'." All such concept formation starts at the material level of very concrete subjects and particular experiences. All ethical thinking starts here as well, building on the basic concepts of what is nonmorally "good" and "bad," the stuff of concrete individual satisfactions and frustrations. It then moves to prescribe what is "right" or "wrong" to do in view of these "goods" and "bads." Thousands of years ago, in the nursery ages of emerging ethics, concepts of this type were noticed and named. Codes of normative conduct, like Hammurabi's (mentioned earlier), were constructed, based on conceptual awareness of what tends to help and hurt businessmen, husbands, wives, and so forth, giving prescriptive ethical-legal guidance on the sorts of conduct that should be maintained within a society of subjects vulnerable to individual pain and satisfaction but engaged in shared policies for common ends.

Sharing is the other great ethical nursery lesson. Not just refraining from randomly hurting others but, much more, recognizing others as entitled to fair shares of satisfaction is vital to eventual maturity in ethical thinking. The concrete nonmoral material of ethics, the frustrations and satisfactions, the bads and goods, can and do characterize the experience of solitary individuals; "fairness," however, is always a pattern involving more than one subject. Fairness is a form of sharing, distributing the concrete nonmoral goods and bads in some normative way among subjects capable of enjoying or suffering them. In this respect fairness is an abstract, second order ethical concept. It depends on the previous discovery of first order nonmoral "goods" (intrinsically satisfactory experiences) and first order nonmoral "bads" (intrinsically unsatisfactory experiences) before it can gain any subject matter of its own. Distributive justice (what some adults call fairness after they leave the nursery) is concerned not simply with the first order ethical principle that nonmoral "goods" should be supported and nonmoral "bads" be suppressed as much as possible, but with the second order principle governing *how* scarce goods are to be shared among subjects capable of enjoying them. If we were to give all the best toys in the nursery to Harry, this would result in his great satisfaction, no doubt; but would it be fair? No! Everyone needs to learn that the satisfaction and frustration of everyone else counts, too. We need to be reminded of the feelings of empathy and sympathy that growing up and learning one's personal separateness tends to overshadow. We need to have our imagination encouraged to *see* how others must see and *feel* how others must feel; that is, we need to be encouraged in the use of mentality to escape the boundaries of our given situation and entertain possibilities in contrast with the actual.

*   *   *

Seeing how others must see, feeling what others must feel, is what Melville J. Herskovits (1895–1963) first named "enculturation." "The aspects of the learning experience which mark off man from other creatures, and by means of which, initially, and in later life, he achieves competence in his culture, may be called enculturation. This is in essence a process of conscious or unconscious conditioning, exercised within the limits sanctioned by a given body of custom" (Herskovits 1948, 39). And so it is, by conscious and unconscious conditioning, that we are equipped to do our first ethical thinking. To acknowledge this is in no way to diminish or impeach ethical thinking. All our thinking, from the heights of mathematical physics to the depths of epic poetry, begins in conscious and unconscious conditioning. Every mode of thinking, however noble, fine, and true, creeps first out of the nursery.

Setting aside the question of the "true" in ethics for attention in the following section, we see at once that ethical concepts can support much that is noble and fine. "Noble" itself is a word with ethical resonances, characterizing great, high-minded, lofty ideals for life. And "fine" can have more than aesthetic reference, including what is pure (refined), delicate in ways of life, opposed to coarse interests and activities. What this illustrates is that the ethical vocabulary is richer and more complex than ethicists usually notice. The staples of "right" and "wrong" are just the beginning. Even they are not used exclusively within ethical contexts: a musical note, though the "right" note, may not sound quite "right," and an attempted rhyme in a poem may feel just "wrong" in context.

The overlapping domains of use we learn through our enculturation into English can be helpful in finding our way to "finer" discriminations in our ethical conversations—either our internal conversations as we deliberate and clarify our ethical views, or our dialogues (and arguments) with others. It makes a large difference whether something we agree was "wrong" was so in a way that was "loathsome" and "disgusting" or merely "unfortunate" and "regrettable." The *emotional* freight carried by these words is crucial to these discriminations in thinking, since "loathing" is a word independently associated with feeling sick or nauseated; in a similar way, so is "disgust." (The former word rises out of the Old High German, *leid*, for suffering or sorrow; the latter reaches us via Romance language stems, the French *dégoût* and the Italian *disgusto*, for tasting bad.) Sometimes we feel our ethical negatives strongly and therefore, to qualify our sense of "wrong," we borrow concepts from other domains of strong negative experience, like vomiting. At other times we need cooler conceptual vehicles by which to temper our ill-temper, for which "regrettable" can serve. This anodyne concept evokes feelings of sadness and loss. When used to qualify one's judgment of ethical "wrongness," it may suggest sadness at the loss of ethical purity by someone one still embraces fondly in other respects. Or, used with reference to one's own acknowledged "wrong" action, it carries the flavor of sadness but not necessarily guilt. To say that one "regrets" one's action does not quite qualify as an apology. It merely acknowledges that the act was "wrong," but many actions are wrong and "regrettable" that are not morally blameworthy. For example, I may sincerely regret that I took my broker's advice to invest in a certain stock. The action turned out to have been "wrong" when the company went bankrupt, but I need feel no guilt for such a mistake. Regret is not the same thing as remorse, which is tinctured with a sense of guilt. If anyone deserves blame it is the broker, since he should have known better.

Similarly, we learn by enculturation the subtle differences between "shame" and "guilt." "Shame" is a word naming the unpleasant emotion (alas, a regularity in the experience of most cultures) of being found in a situation felt to be ridiculous, indecorous, or dishonoring. A naked sleepwalker wandering into a convent might feel intense shame on awakening, but there is no ground for moral blame. "Guilt," in contrast, names a situation, first of all, and an emotion only secondarily. One may *be* guilty of some infraction, objectively defined, but not *feel* guilty about it. Some terrorists, for instance, feel pride in their guilt. But as a phrase in the ethical vocabulary, "moral guilt" names a feeling frequently associated with judging oneself to blame for acts, attitudes, or character traits falling outside the moral norms.

Guilt and blame go intimately together. If one is blameless, there is no need to feel guilt. But "to blame" (derived from the Greek, meaning "blaspheme" or revile) is revilingly to hold someone guilty of violating the norms of regular social behavior that one has been enculturated to expect and approve. The act of placing blame itself is a reproof, a censure. When we blame little Harry in the nursery for knocking down the blocks, this conceptual act categorizing Harry as blameworthy carries the implication that he did in fact knock down the blocks, that such behavior does not in fact fall within the norms of the nursery, and that his act was deliberate, not accidental or inadvertent, which might make it "regrettable" but not "blameworthy."

In the vocabulary of ethical thinking, illustrated by the difference between "regret" and "blame," morally wrong actions, policies, and characters depend for their blameworthiness on the prior attribution (or assumption) of moral responsibility. If the blocks were really kicked over by sheer mistake, Harry might (or might not, depending on the nature of the accident) be blamed for being careless in general, but not for being "evil" or "malicious" in his treatment of the blocks. Clumsy Harry might be just as sorry as the others that the block construction was destroyed. It was not, in this case, genuinely "his act" to knock it down. True, it was his foot that did it, but since feet intend nothing by themselves, they are not "responsible" in the crucial sense. Harry himself did not in the least want what his foot did. Therefore, although a part of his body was causally involved, *he* was not truly acting through his foot. It was not an "act" at all, it was merely a regrettable happening. And if not an act, then a fortiori it was not a "responsible act." We learn gradually through our enculturation that we ought not apply blame words to situations where there is no responsible agent involved. This may take a long time, since it is easy to attribute animistic intentions to objects and events in the world around us. But as we gradually withdraw from such characterizations and focus our ethical discourse on apparent centers of purpose, awareness, and freedom, we come to define, if only through our use (and withholding) of "blame" language, what we mean by "morally responsible."

Such reflections on the language of ethics, through which we do our ethical thinking, could be greatly extended, but my point does not require more elaboration. That point is that beginning with the learning of normal speech, and extending throughout life, we learn (are conditioned) to recognize significant regularities in experience having to do not merely with objects and their characteristics but also with social orderings and expectations, and the feelings—often strong—that are associated with these orderings and expectations. Having some social order for humans is a biological advantage. But we are never enculturated into "some" order in general, but always into "this" order in particular. Therefore, regularity (within a normal range) of specific behavioral expectations, a necessity underlying social surviving and thriving, is strongly felt as important among the normal members of any society. Behaviors falling outside this normal range are shocking to various degrees and felt as threatening the foundations of society.

To summarize: Along with the rest of our language, we have learned to name local normative regularities of behavior. In different social orderings, these local regularities may not be the same (which must be discussed in the next section of this chapter). Whatever they are, they will be recognized, named, and painted with a rich pallette of emotions. First-order core concepts of ethical thinking will deal with *responsible acts* (i.e., deeds done by moral agents open to moral blame and praise), insofar as these acts are liable to *help or hurt* those capable of being helped and harmed (i.e., consequences enjoyed or suffered by moral patients open to moral consideration). Second-order ethical thinking will reflect on patterns and principles in the distribution of these helps and harms.

On the above account of ethical thinking, starting with the noticing of important features in social experience, recognizing these features as regularities, and naming them with symbols we can produce both in the presence and in the absence of the features themselves, it follows that ethical concepts are as universal as any other terms in language. If the features in experience we name as "heavy" are universal within the language community that recognizes this word, so the features in experience we learn to name as "wicked" are also universal. Both words are vague, admittedly, and require a lot of refinement for many social purposes. What amounts to a "heavy" sack of potatoes differs from a "heavy" jetliner; what counts as "wicked" in a witch may differ from a cruel Sultan. But in principle, if enculturation has succeeded, the recognition of what generally counts as "wicked" will be as well within normal curves as will be what generally counts as "heavy." And if it is wicked for you, it will be wicked for me as well. Of course, there are parallel variations here too. What is heavy for me might not be heavy for you, because you have stronger muscles. But the vague concept of "heavy" remains universal, or we would not be able to make sense of these variations. "Variations in what?" we would need to ask. Similarly, what is wicked for me in my circumstances might not apply to your circumstances. But within our common language-community, we can think about these differences of circumstances with respect to the same general ethical concept. The possibility of making excuses for you while pinning blame on me demands a common concept, relative to which excuses and blame make sense.

Still, nothing I have yet said touches on the differences between the language communities associated with different social orders. Even if it is true that ethical thinking is continuous with and shares the logic of ordinary thinking of all sorts, we must remember that language-communities, especially those embedded in very different social experience and structure, can have very different conceptual mappings of the world. Different "ways of seeing" may be associated with cultures dealing largely with forms of snow as against others coping in the context of sand. Different "ways of feeling" may be expected within nomadic warring societies in contrast to settled agricultural societies. Even concepts concerning the "public" physical environment, color concepts, and so forth, may be hard to mediate, as between such different cultures. Thus, granting that some provisions are possible for partial translation between language communities insofar as they think about the physical environment, can this be claimed for ethics? Closer to home, what should we think about the seemingly endless disputes over ethics between members of the *same* language community, the same neighborhood, the same family? Sometimes we argue even within ourselves, first drawn one way, then another, over what to think concerning some particularly dicey issues. When we find ourselves internally conflicted over a difficult ethical decision or assessment, and when we find ourselves confronted with new situations, such as are being raised with increasing frequency by unprecedented technological powers to do hitherto unthinkable things, we cannot fall back on "tried and true" enculturation. Thus, we must ask, when cultures or neighbors clash on ethics, when we find no traditional resolution of our own personal moral uncertainties, is it possible to deploy something broader and better secured than the concepts and beliefs we have picked up by conscious and unconscious conditioning? Are there larger universals and more reliable standards by which we can move from ethical thinking to what could reasonably be called "ethical knowing"?

ETHICAL KNOWING

My answer to this question will be positive. Ethical skepticism is not forced on us. Neither culturally conditioned diversity in beliefs, nor the entanglement of thinking with strong emotional freight, is unique to ethics. An epistemology which recognizes the embeddedness of knowing in the fullness of human life will affirm ethical knowing in continuity with all other areas of knowing, from history to physics (Ferré 1998, 341–73).

Philosophers like to leap immediately to the issues of theoretical knowing in ethics. This is, after all, our own professional stock in trade. But I think it would be useful to build to theoretical issues with a look first at two other kinds of knowing that precede and feed theoretical knowing. These are *practical* knowing and *observational* knowing.

PRACTICAL KNOWING

"Know-how," the learned skills of applying methods to situations—runs deep among species that live by their wits. I am not now preparing to maintain that arguably ethical "know-how" extends beyond the human realm, though I suspect such a case might plausibly be made with reference to some intelligent social species, and I imagine that much anecdotal evidence of quasi-moral "wisdom" could be collected from petlovers around the world. My own dog gives a lively imitation of feeling a guilty conscience from time to time, and at other times she seems torn between inclination and duty. But let us set aside—for this chapter at least—this "deeper" issue of ethical continuities between human and nonhuman beings. Our answer would depend on metaphysical considerations, and we are concentrating here on epistemology.

It can hardly be doubted that some human beings have a talent for practical ethics. They regularly do or say the deft thing that defuses a tense moment; they can be counted on to make the new suggestion that turns a potential lose-lose conflict into a win-win situation; they keep their word and maintain their perspective; they manage over the years to live in a way that glows with its own unity and richness. But they need not also be theoreticians. Their ethical wisdom is not spun from abstractions. How can we understand ethical know-how on the practical level?

Know-how in general is the skilled application of method to circumstance. A method is a general way of doing something, a trick or "dodge" for accomplishing something in the interest of life's urge, as A. N. Whitehead put it, "to live, to live well, to live better" (Whitehead 1929, 8). Every method, however simple, is abstract, since it is applicable in principle to indefinitely many situations. Like a concept, a method depends on our noticing and recognizing regularities within experience, then responding to those regularities with behavioral regularities of our own. Suppose I am thirsty (a regularity in experience) but in a desert place where no visible water could slake my discomfort. My mind could become so obsessed, imagining the physically absent water I crave, that I might (without a method) die of thirst in my frantic, unstructured pursuit of vividly imagined but absent possibilities. But suppose I have the good luck to run across a plump water-bearing cactus, knocking it down in my panic, perhaps, but then seeing and sucking the shiny drops inside. This first time I was saved by luck. But if I notice and remember this happy event, then the next time I am thirsty in the desert, I may discipline my energy by seeking out similar cacti for their lifesaving moisture. A *method* is born when the anarchical capacity of mentality to dwell on the physically absent is self-disciplined by the counter capacity of mentality to remember, recognize, and apply a general mode of behavior to a new situation (Ferré 1998, 344–47).

The success of practical intelligence to serve the interests of life depends on the new situation being "sufficiently like" those earlier situations in which the general pattern of behavior proved useful. If the type of situation is wrongly "recognized," the type of behavior represented by the method may not work. Again, as in conceptual recognition, the crucial features of the supposed regularities in experience must be self-certified as "good enough" to qualify, in this new instance, as a case of the relevant general sort. The difference is that at the level of practical know-how, the recognized situation need not be named with a general *verbal* marker—a sign to be seen or heard, tokens of which can be generated freely in intricate symbolic contexts—but may be addressed by an instance of a general behavioral response.

Just as there is always the possibility of misnaming a situation, so there is also always the possibility of misresponding. But equally, just as natural languages persist only to the extent that their relevant language-communities succeed on the average in recognizing and naming important regularities of experience, so, too, methods rise and persist only to the extent that their users normally advance ends of life with them. Thus, both languages and methods follow the rule of the survival of the fit. It is not surprising that they are so closely allied, since both are expressions of mentality, and since language use itself is a higher order expression of method, one that can reflect on all methods, including itself.

Mental expression through learned methods can be immensely subtle and successful. Practical ethical wisdom is a leading domain where we may be kindled to admiration. Solomon's wisdom, reflecting practical ethical know-how, as most famously illustrated by his method of settling the dispute between two women claiming the same child—he fully (and correctly) anticipated that the real mother would reveal herself by rejecting his "solution" of cutting the disputed baby in half (I Kings 3:16–28)—became the stuff of folk memory and eventually Scripture. Keeping the peace, maintaining fairness in the distribution of nonmoral good and bad, strengthening the positive grounds of social cohesion—all these and more reflect needs of human life to survive and thrive socially. At one extreme, some practical know-how in ethics, as in other kinds of method (e.g., in art or cookery, pottery or the hunt), may reach the level of genius. Most ethical methods, by definition, will be more commonplace and "average." At the bottom of the scale, some ethical methods can be very poor in practice: prejudicial, unfair, destructive of vital goods and socially destabilizing, hardly better than no method at all, perhaps (in the short run before self-destruction) even worse.

Methods—practical knowledge—can be wonderful enhancements to life, but they are not self-criticizing. Once a method is achieved, the tendency of practical intelligence is to cling to it. "If it ain't broke, don't fix it," is a basic tenet of practical wisdom. But since methods are not all equally good at what they do, this practical conservatism may lock a mediocre method in place, resistant to improvement or to alternative ways of doing the same job better. One step toward liberation from obscurantism, the negative aspect of practical knowing, is a keen eye for experience itself. Through watchful awareness, the basis of critical change may be laid. This watchful awareness is what we may call "observational knowing."

OBSERVATIONAL KNOWING

Watchful attention is capable of remarkable feats. In ancient science, for example, the unmatched achievements of Babylonian astronomy, including prediction of planetary motions and even anticipation of eclipses, were made possible by hundreds of years of patient looking and noticing, recording these sightings for long-term recall by priests. The religious beliefs that motivated such attentions turned out less lasting than the observations themselves, in which inevitable errors of uninstrumented looking were cancelled out over long periods of time, leaving remarkably accurate observational knowledge of correlations between observables firmly established. Perhaps Thales of Miletus used this lore for his own successful prediction of a solar eclipse (Kirk and Raven 1962, 79–81).

The ethical domain is another area of experience where long observation of human variables has occurred in all cultures. Two sorts of observational knowledge may be distinguished here: first, the gathering of consensus about what are the basic helps and harms to humans, identifying the nonmoral goods and bads that stimulate our attractions and repulsions; and, second, the tracking of consequences and weighing of patterns, funding observational wisdom concerning common types of practice and whole ways of life.

On nonmoral good and bad, there is a basis in observational knowing, especially at fundamental levels, for considerable cross-cultural consensus.

Much of this is so obvious that reporting on it sounds platitudinous. But observational knowledge at its very best is in search of platitudes: the broader, flatter, and more commonplace, the better. These are the marks of averaged-out errors, agreement based on innumerable sightings taken from indefinitely many points of view. For example, steady observation over the millennia of human experience makes it clear that biological survival, for the vast majority, is a nonmoral good. There are exceptions, of course. People under severe torture may wish to die; some Roman slaves plotted ways to cheat their owners through suicide. But these are recognizably exceptions. Even difficult lives are usually preferred to no life at all. This is a platitude, but an important one for ethics, since taking a life from one who treasures it can be known by observational consensus to be a grievous harm. In addition to this consensus on the *intrinsic* nonmoral good of survival, watchful attention also establishes correlative *instrumental* nonmoral goods, namely, the necessary conditions for survival, such as food, water, air, protection from predators, shelter from extreme climate conditions, and the like. This may sound basic to the point of triviality, but the removal of any one of these necessary conditions would feel far from trivial. Sometimes the obvious needs to be noted. The obvious is what observational knowing is about.

A notch above sheer survival, normal health, biological well-functioning, is a significant nonmoral good. Ill health, even if this does not bring about such an intensity of suffering that survival itself is no longer desired, constitutes a fundamental nonmoral bad to be shunned as far as possible. Mention of suffering brings up another important platitude: suffering is something we shun. Once again, there may be exceptions to this generalization, some real, some merely apparent. Observational knowing is aware that some people apparently *like* to suffer. Some exceptional people find powerful sexual gratification in suffering some kinds of pain inflicted under special circumstances, but the total experience, on balance, is for them net pleasure. Likewise, some self-punishing people seem unable to cope with life if they do not see themselves (and, perhaps more important, feel that others are seeing them) as victims to be pitied. These apparent exceptions duly noted, it is hard to dispute the funded observational knowledge of humankind that pain and ill-health are basic nonmoral bads, "evils" to be avoided. Likewise, robust health and pleasures of body and mind, when experienced, are nonmoral goods in themselves. Health is an unusual case. It is an intrinsic good that is also an instrumental good, when available, allowing many additional goods to be achieved. Whatever is conducive to health, therefore, and to the resulting intrinsic nonmoral pleasures, is also instrumentally good to that extent.

These further instrumental nonmoral goods include physical things, (or the means to acquire physical things, through money or some equivalent power), which can provide the immediate stimuli for intrinsically satisfying experiences of body and/or mind. Wealth and power are nonmoral goods, all other things being equal, because of their ability to assure comfort (defend against suffering) and to bring about conditions in which intrinsic satisfactions are experienced. Funded observational knowing looks at wealth and power with a more skeptical eye, however, since too often these means have a way of capturing attention and commitment, even at the cost of the intrinsic goods they were meant to serve. Legends like that of Midas and the good-destroying capacity even of gold in itself are some of the ways cultures express these long-observed correlations. Cautionary tales in every culture are replete with the significant platitudes of ethical observational knowing.

Richer even than wealth are the nonmoral goods of human society: to-getherness, mutual caring, cooperation, and love. The previous nonmoral goods mentioned are all capable of being experienced alone. Survival, health, pleasure, security, power, wealth, are all in principle capable of being goods of the individual. Love, in the sense intended here, is not. Human society is the sharing of selves, the mutual involvement of persons, the growing that comes from sharing. These are intrinsic goods, deep satisfactions, and press the enve-lope of nonmoral goods toward moral goods themselves. But since a cutthroat pirate crew might find deep social satisfactions in sharing the joys of rape and pillage with each other, we are not yet able to certify even this level, high as it is, as automatically laden with moral good. Observational knowing realizes that there is "honor even among thieves." As observational, this is a finding shorn of theory, but explanation is not difficult. If there were a band of thieves wholly without honor toward one another, the band would quickly disintegrate in cheating, rivalry, and mistrust. Such short-lived bands may come and go, but it seems safe to say that there are no long-term bands of thieves bereft of all honor among themselves. Is this an ethical hypothesis open to verification or falsification? It could be. Observational knowing in ethics, as in science or daily life, offers generalizations open in principle to testing. In this, as we shall shortly see, it offers stimulus for theory.

One more level suggested by ethical observation begs notice before we move on. It involves the unparalleled goods of experienced agency, creativity, responsibility, socially embedded personhood. On Abraham Maslow's scale, this is called "self-actualizing" (Maslow 1970). I include it as a finding of eth-ical observation, not so much one founded on watchful folk experience over the ages as one noticed by a keen, discerning eye. This good, of socially em-bedded personhood, is less frequently encountered in experience than the pre-viously mentioned goods; it is as rare as it is precious; but when observed it evokes the highest level of admiration and attraction.

At this point we have already begun the transition from the first to the sec-ond main function of ethical observation. The first with which we have been dealing was the identification of basic nonmoral goods and bads, states (and means to those states) to be sought or avoided. This first function provides specificity for what I earlier called the "concrete nonmoral material" of ethics, the substantive content for what counts as "helping" or "harming." The second function of ethical observational knowing is tracking the actual consequences of types of behavior, developing lore about what leads to what, and learning to recognize major patterns in the ethical regulation of life. That is, observational intelligence keeps watch on types of ethical know-how, on ethical methods for living, individually and socially.

Practical intelligence is not self-critical. As situations arise and are recognized as of a certain type, response is made of a sort that has worked well enough in the past. Observational intelligence, in contrast, keeps tabs on outcomes. Correlation and generalization are its main products. What are the actual long-term probable outcomes of certain methods? Does bluster and intimidation as a policy of life, for example, realize more nonmoral goods than compromise and cooperation? The findings of folk wisdom on this question are couched in aphorisms and fables. "You'll catch more flies with honey than with vinegar," is one aphorism on the subject. Aesop's fable of the North Wind and the Sun, contesting to see which could get a man to remove his cloak is another. The North Wind blew with all its force, but only caused the man to wrap himself ever more tightly in his cloak; the Sun beamed instead, and soon the man discarded his wrap. The adage attributed to Napoleon is also pertinent: "You can do anything with bayonets—except sit on them."

Not all folk wisdom leans the same way, of course. Adages often conflict. In traditional African settings, one of the primary methods of debate among the village elders is by quotation and counter-quotation from the stock of observational tribal lore stored aphoristically for application. In biblical cultures, similarly, some insist on "An eye for an eye, and a tooth for a tooth" (Lev. 24:20), while others reply: "You have heard that it was said, 'An eye for an eye and a tooth for a tooth.' But I say to you, Do not resist one who is evil. But if any one strikes you on the right cheek, turn to him the other also; and if any one would sue you and take your coat, let him have your cloak as well; and if any one forces you to go one mile, go with him two miles" (Matt. 5:38–41, RSV). What are the consequences of these two contrasting methods for living? Observational intelligence has access to much more data concerning the first than the second, of course, since the ideals of radical nonresistance are far less frequently embodied in practice than the ideals of "getting even." Even so, there are peaceful communities, from the Hopi to the Amish, from which observational knowledge may be gleaned. Interesting efforts are currently being made to use observational evidence of this sort to support a full ethical theory, both personal and social, based upon the principles of nonviolence and self-renunciation (Murphy and Ellis 1996, 115–72).

Observational knowing by itself cannot resolve its own internal disputes. At the level of mere correlations between observed social regularities, there is no way to adjudicate the question *which* outcomes *ought* to be supported and which resisted. Some may stimulate admiration, some disgust, but should these feelings be associated with these observed patterns? Just as ethical know-how needs the perspective of ethical observation, so both need the critical examination of ethical theory.

THEORETICAL KNOWING

As I begin this discussion, perhaps I should offer a clarifying disclaimer on the language I have been using concerning "practical," "observational," and "theoretical" intelligence (Ferré 1995, 30–53; 1988, 344–70). It may seem that I mean to compartmentalize or even reify these three distinguishable functions of mentality. That is far from my intent. Let us leave old baggage behind. "Practical Reason" and "Theoretical Reason" are familiar philosophical terms, carrying many traditional overtones; this is why I prefer practical *intelligence* and the like instead. If it were not for old, misleading associations, it would be legitimate, I acknowledge, to call them forms of "reason," since each has its own mode of validating discipline. Practical intelligence is *active mentality* controlled by *method*; observational intelligence is *discriminating mentality* controlled by *experiment*; and theoretical intelligence is *symbolic mentality* controlled by *logic*. But in each case, in my view, these distinctions are functional only. There are not three faculties at work.

In the first case, practical intelligence, mentality—the capacity to deal with possibilities in their presence or absence—is expressed through action. This is the most widespread expression of mental powers because they can operate wordlessly; they are found in many species. But given this capacity to attend behaviorally to absent as well as to present possibilities, organisms equipped with significant levels of mentality are not fully under control by the external environment. Thus, mental powers could be dangerous disrupters without some internal brake to control them. This needed self-discipline mentality supplies for itself by remembering past successful strategies and turning them into methods, as described earlier.

In the second case, observational intelligence, mentality is expressed through the capacity for discriminating perception. This also seems a widespread phenomenon. This capacity also does not require language in order to operate, and it seems present in many intelligent species. This same capacity to perceive regularities of definite form (i.e., possibilities when present) also functions in a highly "interested" way at the level of practical intelligence, since successful methods depend on rightly perceiving situations in which they should work. But the function of mentality I have been calling "observational" is to discriminate and sort out, freed of immediate practical urgencies, the realized possibilities contained in the experienced world. These discriminations and anticipations are interesting and satisfying in their own right. Perhaps noting these regularities will prove useful some day; perhaps not. At the border between aesthetics and cognition, the need for mental self-discipline is functional—to provide ever more fine detail within larger patterns of expectation. Among human beings, we find these disciplines most developed among artists and experimental scientists.

In the third case, theoretical intelligence, mentality is expressed through the capacity for symbolic construction. Not "another faculty," though enhanced with vast powers by the development of language, mentality still deals with possibilities in their presence and in their absence. But the linguistic abilities to *name* concepts at will, to *manipulate* meaningful tokens of great breadth and discrimination, and to *put together* a mental dwelling place where methods, observations, and understanding are linked together—these abilities transform life for those capable of them and transform as well the other two expressions of intelligence, practical and observational, for those equipped with speech.

As noted earlier, the function of practical intelligence, to discover, apply, and preserve methods, tends quite understandably to resist questions about its achieved know-how. An acquired method is a precious thing. "If it ain't broke, don't fix it" inhibits calls for reform or improvement, calls which are perceived, instead, as threats. The function of theoretical intelligence—to dance freely with concepts, question everything, try to construct better possibilities—is at odds with settled, unreflective tradition. In ethics this can lead to explosive confrontations between defenders of tried and true patterns of living and the critics who have their eye on what they imagine would be a better way.

Similarly, the function of mentality in attending carefully to features of experience, what I have called "observational intelligence," is to notice accurately and describe fully. When this is well done, the quest is over. But the function of theoretical intelligence is to build a structure of concepts in which such accurate observations make sense, fit together, have a point. Especially where there are conflicting reports, the theoretical functions of intelligence, to criticize and question, to probe for connections and look for unity, keep mentality from resting easy, no matter how accurate the descriptions. When observation brings in the harvest, theory threshes the grain and grinds the corn. Then it wants to bake the bread, bake it better than before, and then invent a bread slicer! In ethics, folk wisdom may be willing to rest on the deep insights it embodies. Restless ethical theory wants to know why such regularities may be so commonly observed, why platitudes so often work, but most urgently why conflicts in aphorisms also surface, which of clashing commandments should be followed, and why, why, why one should feel more confident adopting one pattern of life than another.

Ethical theory is in all respects continuous with theory in general. If any theory can give reliable guidance in the face of conflicting claims, if any theory can supply warranted confidence for one line of activity over another, if any theory can qualify for the highly normative achievement word, "knowledge"—then there is no obstacle in principle preventing ethical thinking from becoming a form of knowing.

The continuities between ethical thinking and other domains of perception, thought, and feeling should now be obvious. Ethical concepts, the bricks of ethical theory (Ferré 1998, 358), are formed in the same way that all other concepts are formed, by the "conscious and unconscious conditioning" that constitutes the enculturation of every initiate into a language community. They reflect regularities in experience that are taken in that community to be important enough to notice and name. The descriptive range and affective associations of these concepts fall within the normal curve of average usage, though for technical purposes special definitions in the ethical vocabulary as in any specialized domain may be stipulated, trimmed, and focused for the sake of theory construction.

Construction itself, requiring only the generation and manipulation of abstract symbols, thus liberated from the plodding reins of the immediate environment, is one of the freest expressions of mentality in the universe. Thinking, unbound, loops and soars. For exactly this reason, Whitehead warned against the dangers of "charlatanism" in speculative reason. He expands the warning:

> The world's experience of professed seers has on the whole been very unfortunate. In the main, they are a shady lot with a bad reputation. Even if we put aside those with some tinge of insincerity, there still remain the presumptuous, ignorant, incompetent, unbalanced band of false prophets who deceive the people. On the whole, the odds are so heavily against any particular prophet that, apart from some method of testing, perhaps it is safer to stone them, in some merciful way (Whitehead 1929, 67).

Mentality loosed at the theoretical level turns out to be just as much a hazard as it is when released to deal with absent possibilities at the practical level where survival demands self-discipline by method. The equivalent of practical methods for theoretical intelligence is logic. Logic *is* mentality's method of self-control in the flight space offered by symbols. In inventing logic, theoretical intelligence developed a way to minimize its own dangers of crashing. Logic provides the flight rules for free speculation.

It is important to remember that these rules, too, have a history. They have changed over the centuries, and continue to change. Logic, at any given stage, no less than any other method, is subject to the swooping critiques of theoretical reason even as free mentality flies by the very rules it questions and tries to improve. Still, some fundamental logical constraints are not optional for theoretical intelligence. This internal requirement is given by the nature of its basic function: to help us make sense of experience. There are implicit in this function two broad aspects, in tension but ultimately demanding each other, that must be satisfied. The first requires that our theoretical accounts of experience be *full enough* to cover what needs to be understood; the second requires that our accounts *hang together enough* to form a meaningful unity. These are the constraints on theory that earlier, in chapter 1 and throughout these volumes, I have been calling "adequacy" and "coherence."

Assuming that these other treatments will suffice at the general level, what do adequacy and coherence mean for theories of ethics more specifically? I shall divide my answer into two parts, each in turn made up of two parts. First I plan to look at *individual* ethics, not as though individuals were outside social relations, but showing how individual persons living with other persons might test their standards for assessing their own and others' personal behavior and goals for living, first by reference to adequacy, then by coherence. Then I plan to consider *social* ethics, not as though society and its institutions were not grounded in responsible individuals, but focusing on evaluating right principles for arranging these institutions, first by adequacy and then by coherence. These discussions can be relatively brief, simply laying down markers to be retrieved in part three of this book, where applications will be made to ethical issues raised by the environment, technology, and shaping a postmodern society.

Every person is a society. I will argue for this proposition more fully (as a question of ontology) in the next chapter, but here we can take it simply as a report on the experienced multiplicity of impulses, aversions, appetites, hopes, frustrations, satisfactions, and distractions that need to be contained and dealt with, somehow, within a single skin. There is no doubt that some individuals deal more successfully than others with the clamor inside. Some (perhaps more than generally recognized) manifest multiple personalities (Baldwin 1997). Others, at the opposite extreme, shut down into unresponsive states of catatonic world refusal. But the vast majority, the bell-shaped curve covering the "normal" middle ground, somehow manage to cope with their legions of adversions and aversions while remaining more or less whole. Despite the temptations of a beautiful day, we keep on writing. We resist the third martini, if only to keep our palate sensitive to the fine dinner to follow.

From these experiences and endlessly many more, two great questions of personal ethics arise: First, would it be *better* if there were fewer or more claims for inclusion in our field of awareness? Second, would it be *better* if these claims were organized in some way or were left in their sheer multiplicity?

The first issue is that of "fullness" in human lives. From what I have argued above concerning the nonmoral good, my first obvious response must be that more is indeed merrier. If some goods are good, then adding to them should be better. Eliminating aversions (nonmoral bads) while multiplying adversions (nonmoral goods) leads to larger fullness in satisfactory experience. Or, approaching the question in the other way, cutting out intrinsically satisfactory experiences diminishes the whole. All other things being equal, it would be a shame to lose from a human life the deep joys of walking in nature on beautiful days; and it would be a shame to lose the very different satisfactions of scholarly work, shaping ideas, offering examined thoughts to others. Likewise, all other things being equal, it would be a lesser world without the glow of a good martini; and it would be a diminishment of life to lose appreciation for the tastes, aromas, and appearances of food. The principle of fullness is the practical incarnation of theoretical adequacy. "Exclude no relevant evidence" in theory construction translates to "Scorn no harmonizable satisfaction" in personal ethics. Just as the criterion of adequacy calls for an open door policy for experience, until shown irrelevant, so the principle of fullness calls for the richest possible array of values to be included in a life until some are shown unharmonizable.

Relevance, however, as we saw earlier, is determined not by the criterion of adequacy but by coherence. Adequacy pushes coherence to be broad, but coherence constrains adequacy to be well-connected to the subject at hand. In the same way, the principle of fullness in life demands another countervailing principle, the principle of "wholeness." By wholeness I intend to refer at a minimum to the harmonization every healthy organism must make among its vital parts in the interest of survival. A living entity survives as a whole or not at all. If the interests of sore, tired feet were to dominate the hunt, the interests of the stomach and soon the entire body would suffer. Some rest for the feet may be allowed, but not so much as to undermine the needs of the organism as a whole.

Every personal life needs at least a minimum of internal "cooperation" among its diverse interests, as well as its diverse organs, in order to survive and thrive. This unity may never be perfect in the real world of competing impulses and partial knowledge about consequences. We may opt for the satisfaction of scratching a mosquito bite even though we know it will only make matters worse. We may accept that third martini despite our better judgment. Many smokers, though aware of all the facts, somehow continue to light up. But, granting recklessness, addictions, and irresistible impulses (scratching an itch is just one), the individual person who would survive and thrive must learn to blend adversions and aversions into at least a partial harmony of some sort, however imperfect, in order to get through any day—and, much more, any lifetime of meaningful accomplishment.

We start to learn this as infants. Applying the principle of fullness is easy; we are naturally acquisitive of satisfactions. Wholeness is difficult and very much a learned matter. As individuals we learn vividly from our own experience. We discover by trial and error, for example, what happens to our other satisfactions after we accept that third (or fourth) martini. We discover what will harmonize and what will not. Fortunately, we are not limited to learning from our own experiences alone. As social organisms living linguistically in a culture that has for centuries engaged in observational ethical knowing, we can be warned against dangerous excesses in blind application of the principle of fullness in ways that can destroy both wholeness and eventually fullness, too, in life. The principle of fullness unchecked, for example, might urge one to try heroin or crack cocaine. Addicts report intrinsic satisfactions of such vividness and intensity that nothing else compares. What an apparent shame to exclude these from one's life! But observational knowing reveals emphatically that these satisfactions, though hugely intense, are not harmonizable. They take over a life and ultimately diminish it. Wholeness trumps fullness when fullness itself is threatened by unwary experimentation.

Introducing the funded learning of culture widens our horizon from the solitary individual with whom we began. But in the case of normally social human beings, there are, except for extremely rare "wolf children" raised without human attention, no genuinely solitary individuals. To pretend otherwise, except briefly to make a limited point, would court deception by abstracting from the concrete richness of human experience, in which others play a vital role from the beginning. Each one experiences not only a society within a skin, but also a greater society beyond. Among the urges, needs, adversions, values within the human person—the legion that need not be learned—are interests in and for other significant actors in the individual's lifeworld. Full empathic feelings and the more cerebral capacity to imagine oneself sympathetically in the place of another may not develop for a few years into childhood, but the seeds must be present *in utero* or they would never grow. In a few tragic instances, as in other birth defects, this does not happen, but for the vast normal majority, among the desires of the ego are desires that transcend sheer egotism. Among the satisfactions typically sought by the self in the interest of fullness are satisfactions for others, too.

Such satisfactions often conflict with other urges, of course! The clamor within is full of contradictions and incompatibilities. This is why even in the "solitary individual" there is the felt need for organization, priorities, coherence, the achievement of wholeness that is the "private" analogue of *fairness* or *justice*. True, the sore feet need some attention, but the demands of the stomach warrant still more deference, as do the hungry loved ones back at the camp. For individuals as well as groups, distribution of pains and satisfactions, nonmoral bads and goods, needs to be done under a principle. Even abstracting from any normal reference to loved ones (adopting a fictional Robinson Crusoe scenario), the clamor within the self, from various organs, various personal aims, hopes and fears—for their due share of attention, care, satisfaction, compensation, and so forth—calls for a discipline of functional fairness organized under an ideal of well-being for the self as a whole.

Under a given ideal of well-being, it becomes obvious that one can argue meaningfully whether there are better or worse ways of distributing energy and attention in becoming, say, a hunter. There are good hunters, average hunters, mediocre hunters and, at the extremes, extraordinary hunters and complete failures. Practical knowing, through the discovery, retention, and execution of methods, is at home measuring success and failure under such ideals. A would-be hunter who regularly slights the chore of sharpening weapons in favor of lazy naps by the stream is listening to internal urges and distributing resources of time and energy in a way that is inconsistent with the ideal of successful hunting. Judged by the type of wholeness represented by the norm of a good hunter, this sort of indulgence can be reliably known as a bad decision.

Is this *ethical* knowledge? Not quite. But we are getting close. If someone genuinely adopts an ideal of well-being, the individual, even in solitude, has a standard by which to evaluate his or her approximation to it. An ideal accepted creates the context for obligation. Falling short may evoke feelings of shame and remorse. These feelings need not necessarily be ethical shame or remorse, but they are continuous with the ethical variety. For example, the ideal of a good landing for a student pilot is both goad and reward. Let us stipulate that there is no ethical stake here. Let us assume that no one will be harmed if the solo student pilot bounces the aircraft with great lurching screeches along the runway, before coming to a wobbly halt. Let us even assume that the usual smirking hangar aces are absent from the scene. Still, the unfulfilled ideal of a perfect landing renews its claim, and the perspiring student vows to try again. Let the day come when a "squeaker" landing is accomplished, and (audience or none) the achievement of the ideal is its own reward.

Transition to specifically ethical ideals requires, as we saw earlier in this chapter, the introduction of centers of value which can be helped or hurt. Since one such center is emphatically the individual person around whom discussion has centered to this point, ethical obligation is no stranger even in solitude (though that is not its primary venue). I refer here not simply to the vigorous moral intuition, evident already in toddler outrage, of the moral right not to be harmed by others: "You *ought* not to hurt me; I am precious; I deserve respect." (This explicit affirmation of the self's moral claims may indeed be developmentally first in the order of learning, but it implies a social situation.) I refer, rather, to the moral obligation to defend and nurture one's own excellence for its own sake, for one's own personal sake. One ought not to throw oneself away. A center of value, vulnerable to being harmed, should not be wantonly harmed, even by itself. Intrinsic value wherever found should be respected. This is the basis for the widely intuited duty, all other things being equal, not to commit suicide. It is also the basis for the positive, widely felt obligation to attain an ideal for oneself, to organize one's competing inclinations so as to realize a form of wholeness that includes a satisfying fullness. Every personal self has an ethical calling to honor itself by aiming at rich integrity.

Still, the primary venue of ethics is among persons. The very language of rights and duties, obligations and virtues, rises as all language does out of interpersonal contexts. As we saw, the Code of Hammurabi was an authoritative public formulation functioning to coordinate both regularities of *behavior*— what can be legitimately expected in given circumstances—and *attitudes* toward behavior that can help or harm beings vulnerable to satisfaction or suffering. To this point in premodern and modern history, such "beings" have for the most part been limited to human persons. In the next chapter I shall challenge this limitation and hope to point toward a postmodern basis for a wider, environmentally aware ethics, continuous with but radically challenging to anthropocentric traditions. But the principle is the same. Ethical norms guide legitimate expectations, shape attitudes toward what should occur, and thereby form dispositions to act in foreseeable ways under imaginable circumstances when they arise. In so doing they make the benefits of social order more likely by increasing cohesion and ultimately survival value in societies for which these norms enhance cooperative behavior.

One should not overstate. Ethical norms do not just describe, they prescribe. Unlike "laws" of nature, which are simply reports on regularities as they have been observed within margins of error, laws of ethics can be and frequently are violated. They do not guarantee cooperation; instead, they lay the basis for it, urge it, provide social and psychological rewards for it, and foster internal sanctions against violating it. In many societies where legal, religious, and ethical norms of behavior are not clearly distinguished, there may be harsh external sanctions, as well, for violations. Still, ethics itself provides a framework for the normative coordination of voluntary behavior in matters of help or harm. As long as the behavior concerned is truly voluntary, there will be those who voluntarily scoff at these eminently breakable laws for their own private reasons.

Some "reasons" may be less genuine *reasons* than *causes*, for example, a diminished ability to take a standard moral point of view. Some persons may not have been enculturated in the norms of good and bad behavior as understood by the language community; or they may have learned their values in a subculture (e.g., a criminal family or gang) at odds with the majority codes. They may be among the few "birth defect" tragedies who seem to lack the normal capacity for empathetic feeling; or they may simply have weak mental powers of imaginative place switching, in which the feelings of other centers of value for themselves might be considered. In a very few cases, it may be that there are genuine, important reasons for the rejection of normally expected ethical behavior. It may be that the standard norms themselves should critically be questioned, in the interest of additional information or of other norms taken to be more compelling. And at this point we finally face the question, floating in the background since chapter 1, whether and how we can reasonably criticize or improve ethical norms and whole codes of norms. How do we distinguish between the gangster, the fanatic, and the reformer?

Let us enlarge the question. I wrote in the first chapter that before we were done we should be able to give a principled account distinguishing "the range from saint to psychopath." A fitting conclusion to this chapter would be to try just that, beginning with the psychopath and gangster, then commenting on other major ethical types on the way to the saint and the reformer.

Psychopathic immoralists—famous examples might include Nero, Sade, and Hitler—are by definition abnormal. At its extremes, every normal curve has cases that almost entirely fail to fit the domain at issue. On the viewpoint here presented, ethical psychopaths are legitimately called "evil" by standard speakers, since actions horribly in contravention of standard norms appropriately excite revulsion, outrage, anger, and moral condemnation. Psychopathic actions of extreme cruelty show a radical lack of sympathy with victims who are deliberately harmed. Among many other atrocities, for example, Nero amused himself by dressing as a wild animal to act out sexual fantasies on men and women bound naked to stakes, shredding their private parts with razor sharp "claws." There was apparently no empathy in him. He really did not need to pretend to be a ravening beast; he *was* a ravening beast, emotionally, but one supplied with the additional refinements of human thought and the cultural apparatus of imperial authority. He was in the fullest sense a defective human being, missing something normally present in our makeup as truly as someone born with withered hands. Perhaps ethical psychopaths could be encouraged to strengthen their stunted emotional capacities for empathy or for sympathetic imagination, just as children born with other types of birth defects are sometimes successfully encouraged to work with, or work around, their disability. As I shall contend later, these capacities can be encouraged, strengthened, nurtured, and redirected. But perhaps there are some who are simply hopeless. That is finally an empirical question to be settled outside philosophy books. But if such individuals do exist, they would be outside the domain of the ethical normal curve. Their evil deeds and wicked characters can be meaningfully and rightly condemned from within the ethical language game, but they themselves are not capable of playing that game, and they would not understand—could not resonate to—what we are talking about even if they listened to our words. They must simply be stopped and controlled by superior force.

Gangsters, our next category, are by no means always ethical psychopaths, though some may be. To belong to a "gang" in itself is an ethical situation involving commitments, promises, trust, division of labor, sharing—the necessary conditions of cooperative social life. Indeed, some of the most rigorous ethical standards on our social horizon are those imposed on themselves by members of the secret "families" of the underworld. Perhaps because stealing and murder, beatings and sexual predation, are so prominent in the lives of gangsters (and the risk of associating with true psychopaths correspondingly so much increased), the ethical codes approved and enforced within this subculture are even more rigid than in the "overworld" on which the underworld preys. These involve above all loyalty and silence, but also fairness in work assignments and division of spoils (the nonmoral bads and goods must be justly distributed). On the normal curve of ethical assessment, gangsters cluster at one edge, but those who are not psychopaths are within the curve. They can understand the standard culture's concepts of promise keeping, truth telling, and fairness. They are bound by feelings of sympathy, at least to some degree, for their comrades in crime. What sets them off from the larger society is the specific content of their norms and a trained disregard for the feelings of their victims. The narrow subsociety of their gang receives all their (perhaps meager) store of empathic feeling; promises are to be kept only to one another. What we encounter in the ethical type we are calling the gangster is a *different* ethical code from that of the larger society. Can it be thoughtfully criticized, reasonably known to be inferior to codes nearer the center of the normal curve? I believe so, but defer the argument until other competing types have been outlined.

A different ethical type is what William James called "the boor." Here I refer to someone who is markedly careless about norms of conduct accepted as standard. This carelessness need not necessarily hold across the whole range of social norms. An ethical boor might care about good table manners, stylish dress, and personal hygiene. But for the sake of drawing this type, let us suppose that our boor is boorish in all domains. This boor talks (and kisses) while chewing gum, attends a wedding (unwashed) in torn and dirty jeans, lies and breaks promises whenever more convenient. I describe the boor in these ways to underline the continuity between nonmoral and moral norms. Continuity has been one of the themes of my discussion, and here again it reappears. Flouting norms of etiquette usually harms no one (else) but results in disapproval to one degree or another; flouting norms of ethics is another way of earning disapproval—similar in that way—but also carries the sting of potential harm. Breaking a promise because it is inconvenient harms the disappointed individual, of course, but it also undermines social trust, predictability, ability to plan, the basis for working together, coordinating schedules, and in general damages social order and cooperation. Thus, such carelessness has the potential for widespread harm. Our boor thinks nothing about all this. The momentary inconvenience outweighs such considerations. The boor is not a psychopath. If thought were given to it, the boor could feel sympathy for the hurt and disappointment caused by the broken promise; if attention were paid to the larger consequences for social cooperation, there might be a change in ways. But the boor is a boor, a moral slob, and the effort to think is not made. Only the moment's gratification speaks loudly enough to be heard. For this we hold the boor in some contempt, no doubt, but there is at least some hope. The boor may be located somewhere out of the center of the normal curve, but not so far as we might suppose. Many normal people do not think much about moral norms. The diagnosis, in terms of my previous discussion, can be put in terms of too much domination by the quest for "fullness," with too little discipline by the principle of "wholeness." Immediate interests overwhelm any attention to shaping a meaningful moral character. The boor is recognizable as a type, but this type has no character.

In contrast with the careless ethical slacker, the fanatic is driven by *too much* "character," in the sense of a sharply defined, narrowly focused unity of aims. Though doubtless outnumbered by the boors, there are many examples of fanatics at the turn of the third millennium. Some are willing to destroy hundreds, in principle, thousands of lives including innocent children by bombing buildings, school buses, parks, and airplanes for the sake of one cause or another that, for the fanatic, outweighs every sort of anguish but the particular passion felt by the bomber. Some are ready to shoot doctors—even receptionists—involved in providing legal abortion services. Some walk into busy markets strapped into harnesses of high explosives, their final thoughts focused on vengeance and jihad. On a smaller scale, some break into laboratories and destroy equipment, releasing captive animals into the uncertain mercies of the wild; others drive spikes into trees to create deadly booby traps for chainsaw workers. Ethics becomes a sword. Even nonviolent fanaticism is sharp and cutting. Banishment, exclusion, shunning, excommunication, anathema, the weapons of either/or, are the methods of narrow focus, tightly drawn "wholeness" in the battle against the laxities of "fullness." Values of many kinds, values that can be acknowledged as values (the fanatic need not deny the value of the little children about to be bombed), are sharply subordinated to the one set of supreme values that defines the fanatic's "character." The fanatic is the inverse image of the boor.

Between them, somewhere on a continuum of delicate balances between wholeness and fullness, is the solid ethical citizen. This ethical type cares about right and wrong, feels a degree of sympathy for the well-being of others, learns the standard ethical concepts of the primary language community, and internalizes their norms. For the most part, duty is done, not always happily, but not grudgingly, either, by the solid citizen, and when temptation proves too strong, pangs of conscience punish occasional misbehavior. The solid citizen adopts the practical ethical knowledge of present society and accepts the accumulated observational ethical knowledge of tradition. The solid citizen is disgusted by the boor and repelled by the fanatic. The solid citizen will not agree that "anything goes," as though the principle of fullness—packing every sort of satisfaction into experience—were the sole consideration in life. But, contrariwise, the solid citizen will not agree to burn with the single intense flame that consumes all else. The integrity of our solid citizen may be flawed, but imperfections of character here are in the service of common sense and balanced existence. Our solid citizen is no great sinner, but no great saint, either.

Saints, heroes, and moral geniuses are almost off the normal curve, where it narrows asymptotically at the edge opposite from the gangster and the boor. There are differences between saints and heroes (both types may be moral geniuses), but for present purposes we need not pause to distinguish them. Both are experts in "going beyond." They do what can be recognized by the solid citizen as right, but in a way that goes beyond what could normally be asked or expected. Both are defined by their readiness to go "above and beyond the call." For heroes, the call is to "beyond" duty; for saints, the call to the "beyond" comes from God. In medieval theology, it was held that a special heavenly fund of merit was established and refreshed by the supererogatory acts of saints, that is, acts that went above (*super*) the standard "paying out" (*e-rogare*) required by divine commands. It was on this fund that the Roman Catholic Church could draw freely to make up for the deficiencies of others without violating the demands of God's justice. Theology aside, there is something "extra" admirable, often startling in its context, unexpected, but in retrospect perfectly fitting, often healing, in the supererogatory actions of saints and heroes. Jesus proposed that such startling actions become a way of life for his followers: if someone (say, a Roman soldier) forces you to walk a mile with him to carry his equipment, surprise him, take the moral initiative by gladly walking with him a second mile. If someone requisitions your coat, add your cloak freely, out of love. New creative opportunities emerge when familiar ethical points and counterpoints are transcended in moments of moral heroism like these. When the incognito Christ kisses the Grand Inquisitor, the Inquisitor's plausible arguments are silenced, not by refutation but by innocence. The Inquisitor withdraws, his arguments in tatters, the kiss glowing in his heart even as the old man adheres at least for the moment to his ideas (Dostoevsky 1976, 242–43).

My treatment of ethical types deliberately abstracts from the clutter and ambiguity of actual persons who are usually mixtures of several types.

Historical people who have been given the title of saint, for example, would probably have been difficult to live with. Moral genius, like mathematical or artistic genius, may show itself unsteadily. A real life hero, who has hardly ever done anything supererogatory, may need to confess, with the fictional Sydney Carton, "It is a far, far better thing that I do, than I have ever done" (Dickens 1960, 351). Actual saints run a heavy risk of fanaticism. And concrete historical figures who may legitimately be considered moral geniuses (e.g., Martin Luther King, Jr.) may at the same time exhibit ethical weaknesses (e.g., in sexual liaisons or in scholarly practices) that outrage solid citizens more accustomed to assessing virtue by standard norms than by novel visions.

Still, the novel visions sometimes draw followers, and standard norms are challenged. What then? Are there reasonable ways of criticizing and defending structures of ethical norms themselves? Does ethical knowing extend to the weighing and assessment of ideal types of life and to the modes of social regularity that provide the substance of ethical enculturation in the first place? I would like to deal with this final (and fundamental) issue in terms of one last ethical type, the ethical reformer. Assuming, in the case of this reformer, epistemological standards neither more stringent nor looser than those applicable to the other domains of life (Ferré, 1998, 341–73), how much can legitimately be known in evaluating these final ethical conflicts?

It is worth pondering at the outset why and how "ethical reform" is a possibility at all. If ethical concepts are part of one's enculturation, how can a culture's ethics be challenged? If individuals are morally answerable at last to their consciences, how is it that consciences are persuaded to change? The answer in principle is the same in ethics as in all other epistemological domains: it resides in the power of mentality to deal with possibilities absent from those embodied in the immediate actual environment. It dwells in the "gadfly sting" of what Whitehead calls the "Reason of Plato" (Whitehead 1929, 11), namely, free speculative intelligence capable of criticizing whatever "merely is" against the standard of a "possible better." This is how somewhat successful methods come to be challenged on behalf of more effective ways of doing; this is how accurate observations come to be questioned in the interests of understanding *why* they should be so; this is how useful theories come to be dissected for the sake of still greater understanding. The Reason of Plato is not uniformly distributed across the human population. Ethical reformers are comparatively rare. Likewise, people open to criticizing and educating their consciences are likewise few. Perhaps because ethical norms engage so much feeling, even reformers seldom get started with a simply theoretical examination of the personal or social status quo. Reform needs to be inspired by something. Sometimes, negatively, it is the powerful empathic feeling of a great wrong done to some vulnerable beings not considered in the dominant moral code, but capable of being harmed. Abolitionists in earlier times and environmentalists in ours seem to have traveled this route. Sometimes, positively, a moral genius, saint or hero, may inspire a vision of ethical possibilities for good, not previously entertained, that stimulate thoughtful reappraisal and reform for an individual or a society.

The standards for such thoughtful assessment, as in the case of every sort of cognition, are richness and wholeness (Ferré 1998, 346–47, 349, 359). The richness, or adequacy, of an ethical vision is judged by how much nonmoral good it can welcome, support, nurture for those subjects whose lives are organized by its norms. All other things being equal, the more the merrier! Long faces in ethics, after all, are not adopted for their own sakes. If nonmoral good must be excluded, this is only warranted if there is some *reason* to reject it. Just as the relevance of evidence must not be lightly challenged if a theory is to meet the standard of adequacy, so principled reform in ethics may be justified by the analogous principle of richness. Suffering caused or condoned, satisfaction missed or needlessly rejected, will count prima facie against an ethics, old or new. But, of course, the question of what is "needless" depends on the other primary standard, wholeness. A nonmoral good excluded for the sake of the integrity of a life or of a society does not count as a "needless" rejection. As in other human attempts to think reliably, the great criteria of adequacy and coherence pull (usefully) in opposite directions. Premature theoretical "coherence," pulling in one direction, can lead to overrestricted theories of relevance and thus to rejecting data that might have been illuminating in another theory; undisciplined attention to piling up data alone, pulling in the opposite direction, can confound unity in understanding. In the same way, narrow ethical "integrity," pulling in one direction, can squelch otherwise legitimate satisfactions, condoning pains that could be avoided in another framework; sloppy attention to richness of satisfactions alone, pulling in the other direction, can swamp wholeness in life.

This dynamism is frustrating but fortunate. First, the *frustration* lies in the fact that we can never rest assured that we have gotten the balance finally right, or that our balance between richness and wholeness is the only one that could legitimately be struck. This does not condemn ethical reformers to sheer relativism, since it is not the case on this epistemology that "anything goes." Some codes are manifestly too narrow, needlessly forfeiting nonmoral goods for scant return. Some codes are manifestly too broad, dangerously courting personal or social disintegration. But (frustrating to some), on this epistemology, the reformer may never legitimately claim absolute ethical knowledge. In the end, fallible judgments must be made. Normative judgments are pervasive and unavoidable in all of human knowledge (Ferré 1998, 372–73). Reformers may, and must, sort out better from worse ethical claims and codes, using values learned from the culture to criticize values learned from the culture. There is no other human alternative. Moderate pluralism is the best we can achieve.

But, second, this is *fortunate*, because the moderate pluralism appropriate to the human epistemic condition requires us to keep ourselves open to hearing the well-considered views of others and to keep ourselves critical of our own best-considered views. The happy tension between our primary epistemic standards, richness and wholeness, thus keeps us poised to adapt and grow.

We must *adapt* our ethical posture, whether we acknowledge the fact or not, because new circumstances, unprecedented questions, force us to change. Modern technology has been the primary goad. It is impossible to read straight from ancient texts the ethical solutions to issues (say) of human cloning. This is a new human ability opening new dilemmas. Clues from established positions may abound, and general hints about ways of approaching unprecedented challenges, but all such clues require extension and interpretation on our part. To these types of question, more concretely addressed, I shall return in the final part of this book, "Ethics and Society."

But how can we *grow* ethically, if we do? This is different from adapting and enlarging our ethical repertoire in unprecedented, ethically charged circumstances. It may instead involve finding new answers to old issues, such as capital punishment or sexual exclusiveness. Here the reformer may face the need to help in the delicate task of educating consciences. The conscience, as I have noted several times, is not a static phenomenon. Our conscience starts to form when we first experience empathic intuitions for independent centers of value beyond our own immediate field of consciousness, which allows a moral viewpoint of any kind, and when we learn (and internalize) the norms with which we are enculturated. As Jonathan Bennett's delightful meditation on "The Conscience of Huckleberry Finn" shows, however, the particular content of someone's conscience may be in urgent need of overhaul (Bennett 1974). Huck's conscience condemns him for helping his friend, Jim, escape from the slave catchers. The specific personal duties he unreflectingly acknowledges are violated, to his piercing shame, in being overwhelmed by very specific feelings of empathy for his traveling companion.

How could our reformer help Huck overhaul his conscience? One help would be to encourage him to heed his empathic intuitions. Just as people can desensitize their empathic connections with one another (nonpsychopathic gangsters must learn to suppress such feelings for their victims), so people can be encouraged instead to attend to these feelings. We attempt to nurture empathic capacities in small children; continuing this vector in adults can strengthen a vital sine qua non of a healthy, functioning conscience. But more is needed. Huck is tortured by his sense of having done wrong by following his already strong empathic callings. How can the *content* of an inadequate conscience be turned around? One way is by enlarging the mental domain, stocking it with a richer set of imaginative possibilities to help picture what it must be like to be in another person's place. Here literature (including *Huckleberry*

Finn) can help. Vicariously inhabiting a wide range of viewpoints can help shake provincial assumptions. First-rate fiction can allow us to see through the eyes of the opposite gender, or those of a scornful ruler, a desperate student, or a slave. Teaching Huck to read and giving him a copy of *Uncle Tom's Cabin* might go a long way to help reform his conscience. Education in general—liberating persons by providing them with far wider ranges of mental possibilities than any life career can normally encompass—freeing imaginations as it can from unquestioning parochialism is one of the most important keys to enlarged and refined conscience.

In the end, we need to follow our conscience in the moment of choice. We have no good moral alternative. But we need not settle for the conscience of a child, or of an adolescent. This realization adds an important new dimension to our position. As we noted in chapter 1, in connection with the Paradox of Expertise, we finally must take responsibility. There are no moral experts who can deprive us (or relieve us) of that final accountability for our moral life. But the moral reformer, one (like ours) arguing from the standpoint of an evolutionary, relational, ecological epistemology, will add that we are also finally responsible to see to it that our consciences are as rich and whole as possible. This means we need to listen to each other, to glean as much wisdom as we can from those who have thought long thoughts about ethical matters, to subject our ethical intuitions to criticism and enlargement. And for this we need respectful dialogue. A moderate pluralist, neither know-it-all nor skeptic, can freely acknowledge both the limits and possibilities of ethical cognition and thereby confidently hope to be helped by the insights of others.

CODA: OVERCOMING DISCONNECTIONS

In the foregoing chapter, I have chosen to skip the usual cut-and-thrust of modern ethical fencing, declining to parry in detail the sabres of Hume and Kant, Moore and Ayer, and their many followers. I have opted, rather, to take my own advice "never to permit the gap [of modern skepticism] to open in the first place," by presenting instead "a fuller account of what is involved in [ethical] experience, thought, and knowing" (Ferré 1998, 341). Prolonged attention to those flashing swords, it seems to me, gives them too much center stage, distracts attention from the solid epistemological ground on which ethics stands, namely, the continuities it shares with the rest of experiential, conceptual, and cognitive life.

Now that this primary job is done, it may be well, just as a coda, to show briefly (with chapter 2 as assumed background) how my account speaks constructively to the traditional problems. Why, in other words, we were entitled to walk around the fencing match that has raised so much philosophical dust. These problems were four in number, all assuming a disconnection of one kind or another. Modern ethical skepticism, I believe, depends on one or more of the following: *organic* disconnection, *empirical* disconnection, *theoretical* disconnection, and *social* disconnection. In brief strokes, I shall explain what I mean by these and show how the evolutionary, ecological, relational, experience-based epistemology expressed in this chapter rejects all these purported disconnections.

The first disconnection I call "organic," by which I mean to indicate the sharp separation of ethics from prudence and the quest of all life "to live, to live well, and to live better," in Whitehead's well-known words (Whitehead 1929, 8). Socrates and Plato were understandably shocked by the crass commercialism displayed by Protagoras in offering to teach "virtue" as a mere way of getting along, getting one's way, and getting rich. They wanted a "science of measurement"—a reliable criterion or standard—by which some general perspective could be restored to the completely fragmenting idea that every "man" or every society could be the "measure" of literally everything. But in their revulsion from Protagorean relativism, they demanded perfect and necessary knowledge of a timeless virtue, completely secure from change and from cultural opinion. Mere mores were not to be confused with eternal Good.

My position, too, rejects Protagorean relativism. There are indeed empirically discoverable constants that allow for a "science of measurement" to provide perspective within the cacophony of adversions and aversions experienced by individuals and societies. These are evolutionarily selected constants. A poisoned apple may seem, but not be, good. "Man is the measure" does not work, as Socrates clearly saw. But this does not require disconnection between prudence and ethics. Nor does it justify sealing in heaven some Form of perfect Virtue beyond improvement. On my evolutionary view, norms rose in the quest to "live, live well, and live better." They make possible (and when effective, make more likely) coordinated behavior of all sorts. Normative ideals are a mix of thought and feeling, they organize attitudes, they shape action. Where the felt "ought" of ethical norms differs in weight from the felt "ought" of table manners, this stems from the crucial fact that ethics deals with issues of hurt and help, where beings we care about, capable of being hurt or helped, are at stake. The felt importance of ethics therefore derives from the felt importance of such beings, their real value in the nature of things. This gets beyond epistemology; to this "beyond" we turn in the following chapter.

The second disconnection I call "empirical." Here I refer to the modern mantra that facts and values are entirely distinct in experience. Facts are experienced as entirely neutral states of affairs; values are experienced as approvals or disapprovals, sublimities or despairs entirely independent of the facts. To this I can only reply, "Who says so?" The modern mantra rests on a profoundly flawed account of pervasive experience. All our factual experience is shot through with, is drenched with, is full of—is inseparable from—valuational responses. And all our thinking is likewise pervasively value full. Hume's doctrine of "ideas" is just wrong. He held them, by his initial definition, to be passive copies of our original experience, our impressions, which are full of "force and vivacity." Beginning with ideas as deracinated copies defined by their lack of "vivacity," he could easily move to the conclusion that all ideas (if so abstracted and so defined) are entirely disconnected from the warm impressions of approval or disapproval that constitute our "moral sentiments." Mere wraiths of ideas (so defined) can never in principle move us; our passions, not qualifying as ideas, can never in principle be controlled by ideas. It all follows from initial definitions, but these were ruinous. To this day, philosophers agonize over the issues of "moral internalism versus externalism" (e.g., Sinnott-Armstrong and Timmons 1996, 28–29, 71–74, 162–63, and passim) and the "belief-desire theory" (e.g., McNaughton 1988, 20–23, 47–50, 106–108, and passim) all hinging on Hume's strange dichotomizing of actual experience.

Hume's remarkable and undeserved authority needs simply to be challenged. His abstracting of ideas from the rich context of real human life was, and remains, mischievous. All experience is value-laden, and all ideas are shot through from their birth with judgments. The alleged disconnection is empirically false.

The third disconnection I call "theoretical." This is where the mischief begun with the misdescription of experience comes to fruition in logical consequences drawn variously by Hume, Kant, Moore, and Ayer. Hume, we saw, argued that since rational argument is at home exclusively with ideas, therefore (on his definition of "ideas" and "impressions") the "passions" (directly felt impressions) alone can motivate and alone should rule. "Reason is, and ought only to be the slave of the passions" (Hume 1955, 414), he wrote, insisting on the arbitrariness of our preferences and aversions. We should never attempt to train or educate our value judgments by arguments of fact or logic; the two are entirely disconnected. Kant joined Hume in this dichotomizing of reason from inclination, though he reversed the moral priority. Our inclinations, our moral sentiments, can never teach reason, Kant adamantly maintained. The former deal merely with "anthropology," and inclinations no more than consequences can have fruitful discourse with true ethics, which must be "pure" of taint by mere fact. Moore, in a very different spirit, carried on the disconnection by insisting that no natural state of affairs, no collection of facts, could rise to the meaning of "good." Only a "nonnatural intuition" could supply the meaning for this supreme evaluative term. And Ayer, followed by much late-modern philosophy, drew the inference (left temptingly open by Moore) that if there could in principle be no factual meaning for good, there could be no cognitive meaning at all, just emotional burble, arbitrary ejaculates of feeling directed toward cold, value free fact.

My position has substituted a continuum between value tinged thought and conceptually determinate judgments of value. All our reasoning is done with ideas forged in interest, in noticing, in naming, in subjects of felt importance, in self-certified judgments of usage and appropriateness. All explicitly factual concepts (e.g., the element, gold), no matter how descriptive in primary use, are based on implicit norms—of the good or marginally good or excellent exemplars by which they are learned. All explicitly normative concepts (e.g., sloppy table manners), no matter how prescriptive in primary use, have descriptive content and are subject to public discussion in a shared language. Such shared discussion of "sloppy" can appeal to standards, offer evidence, cite authorities, in much the same way one might argue about the correct application of the term "gold." Normative discussion is not mere venting. Ethical norms, too, are learned, refined, and argued about in much the same way. A reasoned argument about an apparent ethical slip may convince someone that the slip was only apparent and not wrong after all. When this happens, attitudes as well as beliefs change, and with them dispositions to action as well. Our "passions" do not always rightly rule. Seeing the ethical situation more clearly, understanding the larger picture, rightly predicting the consequences, revising beliefs about the pertinent facts—all the benefits of reason—may (*pace* Hume, Kant, Moore, and Ayer) properly sway ethical understanding. And, I would add, the educability of conscience itself is the final refutation of this alleged disconnection between rational thinking and moral sentiment.

The final disconnection I call "social." By this I mean to refer to the atomizing of the individual agent that is so clearly argued in Hobbes, hinted in Descartes, and implicit in much modern thinking about human society. We are taken to be alone, a bundle of wants and fears, bent on maximizing our own satisfactions and minimizing our pains. Any social structures, including modes of cooperative behavior, rise in this context. Moral restraint is external to our inmost motives. Skepticism is to be poured over the entire ethical enterprise. Its structures are artificial. Its norms are arbitrary.

I respond to this claim with a sense that my species, and I with it, have been slandered. The solitary ego as I have repeatedly argued is an abstraction or a monster. I do not hold that everyone without exception has the capacity for sympathizing with others. I do not insist that each child born has empathic links to mother or early care-givers. But I do hold that these traits are normal. To lack them completely, whether due to birth defect or severe childhood abuse, is tragic, since these endowments are the indispensable basis for a functioning ethical life. Hobbes, I fear, may have been accurately reflecting his own personal circumstances, and Descartes, too, was far from socially normal (Ferré 1998, 94–120). I allude to these facts with no intended disrespect for the historic contributions of these cofounders of modern philosophy. But personal quirks, contingent at first, have a way of working their way into the substance of what is shaped by persons. It is not illegitimately ad hominem to raise doubts about the universality of what may have been correctly reported by these two brilliant, eccentric men.

But at this point we are balancing on the knife edge between raising questions about experience, which has been the domain of this chapter, and making assertions about what people really are, which is the task of the next. The two issues, though I have done my best to distinguish them, are not really separable. Probably the deepest root of ethical skepticism is the one drawing on ethical irrealism. Is anything really of value? Does something firm support ethical experience? Does ethical thought run against something that disciplines and warrants it? My answers to these questions will be affirmative. Knowing depends on being. It is time we turned to ethics and the character of reality.

4

ETHICS AND BEING

We are currently living through an age of epistemology, in which the concerns of the preceding two chapters draw more popular attention than do the underlying questions of reality, often dismissed as "mere metaphysics." But these profound questions of "is"—what *values* are, what *human moral agents* are, how ethics fits into the *whole natural universe*—are utterly vital to a sound understanding of what, if anything, "ought" to be. I am uncomfortably aware of the many places in the previous chapter where the epistemological ice threatened to break through to metaphysical depths that I simply decided to speed across. No more skating allowed!

There are two great modern threats to ethics. One of them is skepticism. The other is irrealism. They are inextricably intertwined in various ways. If one believes, for example, that there *are* really no values (irrealism), then this certainly strengthens the case against being able to *know* anything about them (skepticism). Conversely, if one believes that values and obligations cannot be reasonably *known* (skepticism), then there is greater plausibility in the claim that values and obligations do not exist (irrealism). As I said at the end of the last chapter, I believe the order of Being ultimately determines the order of *knowing*. Irrealism, then, poses a deeper challenge to ethics than the skeptical arguments that the previous chapter was meant to answer. This means concretely that the positive ethical position I laid out in the previous chapter will finally stand or fall by the acceptability of certain metaphysically necessary conditions.

These necessary conditions are not particularly hard to understand. Let me state them here at the outset, quite baldly, so that it is obvious what the stakes are in the following metaphysical discussion.

First, the ethical position I proposed in chapter 3 relies on the reality of multiple subjective centers in real relationships. Both sides of this dual requirement are controversial. In late-modern times, subjectivity has become entangled in the still-unfulfilled "modern agenda" to find a place for mind and value in the world of matter (Ferré 1996, 107–273). Despite the fact that, at this writing, sophisticated versions of behaviorism are popular, I must insist on subjectivity as a necessary condition for ethics. Without subjectivity there would be no locus for satisfactions (and pains) that on this ethical viewpoint are the intrinsic values and disvalues. Multiplicity is also essential. Even supposing that there is subjectivity in the universe, why should we think that there are multiple centers of it? Monism has many attractions. But ethics fails to arise not only if there is no subjectivity, but also if there is only one center of subjectivity. Only in the interplay of at least partially independent centers of satisfaction and frustration does ethics emerge. But solitary subjectivity, monist or multiple, is still not enough. The multiple interplay among subjectivities, if it is to qualify as ethical, must be grounded in real relations between the entities involved. Purely external relations, symbolized by the mere collision of billiard balls or gas molecules, does not constitute an ethical framework. I would not dignify the calculations and maneuvers of a room full of pure egoists with the term "ethics." There may be tactics and strategies involved, but as I have made clear, without some bond of empathy or capacity for sympathetic self-transcendence, without some concern for another subject, ethics does not get started.

A second pair of metaphysically necessary conditions for my proposed ethics is a combination, somehow, of real freedom with real responsibility. Causal determinism of the familiar modern sort, largely drawn from Newtonian physics and generalized to all events, would rule out ethics, since the subjective center involved would not be making a genuine decision according to norms but would be transmitting causal influences according to laws. The freedom my ethics requires, however, is not mere randomness. Emitting random behavior is no closer to ethics than obeying necessary impulses. The ethics of personalistic organicism needs a real basis for creative initiation of events, a theory of agency. But at the same time, the creative initiator of events needs to be tied to the world in ways that help account for the decision when it is made and help ground later responsibility for what was decided. Without real responsibility, consequences for ethical decisions would not matter, but on my view they do matter. Without real freedom, norms and principles for ethical decisions would be irrelevant, but on my view nothing is more relevant.

Third, if the evolutionary, naturalistic ethics I have proposed is to be possible at all, there must be organisms in the universe, of which some, at least, have evolved subjective mental powers of recognition, imagination, preference, satisfaction, and language. This may sound utterly noncontroversial to some, but it is not. Evolution itself is resisted by many, but the reality of evolution and the resulting continuities between personal organisms and other living organisms (and both with their inorganic environment) is essential to my ecological ethics. What I call "personalistic organicism" takes the factual truth of evolution with utmost seriousness. Organisms and persons, living entities and thinking entities, bound by developmental ties across time, are essential for the inventory of the universe on my ethical viewpoint.

These three pairs of ontological make-or-break conditions could be enlarged upon, but they should be enough to watch for in the next pages as a metaphysical framework emerges. Can a reasonable worldview be offered that can do them all justice? Thanks to the pioneering work of Alfred North Whitehead, I believe it can (Ferré 1996). Here it can be introduced with special focus on its significance for ethics.

THE LOCUS OF VALUE

The locus of value is experience. This is perhaps the most important metaphysical claim that a Whiteheadian position can make, but at first it may not be clear whether it is metaphysical at all. Is it not perhaps epistemological, in that it is only through experience that we come to *know* values? Or is it just an observation of common sense, since if we didn't experience anything, of course we wouldn't value anything?

Or is it even true at all? Would such a statement about the "locus of value" rule out (*a*) that this vase does not experience anything, and yet (*b*) this vase is valuable? No, it would not. Whiteheadians do not maintain that vases experience anything as vases. They are, technically speaking, nexūs, like rocks, and have no experience of themselves. More, Whiteheadians do not deny that nexūs can be of great value.

Then in what does the value of a valuable vase consist? This may be a complex question, since part of the value may be defined in terms of its market price, part in its aesthetic perfection, part in historic uniqueness, part in sentimental family stories, and so on. Take each one and analyze it further, starting from the last and working back. In what does the value of sentimental family stories and associations consist? In the end it comes down to the pleasant experiences of members of the family (or those to whom they tell their stories), warm memories layered on one another, affections for people gone or present who have purchased, defended, dusted the vase. Without these memories the vase would be just another object.

In what does the value of historic uniqueness consist? Again, it is found in the appreciation of persons who can understand the circumstances in which the vase was created and the length of time it has remained a physical link with those earlier days, also appreciating the fragility of the object and the rarity of the opportunity to enjoy its presence in view of the disappearance of so many of its contemporaries. Remove all the appreciators of these special temporal linkages and the vase would be just another object.

In what does the value of aesthetic perfection of the vase consist? This is the most obvious of all. It consists in the experiences of satisfaction generated by the visual and perhaps tactile examination of the vase: the delicate shape, balanced curves, color, play of light and shadow, smoothness, lightness, coolness, all combined to provide the intrinsic rewards of beauty. Take away every center of experience capable of such subjective appreciation, and the vase (no longer able even to be meaningfully recognized and named a "vase") would reduce to nothing more than a set of space-time coordinates and energy fields.

Finally, in what does the market value of the vase consist? Described monetarily, it is in how many exchange units of money it can be exchanged for, so that those gaining these units can eventually obtain other experiences of immediate satisfaction that the money can be exchanged for. One might obtain other works of art for purely aesthetic experience; or, perhaps (in time of need), alternative experiences might be sought, such as the satisfactions of nourishing food or warm shelter. Without these end-satisfactions in prospect, money alone would lose all its exchange value and the locus of its remaining value would then reside in the more dubious satisfactions of its direct aesthetic appreciation or in the satisfactions of prestige from piling it up. Such prestige would doubtless quickly crumble, once money lost all its exchange value, since without the power of bringing about satisfaction through other goods than itself, merely amassing money would lose its main point. Without experiencers seeking the means to subjective satisfaction, money would reduce to the metal, paper, plastic, or bytes of information that constitutes it. The locus of value—in the end, all value—rests in experience.

This argument may support the view that instrumental values can only be *known* by tracing them back to intrinsic satisfactions in experience, which they make possible, a rather commonsense understanding. But why is it important metaphysically? Here, at this elemental point, we should refuse to accept the great divide between epistemology and metaphysics. This is an issue so basic that the metaphysical and the epistemological are welded inseparably together. In a variant on Descartes' *cogito ergo sum* (Ferré 1996, 138–39), we realize that just as there cannot be thoughts without thinkers, worries without worriers, or loves without lovers, so, in the same way, there cannot be values without valuers. For ethics to be possible, metaphysically, there must be postulated in the universe at least one subject capable of valuing. This is not an unreasonable postulate to make. I trust every reader will find in her or himself the living confirmation that it is actually true. If so, let us explore what else may follow.

*   *   *

To be a valuer presupposes that something (at least oneself) is able to *attend* to definite qualities proffered to experience, to *discriminate* among them, and to *prefer* some to others. Whitehead put this last capacity in terms of "adverting toward" and "averting away from" the discriminated possibilities. For this to happen, the attention span needs to comprise a minimum duration in which the attention, the discrimination, and the valuation are all held together in a unity of experience in which a new coming to terms with the discriminated possibilities is accomplished. This is a moment that has never been before, no matter how similar other past moments have been. And it is a unified moment that is felt as pressing toward a future that matters, even though in that future it will have been replaced by a different moment. In other words, the value being shaped in this moment, the present, has an origin in felt conflicting possibilities drawn from the immediate past, and has a bearing on what will be possible for future moments.

This is what Whiteheadians call "concrescence," that is, making concrete (or actual) some determinate pattern of adversions and aversions, thereby shaping a harmony (with some degree of quality) from initially contrasting possibilities. Each time a moment of open possibility is resolved into such a harmony, something definite is created that, in its moment, never existed before; and in that achievement of new concrete actuality lies a satisfaction, however fleeting. The felt satisfaction of becoming determinately actual crowns the creative moment and is, for the actuality created, intrinsically valuable. For any moment, simply achieving objective actuality out of possibility is its own subjective reward. The harmony of the moment may not be grand, but it has its degree of beauty in itself. Intrinsic value is the value of the experienced moment, however humble, for itself. Great moments of intrinsic value may not come often in the sequence of moments making up a personal career, but each moment, simply by becoming an actual occasion of harmonious experience, is justified by whatever beauty it attains. Since intrinsically satisfying experience is what Whiteheadians mean by beauty, and since beauty is always present when self-consistent actuality blooms from conflicting possibility, the process of concrescence is the process of beauty-creation. Combining the Greek roots for beauty (*kalós*) and for creation (*genesis*), the acknowledgment of a valuer, achieving patterns of preferences that create moments of intrinsic satisfaction, leads to the acknowledgement of *kalogenesis* at the heart of ethics and of actuality (Ferré 1996, 356–70).

I realize that I have been moving rather fast in the above, but before I go back to fill in the pattern with more detail, let me quickly offer more of the broad picture that takes shape from the acknowledgment of ethics and the presence in the universe of at least one valuer.

The presence of a valuer, as I have described the situation, calls implicitly for more valuers. Let me make it more explicit. All I have postulated to

110   LIVING AND VALUE

this point is the experiential center of a creative moment. This may be quite brief. But *internal* to this brief experience of concrescence is the capacity to attend to and discriminate among possibilities arising out of the immediate past, not manufactured in the moment of concrescence but found impinging on the moment from before and along with its origin. Experience has no absolute beginnings. We emerge into wakefulness each day from vaguer modes of experience; every moment of our day has its predecessor moments. At least for any human self that is asked to confirm this postulate, there will be a multiplicity of moments of concrescence, of adverting and averting, of achieving the satisfaction of definiteness. More actual occasions, fading indefinitely into the past, can be remembered; other possible occasions, anticipated indefinitely into the future, are felt within the actual occasion that is constituting the present, adding to the relatedness of the present with the past and to the importance of the present for the future.

Likewise, if deep experience is to be trusted over abstract theories, the valuer, in attending to the data, finds more there than formal possibilities. Formal possibilities are distinguished in the clarities allowed by our mental powers. But concrete actualities from the immediate past are felt through the powerful bonds with a real world that are received by our physical nature. It is a dangerous modern myth that we nowhere experience causal connections (Ferré 1998, 144–62). Down that path lies the impassable Epistemological Gap (Ferré 1998, 165–263). In the experience of reflexes within the physical body, and in the body's interactions with its immediate physical environment, the vague but important links with innumerable other real entities are grounded. These, Whiteheadians call "physical prehensions," which tie all valuers into an actual surrounding world by the experience of causal efficacy (Ferré 1998, 267–303).

Not only by physical prehensions, but also by what Whitehead called "hybrid physical prehensions," through which mental realities can be directly felt, valuers are linked to a real world containing not just physical objects but other centers of valuation as well. The baby does not hypothesize that mother is a locus of love and attention. Once cast into abstract syllogistic form, the problem of other minds looms as very difficult, a matter at best of inference or analogy (when only inferences and analogies are allowed under the rules of the game). But we are not obliged to submit to the dictum that we have no direct awareness of the mentalities of others. There may be no clear sensory awareness, if that is all we are allowed, but why limit "experience" arbitrarily to "clear sensory" varieties of it? Most of our real experience is far from ideally clear and distinct, if our ideals must be taken from Descartes, Hume, and Kant (Ferré 1998, 93–120, 144–62). But those are historically contingent ideals. Experience is much richer than the modern bias toward conceptual abstraction would allow. We prehend both a physical world and the presence of other centers of valuing. These prehensions, both purely physical and hybrid, constitute real relations entering into our makeup and partially determining who we shall become in the moment of limited self-creation.

The idea of limited self-creation can wait to be explored in some detail in the next section. What is central to this section is the concept of the actual occasion, located among a multitude of other actual occasions linked in real relations. On this account of how things are, the locus of value is both individual and social.

First, it is *individual*, because the particular actual occasion of experience, an indivisible droplet of temporal process, creates its own satisfaction as it carves its unique concreteness out of conflict. All value is ultimately grounded in individual actual occasions, both as intrinsic (the satisfaction itself, valued for itself) and as instrumental to some such eventual satisfaction. This is an ethical application of Whitehead's more general ontological principle: "The ontological principle can be summarized as: no actual entity, then no reason" (Whitehead 1978, 19). The basic reason that there are values at all is that there are individual droplets of experience which affirm themselves as of worth. If something is not an actual entity with subjective experience allowing it to be something of value for itself, then—though it may be of great value of other sorts—it is not something of intrinsic value, on which the whole edifice of values is built.

Second, however, the locus of value is also *social,* since the actual occasions of concrescent experience do not develop in ontological isolation from one another, in the manner of Leibniz's windowless monads (Ferré 1996, 189). On the contrary, the initial formative prehensions of any actual entity will be received from the social environment of the immediate past. The multifarious world of just-achieved definiteness reaches into the new moment through real internal relations, both causal and noncausal. Causal relations, to begin with these, set limits to what the new occasion can possibly become, providing at the same time raw material for creating novelty within the bounds of real possibility. If I am hiking in the woods, many possibilities for satisfaction are given in the immediate moment, but among them are not the possibilities of satisfaction that come from flying an airplane on a calm spring morning over meadows and streams. Through these causal prehensions experience receives both the substantial pressure of the "thatness" of the circumstances within which any creative achievement of actuality must be set and the "whatness," the formal definiteness, of the given environment. What Whitehead called "causal efficacy" and "presentational immediacy"—also important for epistemology (Ferré 1998, 293–94)—here work in parallel to provide concrescent experience with both its vague sense of importance and, simultaneously, the more distinct awareness of given qualities, which form the range of formal possibilities that are actually embedded in present awareness. These are the set of possibilities urgently requiring attention for acceptance or rejection, and if rejection, then what would be better in their place? The comparison of the possibilities *actually present* with what *might be instead* is what Whitehead calls "reversion." To take an example: if I walk into a room whose walls are painted bilious green, the formal possibility of bilious green is forced on my attention, because it is embodied in the actual environment, like it or not. "Like it or not?" becomes exactly the question for reversion, a phase of evaluative comparison between the pure possibility of this actually present shade of bilious green with the pure possibility of practically any other color. In this example, after a moment's comparison between embodied possibility and alternative relevant possibilities, I may come down hard against the ubiquitous actual in favor of some absent possibility, perhaps antique white. If that is the result, I have introduced a novel possibility into my experience, that is, the possibility of antique white instead of bilious green, and my affirming this contrast gives me aesthetic satisfaction. If I continue over many more succeeding moments to affirm this new harmony of possibilities against the old—if my aesthetic judgment is allowed to firm into a practical purpose—I will have fostered a disposition to act when circumstances allow me to paint the room a new color. Conceptual reversion, by permitting mental novelty, has contributed to physical changes in the environment. New ideas born in alien circumstances can lead to changed circumstances.

There are obvious ethical consequences begging for attention in this account of causal prehensions and how in the Whiteheadian framework purposes arise and novelties are introduced into the world. These consequences for freedom and responsibility will be drawn out soon in the following section. But first, still focusing on actual occasions as the loci of value, some brief attention must be paid to the phenomenon of "noncausal prehensions" that are acknowledged on this account. Whitehead admits them as "hybrid physical prehensions," by which the mental contents of noncontiguous actual occasions can be felt directly, independently of the physical routes of transmission that dominate our understanding of the physical world. Whitehead's own words are worth quoting:

> Physical prehensions fall into two species, pure physical prehensions and hybrid physical prehensions. A pure physical prehension is a prehension whose datum is an antecedent occasion objectified in respect to one of its own *physical* prehensions. A hybrid prehension has as its datum an antecedent occasion objectified in respect to a *conceptual* prehension. Thus a pure physical prehension is the transmission of the physical feeling while hybrid prehension is the transmission of mental feeling (Whitehead 1978, 30–38).

On this widened understanding of the possibilities of transmission, the dependence of ethics on feelings of empathy for other centers of value whose claims warrant consideration causes no embarrassment. Neither solipsism nor egoism (epistemological and ethical sides of the same coin) need to be allowed through the outer door of respectable hypotheses. We experience other minds as part of the givenness of the larger world. The topic of suprasensory experience may lead in a number of promising directions (Ferré 1998, 281–84, 299–303), but here its main force (allied with standard causal pathways, including caresses, facial expressions, and other physical interactions) is to reinforce the legitimacy of "ethical sentiments," for example, moral intuitions that value inheres in other selves, and to help give firmer ontological standing to the claims of sympathy, which on dominant modern worldviews have enjoyed precious little status.

The main thrust of this section has been to locate in immediate experience the foundations of value. Immediate experience, on this view, is fleeting, each moment of concrescence replaced very quickly by another and another. These moments blossom from the ragged clash of possibility into the harmonious satisfaction of actuality so rapidly that they often give the illusion of substantial continuity—as the many frames of a motion picture give the appearance of smooth flow—but immediate experience, in Whitehead's word, is "epochal" (from the Greek *epochē*, for cessation). Each moment comes to closure. Huge numbers of occasions of concrescence make up a day. Each occasion is bipolar. The physical pole inherits actualities from the immediately given past; the conceptual pole compares the pure possibilities so inherited, both with one another and with pure possibilities not inherited but imagined. It is within the concluding phases of the conceptual pole that an occasion achieves its own unique harmony and becomes fully actual, leaving its satisfaction vectoring strongly toward future occasions yet to form. All this is indivisible, an integral duration, a minimum unit of becoming, containing elements of past, present, and future all woven together within itself.

The metaphysical propositions rather informally developed in this section, introduced as vital for ethics, are also immensely helpful in more general ways, for resolving intractable problems of modern philosophy such as the mind-body problem, the problem of induction, and many more, as in other books I have tried to show. The key question for this book is the status of value itself and its place in ethics. The key answer is experience—immediate, pulsating, relational experience. And in this answer we are provided the one direct glimpse available to us into the internal character of reality. Nowhere but in our own direct experience do we see more than the external features of things. Some might prefer that we refrain even from asking what the inside of things might be like. We speak of "energy" and find ourselves limited to observing changes in location and momentum but without conceptual permission to say anything about what a pulsing field of energy, grasping and being grasped by other pulsing energetic entities, might be like from within. *We* are also pulsing fields of energy, grasping and being grasped, but we are told we would be illicitly "anthropomorphic" if we imagined that human experience offered any analogies beyond our selves. Some, doctrinaire behaviorists, consider it illicit to imagine analogies beyond our skin to other human agents. A few, following the modern logic that finds no room in nature for subjective experience at all, value-laden and unobservable by tools of modern science, denounce the idea that even we ourselves could really enjoy "subjective states." But my view, with other Whiteheadians, is that such denials constitute their own reductions to absurdity. Instead, we hold that our one direct access to reality "from inside" should be appreciated and used as a clue to what reality in general may be like, namely, essentially dynamic, temporal, pulsating, relational, self-constituting, internally complex but consistent, bound to a past, open to a future, and worth something to itself. *There is literally no other evidence.* Is it, then, from some sort of species pride that modern orthodoxy insists human experience is so discontinuous with everything else that analogies should not even be attempted? Perhaps other motives are at work blocking the idea that we could take seriously the idea of our own experience (suitably qualified to suit circumstances) as key to understanding the intrinsic character of things. At any rate I, for my part, do not scorn to use the one source of evidence we do have.

This line of thought will need to be resumed when we turn, in the third section of this chapter, to questions of ethics and nature as a whole. Enough has been said here, I hope, to suggest that a worldview approaching fundamental reality as modeled after immediate experience, while taking immediate experience as also the locus of value, will have enormous implications for an enlarged environmental ethics. But before we turn to nature, we need to think about human society and the metaphysical ground of personal ethics.

FREEDOM, OBLIGATION, AND RESPONSIBILITY

FREEDOM

It is one thing to acknowledge that freedom and responsibility are necessary conditions for a robust ethics; it is another to provide a framework in which these make sense. Dominant modern philosophy seems quite incapable of showing in any natural way how human beings as evolved physical entities can slip the causal chains that (on orthodox theory) bind nonquantum events within the macroworld of human activities. At best, human freedom—in the sense that genuinely different paths might have been taken within exactly the same circumstances—is grudgingly admitted as a reflection of ignorance. Kant's postulate of freedom (in defiance of his deduction of universal scientific lawfulness) rested, as we saw in Chapter 2, on our necessary ignorance of the real world as it is in itself. Empirical postulates of freedom, in contrast, tend to take comfort from our presently blurred vision of the real but hidden microcauses that "must" be at work. E. O. Wilson dismisses both. As for Kant's postulate, "it makes no sense at all in terms of either material or imaginable entities, which is why Kant, even aside from his tortured prose, is so hard to understand. . . . It does not accord, we know now, with the evidence of how the brain works" (Wilson 1998, 249). As to the empirical appeal to ignorance, "Perhaps, as I believe, it can all eventually be explained as brain circuitry and deep, genetic history" (Wilson 1998, 261).

A Whiteheadian, postmodern view of human freedom will also appeal to the brain, and (if "circuitry" can be cleansed of its metallic, hardwired overtones) appeal also to the hugely complex connections that are found in the living, pulsating "circuits" of prehensive feelings that constitute that organ. The brain, we must remember, is organic. Its "circuits" are not soldered or printed. Its connections grow and tangle, reconnect, branch, and tangle some more. The human brain is the most complex structure in the known universe. Whitehead was not a brain physiologist, but advances in neurology continue to accord with his basic analysis of what a significant actual occasion in the brain should look like from within. It should begin with immense richness of information, drawn from receptors throughout the body, amplified and filtered and transmitted through the nervous system and, in the brain, to some key crossroads among the neurons where the event of consciousness is taking shape. Normally, on Whitehead's theory, there is only one such event concrescing in a brain at any one time. He calls it the "dominant" or "regnant" occasion, since, during its moment, it is in charge of the body as a whole, both as the body's prime focus in self-awareness and as the intelligent unifier of the body's response to the information it is transmitting to the brain. Other simultaneous regnant occasions are not ruled out a priori. On a Whiteheadian view, the frequency of multiple personality is a purely empirical question.

Like any actual occasion, the regnant occasion begins with physical prehensions from its immediate environment. These physical feelings are the richest and most varied that can be provided in the entire known universe, because the human brain-environment is a riot of complex feelings of all sorts connected in billions of ways. This unexcelled wealth of physical feelings, at the physical pole of the unified bipolar event that is consciousness, carries incomparably great possibilities for comparison, as the mental pole grasps and considers, evaluates and resolves, the chaos of competing possibilities into a determinate satisfaction. It is just this highly evolved complexity of the living brain environment that makes a regnant occasion so unlike most of the other occasions in the body. The quality of the experience is so rich with contrasts and possibilities that, in this place, normal, dull, unconscious mentality, present throughout the living organism, bubbles up through the sea of unconscious feeling, bursts through the surface, and unfolds in the bright light of full awareness.

Clear human awareness is of possibilities, present and absent. Human awareness has its unclear, semiconscious dimensions as well, as I have indicated. These are the sense of importance and looming reality of the attractive-repulsive world around us that enters experience by causal efficacy. But clarity in consciousness comes from the opposite pole where presentational immediacy rules awareness. This is the domain of conceptual comparisons, symbolism, and language.

Every actual occasion, on the present theory, makes conceptual comparisons and achieves self-determination. The roots of freedom run deep in every droplet of experience. But these protofreedoms in low grades of experience are not important for what they can realistically achieve. Available possibilities are few when environments are simple. Whitehead speculates that one of the few "choices" offered a concrescing electron event is whether to reverse the charge of its inherited field. The vast preponderance of electron events do just this, thus maximizing vividness of contrast while also maximizing conformity to transmitted character. But the massive endurance of the pulsating physical universe rests on an evolved social order among electrons in which they have consistently made the same "choice" over aeons of time, constituted by countless generations of almost indistinguishable events. From this first, *negligible* status at the level of primarily physical events in which the mental pole is no more than a seed or promise, the roots of freedom rise to a second, far *more significant* plateau, when physical events evolve social arrangements sufficiently complex so that the newly evolved entities manifest significant levels of novelty. The latter is Whitehead's criterion for speaking of "living" entities. There is no absolute line between living and nonliving entities; some entities, like cut flowers, can be "partially living," but on a scale, living entities become more and more capable of significant novelty. As growing complexity allows the mental pole to wax in importance, capacities increase for innovating, adapting to changing environments, finding and filling ecological niches, guiding locomotion, sensing, and responding intelligently to the environment.

The human capacity to deal with possibilities free of environmental circumstances, but to deal with them extensively and in disciplined ways through language and logic, has amplified the powers of the mental pole in human occasions of experience to a third, *most significant*, reach not available to any other known species. Prospects remote from the immediate actual situation can become carefully weighed and thoughtfully reaffirmed goals. It takes years of coherently directed activities and enormous memory capacities to become a concert musician or brain surgeon or flight instructor. An ideal must serve as end in view, organizing step after step on the way. Even details of daily activities come under the sway of a distant norm. Ideals of life are included in these guiding mental beacons. But they are not immune to reconsideration, criticism, alteration, as other possibilities come over the horizon of attention or as hidden implications are gradually (or suddenly) revealed. The process of daily life requires continual moment to moment adversions and aversions regarding competing possibilities. A college education, for example, is not decided on once and for all. It is decided on innumerable times, normally by several people, not just the prospective student, first from the period long before applications are submitted, and then throughout the days, weeks, and years it takes to realize, step-by-step, the once-remote possibility. Obtaining a college education is a way of enlarging and enhancing the qualitative satisfactions of a center of value who can be helped or harmed; therefore, it carries significant ethical import. It is also part of a larger ideal of life, both as empowering moral agents instrumentally and adding to the world's stock of intrinsic values. But this moral ideal may or may not be appropriate for every person, for indefinitely many reasons. The ideal-for-me can be criticized in given personal circumstances. "Should *I* spend the resources, accept the sacrifices required?" As we saw in the previous chapter, these criticisms may deal with the criterion of fullness, probing into the adequacy of the goods involved. For example, "Would these efforts lead to bringing about the finest novel achievements and enjoying the greatest satisfactions I, specifically, can aim for? Or do my personal capacities for creation and fulfillment lie in a different direction?" Equally, they may approach from the criterion of wholeness, raising issues of integrity of distribution. For example, "Is it fair for me to absorb these family resources in view of other needs or other persons who could utilize them better?" These questions are of the form: "Is this norm genuinely normative for *me*?" They are mentally entertained challenges that require resolution in the daily conduct of life, and they are resolved, at least for the moment, in the creation of each actual moment as possibilities turn into actualities.

Are these norms freely adopted and freely criticized? On the metaphysical vision guiding this work, the answer must be nuanced. Competing norms are certainly *not* "freely adopted," if this implies effortless, random picking of norms as though from a hat. We come into any moment from a past that partially constitutes us. We do not decide to be conceived, or which historical era will enframe our life. We do not determine our family, our race, our gender, our genetic endowment, or our initial enculturation into the norms of our native language or the language of our cultural norms. Every moment of experience rises out of a heritage from earlier experience. The possibilities we inherit are not unlimited, even with the best education and the most fortunate of life circumstances. If we are free, it is within causally circumscribed bounds.

But, granting all this, human beings are far more free than other intelligent creatures. Our language gives us a method for dealing in immensely precise, detailed ways with abstract possibilities more remote and unreachable than the South Pole. The center of the Earth, the surface of Mars, the corona of the Sun, Maxwell's Equations, the speed of light—even the character of human freedom—become, for us humans and only for us humans, topics of disciplined reflection. In the absence of abnormal circumstances, we can decide on evaluative grounds which of these concepts to incorporate into our continuing experience. This idea is "interesting," the other is "irrelevant," still another is "silly." In the precious duration of our own concrescence, we are not free *not* to determine for ourselves the ideal possibilities we include and those we exclude. Metaphysically, the "requirement that we be free" within the actualizing moment can be interpreted in Whiteheadian terms as resulting from the "causal irrelevance of contemporaries" (Ferré 1996, 346). Past events are *internally* related to our present moment by being physically felt and incorporated in our initial physical phase, but only past events can enter experience in this way. Other events of experience concrescing *during* the duration of my self-actualizing are not actual yet, have no determinate inheritance to give, and therefore are in principle out of causal relation to my experience. We are *externally* related to contemporary occasions, and therefore *in our own moment* of concrescence, we are insulated from causal interference. Achievement of any new satisfaction must be self-caused in the subsequent mental phases, with respect to the norms of our preference alone.

Ethical ideals, open as they are to normative appraisal in ways explored in the previous chapter and mentioned above, are equally subject to normative erosion or reinforcement. For example, perhaps I have long accepted the ethical ideal of married life as appropriate to guide the little steps of my daily existence. But gradually (or suddenly) I find myself confronted by and fascinated with an incompatible ideal of celibate monastic life. Time and again I examine this complex alternative possibility, both for its richness and for its own particular wholeness, and eventually I judge it to be genuinely normative "for me." Here I have a case in which mental comparisons of these possibilities, together with repeated adversions toward the new, have lead to a free—because *norm-led* rather than *cause-pushed*—shift in ethical commitments, and thus to a regime of significantly different "little steps" to be taken in a daily life now much differently guided.

OBLIGATION

As one's guiding norms change, one's set of moral obligations also changes. Ethical freedom has never meant freedom from ethical obligation, but (shades of the Paradox of Expertise!) such obligations must be freely accepted if they are to be genuinely ethical. Here we must be careful to acknowledge that the range of felt obligations is much wider than ethical ones alone. *Artistic* ideals are notoriously provoking and compelling. Artists have starved willingly to satisfy the obligations of their art: to serve, for example, such demanding ideals as the perfect painting, the ideal trumpet tone, the beautiful statue to be released from the stone. *Scientific* obligations, similarly, to such norms as accuracy before the observed facts or honesty before the consequences of theory, are deeply motivating. *Professional* obligations, as well, are only in part ethical concerns for the well-being of others affected; often they reflect the pure ideal of a job well done. *Religious* obligations, likewise, though frequently entangled with ethical matters, are found quite apart from settings in which others are liable to being helped or harmed. Sometimes, as we saw in the case of Abraham and Isaac in chapter 1, they are felt so strongly as to overwhelm all other obligations, including even the ethical.

Ethical obligations gain their distinctness and their particular power because they are always involved with questions of harm and help to beings capable of frustration or satisfaction. In other words, ethical obligations center on the fundamental loci of value in the universe. That is their great strength. But as in all felt obligation, it is the *acceptance* of a norm or ideal as binding on oneself that alone provides traction. If I have not accepted the ideals of trumpet playing as pertinent to me, I will not feel obliged to practice triple tonguing until my mouth goes dry and my jaws ache. If I am not committed to a certain religion, I will feel no obligation to fulfill its rituals. Likewise, if I simply care nothing for the agonies of others, if I feel no empathy for the frustrations of those close to me, if I cannot or do not put myself sympathetically into the place of others and imaginatively feel their joys or pains, then ethical norms will be alien to my experience and ethical obligations will gain no foothold with me. I would then be a person for whom even the widely respected Golden Rule—the norm holding, in effect, that one should take care to nurture satisfactions for others, guided by one's own experience of satisfactions, could be shrugged off with, "Why?" And to such a person, the Categorical Imperative—the norm requiring that the principle of one's actions be universally extended, to cover every member of the "kingdom of ends"—a similar dismissal is available. That everyone is an "end," not a means only, might be accepted intellectually, but in the absence of all sympathy for other ends in themselves, the response might be, "So what?" Likewise, the utilitarian refrain that everyone counts, but only as one, rings hollow or unintelligible without a basis in fellow-feeling.

Fortunately, however, such fellow-feeling, empathic or sympathetic, is a normal fact of life. Even more, for Whiteheadians it is grounded at the depths of reality in the mutual relatedness of all entities, each experiencing its own self-worth and the self-worth of others. Whitehead sees this as the basis both of democracy and of morals.

> The basis of democracy is in the common fact of value-experience, as constituting the essential nature of each pulsation of actuality. Everything has some value for itself, for others, and for the whole. This

characterizes the meaning of actuality. By reason of this character, constituting reality, the conception of morals arises. We have no right to de-
face the value-experience which is the very essence of the universe.
Existence, in its own nature, is the upholding of value-intensity. Also no
unit can separate itself from the others, and from the whole. And yet
each unit exists in its own right. It upholds value-intensity for itself, and
this involves sharing value-intensity with the universe. Everything that
in any sense exists has two sides, namely, its individual self and its sig-
nification in the universe. Also either of these aspects is a factor in the
other (Whitehead 1938, 151).

Whiteheadians who share this vision of the interconnected universe will tend
to be skeptical, therefore, about people alleged to have *no* sense of fellow-feeling. In reality they, too, are connected. If they do not feel it, or have come to
suppress it, this is a learned tactic resting on the power of the mind to abstract
from the concrete feelings out of which the whole web of actual existence is
woven. Such negative abstracting, though based on a magnificent power
evolved by our species, is in this minimizing of ties a misuse of the mental
pole, an overemphasis on presentational immediacy, a habitual dulling of
causal efficacy, a condition which will lead to the starvation of full personhood, even as it denies proper legitimacy to the organic. (For more on this, see
the following section.)

    In contrast, the proper use of our species' mental power of abstraction (not
unique to humans, of course, but far more developed in us than in any other
known species) supplies the other essential side of ethical obligation. The first
side, set in feelings of deep connection, is a necessary condition for ethical
obligation, since without this affective grounding there is no "grab" for ethical
principles, however intellectually luminous they may be. But felt connection
with other centers of value remains only a necessary condition, not by itself
sufficient for ethics at all. Herding animals seem to feel bonds of connection
among one another, but this alone does not count as making them ethical
agents; apparent acts of altruism among kin of many species occur without
suggesting moral intent; infants, still far from the age of moral responsibility,
know empathy without ethics. What is missing in all these cases is the reflective, conceptual, symbolic dimension provided by the powers of abstract
thought. In the previous chapter, I laid out the process by which ethical thinking—in contrast to felt connection—takes place, squarely in parallel with the
other modes of human thought and experience. The crucial point is that concepts in ethics, like all the other concepts we learn for daily life, are universal
in scope. The term "courageous," for example, does not function as a logically
proper name, denoting a single individual. It functions more like "warm,"
which can be used to designate an indefinite host of meanings (but not an

infinite set, since common usage would reject many as unfitting). "Warm" and "courageous" are judgment calls. On my account of language, *all* concepts are unavoidably judgment calls. Speaking and writing is a continual exercise in making judgments about appropriate word usage, certifying one's own performance as one proceeds, while awaiting feedback from the judgments of others in the language community. For all words denoting regularities of experience that have been noticed and named, there will be a central, uncontroversial cluster of situations denoted by each. Here, at the center of a bell-shaped normal curve, users acknowledge paradigm cases, while eccentric uses stir resistance. To be useful, any language must reflect what Michael Polanyi called the "Law of Poverty" (Ferré 1998, 318). An excessively "rich" vocabulary, in which terms fail to do multiple duty in referring to similar situations, would be impossible to learn or remember, and would fail to organize the universe of experience in any meaningful way. The Law of Poverty, as it works in ethics, requires that words like "courageous" and "good" and "wicked" will be used many times in many different circumstances, and therefore that the force of these terms will be general.

When ethical obligation, properly speaking, occurs, two sides are present together. The *felt* concern for one's own value, the value of others, and the value of "the whole," as Whitehead put it, is *conceptually* clarified and generalized by ethical language, language that must be learned, as children mature into morally responsible adults. General concepts, for example, "promising," and "lying," and "fairness" (and all the rest), designate broad types of situations, some more paradigmatic than others. Part of the meaning of these terms is normative. As one learns what "promises" are, one learns that one ought to keep them (the expectations of others will be frustrated otherwise). As one learns the word for "lies," one internalizes society's revulsion against uttering them (social cooperation depends on mutually trustworthy communications). As one learns what "fairness" means, one learns to picture what it would be like, from another's point of view, to be allowed less than a warranted share of some good (it would be painful, and the pains of others do matter). From this learning, and above all from internalizing—accepting for oneself—the standard ethical meanings (affective significance included) that are implicit in one's ethical discourse, one becomes disposed to feel and think in typical ways about general sorts of behavior. One of the key functions of ethical discourse is to help coordinate attitudes and behavior toward socially important types of ideals and practices. To feel moral obligation is to feel the legitimacy of previously accepted normative concepts to guide actions by which helps or harms may be worked upon those capable of being helped or harmed. One finds these internalized norms in the concrescing present, thanks to causal inheritances from their many reiterations in past occasions, but the influence norms exert on lives is only partially based on pressure from the past. They also lure the mind by the pure attractiveness of their ideals. They further admit, by rever- sion, alternatively attractive possibilities. They permit comparisons and force decision. Even when the decision of this creative moment favors further reiter- ation and holding to a steady course, thus rejecting alternative norms, this counts as a decision, not a causal necessity. After many such decisions, the guiding norm becomes increasingly an expression of the self, the qualifiedly free self in the process of creating a distinctive moral character, a character for which it, the free self, must at last be held morally responsible.

RESPONSIBILITY

What is it to be morally responsible? Does my proposed metaphysical ap- proach to the self through its constitutive moments of experience have any special difficulties in answering this question? It is sometimes held that Whiteheadians, like me, who argue that the self is not a substantial, continu- ous "thing" but is, rather, a close-knit society of successive occasions of ex- perience, must have an especially difficult or impossible job in giving a rich account of this key ethical topic. I disagree. The ecological, relational meta- physics of personalistic organicism is actually in a better position than tradi- tional "substance" ontologies to ground responsibility in the postmodern age.

Here is how the problem is supposed to run: How can a self, defined as a series of regnant occasions, be held responsible if the occasion that actually *makes* a morally significant decision at some earlier time is not the *same* occa- sion as the one that, at some later time, is to be praised or blamed, rewarded or punished, for that earlier decision? Imagine some matter of blame. An excul- patory defense is always, "I wasn't the one! It was done by someone else!" But on this metaphysics, the concrescent occasion reaches satisfaction in becom- ing actual, then perishes in its subjectivity, influencing but not determining its successor occasions and certainly not *being* them. It would seem that the same metaphysical "looseness" that allows for ethical freedom, as each moment ar- rives at its own self-determination, will at the same time undermine ethical re- sponsibility. This approach provides no persisting center of subjectivity to take care for its future or to be accountable for its past. No persisting identity, no moral responsibility. So goes the allegation.

I acknowledge that there is no single, persisting center of subjectivity. It certainly is not given in direct experience, which is episodic, interrupted, and inconstant (as Hume pointed out quite effectively [Ferré 1998, 153–54]). Then to impose it by theory seems both implausible and ineffective. It is implausible in a universe that is now understood by post-Newtonian physics to be a network of energy fluxes rather than absolutely continuous "things." Every "thing" is a flow of vibratory reiterations. Even the most solid-looking, persistent object, for example, a great stone outcropping, that has endured in its place since before the origins of life itself is, and has all along been, atomically abuzz with energetic pulsations passing on their formal properties from one brief event to the next. Enduring things are those in which inheritance of properties from one generation of subentities to the next is stable, resistent to disturbance. Substantially enduring subjective "things" (souls?) of the sort postulated by theorists alarmed by the epochal character of personal experience would be a complete exception in the pulsing postmodern universe. They would introduce theoretical incoherence. Where could they come from? How would they be generated? They would float, like elongated subjective temporal wisps, through contemporary spatiotemporal vibratory worlds with which, as contemporaries, they could have no causal relationship. They would reintroduce the worst features of the unsolved modern agenda: mind-body dualism, supernatural-natural incoherence, value-fact dichotomy, humanities-science disputes, and the eviction of value from the world of physics.

At such a huge theoretical price, what would be purchased? Nothing of value. Endurance across time is no guarantee of moral responsibility. Rocks endure. They are not for this apt to be more morally responsible than the ephemeral ocean waves that crash against them. The problem of substantial identity over time is itself a vexed one. On what grounds do we grant that "this rock" has endured three billion years? On what basis do we identify "this wave" as "the one" that formed in midocean and ended against "this rock"? In both cases, though the subjects are different, the answers are the same. In the case of the wave, there is a distinctive continuity of geometric qualities, for example, amplitude (shape), speed (frequency), and though in detail these qualities may vary continuously from a central norm, due to external influences like wind, they constitute a constant formal reiteration distinct from the material stuff, the seawater that momentarily manifests them, then is left behind. In the case of the rock, there is a distinctive pattern of atomic reiterations, energy pulsations with distinctive amplitude and frequency forming in unison with many others in such a way as to constitute a constant reiteration of macroscopic features through microscopic geometric lattices and crystalline shapes distinct from the particular puffs of primal energy momentarily expressing them. The energy pulsates and disappears, while the reiterated information (in this case highly resistant to interference) persists, only to be embodied in new moments of fresh actualization, again and again and again.

What does this have to do with moral responsibility? For the rock and the wave, and for most of the enduring entities of our daily world, nothing at all. They are not so structured internally as to allow the rise of central regnant occasions of highly conscious experience, alive with awareness of alternative relevant possibilities and equipped with organs to initiate changes in the given environment. Without this, they are not moral agents at all, and the question of moral responsibility fails to arise. But human beings, thanks to the complexity of our central nervous system, our evolved sense organs, our multiple organic information channels, and the amazing living brain, can closely consider remote possibilities, likely consequences, and norms. We can initiate norm-guided chains of events through voluntary control over our muscular and skeletal systems. Normal adults find ourselves, willy-nilly, moral agents. We may not feel this so keenly at all moments within our diverse daily lives, but in those moments of morally significant choice there is no doubt, for most of us, that we are responsible moral agents.

But what happens when the moment passes? How does the question of personal identity over time—assuming now a vibratory universe and a correspondingly epochal self—affect the realities of moral responsibility?

We need to avoid doctrinaire absolutes in these matters. Moral responsibility is not an all-or-nothing matter. Some people feel intensely responsible for their future states, for example, making careful plans for their long-term security and taking out large insurance policies in order to be prudent for dependents. Others feel much less connected with their future states, trusting that in future moments they will be able to improvise satisfactions from what the moment then provides. Assuming moral responsibility for past decisions is also a variable. Some embrace present accountability for past acts far more readily than others. Yes, it may be said, this is true descriptively. *Acknowledging* responsibility may vary; but, prescriptively, *being* responsible is another matter.

I agree, but only in part. There is a difference between being morally responsible and accepting one's responsibility toward the past or the future. But the difference is not that the first is variable and the second absolute. Both vary. A metaphysical analysis can help distinguish the two, thus usefully show that we can be mistaken about our degree of moral responsibility. What are the factors that need to be present for genuine moral responsibility? First, there needs to be organic personal identity between the agent and the one being held accountable. Second, there needs to be causal connection between the agent's behavior and the outcome for which the agent is being held responsible. Third, the agent's behavior must be a genuine action; that is, behavior based on a voluntary, norm-guided decision taken in adequate awareness of the relevant factual situation. If any of these should be missing, the person, however ready to accept responsibility, is not in fact responsible and should renounce any pangs of guilt. Some deliberately extreme examples should make this quickly obvious. First, suppose that the agent in question (P_1) is a certified multiple personality, and that the deed was done by a different persona (P_2), without the knowledge, cooperation, or even memory of P_1. In this case, lacking the first necessary condition, P_1 could not be held morally responsible, though the body shared with P_2 was causally involved in initiating the event. Second, suppose that the agent is mistaken in thinking that an event resulted from an action initiated by some deliberate, norm-guided decision of the agent. A woman puts a baby in a basket into the bulrushes on the banks of a stream. Later she hears of a drowned baby downstream from the patch of bulrushes. But unknown to her, the baby in the basket had been removed by a passerby. This guilt-ridden woman may rightly feel remorse for having abandoned a baby, and perhaps for much else, but she is not at all morally responsible for the drowned baby. She had nothing to do with the causal sequence that led to the second baby's death. Third, suppose that a person, limbs flailing in an epileptic fit, sets off a fire alarm in response to which a fire truck collides with a milk wagon. That person's behavior was not a genuine action. Tripping the alarm was not voluntary or norm-guided; it was simply caused by electrical discharges in the brain. The person may cry from sympathy over the spilt milk, but there is no need to grieve over moral responsibility here.

The reverse can also be instructive. Just as some people may be over inclined to accept responsibility when they should not, so others may be under inclined to acknowledge their accountability when they really should. If all three of the above necessary conditions can be affirmed, then to that extent moral responsibility is the case, like it or not. But even here, on this metaphysics, we are not dealing in absolutes. Let us look at each one.

First, the person responsible must be related by "organic personal identity" with the person who initiated the action. What does this involve? In my view the identity of anything over time—whether rocks or waves, candle flames or universities—depends on the reiteration of microcharacteristics in ways permissive of stability and continuous alteration of macrocharacteristics. In the same way, with one specific enhancement, organic personal identity is also a matter of inherited information, perpetuating itself under a rule of constant change. The one enhancement is highly developed mentality, allowing conscious memory and anticipation. Mentality, as the mere capacity to deal with possibility, is always present, but at the level of mature human organisms mentality is greatly developed. Memory is always present in the recognitional capacity of any event for repetitions of formal characteristics in its physical environment. Chemical reactions depend on such capacities for preorganic discriminations among molecules. But in a conscious, wakeful, attentive human mind, memory images can be clear and detailed, linking the present occasion of experience with remote events from which such imagery has been inherited, stored by reiteration in the organic treasure house of the living brain, and retrieved—sometimes easily, sometimes with difficulty, sometimes not at all—by the present concrescing occasion. This retrieval is sometimes done voluntarily, sometimes involuntarily (or even against all inclination), but it occurs as part of present experience, its "pastness," its felt vector from completed actuality, still clinging to it. This phenomenon of greatly enhanced memory is one important ingredient in organic personal identity, adding greatly to the duller memories (the felt organic continuities of complex, self-reiterating, self-nourishing, self-repairing, systems) of the whole body. What event memory adds is inherited awareness of continuity of the whole living, aware person through many changes over time. Metaphysically, this is the key to past-looking moral responsibility.

Future-looking moral responsibility is analogous, but not quite identical, since future occasions of the personal self are not yet actual and therefore cannot in principle be felt in the way that the looming residue of past actual occasions can be felt, both in clear mental event memory and in deep physical prehension memory. Concerning the latter, responsibility for past-looking occasions is supported by prehensions of empathy, in which the achieved satisfactions of past moments of subjectivity now perished press into the present creative moment. We can feel no such empathy flowing from our future moments. Future occasions have yet to become actual and so are never internally related to the present (though present occasions, after future events achieve full determinate actuality, will become internally related to them as part of their past). This asymmetry reflects the grander lack of symmetry between past and future in general, a fundamental fact about the universe that follows naturally from this metaphysical perspective but remains quite puzzling to worldviews like Newton's or Einstein's (Ferré 1970, 278–80; Ferré 1972, 426–45).

Still, if we feel responsibility for our future and it is not empathy, what then? I believe we feel imaginative sympathy. Sympathy is the mental capacity to put oneself into another's place, take on a different perspective as a vivid possibility. In the present concrescing moment, we have two felt "connections" with the yet-unrealized future. One is grounded in the highly developed mental pole characteristic of attentive human experience. It is with these capabilities we can calculate probabilities, understand likely consequences, and imagine vivid scenarios about possible states of affairs in which we might be playing a central role. These are the intellective powers that allow us to look at possible worlds through eyes that are "not yet" our present eyes, but "might be" if certain organic continuities should occur or are not prevented. Perhaps the deepest sympathy of which most persons are capable is the feelingful consideration of their own possible future states. As I remarked in the previous chapter, capacities for sympathetic imagination seem not to be uniform, and this may help to explain why some people are more, and some less, concerned to take responsibility for their futures. Weaker imaginations, weaker inclination to view the world from an alternative perspective, may make for relative unconcern about the future self. But as I also remarked, it seems that capacities for sympathy are subject to enlargement in various ways. Perhaps taking responsibility for one's future can also be a subject of successful moral education.

The other felt "connection" to the future is more analogous to the physical pole. It is less clear, probably less educable, but can be strong, far stronger at times than any ideas alone. It is what Whitehead called the "superjective" character of every concrescent moment of experience. It not only feels its immediate past as inheritance; it also feels itself as legacy for some immediate future. Every actual occasion feels itself a vector toward something. Its particular satisfaction matters beyond itself. Its achievement of determinateness has some weight of importance for what is coming after the moment's own perishing. There will be more moments. Their felt inheritance from the past will be this moment's legacy to the future. In sum, in its *felt solidarity* to the looming future, as well as in its *sympathetic imaginings* of vivid possibilities, the real self—a hierarchical system of reiterating, multileveled energies, no ethereal "mind" or "soul," not even a thin "train of occasions," but an embodied, remembering, anticipating, organic person—shows responsible concern for the branching possible paths ahead, even as it acknowledges responsibility for having covered the ground its many finite steps have overtaken.

In the past four paragraphs, I have been dealing at some length with the first of the necessary conditions for moral responsibility, the requirement that there be "organic personal identity" between the self held responsible for an act or its consequences and the self initiating the act. I have spent this much attention on the subject, because the "epochal" understanding of human personhood, made up of sequential quanta of experience, has been accused of weakness on this criterion. I hope I have shown that—far from weak—this picture of a pulsating, vibrant, relational universe (what I have called the ecological worldview) fits the responsible organic person into the cosmic scheme of things as *exceptionally empowered* mentally but as no *metaphysical exception*, no miracle, no rent in the fabric of nature. It is a position that rises easily from reflection on our actual episodic human experience. It can take account of the phenomenological fact that some persons feel more tightly tied to their pasts or their futures than do others. There really are some quite irresponsible people. There are some responsibility fanatics. This worldview offers a central norm for responsible concern around which variability can be expected. It allows for developmental growth (and deterioration) of organic personal integrity across time. It gives a basis for educating persons into enlarged visions of moral responsibility. Far from a weakness, the epochal understanding of organic personhood is one of the consequences that most recommends it—and thus goes on to recommend the larger relational, ecological worldview with which it coheres.

The second and third conditions for moral responsibility are not unique to this worldview and can be much more briefly noted. The second condition, causal connection between the morally relevant act and the morally relevant outcome, is a serious problem for popular modern metaphysical positions in which causal connection itself is a mystery, but my postmodern metaphysical approach has no such problem. Physical prehensions bind the universe into a relational network of evolved societies nested in larger societies, where physical conformity has become the overwhelming rule in nature. Inheritance undergirds all structure, and causal continuity can be traced from an initiating action to its significant consequences. These are ultimately matters of probability since there are no iron laws determining causal events; but the so-called problem of induction, as I showed in an earlier volume, dissolves on the present worldview (Ferré 1998, 295–99). Figuring out the empirical details of causal sequences is a job for scientists (as in criminal trials), but this is no special philosophical problem for a Whiteheadian viewpoint.

The third condition, that the morally relevant act be initiated by an informed, voluntary decision, one guided by norms and not forced by causes, was the subject of the first part of this section. Again, on this analysis, the criterion can be met by degrees. "Adequate information" is not an all-or-nothing matter. There are some situations in which ignorance is a full excuse from moral responsibility; contrariwise, there are situations of culpable ignorance. Most of the time we find ourselves somewhere between the extremes, somewhere under a bell-shaped normal curve in which "enough" must be a matter of sober judgment solved by no neat algorithm. "Voluntary" is also on a sliding scale, as my previous discussion should have made clear. Powers of mentality are not equally distributed, even for a single person over a single day. Fatigue or drugs or illness may dull imagination to the point where the process of reversion is low-grade, creative alternatives are minimized, and causal conformity mainly rules. Some persons trapped in some circumstances of life may rarely know moments of full voluntary action. Even those who do may experience them sporadically. On this bipolar understanding of human personhood, the causal, physical pole is always heavily present, and the conceptual, mental pole is flickering at best. But again we find ourselves—as seems quite appropriate to the facts of experience—within a normal curve where some actions are borderline voluntary, some are outstanding cases, and most are somewhere between these extremes, in the real world of mixed motivations where full moral responsibility is a matter of judgment. For legal purposes, society tilts toward the view that actions are voluntary unless proven otherwise, and this is doubtless wise social policy. But philosophers will likely see more shades of gray. Still, our lives are full of reasonably clear cases of free, norm-guided decisions, reiterated over long periods of time in our attitudes and actions. For these voluntary decisions and their many consequences we can hold ourselves morally, as well as legally, responsible.

One final note on moral responsibility needs to conclude this section. I have been concentrating on personal responsibility. This is justifiable, since personal responsibility is the paradigmatic case; on my view, without personal responsibility there would be no responsibility at all, just as without individual centers of subjectivity there would be no value at all. But on my ecological worldview of personalistic organicism, there is a wider scope for moral responsibility. The individual is not alone. The social environment limits and allows the individual to be just that individual, in that time and place, and the morally responsible individual contributes to what the social environment shall become.

Just as an individual is not whole without others who enter intimately into the internal relations that partially shape concrescent characters, so an individual normally takes responsibility for more than just the future well-being of yet unactualized moments of private experience. Parents take responsibility for their children and for each other. Doctors take responsibility for their patients. Teachers for their students. The network of responsibility widens, ideally, to include the whole social fabric of mutual dependency and mutual aid. We generally recognize and approve, as long as the bonds of responsibility are not exaggerated. This metaphysics acknowledges legitimate external relations as well as internal ones (Ferré 1996, 316–24). If responsibility comes in degrees, even within the lives of individual persons, so much the more must we recognize a sliding scale of responsibility in social contexts. I am responsible for keeping my dog off my neighbor's lawn, but I am not responsible for putting my neighbor's child through college. I am morally (and legally) responsible for paying my school taxes to help everyone's children in my school district gain the liberating satisfactions of education, but I am not morally (or legally) responsible for getting everyone in my community to go to church, however great the benefits may be. I shall return in more detail to these reflections on social life in the final part of this book. The main point for now is to remind ourselves that moral responsibility is not merely a private matter. As we are social entities, so we are connected with moral strands of varying thicknesses and textures.

Less frequently appreciated, but important to recognize, are the strands that tie us as persons to the history and moral character of the society that nourishes us, shapes our identity, and requires our loyalty. Many in our individualistic age object to the very notion of "collective responsibility." If I *personally* had nothing to do with the oppression of your ancestors, so it is hotly argued, then I have no responsibility whatever for the consequences that have been visited on you. Tough luck. I am not to blame, and therefore should not be expected to share in any indemnification of the wrong done to others by others. Let us compete, therefore, free of guilt and subsidies. And let the better qualified prevail!

This line of argument presupposes a different, more atomic metaphysics than my own. I agree that the beneficiaries of social misdeeds in the past should bear no guilt, assuming they have done no wrong, but avoidance of personal guilt does not equal escape from social responsibility. Suppose, for a simple example, that one member of a family, unknown to the family, is an expert embezzler who brings home large fortunes supposedly earned. The family prospers, its members live in a great mansion, go to the finest schools, make the most profitable contacts, enjoy successful careers. When the embezzlement is discovered, these family members are not *guilty* of the crime. But they *are* in very significant part *who they are* because of their membership in and solidarity with the family. Since they have so greatly *benefited* from the dishonest proceeds, they are on my view morally responsible to join in making restitution to those who have been defrauded, even at considerable personal cost to themselves. By the way, they are in an excellent position to do so, since they have used their illicit wealth (however innocently) to create more wealth and access to wealth than they could otherwise have gained.

Now suppose, in contrast, that these family members had at some point learned about the fraudulent source of their good fortune. Suppose they kept it their "dirty little secret" as long as possible, and then fought to keep it from coming to the attention of the authorities, doing all they could, by intimidation of witnesses, destruction of evidence, and the like, to keep their cash cow alive. What then is the moral situation? Besides full restitution, punitive damages would seem appropriate. This predatory family had assumed a large share of responsibility for the crime begun by one.

What of the next generation? Suppose the original embezzlement had been from a widow's trust, and the widow's children and grandchildren were forced as a consequence into poverty. Educational doors were closed to them. Social graces were a luxury they could never afford to learn. They became society's trash. Do the innocent children of the guilty family have any moral responsibility to endure some costs, moderate perhaps, but enough to be felt, in order to make restitution for their parents' sins? On this metaphysics of relationship, the answer is yes. The principle of fairness in distributing nonmoral goods would urge a special responsibility on the innocent children to do justly by their parents' victims. Others in the larger society may also have a general responsibility to help, but the strands of responsibility are thicker and pull more tightly on the collective beneficiaries of a collective injustice. Social responsibility is not only something we freely take; it also provides a norm that may legitimately oblige us to give. Here the topics of this section—freedom, obligation, and responsibility—come together, rolling in the familiar dust of daily debate. We must return to this, and more, in the final part of this book.

PERSONS AND ORGANISMS

To this point, I have made no secret of the fact that I accept nonhuman centers of value as an essential part of my worldview. I have taken it as literally true, for example, that my dog has felt needs, joys, frustrations, pleasures, pains, fears, preferences, and in general values of her own. We are not talking in an "extended sense" when we say these things. They are part of the original meaning of those terms, centrally embraced within the bell-shaped normal curve of their origins in what Mary Midgley calls the "mixed community" of people and animals wherein human language first took root (Midgley 1984, chap. 10). To reduce the literal scope of "satisfaction"-terms to exclusively human reference depends on a modern metaphysical restriction, a shrinking from supposedly illicit "anthropomorphism" that depends for its pejorative meaning on first drawing fixed, tendentious lines between the human and everything else. Such linguistic lines would not have been possible without prior alienation between human culture and wider nature.

On a more ecological metaphysics, informed and inspired by postmodern environmentalist intuitions (Ferré 1996, 297–304), we can now reopen the question of human ethical obligations and responsibilities to a wider realm of value-centers than human ones alone. Environmental ethics needs to be a deepening of, an extension from, what I shall call culture ethics. Anything short of continuity is in danger of falling into ethical incoherence (Ferré 1993, 441–53). An environmental ethic, that is, must not be created as an unconnected annex to a culture ethic offering simply "different" norms. What should we think, what shall we do, when the interests of culture and nature seem to clash, and when their simply "different" norms conflict (Ferré 1996, 301–302)?

Still, nature and culture have long been contrasted. And there is much to contrast. Culture is the domain in which voluntary purposes are significant ingredients in shaping history. Nature is the domain of unconscious causal evolution. In culture, individual personhood is nurtured, expressed, and defended. In nature, the good of the species outweighs the good of the individual organism. Any environmental ethics will need to span some wide gulfs between nature and culture. Can a unified ethics applicable to both contexts be supported by a Whiteheadian vision of reality?

I believe the analysis of persons and organisms allowed on this metaphysics permits just the sort of continuities and contrasts needed for a coherent expansion of culture ethics to include environmental ethics. I have named my position "personalistic organicism" (Ferré 1996, 1998). Let me now explain its implications in terms of a larger, more inclusive ethics.

"Organicism" is the genus term, and "personalistic" the differentia. Let me start with the idea of an organism and leap downward to the ultimate pulses of creative energy that make our universe. Then I can work back up to the human, to persons and beyond.

Whitehead called his own position the "philosophy of organism." By "organism" he meant an entity that is internally dynamic and essentially related.

That is, an organism would contrast with the common modern conception of a particle, inert and dependent on "impressed forces" from outside itself. It would also contrast with the modern conception of things as basically independent of each other, "atomic facts" about which true propositions could be affirmed quite apart from reference to any other facts, things that would be what they are in any location. An organism, in contrast, is never "simply located." It is always what it is, in significant part, because of its environment. Tear an organism out of its network of environmental relationships, and it would not remain the same organism. Perhaps it would not die, but it would certainly be different.

One of the deepest insights of scientific ecology is that "everything is related to everything else." Eugene Odum's great textbook defines ecology as the science of relationships between organisms or groups of organisms and their environment (Odum 1971, 3). To call Whitehead's "philosophy of organism" ecological is to recognize that for this philosophy, the universe itself is ultimately composed of organisms or groups of organisms in relation. This means, for organicism in one (technical) sense, there is nothing in the universe that is not at heart organic. The briefest subatomic event is dynamic and essentially relational. In this sense, organisms go "all the way down" to the smallest, most insignificant puff of reality.

This is counterintuitive for normal speakers who make a major distinction between the organic and the inorganic. And there is such a big, obvious difference between microbes and grains of sand, between fish and the water they swim in, that organicism needs to slam on its brakes. It must quickly acknowledge that such differences, which really do exist, can be dealt with in a natural way. Otherwise it could be dismissed as a silly position, not worth the time to refute.

Whitehead's way was to distinguish between actual entities, which are always internally dynamic and essentially related (always organisms) and the macrocharacteristics of groupings of these entities when socially organized. On Earth a grain of sand made up of crystals of worn or disintegrated rock is most likely to be silicon dioxide (quartz). The silicon element is an enormous presence in the universe—in the Sun, in meteorites, as well as Earth, where (next to oxygen) it is the most abundant element—but it does not appear "naked" in nature, only in combination with other elements. A silicon atom alone is a society of fourteen negatively charged electrons in pulsing relationship to each other and balanced by a complex, positively charged nucleus. Each of these atomic components is dynamic and essentially related, an "organism" in the technical sense. But silicon atoms do not thrive alone. Making up the quartz crystals in a still larger society of dynamic relations are two oxygen atoms, each with eight electrons pulsing in complex energetic relationship with each other, with their nuclear events and with the society of charges and forces we call the silicon atom. For the philosophy of organism, this is the microscopic locus of being and value. Each electronic or nuclear event is essentially related to its predecessor state and leaves its own achieved integration as a legacy to its successors. Each grasps its immediate atomic environment and makes something definite of itself in its unimaginably short duration into actuality. Each achieves its tiny satisfaction, its small flash of beauty before perishing.

The grain of sand, in contrast, does not move of its own accord. It fits the model of inert stuff for which it and things like it were the original inspiration. It is more or less the same grain of sand wherever on the beach it may be tossed by wind or wave. Superficially, it is "simply located" and relatively indifferent to its changing environment, up to a point. In these respects it is the paradigm of inorganic matter. As a loose, gritty particle of disintegrated rock, it *does* nothing (qua grain), *feels* nothing (qua grain), and has no intrinsic value (qua grain). For organismic philosophy, inertness, simple location, and indifference turn out to be emergent properties, only achieved after reaching certain levels of complexity, where social order has evolved in ways that support perpetuation of pattern through stable reiterated structure. They are the drab properties of "enduring" things, exoskeletal features, supervenient on the vivid dynamism of perishing moments of intrinsically valuable activity. The inorganic realities are the derivative realities; metaphysics must not be based on them.

Neither should ethics be so based. Ethics needs to guide us in giving due respect to value wherever found. This requires us to be clear about different kinds and orders of value if we are to attain a unified and coherent ethics for environment and culture.

Postmodern physics, the stochastic science of relational energies, gives personalistic organicism its framework of pulsing, self-affirming moments of actuality found in evolved social configurations of regular reiteration. On this view, the intrinsic value of subatomic events is individually tiny—so brief and so far from vivid as to be negligible—but collectively huge. The physical universe vibrates in mighty chorus, affirming every moment its new perpetuation. And toward this silent music of the spheres, the human ethical response is only appreciation. There are no other obligations. At this level, there is nothing we can do about the immense fields of beauty constituted by the concrescing of actual occasions in themselves. They cannot be harmed or helped. But they can be appreciated. One order of appreciation might be at the level of physical cosmology, looking outward from Earth to the fascinating universe still dark with missing matter and with mystery but the glowing context of all known things. Another order of appreciation might instead be microscopic. Materials science at the creative interface between physics and chemistry now allows a postmodern vision of what might well be called "neomatter" to replace the old, modern sense of matter as inert, asocial, and value-free. One postmodern materials scientist, Pierre-Gilles de Gennes, working in polymers and liquid crystals, expresses his appreciation warmly: "Liquid crystals are beautiful and mysterious; I am fond of them for both reasons." (de Gennes and Prost 1993, vii). The self-organization in polymers, as we are learning, is nothing short of vast, and sets us imagining the road toward living organisms, capable of self-repair and reproduction (de Gennes 1990).

Physics, chemistry, materials science have all entered a new era in the new millennium. Dynamism and relation are no longer alien. Even value-language appears in science texts. But for ethics, the primary values in these domains are instrumental ones. The intrinsic values of the material universe may be fitting for our appreciation, but since there is nothing we can do to help or harm them—even radically altering chemical states, as by burning, will not hurt the electronic or protonic occasions involved—the ethical focus turns to how we might use them, well or badly, in the pursuit of our own human satisfactions or in connection with other entities that can in fact be helped or harmed.

Although the intrinsic values involved in material things are individually trivial and collectively beyond our practical reach, the instrumental values of the physical universe are immense. This is so obvious it almost embarrasses me to write it, but honor must be given to each value according to its kind and degree. One does not need to become "materialistic" in any objectionable sense in order to recognize matter as the sine qua non (in this universe, at least) for the achievements of all the "higher" satisfactions we crave and admire. It provides the means for everything, including our bodies and our brains. Let no one say "merely" instrumental value. If instrumentally valuable, then *really* valuable. It would be a fatal error for ethics to honor only intrinsic value. Everything deserves respect according to its degree and type of value. Confusing instrumental with intrinsic value is unhelpful, but despising instrumental value is perverse.

Postmodern science is finding the "line" between complex forms of matter and simple forms of living things hard to identify. This, from the viewpoint of personalistic organicism, is exactly as it should be. There is no fixed line. Liquid crystals and polymers act in fascinating, mysterious, and beautiful ways; viruses act a lot like crystals. Viruses cannot reproduce—cannot be what they are—without a living host. Are they "dead" matter? Are liquid crystals "alive"? The philosophy of organism rejects these dichotomies. These are matters of degree, inescapably calling for a qualitative judgment about the application of words if distinctions need to be made within the unbroken continuum of nature. For organicist philosophy, the key variable is the production of relevant novelty in environmental context. The virus in the context of a living host adapts and mutates and qualifies as a living thing. Outside any living host, in the "inorganic" environment of inert, enduring physical structures like test tubes, the virion is an inert, nonliving structure, too. The electronic and protonic occasions of its atomic level are, of course, as active as ever, but as a structured material thing reiterating the supervening patterns of nucleic acid and protein molecules, it is not a living thing, as we humans like to draw lines.

Bacteria are a different story. Although extremely small and with a nucleus composed of only one chromosome, they are single cells of components organized in such a way as to perform by themselves all the functions of nutrition and reproduction, often even locomotion, needed to be classified unambiguously as "living." In thousands of species, they have evolved to manage amazingly varied environments, from the almost airless upper atmosphere to boiling sulfurous vent holes in the ocean floor.

Again, speaking ethically, we are primarily concerned with instrumental values when we deal with viruses, bacteria, and other microbes like the blue-green algae. It is not clear whether any of these could be thought to have a significant "life of its own." The virion is not even alive. Bacteria, though alive, reproduce mainly by fission, dividing into endless generations of identical twins without an identifiable "parent," thus raising problems about what "its own" could mean. But urgent questions of instrumental value and disvalue are raised by the capacity of viruses and bacteria to help or harm other organisms for which "good of its own" has a firmer basis.

Turning to plant life, those multicellular primary producers whose cell walls are characteristically stiffened by cellulose, rather than the murein (sugar and amino acid) of bacteria, we find a similar ethical situation. Green plants are capable of capturing the energy of sunlight, using it both for their own life needs and for manufacturing (from carbon dioxide and water) the starches and sugars essential, directly or indirectly, for all plant and animal life. Although algae and some bacteria are also capable of photosynthesis, the green plants are what all animal life depends on. Since this is so, the instrumental value of these plants is enormous, for the insects that suck on them, the grazers that graze on them, the birds that eat the insects, and the carnivores that hunt the grazers, as well as the human race that depends on all of the above. Phytoplankton in the waters, and grasses on land, provide the necessary conditions on which the rest of the food chain depends. Individual blades of grass, like single diatoms of plankton, may have low orders of intrinsic value, but this is many times compensated by the instrumental value they represent to all the species that depend on them. If a human being were forced to choose between the good of a blade of grass, for example, and the good of a hungry horse, the more complex and vivid good of the horse would normally far outweigh the dull, unconscious good of the blade of grass, or several, or many. But if the choice were to be between an individual animal, or even a herd, and the health of grasses generally in an ecosystem, the weight of the good might well swing from considerations of intrinsic satisfaction for the few (the horses) toward instrumental good for the many (the grasses).

There are other ethically relevant ontological differences between horses and grasses than the fact that one is a consumer and the other a producer of the foodstuffs necessary to energize life. Green plants are multicellular. For Whiteheadian philosophy, a plant is a society of societies of cells (each cell its own complex society), all organized to work together for the needs of the plant as a whole. The plant as a whole has objective interests, for example, in maintaining its place in the sun, in reaching adequate supplies of water, in successfully reproducing its kind, and the like. One could say that it has an "objective good" in fulfilling its "objective interests" insofar as possible. But does the plant as a whole have *subjective* interests or a *subjective* "good for itself"? This is difficult to determine, though Whitehead himself was somewhat skeptical on the question, pointing to the absence of a central nervous system. The complex plant society, he believed, is organized more like a democracy, in which cooperation is less centrally controlled, than are animal societies, characteristically focused in perception and action by a "ruling" occasion. If this is so, then there is no unified subjective good for a plant, just as there seem to be no channels for sending feelings of pain to a central locus. I might reserve judgment a bit on this question, since recent empirical research suggests that some plants do send electrical signals triggering self-defense measures (Ferré 1996, 332–33), but it seems most probable that the plant kingdom is not characterized by vivid, centrally focused experiences of a sort comparable to those of the animal kingdom. The individual parts may be vaguely sensate, but they are not organized to share perceptions with a central locus of individual identity. Therefore the objective good of a plant is likely to be instrumental (to its health, growth, reproductive success, etc.), while any subjective goods within plants are likely to be vague, diffused, and ineffectual. Ethically, then, the horse is at least not causing pain as it grazes across the meadow, and humans need not feel a guilty conscience while eating a lettuce salad. All life except the primary producers (bacteria, algae, and green plants) live on other life. "All life is robbery," as Whitehead said (Whitehead 1978, 105). For a purely "biocentric" ethic, such robbery, since life is taken, would be a crime, or at least a tragedy. But for the philosophy of organism this need not be the case. The central value of personalistic organicism (Ferré 1996, 340; Ferré 1998, 366–67) is the generation of beauty in experience, *kalogenesis* (from the Greek *kalós*, or beauty). Therefore my proposed environmental ethic will be neither biocentric nor anthropocentric, but *kalocentric*. The main ethical concerns will be support for creation of beauty in experience, wherever it occurs, and for making good judgments about its richness and intensity.

The grazing horse, here representing the animal kingdom, is in fact differently organized from the plants in the meadow. The horse is also a complex society of societies, composed of cells of many varied sorts, organelles and organs delicately interrelated but with ethically relevant centralization of feeling and information in a complex living brain. Everyone, even doctrinaire behaviorists, acknowledge that horses are intelligent creatures, on any definition of "intelligent." On the present worldview there is no question that horses are subjectively aware as well. Anyone who has become directly acquainted with horses will have an inclination—suppress it or not—to attribute interiority to these magnificent animals. They have characters of their own (I might even say "personalities," were I not saving the concept of "personal" for a more technical use). It is most natural to say that they feel fear and affection, pain and pleasure, resentment and joy. Why suppress this natural inclination? Only modern philosophical prejudices stand in the way, and they have led only to confusions and dead ends. My kalogenic organicism leads me to assert that the horse's experience, by analogy to our own, is episodic and creative of complex satisfactions from moment to moment. Satisfactory experience is the basic meaning of beauty, some more or less rich, more or less vivid. The complexity of the horse's organic connectedness, supporting a finely tuned nervous system culminating in a large brain, allows a very rich harmony of experience to be achieved from concrescent moment to concrescent moment in a train of ruling occasions. Vision, hearing, smell, touch, taste, kinesthetic awareness of movement and bodily organs, all these pour into the receiving occasion and achieve definiteness, harmonization, that is, beauty, in the moment of subjective actualization. The horse is a high order creator of beautiful experience. The many living blades of grass taken to make these events of kalogenesis possible are well sacrificed.

I chose a large-brained mammal as my prime example to make this point easier to accept. I would, however, boldly extend the argument downward in the animal kingdom (where "down" and "up" are scales of organic complexity, especially neural complexity), to non-mammalian life, including birds and worms, octopi, fish, and clams. The lowly clam is not a highly intelligent creature. My worldview leads me to believe it has a subjectivity, but if so it is extremely dim. The clam has a nervous system, featuring three pairs of interconnected ganglia, but no central brain. It is doubtful whether a clam has a single subjective "good of its own," therefore, but probable that it feels a vague, far-from-conscious contentment as it digests its particles of food and respires through its siphon. This is beauty of a sort. We would find the harmonies and intensities extremely boring, no doubt, but all other things being equal, a kalocentric environmental ethic would respect this good of its kind and counsel its nurture. "As happy as a clam" has genuine meaning on this philosophy.

But all other things are seldom equal. A hungry sea gull may be cruising the beach in search of nourishment for its own kalogenesis. For the sea gull, the clam is fair game. This is as it should be. The food chain has genuine meaning on this philosophy.

This is true, too, for predators which cause subjective pain in their prey. Pain is a nonmoral bad for all subjectivities, including the gazelle being torn alive by the leopard. But pain is not an absolute bad. I shall need to postpone until Chapter 7 my general discussion of the problem of evil and ugliness in a kalogenic universe, but this is a good place to alert the reader that personalistic organicism is not sentimental "Bambiism," out of touch with the realities of predation in nature. Holmes Rolston is right when he insists: "A morally satisfactory fit must be a biologically satisfactory fit" (Rolston 1988, 58).

Predation reminds us that the well-being of individual organisms is not the only concern of an adequate environmental ethics. Biodiversity also matters. The well-being of species matters. Ecosystems matter. Habitats matter. Just how do they matter—how do the various goods involved cohere with one another—for this philosophy?

I have already stated that the ultimate locus of value is individual subjectivity, the concrescing actual occasion of experience. Biodiversity, therefore, cannot be an intrinsic value, since it represents the state of a system rather than the actual experience of any of the members of the system. It can, however, be a compelling instrumental value which, multiplied by indefinitely large numbers of kalogenic individuals, can outweigh the intrinsic value of individual organisms. An ecosystem is richer for its predators, and the symphony of satisfactions enlarged. Further, a species is enhanced by the culling of its weaker members. A species has no *intrinsic* good for itself, since there is no central locus for a species' awareness. It is not that kind of entity. A species is a temporal formal entity (Ferré 1996, 329–30). It is temporal because it has a history: it arises, endures, goes extinct. It is an entity because it has properties of its own. Besides its historical properties, it can "thrive" or be "endangered." A species' specific properties are distinctive. An individual organism can die, for example, but an individual (unlike a species) cannot go extinct. An individual's death, indeed, can help its species thrive, as in times of overpopulation. But this temporal entity is not a particular thing, it is a formal entity, that is, one that only exists as an abstract possibility, except through the concrete actuality of its exemplars. As a formal entity, it serves as an ideal type against which individuals can be measured by intelligent organisms capable of measuring. By thriving, if it does so in the cooperative and competitive world of individual organisms, it offers the possibility of a type of kalogenesis that would not be available in the event of its extinction. Species (unlike individual organisms) have no intrinsic good for themselves, since they have no center of awareness of their own for satisfaction or suffering. Further, they are not the sort of entities that can *do* anything, since they are not agencies. As noncausal, therefore, species are not instrumental goods, either, at least in the unconscious domains of nature where pure possibilities have little practical effect. In culture, however, where mentality is much at work, a species as an ideal entity can be an instrumental good, for example, in shaping protective legislation. Species are important but mainly for humans.

This is not the case for habitat. Habitats are as concrete as species are abstract. They provide the necessary condition for large numbers of organisms to thrive. A pond, considered as mere water contained in earthen banks, is not in the first instance intrinsically valuable. The atoms in the molecules of hydrogen and oxygen making up the H_2O would sing their actuality-affirming chorus whether or not they were evaporated into the atmosphere or drained into the ground below. The configuration of these molecules into the form of a pond is inessential to their value in themselves. But the pond is an important *aggregate* entity (Ferré 1996, 326–27), because it provides the means for many *organic* entities to survive and thrive. As a habitat, it becomes a *systematic* entity, whose various parts and elements are intimately linked in self-sustaining rhythms and feedback loops (Ferré 1996, 327–28). The living organisms that swarm in the pond, from the microorganisms that make the "water" of the pond not merely H_2O at all, but a soup of life-affirming entities, to the otters on the bank, feeding on the fish, crustaceans, amphibians, turtles, and even birds and small land mammals supported by the pond, represent intrinsic values. The pond, qua either aggregate entity or systematic entity, is nothing less than essential habitat, therefore enormously high in instrumental value. If we care about the carriers of intrinsic value, we must care for their habitat. This is why protection of habitat is of such pressing concern to any adequate environmental ethics.

Over the past few pages, I have been emphasizing the "organicism" root of personalistic organicism. But inevitably the "personalistic" qualifier has edged into the discussion. When I refer, for example, to the role of the "species ideal" in defining endangered organisms and guiding protective legislation, or, more generally, when I point out implications of an organicist viewpoint for environmental ethics, something beyond the scope of organicism enters the picture. On my view, all organisms are dynamic and relational; all organisms are bipolar, with both physical and mental attributes; all organisms have some degree of intrinsic value; but it is not the case that all organisms are personal. Whitehead named his position the philosophy of organism, and at one point I tried to make do with just organic categories (Ferré 1976). I stressed the organic virtues of creativity, homeostasis, and holism, that is, I called for *growth and innovation*, but always *under constraint* by negative feedback loops, these themselves established by free information flows between differentiated parts of a whole in *mutual relation*. But on reflection I realized that even if these categories are adequate for "healthy life," they alone are not sufficient for "ethical life" (Ferré 1989, 231–41). Something uniquely important is omitted: precisely the unique importance of individual persons in culture, far beyond the importance of individual organisms in nature. A set of categories suitable for a thriving pond habitat, for instance, where the burgeoning growth of frogs is maintained within healthy limits by complex, holistic predator-prey relations, may be glorious organicism but is no ideal model for human society. Therefore organicism needs, in my view, to be qualified as personalistic.

Does this break the continuity between nature and culture? Does it force a dichotomy between environmental and culture ethics? I think not. If persons are in the first place organisms (though organisms with especially well-developed mental capacities leading to special needs and powers) then metaphysical continuity is established, offering a sturdy bridge across which ethical continuities (properly qualified to context) can also travel. We shall cross that bridge repeatedly in Chapter 8.

I have already suggested more fully (Ferré 1998, 307–34) how persons arise within at least one set of organisms, human ones, who have evolved enormously complex brains in bodies that can perceive and manipulate the world, can vocalize and socialize, creating language, can imagine and plan by use of symbols freed from the immediate environment, and can guide behavior by ideal norms. Persons, on this analysis, are constituted developmentally by organisms with these powers. Persons are not born, they create themselves across time. Sequential ruling occasions first inherit ideals of character that have been responsibly shaped by predecessor occasions, then consciously affirm or refine them, and finally pass them on. Persons, on this understanding, are living beings complex enough to be conscious and free enough to be responsible.

Persons are defined not by a living body only, however, but by character. In principle (and sometimes, it seems, in practice) a single body may give rise to several persons, in cases of multiple personality. Each person has a different character, perhaps different memories, certainly different ideals.

"Person" is a threshold term and, for good reasons, a social construct as well. A newborn human is not yet a person, on this view, but is *potentially* a person, and this real potential for gaining personhood is so significant that human social institutions rightly *treat* such precious little organisms as persons, even though they have not in fact yet passed the threshold. Human beings can also lose personhood. Sometimes this loss has been deliberately inflicted, as against slaves or prisoners of war, when consciousness, character, and responsibility were undermined or stripped away. For personalistic organicism, this is a monstrous moral transgression. It need not, however, be done deliberately. A hopelessly comatose invalid is no longer functionally a person, on this view, but may still qualify for special protections. This invalid *has actually* been a person, and this achievement is so significant that human social institutions tend understandably to treat such precious veterans from the personal world as though they were still persons. Legally they remain persons. Whether this should be the case in all circumstances requires sorting out conflicting norms and weighing alternative goods. Different cultures have answered such matters differently, and changing medical technologies are currently challenging traditional answers within late-modern culture. I shall return to this issue at the end of Chapter 9.

Being personal is enormously important. Why should this be? What makes personhood, its potential and actual achievement, ethically so crucial? The answer once again lies in kalogenesis. The capacities of human thought and feeling allow the most intricate as well as the most vivid harmonies of experience to arise, offering interplay of the prehended actual with a vastly expanded domain of the possible through language and imagination. Persons are able to take account of the distant future with fear or hope, depending on the possibilities dwelt on. Through enhanced mentality, a person can enjoy more delicacies of refined experience, and can suffer more exquisitely, than any other known center of aversion and adversion. Persons alone, through their qualified freedom, can know the anguish of responsibility and the pangs of conscience. Persons alone quake in terror before the mysterious divine, and persons alone know the ecstacy of religious transfiguration.

Are there any other persons besides human beings? We really do not know. It is not enough to acknowledge sentience or even intelligence in other species. The personal qualities of life depend on free manipulation of symbols and purposeful engagement with a practical world. These seem lacking even in the most intelligent creatures with whom we share this home planet. Perhaps if the cetaceans—dolphins, whales, and porpoises—had lived on land and evolved hands with which to manipulate a stable material environment, they might have evolved personal life. They are highly adept at vocalizing, and they are impressively intelligent, but even the most hopeful research has not revealed dolphins to be persons. Their intrinsic value must be ranked near the top of the scale for organisms, but the transcendently beautiful achievements of personhood are not to be found there. The same seems true for primate research. As far as we know, on Earth only humans are persons.

Might there be persons in other parts of the universe? Of course there might. Personalistic organicism is not in the least anthropocentric in understanding personhood. It is a set of powers: of consciousness, freedom, and moral responsibility. Any organism that rises in complexity so as to acquire such powers is welcome to the club. The question is often put in terms of "alien intelligences." From the viewpoint of personalistic organicism this is not quite adequate. Intelligence is a factor in personhood, but only one. If intelligence is taken as purely theoretical, just the acquiring of concepts and the capacity to manipulate them, then this sort of intelligence might assure *consciousness*, since (on this viewpoint) consciousness is nothing other than a level of intensity reached in making mental comparisons of pure and embodied possibilities. But if "alien intelligences" are only that, then they are not yet *persons*, since personhood involves agency led by norms, and agency is doing

something, making a difference, intervening in the world. Personhood also involves moral responsibility, feeling the world, having empathic relations with
other centers of value, and sympathetic imagining how the situation would feel
from another's viewpoint. The moral point of view depends on such a capacity
for fellow-feeling. Therefore, if aliens are persons, they must (on this understanding of persons) be capable of empathy and of recognizing norms as universal in meaning and obligatory in force. Must such aliens share the specifics
of earthling ethics? Probably not. Even earthlings differ with one another in
important ways. But if our aliens are morally responsible persons, rather than
amoral intelligent forces of some sort, they will at least accept their obligation
to respect the unique intrinsic value of personal kalogenesis against wanton
destruction. In other words, they would not eat us, at least without good reason. But if, forced by the exigency of some greater cause, they were required
to eat us, they would make sure our sufferings, physical and psychological,
were absolutely minimal.

Such considerations, facetiously intended or not, return us to the ontological background of environmental ethics where real interests conflict and
where holism does not rule out pain. We must remember that persons are only
persons if they are first organisms. Persons need to eat. Persons want their
place in the sun. Persons can become food for predators, and persons can be
predators. In the modern era, persons became the most effective and dangerous
predators in the history of the world. How shall persons—organic beings with
a conscience—relate to the environment, to nature, appropriate to the postmodern norms of personalistic organicism?

These specific applications, and others, will engage us in the final part of
the book. Before getting there, we need to consider the widest environment of
all, the value lens through which all ethical judgments are colored, consciously or not. Rich with both preferences and beliefs, I call this ultimate
context religion.

PART TWO

Ethics and Religion

5

CONTEXT OF CONTEXTS

All meaning depends on context. Ethics is no different in this respect from medicine or detective work. The "same" set of facts turn out not at all the "same," depending on the framework taken as appropriate for the situation's interpretation. If thrusting a sharp knife into someone's abdomen is understood as part of a crime, it is subject to moral condemnation, but if the sharp knife is a scalpel and the act is done by a surgeon in quest of the "victim's" health, then the ethical situation is entirely different. Beliefs about the ethically relevant facts defining the situation are all-important for the guidance of attitudes and life.

"Religion" is what I call whatever provides the final, governing context of our lives. This is not just a matter of beliefs. Feelings and actions are religious context-providers, too. Still, extremely deep and maximally relevant beliefs are basic to religion. Every context has a context, and each wider context can redefine the situation for all the lesser contexts within it. In pure theory this progression could ripple outward forever; in which case, there would be no functioning religion, but only clusters of proximate meanings offering ad hoc guidance. Some postmodernists think this is the best we can do and seek to make a virtue of living without ultimate contexts. But in real life this seldom happens. We do not live in pure theory, but among the debris of decisions made, preferences formed, investments risked, habits shaped, and institutions built on the assurance that some governing context will not let us down. In fiction or imaginative film (e.g., *The Truman Show* [1998]), we may play with the concept of systematically delusive contexts "rigged" to give misleading meanings to daily events. But outside fiction or paranoia, the implacable economies of life grind away the theoretical possibility of elaborate stage settings, and leave us with a limited range of religious world models from which (we find) we have already attended closely to one or two. William James would have called them "living" options (James 1948); that is, they have some real appeal as providing a context of contexts for our lives.

When we have religious doubts, it is not usually a struggle between a recognized religious tradition and nothing at all, but between a familiar set of context-providing images and another competing set that would, if accepted, also function to provide a context of contexts, only differently. Often (so strongly does society tend to identify some particular ultimate imagery with religion as such), people think of themselves as torn between "religion" and "no religion" when this occurs, but that is a mistake. Whatever provides the context for all other contexts of meaning is functionally religion. It may involve a God or gods, or it may refer to swirls of mindless matter in a gradually cooling universe. These are significant religious alternatives in our own cultural framework. They vie to interpret the meaning of ethical situations confronting life. They involve characteristic attitudes, feelings, and dispositions to behave, as well as complex theoretical and imaginative consequences.

RELIGIOUS WORLD MODELS

Since I used the expression, "religious world model," in the previous paragraphs, I owe the reader an explanation of what I mean by RWMs. Taken in reverse order, the three component words tell the tale: (1) an RWM is a *model*, which indicates that it stands for or represents something else, (2) an RWM represents the *world*, which means that it is comprehensive in its reference to the entire universe, and (3) an RWM is *religious*, which entails that it is emotionally "hot," engaging intense valuational affect. All three components are necessary conditions. Lacking intense value resonance, we might have an interesting metaphysical model—a purely theoretical world hypothesis—but we would not quite have an RWM. Lacking full comprehensiveness, we might have a powerful metaphor to shape thought and feeling in some domain, but again not a full RWM. And without referential function, we might have a strong organizing image, an image capable of guiding attitudes and shaping actions, but unless it is used for guiding thought as well, it is not an RWM (Ferré 1983, 71–90).

My use of the term "religious" may be objectionable to those who are accustomed to think of religion primarily in doctrinal terms (the content of belief rather than the quality of the believing) and, even more, in terms of familiar biblical doctrine (e.g., belief in God, the Ten Commandments, an afterlife, and so on). My plea to such readers is to remember that religion is not identical with Christianity or Judaism or other familiar religions of our culture; that well-recognized religions exist with very different beliefs (classical Buddhism, for example, has no place for God in its scheme of things); and that what ties all religion together is *worship*, the acknowledgement of some compelling value (worthship), rather than specific *doctrine*, which tends to arise in support of intensely felt value.

The one shared mark of all religions, as I see it, is the power to affect the whole range of human life, both personal and social, by rising from some sense of supreme worth (the sacred), to mold how people act, feel, perceive, and think. Anywhere we find such power, however dissimilar it may be from the familiar religions of our culture in other respects, I propose to call it "religious." If some readers would prefer to think instead of "religion-like" phenomena, they are welcome to do so. What counts is that my language not confuse anyone by suggesting specific doctrinal content where none is intended. Conversely, it is important that conventional linguistic usages do not block us from seeing the many ways in which it may be fruitful to apply categories and techniques from philosophy of religion to what are often labeled as secular matters.

Whichever names we use, it is clear that we are deeply influenced, today as always, by value-laden conceptions of what the world is like. During the last four decades of the twentieth century, people have become increasingly conscious of the degree to which our relations to each other and to the natural environment have been shaped by visions of nature (and our species' place in it) that are historically contingent and in many ways regrettable (White 1967; Elder 1970; Roszak 1973; Ferré 1976, 1996; Hargrove 1986; Rasmussen 1996; Rolston 1999). The tragedy remains that such growing awareness of the presence of RWMs in the background of social and environmental practices has had to wait a long time and remains mainly limited to intellectual elites. In consequence, vast numbers of active participants in current history continue unaware of the religious roots of the present cultural and environmental crisis, and therefore of how they might be implicated both in the root problems and in their potential remedies.

Historically, the potent, comprehensive, idea-generating images we are interested in may well have come from agricultural practices, or sexual interests, or hunting rituals; to this list we should add today's political imagery, economic preoccupations, advertising messages, and aesthetic intuitions. Psychologically, it would be fascinating to reflect on the two hemispheres of the human brain and whether in some cases our RWMs are more readily traceable to the right hemisphere's engagement with patterns, while in other cases RWMs arise from the left brain's hunger for linear explanation. Such quasi-psychological speculations might be interesting to pursue in another context, but not here.

For now, I shall be content to introduce the parallel and contrasting ways in which traditional mythic metaphors, on one side, and central scientific ideals, on another, may ascend to the level of RWMs that deeply influence our daily lives by offering a context for contexts of ethical meaning. My point is not to catalogue every possible source for RWMs, but to show how they may come by different paths from more than one source, and that one of these sources for our society is science. If I can show this, then it will be clear that science is even more significant in our culture than is normally recognized. It contributes to our basic knowledge and technology and also to our ultimate, value-laden vision of things. At the same time, it should become clear that religion is even more pervasive and influential in our civilization than modernity's brash secular front might suggest, because religion shapes not just formal worship and official ethical codes but even the basic attitudes and real policies with which we approach each other and the world we live in.

TRADITIONAL RWMS

Humans are myth-making animals. By "myth" in this context I do not mean to imply anything false or outmoded. I mean rather to refer to the stories which provide a framework of intelligible order and moral guidance for the originating, storytelling community (and for others who may make the stories their own). Such stories make use of familiar value-laden images to help us cope with the strange and threatening, and to help us find comfortable orientation with the daily routine. Especially helpful in both these functions are stories about ancient (or even absolute) beginnings, when everything was much clearer and purer than in today's mixed situation. (Plato's use of such a story of "beginnings" in his *Timaeus*, as we had occasion to observe at the outset of this trilogy [Ferré 1996, 52–55], is an especially good example of mythic form being put to philosophical use.) In "those days" things could be seen for what they really are, good or bad, mischievous or noble. Confusion, we can hope, will end again in the distant future, too, when everything is again somehow sorted out. Stories of genesis and stories of "last things" are both well-suited to overcome the ambiguities of the present. Some of these stories are aetiological (like ancient "just-so" stories), providing an explanation for the origin of a tribe's special practices regarding, say, a holy place or an ancient feud. Some are more comprehensive, depicting the gods (or God or other ultimate powers) and the circumstances of creation itself. Most important, all such stories are deeply freighted with values for those who rely on and find personal or group significance through the images they evoke.

I believe that these images, which may be called "organizing images" because of the role they play in organizing the perceptions and values of those who dwell on them, might become in the full sense *models* for the understanding of the world if, in addition to their several value roles, they are also taken seriously for *thought* as well. This thought-guiding function need not always surface. A metaphor, for example, such as the Lord as my "shepherd," may be evoked mainly for emotional needs. I choose this image from the Twenty-Third Psalm, because it is plainly and explicitly poetry. Like any metaphor, it must be acknowledged as false on the literal level. The Almighty carries no shepherd's crook, no rod or staff. But it is an image of proven power to attract and comfort. It helps one feel, behind the often contradictory appearances, a companion who cares; it assists one who takes refuge in this image to perceive the world and one's entire career through life as a journey with a strong companion and a secure destination. It gives needed encouragement.

Often, in addition to the evocative powers of such images drawn from the mythic tradition, we find that these metaphors provide aids for generalized thought. The organizing image becomes a *model for thinking*, as well as a *metaphor for feeling and perceiving* the whole of reality (Ferré 1967, 373–405). The Lord is not only "Shepherd," but also "Shield of Abraham," and "Rock of Ages." Such metaphors are mythopoetically coherent but literally inconsistent; a shepherd obviously cannot be a rock, useful shields are not made from stone. Yet if such metaphors are taken seriously within a faith community at the level of valuation, there is a strong tendency to take them seriously also at the level of thought. What is it that this typical mosaic pattern of images can be thought to be saying about the general nature of things? Is it not saying at least that *there is protection*, and that the protector is personal, caring, aware?

As an *organizing image*, a metaphor's power of stirring values is vested in its vivid concreteness as it captures attention and consent. As a *model* (a RWM) the metaphor's function is to suggest general respects in which the profoundly real may be thought to resemble features of the familiar and treasured. In this way the image becomes a model and the model gives rise to theory, a structured and logically disciplined effort to conceptualize the unknown with the materials of the known.

Religious theory, on this view, functions as metaphysical theory but is always derivative from the value-drenched imagery that constitutes its leading metaphor. The highest flights of theological construction, no matter how coherent and adequate they may be intellectually, return again for their religious authority to earth in poetry, whence they were launched. One can see this with special clarity in connection with doctrines about God that spring from the key Christian metaphor of God as "Father." The image, however objectionable to those offended by gender specificity (Ferré 1996, 290–97), is deep within the Christian RWM. This is what makes the struggle over gendered language in theology so fraught with deep emotion on all sides. It runs deep. It is dramatized in such parables as the Prodigal Son, where the fatherhood of God is quite explicit; it is reinforced in Christian liturgy with the constant repetition of the Lord's Prayer, beginning, "Our Father, . . ." In all this, God is admittedly not properly to be *thought* (even by most traditionalists) as literally a gendered being; yet the metaphor has great weight both for stirring potent *feeling*, and organizing or reinforcing certain patterns of *acting*.

Religion, though initially rooted in feeling and action, is a fully human phenomenon generating thinking, too. The potent organizing image of God as Father demands thought. What are the features in respect to which we might be entitled to think as well as to feel this vital image? One respect must have to do with the *generative* function of literal fatherhood. Theological doctrines of creation stem from this feature, and with them subtle discussions of the similarities and differences between human creative activity and the divine. Another respect might focus on *moral authority* and rulemaking within the family. Moral theology rises from this general feature. Still another feature modeled by the fatherhood image is that of *continuing power*. Doctrines of providence, God ruling the world and guiding history, root here. Still further, the father is ideally *unifier* of his family. Theology of the church, ecclesiology, as well as ecumenical theories find footing in this feature. And above all, paramount to the Christian metaphor itself as stressed in stories of Jesus' own spirituality, is the feature of God's *fatherly love*. Theology of salvation, Christology, eschatology, and more, arise from attempting to think appropriately in the light of this aspect of Christian imagery.

In sum, potent valuational images are primary to the RWMs that derive from the ancient mythic traditions. Insofar as these images are effective in organizing lives and profoundly influencing feelings, there is also strong motivation to *think* as generally and as consistently as possible in their terms. In that role, as undergirding the effort to construct an intelligible pattern of relationships between familiar things for the sake of representing fundamental reality as a whole, such metaphors that offer organizing images become RWMs through which we perceive, perform, and relate ideationally to our world.

SCIENCE-GENERATED RWMS

It is less often noticed that RWMs spring also (by a different route) from modern science (Ferré 1996, 148–59, 174–82, 307–16). Science seeks to explain as well as to control the world we live in. Its theoretical aim (together with other practical aims) is toward understanding as well as prediction. But explanation is an inherently open-ended process, similar to the way contexts expand indefinitely. The principles used for explanation are themselves subject to a demand for explanation. Once this is supplied, by invoking further (or wider) principles, these, too, will be subject to still more explaining. The quest for understanding would seem forever unattainable. Though apparently inevitable in theory, this frustrating situation seems not to come about in practice. Scientists at any given time believe that they understand tolerably well what they are studying, even though they know full well that in the past scientists have held views long since overthrown (Kuhn 1970). They recognize that they do not have the "final" truth, perhaps, but neither do they have an obligation to give up their efforts in despair. The logical platitude that every explanation remains unexplained as long as the whole hierarchy of explanations is unexplained does not require that. Instead, working scientists in any given era take for granted certain principles as not requiring explanation, as being understandable "straight off," as it were, on their own credentials. These principles, which Stephen Toulmin named "ideals of the natural order" (Toulmin 1961), just "stand to reason," "feel transparently appropriate." When one gets to one of these ideals of the natural order, one has reached the end of the line, one has hit the bottom deck in the quest for understanding.

In Newtonian physics, for example, a body will continue in uniform motion in a straight line (or will remain at rest) as long as no forces are acting on it. Changes in motion—starting, stopping, speeding up, slowing down—need explanation, but in the absence of such changes, uniform straight line motion just "stands to reason." What else would a body do with itself? That is just the way nature is, ideally, when all the perturbations and confusions of daily life are removed. We may never be able actually to experience such a state of affairs (which is part of what is meant by its being an "ideal" of the natural order), but we can approximate it. As we do, no further comment or explanation is called for.

That this readiness to accept some bottom deck to the otherwise infinite regress of explanation is not without its historical risk is obvious. Ideals of the natural order are subject to displacement. They are displaced with difficulty, but it happens. For example, prior to the Newtonian ideal of unaccelerated *straight-line* motion as "standing to reason," astronomers took as wholly natural and without need for explanation the ideal of uniform *circular* motion. As Stephen Toulmin put it, Nicolas Copernicus declared

> ... some sorts of natural happenings stand to reason, being self-explanatory, natural, and intelligible of themselves. The task of astronomy ... was complete only when all the celestial motions were displayed as explicable in terms of "the principle of regularity". What was this principle of which Copernicus wrote? It laid down that, in Nature, all bodies which are in their proper places move uniformly and regularly—and this, for him, meant that they moved along tracks composed out of circles, each of which was revolving at a constant angular rate about its own proper centre (Toulmin 1961, 39).

Galileo, too, who came close to anticipating Newton's law of inertia in picturing the motion of a ship to be just as "natural" as its being at rest (it takes the imposition of a force to slow down a moving ship just as much as it requires a force to speed one up), still retained the ideal of circular motion as being directly intelligible.

> For what he envisaged as his ideal case was a ship moving unflaggingly across the ocean along a Great Circle track, for lack of any external force to speed it up or slow it down. He saw that uniform motion could be quite as natural as rest; but this "uniform motion" took place along a closed horizontal track circling the centre of the earth; and Galileo took such circular motion as entirely natural and self-explanatory. He does not seem to have regarded the ship as constrained by its own weight from flying off the earth on a tangent—the image which can clearly be found in Newton (Toulmin 1961, 55).

Thinking of circular motion as "natural," and feeling toward this ideal that it simply "stands to reason" as "appropriate," is quite different from taking a similar view of straight-line motion. Theoretically, on the first position, no questions need to be raised about what keeps the planets in their closed orbits or what keeps massive bodies moving along the curved surface of the Earth. Those would not be phenomena to be accounted for; they are simply natural, the way things ought to be. But on the second position, that of Newton and his followers, the provision of a force, gravitational attraction, was necessary before proper understanding could be achieved. One could say that the theory of gravitation was unnecessary for Copernicus because of his ideals of the natural order, but necessary for Newton, holding different ideals. The ideal of what *ought* to be in nature had changed. What simply "stood to reason" for pre-Newtonian thinkers had been penetrated to a new "lowest deck," and the content of theoretical explanation itself had to be adjusted to match.

To generalize, ideals of the natural order set the challenge for explanatory science at any given time. They are vital to the explanatory process both in posing the basic problems that are acknowledged as needing to be answered and in providing the stopping place of presumed intelligibility in what otherwise would be an endlessly frustrating abyss of unexplained explanations.

Yet the theoretical implications of these ideals are only part of the story. They are also intimately related to still broader value-laden assumptions drawn from the cultural context out of which they arise and then on which, reciprocally, they exert an influence amplified by the prestige of science. The Copernican ideal of natural circular motion, for example, did not by any means originate with him. On the contrary, it was a pre-Ptolemaic, pre-Aristotelian ideal of astronomical explanation set by Plato as a challenge to his successors. His challenge was that they account for the complex appearances of the heavens by appealing to none but "perfect" uniform motions (Plato 1985b). Behind

Plato's requirement was both a philosophical and a deeply religious motive. First, only the perfect forms are fully intelligible; second, reinforcing this thought, the heavens, being divine, would be desecrated by being thought in any terms short of perfect motions (Ferré 1996, 52–54). Even earlier than Plato lay another great tradition, that of Pythagoras, who had taught his followers to think of the real as identical with the perfect intelligibilities of number and to hold the principle of "limit" as "good," opposed to the "unlimited" as "bad" (Ferré 1996, 26–30). Deeper yet, enfolding much of Greek thought and perception, was the cultural premise that the perfect forms were the closed or limited ones. Why is a circle more "perfect" than a zigzag or an endless straight line? To the culture that built the Parthenon, with its firmly limited lines and graceful, closed proportions, the answer was obvious. In the context of ethical thought stressing the avoidance of the *hubris* of excess, preference for the limited above the unlimited, for the self-contained circle above the alarming craziness of erratic motion—all these were too plain to require argument. Behind the explanatory ideals of Copernicus and Galileo, and far below the conscious surface of the scientific specifics being investigated, were profound visions of the nature of the cosmos, premodern visions shot through with intuitions of basic values.

Modernity, expressed in Newton and his ideal of straight-line motion, runs equally deep with implications for ultimate reality and value. Scientific specifics were the immediate reasons for Newton's shift in ideals; he was interested in explaining a wider range of phenomena than could have been done without penetrating below the ideal of uniform motion as "bottom deck." He was successful in this; his revolution in ideals was not on its face a clash of underlying philosophical and religious worldviews. But the clash did go this deep. The image of the straight line without beginning or end, as the ideal form of motion, had its own roots in early Greek thought. This minority tradition was defended by the atomist, Democritus (c. 460–c. 370 B.C.), who pictured the universe as a collocation of impenetrable, unchanging particles falling endlessly in the void of space. Not the atomism, but the positive affirmation of infinite lines and endless space was continued and enlarged by the unorthodox speculations of Nicholas of Cusa (1401–1464) in mind-bending mathematical analogies between the infinity of space and the infinity of God. The same rejection of the finite was dramatized in the martyrdom of Giordano Bruno (1548–1600), burned at the stake for his stubborn assertion of the infinity of worlds (see Ferré 1996, 33–36, 102–109, 116–17). By Newton's time (1642–1727), supported by the premodern Christian spirituality of infinite aspirations, space was no longer ideally bounded by the sedate limits of form. On the level of theory it had to be assumed infinite within the Newtonian scheme. Now, bolstered by Newton's scientific prestige, the conception of infinity itself could also be embraced as something good and exciting rather than unthinkable and threatening. The Christian cathedral, with its often asymmetrical vertical lines aspiring heavenward, thrusting ideally forever up and out, could provide a religious analogue for this shift of sensibility, contrasting in every way with the firm-lidded temples of the form-loving Greeks. Likewise, the "excessive" saints seeking God's boundless love in hair shirts lived far from the moderation of the Hellenic ideal. Here we find a value universe that is open-ended, not curved in upon itself. And the religion of progress, faith in human culture ascending forever on the endless inclined plane of historical development, would soon follow the Newtonian shift from the bounded to the boundless ideal of the natural order.

What I am illustrating is more complex than the relatively simple emergence of RWMs from traditional mythic imagery, since theoretical considerations from science play a powerful part. Admittedly, they play only a *part* in the example I have chosen, since the classical preference for the finite had already encountered its diametric opposite in Christianity, with its spiritual embrace of infinity. These antithetical preferences wrestled with each other through the late premodern period. The visionary Nicholas of Cusa and stubborn, martyred Giordano Bruno insisted on thinking in accordance with the spirituality of the infinite. In contrast, Copernicus, though a devoted ecclesiastical official, retained in his theorizing the preference of the ancient Hellenes for closed, uniform circular motion as an explanatory ideal. Even the prototypically modern Galileo clung unreflectingly to this ancient ideal of the natural order. But with the triumph of Newtonian science, the ideal of the endless straight line in infinite homogeneous space became a spiritual and theoretical talisman for modernity. Newtonian science secularized the ideal of the infinite and broke the hold of Plato's "perfect circles" on the imagination of a civilization, making a world suffused with the idea of progress and endless expansion in knowledge, wealth, and power.

The Influence of RWMs

The importance of noticing our RWMs, whatever their source, is precisely their importance! Ultimate values are pervasive in shaping society. Noting key religious metaphors provides the key to becoming more self-aware, as individuals and as a civilization, about why we have become as we are, and where we may be headed.

Consider two examples: one RWM drawn from a traditional source in organizing imagery, the other from an ideal of science.

Paternalism, as we saw, is one of the major organizing images of traditional biblical religion. This is by no means universal. Powerful images drawn from maternal values dominated the imagination of some ancient cultures and are no less worthy of analysis. But the cultures from which the biblical religions eventually emerged were deeply inspired by maleness. Values of fatherhood are profoundly part of human experience, and it is clear that they were functioning to organize life in families, villages, and nations long before our biblical tradition incorporated and modified such father imagery into what we think of today as the Fatherhood of God. From Sky God to Zeus, from Jehovah to our Father in Heaven, the high concepts of rule and responsibility, moral principle, generativity, brotherhood and sisterhood of men and women under a cosmic father—all these themes were expressed and reinforced by traditional organizing imagery centering around the phenomenon of paternity.

It would be difficult to overstate the pervasive influence of this RWM, older than Christianity but strongly supported in Christendom by the theology, liturgy, and spirituality of Christian faith. The language of prayers and hymns, despite recent attempts at liturgical and hymnbook reform in some denominations, seems almost ineradicably masculine. Taken-for-granted political structures, whether presidential or judicial or congressional, are deeply hierarchical in structure. So are the structures of our economic and academic institutions. So deep are the conceptions we internalize about ourselves in a world of rules and authorities and father figures, it seems hardly to make a difference whether a woman is filling the place of the father figure in judicial robes or in the pulpit or in the prime minister's office. The structures and standards themselves are paternalistic, and the policies of Golda Meir or Margaret Thatcher turned out to be hardly distinguishable from those of male counterparts.

In recent decades there has been serious discussion of patriarchy as a problem (Ferré 1996, 290–97). The charge has strongly been made that our stress on *hierarchy* leaves community underattended, that our emphasis on *rules* leaves insight undernourished, and that aggressive, competitive, "testosterone" values lead to conflict, exploitation (of persons and of nature), and to the horrors of war. These are serious charges, in need of attention from any who are concerned for the spiritual health and future course of civilization. Has the "Father in Heaven" RWM led us astray toward the rape of the Earth, exploitation of the weak, and the risk of general catastrophe?

Progressivism is another key characteristic of modern civilization. Unlike most human cultures, the modern industrial world has operated with an open-ended sense of possibility and without much consciousness of limits. Led by the dynamic example of science, with its endless vistas for refinement and cognitive growth, and driven by the industrial power of science-inspired technology, our modern civilization has assaulted the future with aggressive confidence in its destiny. It is true that naive confidence in inevitable progress suffered deep wounds from World War I and its aftermath, but in the rest of the twentieth century modern technological civilization did not easily relinquish its mythic faith in growth. Now, dealing with the realities of global warming and overpopulation, we are confronting the limits of the progressive RWM supported by Newton's scientific vision of infinite openness. It appears that the heady image of limitless motion along an endless line is proving, as an RWM, to be dangerous. Was this ideal applicable only to an unusual era of ample resources and relatively vacant spaces? Will its influence destroy our biosphere, and us with it? Can alternative RWMs be found to guide our basic perceptions and practices, to shape our institutions, in the building of a post-modern civilization that can live more gently on the earth?

My long-held view (Ferré 1982, 261–71; 1996: 305–38) has been affirmative on this question, pointing to the postmodern science of ecology as the fertile source of RWMs that may help change the thinking, attitudes, and institutions of those who absorb their significance. Not since the Newtonian revolution at the start of the modern age have the valuational overtones of a science so captured the imagination of so large a segment of society. The ecology "movement" in the United States and Canada, the phenomenon of the Greens in Germany and elsewhere in Europe, coupled with the widespread sense of disillusionment and the need for something profoundly different among many in modernized societies at the opening of the twenty-first century, makes it thinkable that the immense historic phenomenon of the modern world—its social structures shaped by paternalistic values and its mighty military and industrial machine patterned after Newtonian progressivist images—may be giving way to a new configuration of values and images, leading to new relationships to the environment, new technologies, and new social arrangements.

The RWMs that arise from ecology as a pioneer postmodern science guide thought and feeling toward mutuality rather than hierarchy, and toward cycles rather than open-ended straight lines "upward and onward." Consider first the emerging RWM of *mutuality*. Against the image of the Sky God, always associated with paternalistic, hierarchical religions, again is posed the image of Mother Earth, or Gaia (Lovelock 1979). The model of infinitely complex interaction among symbiotic organisms replaces the picture of kingly rule. The internal evolution of richly supportive *modi vivendi* contrasts with the external enforcement of decrees. The political consequences of such revolutionary changes in basic ideals are difficult to anticipate in detail, but it is clear that if ecology-generated RWMs become typical of a future civilization, these consequences will be profound. I shall return to these themes in the final part of this book.

Second, imagine the difference to our technological and economic life that would be made by substituting the RWM of the *circle* for the progressive, infinitely extensible line. At the dawning of the ecology movement, Barry Commoner struck a profound chord with this image in his classic book, *The Closing Circle* (Commoner 1971, 298–99). Nature *will* close the cycles that humanity attempts to force open with progressive, dominating ways. The question is whether we cooperate with the wisdom of nature or be crushed. Newton's infinite line may have been an ideal for physics before Einstein, but it is no viable ideal for a world grown aware of ecology. Sufficiency, balance, equilibrium, symbiosis, fulfillment within limits—these are new ultimate ideals from ecology that may be in the process of replacing the progressivists RWMs of the modern era.

In all this we have been discussing contexts, and the contexts of contexts, in which beliefs and attitudes toward our world as a whole are shaped. The context formed by taking infinite straight-line motion as "standing to reason" and "appropriate" and "right" is quite different from the context provided by thinking of great cycles as "proper" and "necessary" and "good." These are simple examples, deliberately made so for the purpose of illustrating how ideal images may function subtly but pervasively in ways not traditionally identified as "religious." Matters become quickly more complicated when other profound preferences enter, as in the vision of a universe seen through personal traits in various forms of theism, or in the more austere ideal of perfect regularity and ultimate intelligibility shorn of any personal characteristics. The logic of these context-providing RWMs is the same, though far more tangled. Simple or complex, they provide the final context for considering the meaning of individual lives and the cosmos containing those lives in connection with all other things. They offer the final basis for justification in ethics by offering normative backing for more specific norms of conduct when these are challenged. In this way ethics is continuous with religion, the stopping place not only for explanation, but also for evaluation. Religion is not ethics but, as the most intensive and comprehensive way of valuing, embraces ethics by providing a value drenched vision of the finally relevant state of affairs within which all ethics finds its moorings. But since RWMs differ, and since these differences have ethical consequences, we need to ask whether even ultimate contexts can be subjected to reasonable assessment, whether even final standards of right and wrong can be subjected to responsible judgments of better or worse.

ASSESSING RELIGIOUS WORLD MODELS

It would be naive to expect too much of logic, in the sense of "pure reason," in settling disputes among the candidates for outermost context and deepest value. But if pure reason is imagined stripped of all preferences and judgments, this offers a narrow, abstract view of logic. Life is much larger than this sort of logic. Instead, if we adopt the approach to logic proposed in Chapter 3, that it is "mentality's method of self-control in the flight space offered by symbols," or "the flight rules for free speculation," which function to provide a way to minimize "dangers of crashing," then it makes sense to look for a "logic" of assessment even of RWMs. By logic in this fuller sense is meant normative methods for the conduct of the mind in contemplating images and symbols. In this case the images and symbols are proffered as clues to ultimate reality and its value. Are they good clues or just will-o'-the-wisps? This is what we would like somehow to answer without excessive dogmatism or arbitrariness.

The situation is made more complicated by an obvious circularity. Normative methods for conducting thought are always themselves in a context. This context has profound implications for these normative methods. The norms of sound thinking are expected to assess their own legitimating norms! Or, to reverse the situation, perhaps logic's larger context is inhospitable to the enterprise of applying flight rules to mentality at all. There are RWMs that spurn "reason" as hopelessly corrupt, or hold that conceptual thinking is the enemy to be escaped in favor of other states of mentality. If these intensely value-laden beliefs set the context of contexts, then would it not be wicked (or at least self-defeating) to persist in assessing, considering, deliberating about alternative ultimates? Indeed it would, for those whose final context is provided by such RWMs. They will feel obliged to avoid debate, comparison, and weighing of RWMs. We must all, including those whose context of contexts excludes all kinds of "logic," start from where we find ourselves. There is nowhere else to start.

Still, to start somewhere is not necessarily to end there. Even those most firmly braced in their "Theological Veto" of rational criticism (Ferré 1967, 23–29) may suffer what will feel to them a "loss of faith" after the buffeting of turbulent events. For those of us who have not started in the context of antirational RWMs, this may appear not disaster but opportunity. A richer vista of possibilities opens. The principle of adequacy yearns for "more," even at the outer level of competing worldviews. Why settle for a single possibility when one might consider several? But "more" cannot be the last word. Stopping with sheer multiplicity seems out of the question, especially practically, when decisions must be made within some context or other. Life must be lived with decisiveness and some constancy of direction if we are not to drift or self-destruct. Not just richness but wholeness, too, is a basic demand of healthy life.

These norms, criteria, requirements—they are all three—occupy the "bottom deck" of my own sense of what "stands to reason." Richness and wholeness (adequacy and coherence) are for me justifiers in need of no further justification. I will now say a few words about them, explaining why I find them compelling, but this will not be an attempt to "prove" them, at least not in the sense of "proof" that demands arguments that must coerce every rational mind. Why? First, there is no rationality without prior normative judgments (on the meaning of terms, on the appropriateness of rules of inference, and the like), and where genuine judgments are called for, there can be no coercion (Ferré 1998, 267–373). But second, justifiers are not the sort of result that can be expected to emerge at the conclusion of an argument, no matter how valid, unless the premises of the argument already contain normative terms that everyone acknowledges as justifying the conclusion. This prior acknowledgment cannot be forced by the argument that depends on it.

I find myself in a position (which I believe is shared with many) where I judge "straight off" that *more* of something preferred—all other things being equal—is better than *less* of it. This underlies the norm of richness or the criterion of adequacy. I also find myself judging that organization, focus, or harmonization of what is preferred is no less vital, so that preferences will not excessively conflict with one another but, so far as possible, support each other in a *unity* of well-being. This underlines the norm of wholeness or the criterion of coherence. I can imagine that someone might start from a different place. But, frankly, I find it quite difficult to sympathize with such an imagined preference for *less* rather than more of what is preferred or for *disunity*, instability, or self-hindering in life or thought. I acknowledge that there is nothing strictly coercive about these fundamental norms, yet I find them powerfully attractive, and I confidently expect richness and wholeness to be judged worthy of "bottom deck" status by others as well.

Such expectations can be supported, though not coercively established, by reflecting on the criteria themselves. One striking benefit is the *breadth* of their applicability. Richness and wholeness reflect the needs of healthy life, from the level of individual one-celled organisms, through ecosystems, to the level of the biosphere itself. They define "health." They also constitute normative standards for human "practical reason" in daily affairs. And in "theoretical reason" they apply in every field of thinking, urging adequacy of data and coherence of theory. Besides such breadth they serve to provide *unity* of pattern to our understanding of such diverse areas in a single conceptual focus.

This is circular of course. To consider how pleasingly many different domains can be included, and to judge this a "benefit," is already to agree that richness is to be preferred over poverty; to take the provision of pattern for understanding as a "benefit" is already to affirm wholeness over disintegration as the goal. But such comprehensive circularity is not vicious. We should *expect* reasoning at this outermost level, where we are talking about the justifier of justifiers or the context of contexts, to remain inside the grand "virtuous circles" set in motion by a worldview and the epistemology that comes with it. If our basic justifiers do not finally justify themselves, what else could possibly rise to the task?

The original question for this section was the possibility of reasonable assessment of religious world models. The foregoing remarks should temper any tendency to arrogance in this task, but this task still awaits. We next need to state how the criteria—assuming our starting place is not inhospitable to the values of richness and wholeness in life and thought—might apply. I believe that RWMs can be weighed both in their direct value-organizing role, as organizing images, and as conceptual models for theory. There is considerable parallelism in the assessment of these two roles, but there are interesting differences, too.

RWMs and Practical Reason

Rather than conduct this discussion on a purely general level, I prefer to take as a running example the imagery of theism. Theism, worship of a single God with such personal traits as goodness, purpose, and free agency, is the most common form of religion among the likely readers of this book. It will therefore make a familiar illustration while still remaining general enough to include the main religions "of the Book," namely, Judaism, Christianity, and Islam, and their many expressions in more particularized schisms, denominations, and sects.

One of the practical functions of theistic imagery, prior to its role in shaping theory or even action, is emotive. God-language evokes attitudes and focuses feeling in powerful ways. "God made the world," for example, may owe a great deal of its meaning to the sense of security it fosters in those who hear or use it. "God is on our side" may function powerfully to buoy up sinking hearts; it may be that its emotive function is so valuable to those involved that this largely accounts for the determination of its users to retain such expressions, "come what may." This capacity of religious imagery to generate fierce retentiveness among its users has notable implications for theories that are articulated along their lines, as we shall soon see. In addition, it is quite evident that many uses of this language in connection with worship, both public and private, are deeply immersed in emotive significance, for example, theistic language may evoke thrills of anticipation and importance, moods of penitence, feelings of acceptance. Theistic language may also express sorrow, determination, and awe, and above all the unlimited adoration in which the religious consciousness most fundamentally expresses itself.

It is hard to maintain for long that the emotive meaning of theistic discourse is its only meaning. Even aside from other noncognitive functions, such as I shall soon introduce, it is difficult to see how the emotive meanings of theistic language can function apart from the introduction of some kind of dependence on descriptive meaning. Sheer gibberish does not evoke penitence or express feelings of confidence and adoration. If "God is on our side" is able to arouse or express reassurance, this is finally possible only because the user of the language understands something by it. This something is provided in the first instance by the imagery of a great, powerful, good person in charge of the universe.

Emotive powers of language are in general parasitical upon the provision of some kind of descriptive content. The words used in theistic contexts are likewise given their meaning because we know how to use them, within our familiar bell-shaped normal curve of common usage, in daily settings where descriptive content is reasonably clear. The words we employ about God, for example, "loving," "powerful," "wise," and the like, borrow descriptive definiteness from ordinary usage. It is this descriptive definiteness that underlies whatever emotive power religious language possesses.

Provision of contextual definiteness for theistic language is not only *logically* essential, if feelings are to be evoked, it is *religiously* essential as well. At root, squeamishness about anthropomorphism is just embarrassment about what makes real theism possible (Ferré 1984a, 203–12). Ludwig Feuerbach was justified therefore in thundering:

> Where man deprives God of all qualities, God is no longer anything more to him than a negative being. To the truly religious man, God is not a being without qualities. . . . The denial of determinate, positive predicates concerning the divine nature is nothing else than a denial of religion, with, however, an appearance of religion in its favour, so that it is not recognized as a denial; it is simply a subtle, disguised atheism. The alleged religious horror of limiting God by positive predicates is only the irreligious wish to know nothing more of God, to banish God from the mind. . . . He who earnestly believes in the Divine existence is not shocked at the attributing even of gross sensuous qualities to God (Feuerbach 1957, 14–15).

Besides the keenly felt emotive function of theistic imagery, there is a practical function often called "conative." We "do things" with words (Austin 1962). Language can function to *change the situation* in direct ways. When someone in the due course of an auction sale says, "I bid five dollars," and the auctioneer says "Done!" the situation has been changed; something has been accomplished.

What has happened here? Are the buyer and the auctioneer describing some happenings going on behind the scenes, apart from their words? No, the words *are* the happenings. In their context, they function to make a contract, to transfer ownership, and to put the bidder five dollars in debt to the auctioneer. Language here is employed to perform actions that might equally well have been accomplished by waggling a finger or banging a gavel. It is an instance of what is called the "performative" use of language. As such it is not subject to questions about its "truth" or "falsity," since it is not *asserting* anything to be the case but instead *making* something to be the case.

Performative uses of language of this sort, of which there turn out to be many, may be characterized as having a conative function from the Latin word *conari*, "to endeavor" to *do* something. In the appropriate contextual circumstances, when language is used to make a promise or to place a bet or to take an oath or to declare a truce, or the like, we find the conative dimension of meaning. And the language of theistic imagery is rich with such uses.

One important conative function of theistic language is the endeavor to affirm or commit oneself to a whole way of life. When serious and sincere use of a religion's key discourse is made (contextual circumstances continue to be crucial), this use itself may constitute the speaker's attempt to place the central values of that religion in the position of highest priority in his or her life. When, for instance, a Christian theist says, "I love God," such a statement may be understood, on this conative interpretation, as endeavoring to commit to a life of love for all humankind. There is a New Testament warrant for such a performative linkage: "If anyone says, 'I love God' and hates his brother, he is a liar . . . " (I John 4:20, RSV).

Not only would this be a "doing," it would be by far the most important "doing" that can be done. Organizing basic values, attitudes, and dispositions for behavior will have a profound impact on all aspects of life. But again we can see that conative meaning, like emotive, is dependent on the provision of some kind of descriptive context. In the case of our example at the auction sale, we know that there is considerable performative difference between the meaning of "I bid five dollars" and "I bid fifty dollars." The language employed, for all its performative use, is not without descriptive content. And this definite content is essential for the very possibility of "doing things" with our speech.

In the case of theistic language, if there is a conative use—for example, to commit oneself by means of it to a life of Christian love rather than of Nazi hostility—then there must be a distinguishable descriptive context that undergirds this possibility. Again this content is supplied by theism's ultimate imagery. Just as the expression "I bid five dollars" is not, in context, functioning to describe anything, but its conative meaning is clear only because "bidding five dollars" can be used descriptively in other contexts, so "God made me" has multiple contexts of use. If it can have a conative use, it must first have other uses. That is, "God making . . ." and "God acting . . ." and "God loving . . ." expressions must have descriptive uses at least within the imaginative stories of religion. It is by their ultimate imagery that theists are given a basis for the eliciting and ordering of values. Out of all the possibilities, a few intimately interconnected aspects of human experience are displayed in this imagery as deserving unlimited adoration and as being inescapably relevant to all our existence. These selected aspects are those of human personal experience at its best. God, the object of the committed theist's most intense and comprehensive valuations, is pictured as supremely *aware* and supremely *good* in the exercise of sovereign, creative freedom. Within particular theistic religions like Judaism or Christianity, God is imaged as much more than this: for Judaism, in particular, God is seen as the righteous law-giver motivated by steadfast love, and for Christianity as the self-giving, creator-savior whose triune nature is the paradigm of perfect sociality and perfect unity in the life of the Trinity.

But even at the more general level of theism, we find definite selection of values, from the personal rather than the impersonal, and the theist's own evaluations are strongly elicited from this range. What is most important in the ultimate scheme of things? The theistic image points to vividness of consciousness, to creative freedom, to moral excellence. What is most relevant, ultimately inescapable, in the last analysis? Theism points to the qualities of richest human life as the basis of its representation of the most comprehensive value. In so doing, it urges a way of life and a set of distinctive attitudes.

Once this is granted, the question remains how practical reason can assess such a way of life and such attitudes? My answer, no surprise by now, will be in terms of practical *adequacy* (richness or fullness of life) and practical *coherence* (wholeness or integrity in life). But at this frankly practical level, it may be wise to add one more openly pragmatic standard, that of *effectiveness*. In the next few paragraphs I hope that all three can be made clear.

Valuational adequacy. The adequacy of theistic imagery functioning as a value focus for basic attitudes and policies of life is to be measured by the extent to which theists are able to include a rich array of values within its scope; to the extent, in other words, that they are not led on its basis to ignore or distort values that are perceived by them as genuine. Failure in coverage is a mark of inadequacy relative to the needs of the person who relies on the imagery.

Specifically in terms of the ultimate imagery of theism, which commends, as we have seen, personal values above all others, the question must be raised whether the awesome values of impersonal natural processes or the compelling values of biological rhythms, for two alternative examples, can be included naturally within the life-style of persons who find all of these worthy of inclusion within their range of basic values. A reasonably confident theistic answer to this point can be conjectured: there is nothing necessarily exclusive about the personal focus of theistic value-imagery. Personal values do not rule out biological ones but are, in fact, intimately associated with them in our experience. Likewise, the values of mechanical stability are not necessarily in conflict with personal values; frequently the latter are expressed through or made possible by the former. Theistic imagery, therefore (it may be argued), fares well on the criterion of adequacy: personal concepts can without straining include organic or other impersonal ones, arguably more easily than mechanomorphic or biomorphic imagery can include personal values without distortion or reduction. And if so, anthropomorphic theistic imagery has a reasonable claim on any who judge the success of ultimate imagery, in part at least, in terms of its capacity to stimulate and sustain valuational fullness in the lives of those who adopt it.

Valuational coherence. Religious imagery cannot be measured simply by its powers of inclusion, however, despite the need for adequacy; it also should organize values and give the life lived under its influence a more or less definite form. The priorities implicit in this imagery will provide a basis for orienting the general preferences and policies of people in a unified way. To the degree that people avail themselves of this basis and actually guide their lives by it, their most basic personal policies in behavior should not only avoid interference with each other, internally, but actually should pull together in mutual support. In this way the ultimate images of a religion perform a significant role in orienting or organizing the lives of those who accept them, offering a measure of personal form and unity in place of chaos or disintegration. And as a social phenomenon, the religious community's common allegiance to generally shared imagery can contribute to the cooperation in the pursuit of agreed ends that is the precondition of civilization.

Again a challenge can be put to the ultimate imagery of theism: even acknowledging the relative valuational adequacy of this imagery, can it supply a sufficient degree of *system* to give differentiation and focus to its scope? Once more we may conjecture that the theist can return a reasonably confident answer. The imagery of theistic religions can function to express clear subordination as well as inclusion. Impersonal values, however compelling, are constantly subordinated to personal ones; impersonal structures, though awesome, are depicted in this imagery as made for persons, not persons for impersonal structures. Here is the valuational significance of the theistic insistence that "God made the world"; and here is the valuational force of the anthropocentric image of the physical universe which, despite its cognitive perils, may not lightly be repudiated or "demythologized" by theists without the most serious consequences. Likewise, biological values, though intimately associated with personal ones and worthy of high esteem in their own right, are kept vividly subordinate to personal values of appropriate kinds. Not merely to live but to live *well*, according to a specified set of personal values, is the supreme life-organizing demand of the imagery of the various theistic religions, all of which are prepared emotively and conatively to support their adherents in sacrificing mere biological survival, if need be, for the sake of comprehensive personal values held with supreme intensiveness.

Valuational effectiveness. In this discussion of valuational criteria we must guard against supposing that a person's values are simply given, fully developed, apart for the conceptions by which she or he lives. Ultimate imagery *elicits* approval, *molds* attitudes. It does not merely summarize or represent independently attained value systems. Once again we find circularity in root matters: religious conceptions deeply influence the very attitudes that, in turn, provide the basis for what will count as valuational "adequacy" and "coherence." Theism, in particular, cultivates a disposition to venerate personal values as over against mechanistic or purely biological ones. Here seems to be another clue to the difficulty of resolving religious disputes. This disposition may strike an individual as "adequate" because it includes preferred values; but these values have largely been elicited by theism itself. Theism may strike the same individual as "coherent" because it organizes basic values into a viable system, but this system of priorities as itself been at least partly shaped by theistic imagery. Unless some way can be found to break into or out of these self-validating circles, the "tests" of the reliability of RWMs do not appear particularly potent.

In consequence, "effectiveness" must be basic to the other two tests, at least at the level of practical assessment. The importance of "adequacy" lies in the desire to make life full; the importance of "coherence" lies in the concern to keep life whole. Both are motivated ultimately by the underlying criterion of practical reason: long run success in living well. RWMs mold values as much as they reflect them; as a result short run applications of criteria like adequacy and coherence may suggest Ezekiel's "wheels within wheels—way up in the middle of the air." But *effectiveness*, the actual capacity of an RWM to serve the perceived life needs of large numbers of adherents over long periods of time, brings the circle down to earth.

"Long periods of time?" "Perceived life needs?" How do we make such standards precise? There is no way. Nor is this a theoretical matter in which such precision would seem to be called for. Still, decisions are made and changes gradually do appear as the collective judgments of real men and women cumulatively register over time. In the historical perspective, clear cases of valuational ineffectiveness can be found. Religions are born and die. Theism, too, has been and can still be altered in important ways with shifting assessments of its valuational effectiveness.

For practical reason, therefore, effectiveness is basic. If you find yourself unable to live by theism's imagery, God is dead for you, no matter how adequately and coherently it may be able to deal with values that are not *your* values. Conversely, if you find yourself grasped by the unconditional value represented in some fundamental imagery, then the motivation to *think* in its terms—however difficult it may be to develop a viable theoretical structure for it—is strongly supplied. We seem therefore to be edging back toward the possibility or necessity of serious argument, albeit perhaps in a gentler, postmodern key, about the merits and defects of theism's ultimate imagery for thinking.

RWMS AND THEORETICAL REASON

There are no absolute breaks between practical and theoretical functions. Practical ones, such as the emotive or conative, require some context of descriptive definiteness in order to stir emotion or stimulate action one way rather than another. Possessing descriptive definiteness is not quite the same thing as asserting a factual proposition, but it is on the same continuum. An image or story that functions to evoke feeling in one situation could do more than that in another. Besides stirring to action, it can also suggest a way of looking at the circumstances, a way of interpreting what is the case. This suggestion need not be clearly articulated. But in a quasi-cognitive way, it may help draw scattered items together into a pattern that might have been missed without the mental set provided. Since nothing, strictly speaking, has been asserted, nothing is open to verification or falsification, but suggesting a pattern is not far from proposing a simple theory about what is going on.

RWMs function in the full range spanning the emotive (quasi descriptive), conative, quasi cognitive, and elaborately theoretical. At the explicitly theoretical end of the spectrum, they function as normal models do in any theoretical enterprise, but they differ from nonreligious models (e.g., in the sciences) by remaining indispensable to thinkers who do not just use them but, more profoundly, are *inspired* by them in a deeper way than models normally inspire their users.

A word on models in general may be useful here. In the most general sense a "model" can be anything used in any way to represent anything else. In this they differ in type. Some, as every child knows, are capable of being built and even being made to work, like certain scale models and mechanical models. Others, "conceptual models," may be merely drawn on paper, described in words, or entertained in the mind. They range in ideational type from the comparative concreteness of imaginable mental pictures to the formal generality of mathematical analogues.

Models differ, too, in terms of their *scope*. What is the subject matter they are taken to represent? Often a model may be used to stand for a single thing (e.g., the Eiffel Tower); equally often models are intended to represent whole classes (e.g., the hydrogen atom); and sometimes models are used to refer to even vaster domains of subject matter (e.g., the expanding universe).

This variety in type and scope reflects the variety of purposes that people have in using models. In some contexts (e.g., classes in art appreciation), a scale model with quite particular scope (e.g., Michelangelo's *David*) may assist our aesthetic grasp of the spatial proportions of a huge or distant statue; in other settings (e.g., classes in physics or astronomy), we may call on a conceptual model of wide scope to provide a sense of intuitive familiarity for what is too small or too large or otherwise unavailable for direct observation; in still other enterprises (e.g., airplane design), we may need a working model to anticipate flaws in a wind tunnel without the expense and danger of building and testing the real thing. The catalogue of potential uses of models is limited only by the range of our purposes. Even within the few enterprises I have mentioned, I have not come close to exhausting their varied functions. In the case of microphysics, for example, a good conceptual model not only offers a sense of intuitive interpretation for the otherwise bare formulae of the physicist's theories, but also can illuminate relations that might otherwise have been missed among theoretical domains, and can suggest fruitful new problems for consideration. These roles of interpretation, integration, and heuristic stimulation, indispensable for purposes of satisfactory understanding, are what make "explanatory models" valuable in cognitive enterprises.

When theoretical reason meets RWMs, the standards of explanatory models become relevant to any assessment. What should a good model provide in a theory? First, although they are usually found entangled around one another, it is important to distinguish models from the theories they interpret. Models are so often confused with theories that it is useful to have a phrase for what in a theory the model is not. The model is not the "abstract calculus" (Nagel 1961, 91–93) that provides the logical structure for a theory, whether this be mathematical formulae or assertions in ordinary language. This calculus, uninterpreted by any model, is liable to be a highly arbitrary set of symbols held together by formal rules. It has a definite formal structure. When its symbols are connected somehow to specifiable elements of experience, it can have powerful applications, particularly in drawing inferences about new experiences to be expected.

This abstract calculus can in principle function without the help of any model, but a good conceptual model can add a great deal to the abstract calculus. First, it can bring *ideational definiteness* to what otherwise must remain highly indeterminate. A set of "implicitly defined" symbols and formal rules may make some kinds of calculations possible, but the concrete sense of subject matter needs more than this, especially when the subject matter is of a sort that, for one reason or another, is not open to immediate observation (e.g., the inner structure of an atom, the gradual processes of geological change, the workings of an economic system, or the remote events of the solar system's origin).

Second, in giving ideational definiteness by its concrete representation of a subject matter, a model can help a theory achieve *conceptual unity*. Ideally, it can do this in two ways: (1) internal to a single subject area it can suggest additional ways in which the data go together, new areas in which to establish theoretical connections, for example, as a hydraulic model of an economic system may reveal relations between data that had previously been conceptually isolated; (2) a model may draw together several presumably different subject areas by suggesting hitherto unsuspected similarities of form or structure, as the model of the molecule was able to do in helping to unite the fields of thermodynamics and statistical mechanics.

Third, a fortunate model may have the effect of suggesting potentially fruitful *lines of inquiry*. These sometimes lead to making new discoveries, as the Big Bang model of the universe helped suggest fascinating applications of radio telescopy to research in quasars.

These are ideal cases. Sometimes models may actually inject confusion and disconnection, as in the so-called paradoxes of light, wherein some of the physical data are best interpreted by a wave model, other data most naturally accounted for on a particle model, but the two models are mutually exclusive. The paradox, we find, arises from attempts to take the models literally and to push them beyond their appropriate logical limits as models. Quantum mechanical formulas are capable of dealing consistently, though highly abstractly, with the data; the conflicts and contradictions arise only in our images. It might be argued, in consequence, that sometimes greater understanding is served, after a point, by putting away the models and relying on imageless mathematical theory alone. The aura of intelligibility or "grasp" may indeed be missing from thought shorn of aid from models, but sometimes (especially when purely theoretical purposes are being served) such an aura must be sacrificed for more basic cognitive interests, such as consistency and adequacy to the evidence.

Clearly, caution is required in the employment of conceptual models. Still, with vigilance, models can be of immense value for purposes of cognition. Summarizing: they can provide conceptual definiteness, suggest connections in the subject matter, relate fields to one another, indicate new lines of investigation, and afford a sense of the familiar and intuitively intelligible. The benefits go both ways. While models can *interpret* the abstract calculi of theories, these calculi can *articulate* the formal implications of a model's properties to explore what in detail it means to take the model seriously for thinking. Sometimes, especially in the sciences, awareness of these implications will loop back to amend the model or even replace it. For science, the formally articulated theory, logically laid out and empirically linked, has priority over any of its models, since purposes of empirical prediction and control are dominant, and thirst for understanding is not committed in advance to concrete visions of how things should be. Religious thinking, in contrast, is not equally free to modify or discard deeply valued models. This is the main difference between RWMs and their secular cousins in science and metaphysics.

Most of my examples of nonreligious models have been from the sciences, but these differ in two ways from RWMs. First, they are not valued in the same intense way (though valued they are for scientific purposes); and, second, they are not taken as comprehensively relevant (though relevant they are to a specific domain). In science, models do not function as "religious" or as "world" images. This is deliberate and wise. The sciences profit from being limited to specific subject matters. What they lack in comprehensiveness they make up in concreteness and precision. Imagine the confusion if every science had to take absolutely everything into account! Even the so-called theory of everything sought by some cosmologists is not concerned in coping with the elusive puzzles of human theorizing itself.

But the mental urge for conceptual unity seems boundary-indifferent. At least some of the time some people are open to all-inclusive questions: What are the inescapable, basic features of reality? What is the underlying character of the "sum of things entire"? Is there any fundamental pattern to everything that is? Which (if any) features of experience are the realities, and which the temporary or derivative appearances? Why should anything at all be, rather than nothing?

Most of us do not take time to give such questions sustained critical thought, but a few bold persons attempt to push these questions as far as they can take them, and to supply reasoned answers. In so doing they are thinking metaphysically, at the outer limits of speculative thought.

In my view the defining mark of metaphysical thinking is its all-inclusiveness. Metaphysical thinking needs to be critical if it is to perform its function of providing intelligibility, but in this it is not unique. Every worthwhile theory needs to meet the same basic critical standards. What is essential and distinctive is the reach for comprehensiveness. Thus, when metaphysical thinkers use models (and they must), metaphysical world models (MWMs) are distinct from the conceptual models of science primarily in scope. Like other conceptual models, a metaphysical model is intended to provide conceptual definiteness, to suggest connections among apparently diverse things, and to offer the sense of intelligibility that theoretical enterprises seek. Therefore an MWM is drawn from some particular aspect of experience that is judged to be potentially illuminating for all experience and is relied upon to give initial conceptual definiteness—a vision of reality—to what otherwise is simply too vast to have form. The MWM is explored to discover the interconnected patterns in things that such an angle of vision may reveal. And it is valued for its capacity to help make sense out of the otherwise alien complexities of the total environment in which thinkers find themselves living.

Well-chosen MWMs must lend themselves to articulation in metaphysical theories that are themselves capable of self-consistent elaboration, spelling out in depth and detail the structures of reality as suggested and made concretely vivid by the model. If such a theory performs the conceptual job expected of it (the criteria for which I shall lay out in a moment), the model that suggests the theory and gives it concrete interpretation is to this extent accredited or commended for acceptance. That is, we may responsibly use it to give conceptual definiteness to the otherwise empty or abstract phrase, "ultimate reality." If, though, a metaphysician's theory develops in directions that require modification or abandonment of the initial model, then the model must be expendable. The model, for purely theoretical metaphysical speculation (assuming there is such a thing), remains ancillary to the demands of theory.

I now am prepared to argue that in all logical respects except this last one, anthropomorphic theistic imagery can function on its speculative side as a vivid metaphysical model. It can, when so used in theorizing, give conceptual definiteness to the ultimate nature of things by picturing all of reality as constituting either creature or creator, each with specifiable characteristics. It can suggest patterns and unity in the totality of things in terms of its representation of the various relations between the entities so pictured. And it can give a sense of intelligibility, an aura of meaning and familiarity, by virtue of the appeal to personal purpose, volitional power, and moral principle as ultimate explanatory categories.

An RWM, then, is simply an MWM that has the additional characteristic of pointing to what is most intensely and comprehensively valued, often by a worshipping community in which some are motivated to think carefully in terms of their most precious imagery. On this understanding of religious imagery, it is far from limited to making literal, falsifiable assertions of fact. Fundamentalism rests on an impoverished logic in which literal assertions are given too much status. It is as though RWMs could only be honored by describing photographable fact. This is a profound mistake in judgment. It gives too much credit to photographable fact and too little to the powers of religious imagery to stimulate the sorts of creative thinking that can unify thought and heal lives.

This thinking, theorizing stimulated by intense valuing, can be critically assessed to the extent it shares the goals of all theory, and thus the RWM that inspires the theory is to this extent assessed, too, by theoretical reason. Insofar as theistic religions are interested in the rational justification of their theocentric vision of reality, it appears that it must be done, if it can be done, by displaying the success of the theistic model in concretely suggesting or interpreting some viable metaphysical theory (or theories). If this can be done, then theists will be reasonably entitled to use their imagery not simply for practical purposes but also for "thinking" their world.

Assessing models in a theoretical context is mainly indirect, the verdict on a model is reflected back from the strengths or weaknesses of the theory that articulates it. But one criterion is direct, the question of the "fit" between model and abstract calculus in a theory. This needs to be addressed before other criteria of assessment are relevant. Is the model appropriate to the theory it purports to interpret?

Theoretical appropriateness. The first crucial measure of the cognitive power of theism will be the discovery of how well conceptual structures of unlimited range, supposing for the moment that such structures exist, can be judged to fit the primary model. Such structures may either be made to order or, as has usually been the case, adopted from philosophy with some alterations. But whatever their origin, the cognitive justification of an RWM depends on acceptably appropriate linkage to some theory.

At this point, the one major difference in the logical status of theistic imagery from other metaphysical world models becomes noteworthy. For the purposes of pure theory, as noted above, a model must be subordinate to its theory and must be alterable or disposable according to the dictates of theory. But theistic imagery is not used, even on its speculative side, for theoretical purposes alone. As long as it remains *religious* imagery, the motivation to think in its terms is overridingly practical. This sounds hugely divergent from what "pure" metaphysicians suppose themselves to be doing, but in real life may not prove so different, after all. Despite cool façades, metaphysical models, "visions of ultimate reality," are never held entirely dispassionately. All thinking, even at its most abstract heights, inevitably involves judgments and values (Ferré 1998, 372–73). A metaphysician's views of world and self, as well as deep intuitions of what counts as "decent" order and "acceptable" intelligibility, are wrapped up in the conceptual models used. Theories may be overhauled and rethought to preserve, if possible, a fundamental vision of reality. Theoretical dispassion is always a matter of degree. Still, granting all this, a difference of degree becomes a difference of kind when religious imagery is at stake, since religious imagery is above all a supremely intense value phenomenon by which, for the sake of comprehensiveness, people also often try to think.

Theory, the abstract articulation and explication of the model, becomes the subordinate partner in religious thinking. Various theories may be seized upon as the conceptual vehicles for a common RWM, as can be clearly observed in the history of Christian doctrine (Ferré 1996, 75–103). Plato's abstract metaphysical scheme was used for a millennium to articulate the central model. Aristotle's significantly different scheme emerged with the recovery of Greek texts in Europe to challenge and replace Plato's. Recently, still others, conceptual structures borrowed from Hegel or Heidegger, Whitehead or Wittgenstein, may also be employed to give articulation and application to the value-drenched model at stake.

Each theory has its own abstract formal structure, differing from the others. This structure may be more or less suited to the natural explication of the key points in the RWM's own more concrete formal structure. Each theory, conversely, may eventually influence which structural features of the model should be considered crucial. The influence, for example, of Platonic and Aristotelian theoretical vehicles for Christian imagery drew into the foreground those aspects of the Christian model wherein God's changelessness, self-sufficiency, majestic solitude, and the like, are portrayed. Contrary tendencies to picture God as mutable, developing, or essentially related to the world were interpreted as "merely figurative" (because not open to explication on those theories) and thus were deemphasized. The "fit" of model and theory is thereby aided by the reactions of a powerful theory upon the model, influencing how it is seen. But in the end it is the theory that must be appropriate to the model; theistic imagery, in its speculative as well as in its life-orienting use, remains primary because it is the focus of ultimate valuation.

How is this "fit" or appropriateness to be appraised? That this is a primary requirement is clear, but that there are any clear standards of "fittingness" seems more dubious. It is a fair question, but one to which no easy algorithm can be applied. In the last resort it would seem to be up to religious believers themselves, collectively and individually, to determine the appropriateness of the "fit" between their RWM, their primary "vision of reality," and any particular theory. How is this in practice determined?

I think the fit of one's imagery to the abstract theory intended to articulate it is finally decided in the same way that one determines the fit of the words one chooses to express one's own thought. Each of us engages in the activity of judging the appropriateness of his or her own choice of words: "Such and such a way of putting my thought was not quite right; this other way would be better." But we cannot possibly judge the appropriateness of the manner of our articulation of thought by any precisely articulated standard, as though our thoughts were already articulated somewhere for purposes of comparison before we started articulating them. No, it is the very process of first articulation that we are judging; and therefore the judgment must be by means of some prearticulate—essentially unformulable and imprecise—sense of confidence ("That time I said just what I meant") or of discomfort ("No, that wasn't quite the right way to put it") that guides us (Ferré 1998, 305–307).

In a similar way, theists look to a theory to give articulation to a guiding RWM. And in a similar way, theists must in the last resort simply trust their (and their coreligionists') "feel" for the appropriateness of the conceptual structure to bring out what is most important in the prearticulate vision. It is quite possible that no theories will be felt as perfectly appropriate, but this is a common experience in ordinary uses of language, too—never to find exactly the right way to articulate something, especially something that means a great deal to the speaker. This fact certainly does not argue against the possibility of finding ways of articulating thought that are more (or less) appropriate than others. We judge such matters all the time.

Assuming that this first prerequisite, the criterion of appropriateness, has been sufficiently well met for theists to accept some conceptual scheme as a reasonably well-fitting articulation of their ultimate imagery, the success of the scheme itself in fulfilling its appropriate function must be assessed. What is this function? Ideally, it is the self-consistent elaboration of an integral, or internally well connected, way of thinking about the totality of things. In other words, metaphysical theories in order to do their job must satisfy the familiar twin criteria (now in their theoretical, rather than practical application) of *adequacy* and *coherence*.

Theoretical adequacy. Since RWMs and MWMs are designed to interpret theories dealing with questions of unlimited scope, only a fully comprehensive scheme will be adequate to all the varieties of experience and knowledge that must ultimately be integrated. "Adequacy" requires that, at a minimum, no important ranges of human experience and interest be ignored or denied or (as is sometimes said) "explained away."

Where lies the line, we may wonder, between legitimate *explaining*, by showing a particular object of interest to be an instance of something else already familiar, and *explaining away* by illegitimate reduction? This is another matter for human judgment. Since there is no algorithm available, the question cannot be resolved in the abstract. Even in the sciences these issues raise hotly debated judgmental disputes. But the actual practice of inquiry shows that there *is* a difference between the two, though perhaps no a priori line can be drawn.

In large part we seem thrown back upon the intuitions of those most affected, whose own cognitive interests and personal experiences are being considered. Do they find the conceptual proposal illuminating? Or do they sense something essential lost by the particular abstractions being proposed? If the latter, and if this sense is long sustained, then the verdict of inadequacy will follow.

What is an "acceptable" level of adequacy? The more of it the better, of course. But perfect inclusiveness, the level of adequacy that satisfies everyone's sense that *all* aspects of experience have been considered without distortion, is doubtless an unattainable ideal. Especially is this apt to be so if some elements in the data must be subordinated to other elements, or be put into unfamiliar associations. But problems are compounded by the fact that subordination and unfamiliar association are the inevitable effects of any powerful conceptual ordering; something that is directly sought by the other great criterion, theoretical coherence.

Theoretical coherence. Ideally, successful thinking about the whole of things calls for conceptual unity, the provision of internal connection that would replace fragmentation with integrity. But in real life internal connection is never perfect. In fact the more "adequate" a theory attempts to be, the more difficulties are presented for the achievement of "coherence." Scope and system are polar notions. The more tightly knit the system, the more temptation there is to exclude or explain away parts of the data; but the more rich the system, the harder it is to retain unity. This is especially true if our knowledge and experience are constantly growing, stretching old coherences to the bursting point (Ferré 1998, 355–65).

Still, despite all the difficulties involved, it remains the case that discoverable disconnection is a defect. The more the various elements of a scheme can be shown to involve one another, the more nearly integral, and therefore the more successful, it may be counted as being.

What is the "acceptable level" of incoherence that can be tolerated in a conceptual scheme intended to represent the whole of things? To ask this question in a vacuum is not likely to be any more fruitful than to ask a scientist, apart from particular cases, how much "complexity" can be tolerated in a theory before the standard of "simplicity" is hopelessly violated. The answer in both cases will depend on the available alternatives and the consensus of experienced investigators. No one can say in advance how such tests are going to be applied. And yet they remain important for the working inquirer. Human judgment is inescapable.

The process of human inquiry is not the mechanical affair that is sometimes depicted in simplified logic texts, but neither is it a matter of pure whim nor of arbitrary preference. Adequacy and coherence are not, any more than simplicity or elegance, criteria that lend themselves to programming in computers (though computers might be able to help at certain points). Still, at the level of comprehensiveness appropriate to the speculative function of theism, these happen to be what inquirers must work with.

But "must" inquirers work at all in this maddeningly all-inclusive field? It can be upsetting for those who love clarity and precision, for those who mistrust judgment calls and seek to minimize the visible role of values. The fact is that metaphysics and theology are optional for theorizers made uncomfortable by the vertigo of conceptual agoraphobia. Both these "omnirelevant" fields have been marginalized in the late modern period. The more prestigious intellectual work has been conducted in bounded domains with apparently safer methods, such as in the well-fortified special sciences or in modes of philosophy inspired by science and mathematics.

Therefore, I should amend my previous statement. Adequacy and coherence, with their acknowledged internal tensions and with all the inevitable human judgments implicit in their application, are all that inquirers have to work with *if they opt to work here at all*. There are many reasons, some religious (as we saw) and some secular, both practical and theoretical, why one might opt against it. Not all thinkers have an aptitude for such high conceptual flying, nor would the intellectual world be a richer place if everyone concentrated on metaphysics and theology. Quite the contrary. The latter, the comprehensive thinkers, need the work of patient empirical scientists, logicians, historians, mathematicians, and so forth, to feed their need for the most reliable data possible at any given time. Since metaphysical and theological ways of thinking are critical as well as comprehensive, the discipline of other disciplines is essential.

But without the risk taking of the outermost explorers, no one would be focusing squarely on the context of contexts. The assumed context for ethical decision making—which will guide attitudes and actions whether or not it is made explicit and examined—would be left unassessed. Perhaps, if not checked for adequacy, this context of contexts will leave important elements out of account; perhaps, if not scrutinized for coherence, it will be fragmentary and internally self-defeating for life as well as thought. It takes nothing away from the less comprehensive disciplines to acknowledge that the comprehensive ones are doing important work. In the end they help define what true "importance" means.

6

QUESTION OF GOD

Is the context of all contexts a unified cosmic experiencer, benevolent and all-knowing, an actual agency with purposes and causal powers? In other words, should God provide the ultimate framework for understanding ourselves and the universe, and (directly or indirectly) for coloring all our ethical judgments and actions?

A number of religions, including the dominant ones of Europe, the Middle East, modernized Africa, North and South America, and Australia, affirm such a context (with specific variations) as ultimate. Many more religions could be added to the list from tribal Africa, South Asia, and East Asia, if restrictions on God's "unity" and other superlatives were to be dropped and gods, or deified ancestors, or other personal and quasi personal powers were to be taken as sufficient for the final context. The pull of personal categories is widespread and strong.

This chapter aims to ask the question of God or god or the gods with respectful, if critical, attention. First let me explain my practice of capitalizing (or not) the word "God." When I write the word with an initial capital, I refer to the theist's omnipotent, omniscient, unitary, unique, perfectly good, immaterial, fully actual divinity. Moses' Jehovah, Jesus' Father in Heaven, and Mohammed's Allah can be understood as prominent instances of this concept of God. In the history of thought and worship there have been many more, but these three instances should anchor the abstract notion of the theistic God to concrete, familiar faiths. There are significant differences between and within these faiths, but several central commonalities bind them in even more significant ways (Ferré 1967, 122–26). First, for all of them God is ideal but no mere ideal. That is, God is actual, and supremely so. God is the prime actuality, the context for all actualities. God's actuality is finally responsible for any other actualities that are, and without God there would be nothing actual at all. Next, there is no other actuality like God. God is alone in providing the final context for all things, without a second. This may not rule out sociality in God (this is an unresolved dispute that both Judaism and Islam have with Christianity's doctrine of the Trinity), but all agree that any social richness in God's experience cannot undermine God's perfect unity or challenge God's uniqueness. Beyond this, God's unique actuality is fully aware, both inwardly of the divine nature and outwardly of anything else that may exist. God's knowledge is perfect. But God is not a passive cognizer; God has preferences, purposes, and engages in actions. This makes it logically appropriate to use ethical language about God, for example, that God is just, righteous, faithful, or perfectly good. Different theistic religions specify these qualities in somewhat different terms, painting "perfection" in different hues, one stressing justice, another inscrutable faithfulness, another love, but all insist on using morally positive terms about God in their religious practices even though in their theory some may declare God "beyond good and evil." But if "beyond," God is always beyond in the "good" direction, not the "evil."

When I omit the initial capital, "god" refers to a theoretical entity occupying the logical space of God, that is, the outermost context for ethics and explanation, but the lower case word should not necessarily imply the various perfections suggested by the honorific capital. Shorn of its initial capital, "god" should also not stimulate the reflex that makes God function as a proper name, instantly complete with personal pronouns. Writing about "god" should instead remind us that for critical theory, asserting personal traits for the context of contexts needs to be earned by argument rather than granted *honoris causa*. Perhaps a concept of god, if an appropriate theory can be defined and defended, will turn out worthy of articulating what religious people have called God, or perhaps not. In the end, if I am right in what I argued in the previous chapter, such a finding will not be up to anyone outside the religions that worship a variety of specifications of God in multitudinous ways. But before reaching that point of decision about "appropriateness," theory can be important. For those of us who find it legitimate or even obligatory to think carefully about our ultimate context, theory can warn us away from attractive but unreliable fancies and in the process point us toward sounder candidates for possible interpretation by our vivid, living, religious world models.

QUESTION OF PROOFS

The traditional proofs for God are and have long been in disrepute among philosophers. They remain of interest, however, even among professional theorizers, partly for historical reasons—there is a vast amount of subtle literature on the topic—and partly, perhaps, because the stakes are so high. They also continue to tease the minds of such persons as clergy, or youthful experimenters with religious ideas, or others who feel that something so important as the question of God's actuality for providing the context of contexts must somehow be accessible to conclusive demonstration.

I have long been teased with these issues myself, and wrote my doctoral dissertation on the subject. Now I think they have continuing legitimate functions, but those functions do not include coercing agreement to propositions. There are unavoidable matters of judgment that arise in every theistic "proof," making them suggestive at best but never knockdown demonstrations.

The theoretical proofs for God can be grouped into three families, which among them cover the possibilities in the way that "no," "all," or "some" exhaust the logical possibilities for quantifying premises in arguments. The first family, which I shall call "Perfection" arguments (traditionally "Ontological" arguments), makes use of *no* factual premises, relying instead on necessities of meaning. The second family, which I name "Causal" arguments (usually "Cosmological" arguments), stakes its ground on *all* factual premises, whether taken together (in the sense of the "entire sum") or individually (in the sense of "any"). And the third family, which I refer to as "Design" arguments (technically "Teleological" arguments), rises from *some* factual premises selected as especially significant. In addition to the three families of theoretical proof stands another family of "Moral" quasi arguments. My aim in what follows is nothing exhaustive, but simply to show how in each family human judgments—rationally rejectable evaluations—are inextricably entwined.

The Perfection family of arguments has been offered in many different versions by thinkers premodern, Anselm; modern, Descartes, Spinoza, Leibniz (see Ferré 1996, 88–90, 139–40, 142–48, 189–91); and contemporary, Hartshorne (1962). Shared by all versions is agreement that God is absolutely perfect, unlimited, lacking in nothing. If a greater could be conceived, then the greater, replacing the lesser, would become the correct conception of God. By definition, God is that than which nothing greater can be conceived. This definition is a priori: absolute and secure, dependent on *no* factual premises, *no* deliverances of experience. It would hold even if there were no world of factual experience.

From this it follows necessarily, in this family of arguments, that God must actually exist. Failing to exist would be a serious lack, a huge imperfection ruled out (once we understand God as entailing absolute perfection) by the fundamental meanings involved. Denying the existence of God cannot rationally be done, since it would involve a logical contradiction, namely, both affirming and disallowing all perfections in God. Since God's existence cannot rationally be denied, then asserting it is the only logical possibility. That "God exists" can be known to be true as soon as it is fully understood, so this family of arguments insists.

It is an old, distinguished family and deserves respect. On close examination, the argument is capable of stimulating tantalizing gestalt-switch games. Some philosophers report that they are inclined to accept it on Monday, Wednesday, and Friday, but reject it on Tuesday, Thursday, and Saturday (on Sunday God gives even philosophers a day off). As an argument, it obviously points up something fundamentally important about the uniqueness of the religiously powerful concept of God it revolves around. An early matter of judgment is whether or not to accept this definition as appropriate to one's religious tradition and/or one's linguistic intuitions. Taking "that than which nothing greater can be conceived" as logically equivalent to "God" is not optional for the argument, but it is optional for persons. Other definitions of "God" abound. Defenders of the Perfection argument will rightly point out that the tradition equating God with absolute perfection is old and widespread, but it is not the only tradition, even within Judaism and Christianity. They may assert that it is the only *correct* tradition, but this again is a value judgment, not at all coercive for those who prefer another usage. The argument will not work given other meanings for "God." Nothing but the sole all-perfect One has ever been considered an appropriate subject for a Perfection argument. No finite thing, even considered perfect of its kind (e.g., a perfect island, a perfect soprano, or even a Lord of Hosts), could be proven actual by the argument, since something greater could always in principle be conceived. The Perfection argument, if it works at all, works only for what is defined as beyond all conceivable limits, the possessor of everything valued, that for which one is not prepared to acknowledge shortcomings of any kind.

But here again we come upon matters of judgment. Conceptions of perfection, even absolute perfection, will differ, depending on what components are valued initially. It is easy for world-affirming Westerners to agree, without much reflection, that "actual existence" is to be preferred to "nonexistence." Since Plato, at least, there has been a nearly automatic identification of Being and goodness (Ferré 1996, 46–55). The Perfection argument hinges on that evaluation. Without it there would be no argument, since no conclusion about God's existence would follow. But Easterners, steeped in traditions of world-denial and longing for release from the wheel of existence, might make a different evaluation. So might a Westerner, such as Hamlet, deeply exploring the positive possibilities of nonbeing. If actual existence is not judged to be a perfection, however, the Perfection argument is derailed.

If "mere" existence might not be judged even always a good thing, then "necessary" existence, the inability not to be, will turn out no necessary perfection, either. Quite independent of Kant's famous logical challenge to treating existence as a predicate (or property) at all (Ferré 1967, 202–203), judgments may differ on the evaluation of existence, both contingent and necessary. Therefore, there is a new, non-Kantian, sense in which "existence is a perfection" may intelligibly be refused. It may, of course, be intelligibly accepted, too. Here is a place where the gestalt-switch game may start. But in either case, the Perfection argument turns out not to be the knockdown proof for which some of its proponents hoped.

The second, Causal, family of arguments for God depends on the actual existence of anything at all. It is not selective. For this argument, offered by such great thinkers as Aquinas (Ferré 1996, 97–98) and Descartes (Ferré 1967, 136–38), a whole universe is no better as an initial premise than a single existing self. Aquinas offered three versions of the argument in which moving things, caused things, and contingent things, singly or together, took turns on center stage as premises for inferences to a Prime Mover, a First Cause, and a Necessary Being "whom all know as God." Descartes, after proving his own existence as a thinking thing, took this discovery as sufficient to prove the necessary existence of God. The logic of the arguments within this family all have the same structure: Anything at all that exists either accounts for itself or not. If not, then it must be accounted for by something else sufficient to the task. That something else, in turn, either accounts for itself or not. If not . . . , in the end it is unthinkable that the regress could go on forever, leaving the whole sequence and the presently existing datum unaccounted for. Therefore, since there is something (the datum), there must be something that accounts for itself, on which everything else that does not account for itself depends.

"And this everyone understands to be God," remarks Aquinas, treating it as something obvious, as he completes his first version of the Causal argument (Aquinas 1948, 25). But does this follow in any logically required way? It may indeed be a transition that many in the Hebrew-Christian-Muslim traditions are glad to make, but it takes a major value judgment to do so. There is nothing inherent in the idea of accounting for the facts of motion, or accounting for causal sequences, or even accounting for the existence of everything from oneself to universe, that compels *worship*. The appeal of the argument is to an explanatory stopping place, not to anything necessarily divine. If the sequence simply must be stopped (and this "if" itself is a matter on which fully informed judgments may differ), then the *character* of what stops the infinite regress remains an open question, just as long as the abyss of infinite regress is somehow avoided. No personal characteristics are required by the Causal argument, even if it is judged completely successful. In principle, the Unmoved Mover could be completely unconscious, the First Cause could be purposeless, the Necessary Being could be malevolent, as far as the argument is concerned. All that is required by the argument is that the question "why?" be finally brought to rest.

What sort of explanation could achieve this goal? If the first premise of the Causal argument is that everything needs to be accounted for; if it is then found that only something that accounts for itself can stop the sequence, why should "the world as a whole" not be sufficient? If "the world as a whole" is rejected because we do not know *how* it accounts for itself, then why should "God" not be rejected on exactly the same grounds? If it is replied that "God" is defined as everlasting, without beginning or end, then why not define "the world as a whole" as everlasting, in the same way? If this is opposed by reverting to the first premise, insisting a priori that everything "worldly" needs to be accounted for by something else, why not ask why "God" escapes the same theoretical requirement? The answer is likely to be that "God" is perfect, lacking in nothing, especially in existence, and is consequently necessary. But this, we recognize, is the Perfection argument again, which rests on many value judgments. The purely theoretical "why?" has no legitimate stopping place. What allows the infinite regress to end is not theory alone but the value-laden, functionally religious judgment that one's theorizing has finally come to what "stands to reason," what "ought to be," what "justifies itself."

Candidates for this stopping place differ in character. Certainly the religious conception of God is one powerful candidate, but in contrast some have preferred others, including various consortia of deities, or uncreated and indestructible matter, or inexplicable chance, or primal cosmic energy, or an ever evolving universe. These are truly matters of profound preference, not issues forced by evidence and logic. The Causal argument, if it works at all, rests on the barest of all evidence—sheer existence of something—and its logic presses only to seek what might be a plausible place to hand over the theoretical quest to a far from coercive judgment of finality.

The arguments from religious experience, or the arguments from mystical illumination, are sometimes treated as a separate family. Perhaps this is because the worship-inspiring properties of God are so obviously central to this set of arguments. Here God is allegedly seen as holy, loving, just, and so forth, not simply inferred from motion, causes, or contingency. But insofar as religious experience offers data for an *argument*, and not simply a way around all arguments by asserting immediate awareness beyond the need (or reach) of all theoretical warrants, these data are not in principle different from the others. They are events in experience used to launch their own versions of the Causal argument: "An experience of an awesome presence has occurred; it does not account for itself; therefore something must account for it." But again it is a matter of judgment whether such psychological events should be accounted for as veridical "sightings" or "encounters" with an objectively existing cause resembling the qualities of the experience, or should instead be accounted for in other terms. A cause may be called for, but perhaps the categories of explanation should be drawn from psychology or physiology rather than religion. One does not need to be quite so radical a gastronomic reductionist as Scrooge, who at first tried to explain his encounter with Marley as "an undigested bit of beef, a blot of mustard, a crumb of cheese, a fragment of an underdone potato" (Dickens 1988, 19), but many causal explanations of mystical experience may be offered, from repressed sexuality to brain chemistry. Perhaps, theists may retort, these are ways God has wisely chosen to channel the divine presence to finite human organisms. Perhaps, but this is no longer the Causal argument, which merely seeks a stopping place in a cause that has no need of further explanation. This new reply has the distinct sound of the Design argument, next on the agenda.

The family of Design arguments is much more selective about its evidence. This selectivity is its great strength, and also its great weakness, at least if any of its exemplars should be mistaken for a knockdown proof. Of all the theoretical arguments, this is the best loved. It uses wonderful features of our cosmic habitation to warrant inferences to an at-least-equally wonderful architect, purposefully responsible for them. The specific features chosen can be quite various in this family of arguments. Aquinas pointed simply to "natural bodies" which, despite lacking knowledge, regularly work well together to produce the "best result" (Aquinas 1948, 27). Kant acknowledged the starry heavens above as evidence of wonderful "order and system" (Kant 1929, 259). William Paley wrote a large book detailing the intricate internal organization of animals, birds, and fish as proof that they, just as much as a watch, must be considered products of intelligent design (Paley 1963). More recently, many have appealed to some purposeful "anti-chance" in overcoming the improbabilities of life organizing itself within the comparatively brief window of opportunity afforded by the cooling Earth (du Noüy 1947, 26–39). Currently, much interest is directed to the remarkably "fine tuned" character of the physical constants shown by the early universe, without which no world like ours, no life on Earth, no personal intelligence could ever have evolved (Davies 1982; Peacocke 1993; Polkinghorne 1994; Murphy and Ellis 1996). This latest discussion has revolved around the "anthropic principle," holding that a good guide to understanding the earliest stages of our universe is the extremely improbable (but significant) fact that it gave rise to the human species now speculating about it. I shall return for a further look at the anthropic principle in the following section of this chapter.

It should be clear that human judgment enters early when the Design argument is deployed. As an opening move one must decide what, out of a wide array of evidences, should be selected as best for the case. This choice tends to change with the state of science. Coordination between "natural bodies" not understood in one age, thus open in that age to explanation in terms of intelligent design, may be differently accounted for in another age. The most dramatic example of such a shift is the publication of Paley's *Natural Theology* (originally published 1802) within mere decades of Charles Darwin's *Origin of Species* (1859). Ironically, Darwin (with all other undergraduates) was required to study

Paley's book while a student at Cambridge, less than a decade before his famous voyage on the *Beagle* and his development of the idea of natural selection as an alternative explanation for the amazing intricacies of organic life. After Darwin, virtually all examples of the Design argument have begun by assuming evolution, then have worked toward the same conclusion with quite different evidences of providential design found within the new framework.

Another key judgment underlying this argument is the decision how far one should extend the principle of *self*-organization, instead of relying on the hypothesis of an *external* designer. It is interesting to note that Aquinas, despite his famous Aristotelianism, rejected (at least for the purpose of the Design argument) Aristotle's own stress on the immanent teleology of things (Ferré 1996, 55–63). If organisms are truly self-organizing, their difference from watches is underscored and the need for external "watchmakers" diminished. The use of the plural in "watchmakers" reminds us of another evaluative judgment needed, namely, how much unity should be assigned the alleged intelligence behind the regularities of the world? There are many different kinds of systems in our experience. Must all of them be attributed to the same purposive agent? Could the evidence selected not be even better accounted for by a team of designers? Even Paley admitted that there is no coercive evidence for a single personal agent behind the many systems: "Certain however it is that the whole argument for the divine unity goes no further than to a unity of counsel" (Paley 1963, 52). But a team or a committee is capable of reaching "unity of counsel." Is this good enough to prove the existence of God?

Still harder judgments need to be made. How great, really, is the intelligence of this committee (or this God) in light of the facts? Wonderful though we may find the organization of the world and many things in it, it is possible to imagine improvements. A world without the useless human appendix would be a world without appendicitis. A world without wisdom teeth would contain less impaction. And so on to more serious proposals. The Design argument may reach to "great" and "wonderful," but surely not to "perfect" wisdom in the designer it proposes. Even more painful for the argument is the problem of pain and disorder. Pain in limited quantities may be a vital organic benefit as a danger signal, as Paley argues (Paley 1963, 61–68), but there seems to be a huge superabundance of pain among persons and in nature for this defense to seem plausible. "How much is too much?" is exactly the sort of judgment that is now unavoidable. If the judgment on pain, illness, earthquakes, tornadoes, and the like, turns out "too much," then a judgment needs to be rendered not only on the perfect intelligence of God but also of God's goodness. The intractable problem of evil is the nemesis stirred by the Design argument. There are defenses, though when it comes to animal suffering they seem far from satisfactory (Ferré 1986b). Still, all the arguments and counterarguments rely on judgments of the deepest sort, drawing on moral intuitions as well as intuitions about the appropriate use of religious superlatives for God. The Design argument, from beginning to end, rests on a skein of value judgments.

This in itself is nothing shameful. All human reasoning depends upon judgments of importance, appropriateness, conceptual fit, and other norms of one kind or another (Ferré 1998, 314–73). But there are degrees to which conclusions are based on judgments that can be plausibly rejected by other persons with equal information and intelligence. The three families of theoretical theistic arguments are found on the high end of this scale. Even higher on the scale of "plausible rejectability" is the Moral quasi argument for God, since it is openly an appeal to moral intuition. Most members of this family of arguments do not even claim theoretical status, but as in Kant's version, acknowledge that they are exercises of practical reason (Kant 1956, 128–36). The argument itself, in Kant's classical statement, points out that we have a practical need to assume that the two great goals of human life, morality and happiness, can be fulfilled. We discover no causal connection (or even correlation), so far as the empirical evidence is concerned, between moral virtue and the rewards of happiness. The motivation to do one's duty is entirely independent, and often contrary to, the motivation to happiness. "Nevertheless," Kant says,

> in the practical task of pure reason, i.e., in the necessary endeavor after the highest good, such a connection is postulated as necessary: we *should* seek to further the highest good (which therefore must be at least possible). Therefore also the existence is postulated of a cause of the whole of nature, itself distinct from nature, which contains the ground of the exact coincidence of happiness with morality (Kant 1956, 129).

Since such a "ground" will have to be able to *know perfectly* the motives of the people whose virtue is being assessed, and to *control perfectly* the empirical circumstances that make for happiness, as well as to *act in a perfectly lawful*, just manner in correlating the two independent variables, this "ground" is divine.

> Now a being which is capable of actions by the idea of laws is an intelligence (a rational being), and the causality of such a being according to this idea of laws is his will. Therefore, the supreme cause of nature, in so far as it must be presupposed for the highest good, is a being which is the cause (and consequently the author) of nature through understanding and will, i.e., God (Kant 1956, 130).

God is a "reasonable" postulate if one thinks according to the twin practical necessities of morality and happiness, Kant concludes, but this remains only a matter of *practical* reason. It is not a requirement of theoretical reason. As he puts it, "it is morally necessary to assume the existence of God." But then in the next line he adds: "It is well to notice here that this moral necessity is subjective, i.e., a need, and not objective, i.e., duty itself. For there cannot be any duty to assume the existence of a thing, because such a supposition concerns only the theoretical use of reason" (Kant 1956, 130).

The Moral argument for God then lays no claim to coercive theoretical proof. It is not a theoretical proof at all. Given a readiness to respect the pure call of duty, given a willingness to affirm the importance of happiness, given a sense of the appropriateness of the ultimate adjustment of happiness to moral virtue, and given that one is prepared to affirm that this highest good must somehow be possible for life to make moral sense, then it makes moral sense to postulate a being capable of bringing this about. This postulate is not to any degree knowledge. It does not even carry a degree of probability, since as Kant admits, it is entirely dependent on "subjective" factors.

There are other members of the Moral argument family that are not quite so pure as Kant's. Sometimes it may be argued that if "good" purposes finally triumph over "evil" ones (if a crime turns out not to have paid, or if a cruel ruler is defeated in a "just" war), then this shows that "God is in Heaven, after all." But it should now be clear that this is a disguised version of the Design argument, in which the evidence selected to show providential "design" is defined in moral categories. A large degree of "plausible rejectability," due to the selectivity of this argument and its dependence on other value judgments, remains and is even intensified by the many ethical judgments involved. And, as in other applications of the Design argument, this hybrid Moral argument raises the problem of evil by calling for counterexamples about crimes that *do* seem to have paid and cruel dictators who manage to *win* their battles, avoid retribution, and die happily in their beds.

Another hybrid Moral argument is grafted to the Causal. It can be argued that morality would not exist if God did not. But if this is not a disguised Design argument, holding that no one would be moral if God had not *designed* or *intended* it so, then this is another case in which the universal scope of the Causal argument is again illustrated. Anything that exists, including morality but also gross immorality, can start the regress toward a cause capable of accounting for it. There is no guarantee from the Causal argument that the *quality* of the datum will be manifest in the ultimate cause. If the existence of morality is supposed to prove a good God, might the existence of immorality prove a wicked, disgusting one? To guard against this scoffing challenge, theists may be tempted to insist that only positive perfections can be thought to characterize God. The very meaning of God entails it. But this, alas, is only to call for help from the Perfection argument, whose limitations as a coercive demonstration have already been laid bare.

The point hardly needs further belaboring. All the families of theistic "proofs" are deeply dependent on value-laden judgments. This makes them plausibly rejectable, but they are not without jobs to do, when the circumstances are right. Clearly the circumstances will not be right for their use when facing a determined agnostic or a committed atheist. They do not make good offensive weapons. Or, to change the metaphor, they are not tools that can be expected to grip on every sort of surface. Something attitudinal must be granted for them to gain a purchase and start to work.

No amount of information without key evaluative attitudes will lead to religious conclusions. In overlooking this attitudinal prerequisite, traditional users of the "proofs" have misread the nature of the religious response and its relationship to facts. Learning a list of the particulars concerning the structure of the human eye, for example, leads nowhere—except perhaps to a degree in anatomy. Even in the sciences the facts are taken in a value structure and are given significance as part of some human interest. Naturally, the human interest undergirding the Design argument, for example, is specifically different from scientific interests. Contemplating the optical facts with an attitude of wonder and awe at the marvels of our organic system, as Paley did, may lead to worship the Wisdom that devised and now sustains us. Even the facts on which the Moral arguments rely are without religious significance unless taken as religiously significant. A feeling of moral obligation may be interpreted merely as the irritating residue of parental training. Likewise, on the Causal argument, a feeling of holiness may, as we have seen, be shrugged aside as a spooky reminder of our primitive ancestors, or on other grounds. But attitudes of respect for morality and the readiness to accord a place of importance to religious experiences may transform these phenomena into pointers toward something worth worshiping.

All of these arguments require what can be called "apprehensional premises" (Ferré 1961, 189). These "premises" may or may not be present. It should not be thought peculiar that theological arguments require for their success something beyond what is contained in the arguments themselves. All arguments—even the proofs of logic or mathematics—are in an analogous position. Proofs in formal logic depend, for example, on prior decisions expressible in a "meta-language" concerning relevant axioms and rules of formation and transformation. Attitudes of readiness to accept these rules, and to continue to abide by them even when difficulties arise, are essential to the discipline. Scientific arguments, too, depend on factors not included in the arguments, such as semantic rules which must be accepted for interpreting perceptions on which the arguments are founded and to which they are intended to return. The theistic arguments, analogously, require an unusual supplement, a personal *attitude*, without which they are impotent. The Causal argument, for example, requires that one admit that there is a problem involved in the existence of individual things which do not cause themselves. Above all, this means that we—who are included in the class of beings which did not cause themselves—must be ready to admit that there is a problem about our own being. To admit this, however, requires (among other qualities) a certain degree of humility. We may prefer to refuse the idea that there is anything to wonder at in the existence of anything. We may reject the idea that we might not have been. If we do this the Causal argument is crippled. Withdraw the apprehensional premise of awe and respect from contemplation of "the starry heavens above and the moral law within," and the Design and Moral arguments are wrecked. Refuse to grant numinous overtones to thoughts of absolute completeness and self-existence, and the Perfection argument is shorn of its power.

This may help account for the notorious fact that the arguments for God are more effective with some people than with others equally intelligent and well-informed. This is not uniquely the case in religious matters. Philosophers have long realized that there exists no formal criterion for producing belief or dissipating incredulity through nondeductive arguments, arguments to the effect, for example, that some regular sequence of events is a "universal law of nature." Some may be convinced after a few instances of a happening that the relations between A and B is a law of nature or a fully dependable regularity. Or some may remain skeptical for much longer periods of time. Similar issues rise in connection with falsification. When has a "law" been falsified? How long can one hang on, dismissing apparent falsifying results as "mere anomalies" to be dealt with later? There is no algorithm to answer this question. It is a matter of judgment, and judgments differ. In like manner, determining the effectiveness of a theistic argument is a matter of judgment in which personal traits will be crucial. Given humility, a sense of wonder, a readiness to take seriously moral, aesthetic, and religious experience, the arguments for God may have considerable power to direct attention and offer encouragement. Confronted by opposite traits, the arguments will bear no fruit at all. A postmodern suggestion to opponents struggling over the theistic proofs would be to "lighten up," therefore, and notice how easily arguments of this kind become disguised clashes of fundamental valuations rooted in human personality.

A qualification should be noted before turning away from this kind of clash between a theist and what might be called a "hardened unbeliever." First, personality considerations should not be overinterpreted as unalterable traits of character. Both what is loosely called "the climate of opinion" and more specific pressures of education may do much to form the personality considerations at work. For example, the sense of what is a "rational" question or a "rationally satisfying" answer may be greatly affected by the sort of answers to questions which an individual is *accustomed* to asking and *trained* to find satisfactory. If one lives in an intellectual climate where one is accustomed to being satisfied only by answers in terms of what Aristotle called "material" or "efficient" causes to questions starting with "why" (Ferré 1996, 60–62), then such a one is likely not to feel the same sort of needs for rational satisfaction as is the person whose intellectual practice demands explanation also in terms of "final" causes. To the former, much theistic debate will be both incomprehensible and redundant, while, to the latter, it will be charged with maximal significance. A great deal depends on the way in which our minds have been furnished before we approach theistic argument. "Rationality" does not mean the same to all regardless of experience, education, or interests.

Dropping the "hardened unbeliever" and turning, instead, to dialogue with someone with apprehensional premises less firmly set against the topic, we may find still further uses for the theistic arguments. In this more hospitable climate, one may hope, through the arguments, to show a person who is prepared in humility to revere what can be shown worthy of reverence, that reverence for God is not incompatible with intellectual integrity. The Causal argument, for one, may be used to instill a sense of wonder before the mystery of existence, to draw attention to the dependence of all finite things on something vastly beyond themselves, and to suggest by analogy the dependence of the aggregate of these dependent things (including oneself) on something awe-inspiring, fittingly modeled by the RWM of some great theistic tradition. The Design argument, similarly, may reinforce an appreciation of the universe in which we find ourselves and may lend some weight to the claim that intelligence, far from being a biological accident in a meaningless swarm of stars, must be involved in the very fiber of the world's being.

These arguments need not always require dialogue with others. They may have uses in solitary meditation as well. Someone inclined to faith in God can by their means make sure that his or her faith is not contrary to careful thought. In so doing, the dimension of intellect is added to the worship of God. Religion at its highest cannot violate or neglect any part of complex human nature. If faith stifles reason, faith is bound to be insecure and unhealthy. More positively, theological arguments give believers an opportunity to worship with their minds. In the Design arguments, a theist can praise God for the wonders of creation; in the Causal arguments the theist asserts confident dependence on the One on whom all things depend; in the Perfection arguments (which are only properly understood in this light, I believe) the theist can affirm all existence as good and enlist thought itself into the service of the Perfect One.

From purported demonstrations to acts of worship, the theistic arguments have been wrung through many changes in this discussion. I have tried to show that arguing about God is a many-layered activity, involving a number of dimensions besides logic. I hope my readers will keep this in mind through the following pages, where I add some more personal answers to religious questions about the cosmos. My life experience, enculturation, training, preferences, and temperament will all be showing, as inevitably they must. Obviously this will be no attempt at "hegemonic control" of anyone else's views. Within the spirit as well as from the logic of my position, I am content to hope that some readers will find empathic resonances which might help them in the weaving of their own grand narratives of ultimate context.

QUESTION OF PURPOSE

If we remember that the question of God rose out of the search for a final ethical context, we will keep our focus on the meaning of metaphysics for living. What difference for our attitudes and actions does it make whether God or god or gods—or something else—should provide that context?

Not much difference would come from the assumption or discovery that a great Cause, character unknown, lies behind the universe, without which nothing would exist. There is no clearly appropriate ethical response to such a bare metaphysical context of sheer causal dependency. Some might suggest that gratitude, at least, would be in order, but why should gratitude be given for a fact accomplished without motive? A benevolent purpose behind the giving and sustaining of life, might warrant gratitude for the satisfactions of existence, but mere dependency is not a guiding norm. It does not shape attitudes, nor does it guide decisions about what to do if everything is equally, indifferently causally dependent. Might this lead to support of democratic policies, since all finite entities are in the same contingent condition, or, instead, to hierarchical policies in emulation of the causal chain on which we hang? Should causal contingency motivate us to be more tender toward others, more sympathetic to fellow finite beings, or should it validate our inclinations to stamp out opposition before we ourselves are stamped out? A First Cause, even a Necessary Being, may be an impressive cosmic fact but is not automatically worthy of worship. As a context of contexts it gives no ethical guidance unless, coupled to its causal efficacy, there is some basis for judgments of better and worse.

My shorthand for such a basis is "purpose." By this I mean to include explicit plans, of course, but also general tendencies that emerge from preferences. For this reason I consider the Design family of arguments, for all this family's flaws, to be the most relevant for the ethical context of living. Looking to the universe as resultant of preferences, looking at our lives as part of an ongoing process furthering more general tendencies, is the ethical point of dealing with metaphysical worldviews.

My own preferred worldview, personalistic organicism, stresses the presence of purpose, mind, and the creation of value in nature. It is a "kalogenic" (beauty-creating) naturalism, so named because in my view the fundamental value born in the self-actualization of each momentary entity is beauty, defined as intrinsically satisfactory experience (Ferré 1996, 339–82). My worldview is inspired by the speculative philosophy of Alfred North Whitehead, who developed a quantum *organicism*—a "vibratory universe" (Whitehead 1925, 36) based on fundamental events—aimed at broadening the adequacy and increasing the coherence of any philosophy of *mechanism* that assumes the world is made up of "particles" with no degree of subjectivity or internal relatedness. Orthodox modern worldviews have been mechanistic in this sense; that is, they have resisted including any trace of mind or value in the natural universe, restricting these characteristics exclusively to humans (Ferré 1996, 107–82). In so doing, mainstream modern thinking has managed simultaneously to undermine human respect for nature, seen as valueless in itself, and to create an insoluble mind-body conundrum with disastrous implications for *metaphysical* coherence, *epistemological* self-confidence (Ferré 1998, 93–263), and *ethical* adequacy.

My debt to Whitehead is deep, as I have acknowledged gladly in staking out my own metaphysical and epistemological positions in earlier volumes. I have made significant adjustments, particularly by explicit stress on the "personal" to complement Whitehead's "organic," and have made extensions to topics he touched lightly, or not at all. I think Whitehead would for the most part have welcomed these modifications and applications. In connection with God, however, I suspect he would have resisted. My kalogenic naturalism agrees with Whitehead's "bottom-up" approach to the world but, in contrast to Whitehead himself, is less convinced of the additional need for God or a god, a single unified cosmic entity in constant relationship with the world, to complete the cosmic picture (Ferré 1996, 363–70). At this point, it seems, I need to wrestle with Whitehead himself, at least with the Whitehead of *Process and Reality*, where the doctrine of God as an actual entity is most fully developed.

This doctrine is a sensitive one, since one of the key motives for the continuation of Whitehead scholarship after his death in 1947 and until the present has been theological. "Process theology" has become a significant industry, a lively subdiscipline in which some of the best theological work of the late twentieth century has been accomplished. I am not a process theologian, but "full disclosure" should reveal that I am closely allied to, and enjoy warm ties of friendship with, the men and women who lead and sustain this movement. That said, it should be obvious that my own motivations in writing the present trilogy of books from a Whiteheadian-*cum*-Personalist perspective have been more generally philosophical. My initial introduction to Whitehead, while still in high school, was through reading *Science and the Modern World* (1925), a gift from my father, who had been Whitehead's graduate assistant at Harvard. My father, a theologian, was absorbed in the question of God, but did not much avail himself of Whitehead's ideas in this area, preferring a more classical conception radically rooted in (and transformed by) taking infinite, self-giving love, or *agapé*, as central for interpretation (Ferré 1951). My first attraction to Whitehead, instead, was as one who could allow me to embrace the best of science, answer Hume's doubts about inductive causation, and shake me awake from the seventeenth-century's bleak vision of a universe "cleansed" of all qualities and values. Despite my early work in theological language (Ferré 1961; 1962), Whitehead's doctrine of God remained in the background.

The doctrine itself is somewhat indistinct, coming from different periods of Whitehead's thought. The two most important early expression of Whitehead's views on God, were written at almost the same time, both for the Lowell Lecture series in successive years, 1925 and 1926, presented at King's Chapel in Boston. The first was published as *Science and the Modern World* (Whitehead 1925); the second was *Religion in the Making* (Whitehead 1926).

In the chapter, "God," in the first of these books, Whitehead opens by praising Aristotle for following his argument where it led, dispassionately, to a First Mover. This Mover was required by Aristotelian physics, in which motion did not "stand to reason," thus needing explanation. Now, ever since Newton, physics recognizes motion just as "natural" as rest. Under these circumstances, there is no more need for an Unmoved Mover than for an Unstopped Stopper. At least Aristotle's God was not an arbitrary intrusion into thought but instead a logical requirement of his system. Such dispassionately metaphysical thinking "did not lead him very far towards the production of a God available for religious purposes," Whitehead recognizes, then adds: "It may be doubted whether any properly general metaphysics can ever, without the illicit introduction of other considerations, get much further than Aristotle" (Whitehead 1925, 173).

His own purely theoretical requirement is analogous: "In the place of Aristotle's God as Prime Mover, we require God as the Principle of Concretion" (Whitehead 1925, 174). What "requires" this is the basic Whiteheadian account, as we saw in Chapter 4, of all reality as made up of events coming to concreteness, depending, for the initial phase of their particular character, on the range of possibilities provided by the immediate environment (Ferré 1996, 262–73). The environment, constituting the immediate physically prehended past, both provides and limits possibilities for new concrescence. Every actuality is "in essential relation to an unfathomable possibility," Whitehead points out, and "every actual occasion is a limitation imposed on possibility" (Whitehead 1925, 174). But there are no single occasions. All are related. In their togetherness an actual universe is woven out of possibility by process. Still, there are too many pure possibilities to account for why just *this* universe is actual rather than an innumerable set of others. Actuality is an achievement of value. How account for the fact that just *these* values are selected rather than others?

> Thus as a further element of the metaphysical situation, there is required a principle of limitation. Some particular *how* is necessary, and some particularization in the *what* of matter of fact is necessary. . . . [We] must

provide a ground for limitation which stands among the attributes of the substantial activity. This attribute provides the limitation for which no reason can be given: for all reason flows from it. God is the ultimate limitation, and His existence is the ultimate irrationality. For no reason can be given for just that limitation which it stands in His nature to impose (Whitehead 1925, 178).

Whitehead postulates God as the final ground for there being anything definite despite the "unfathomable" superabundance of possibility. Like the Causal argument, which it resembles, this one rests on "all or any" concrete data being given, and is indifferent to whether the actual world is a paradise or a torture chamber. God's nature is totally inscrutable. Unlike the Causal argument, however, and despite Whitehead's use of the traditional language of personal pronouns and talk of "His nature" causally "imposing" arbitrary limitations, this argument does not purport to require an actual causal entity at its conclusion. "God is not concrete," Whitehead writes, "but He is the ground for concrete actuality. No reason can be given for the nature of God, because that nature is the ground of rationality" (Whitehead 1925, 178). God, at this period of Whitehead's thought, is a Principle, not an actuality.

Whitehead thinks that this metaphysical requirement provides the logical space within which religious persons may fill in the details, depending on actual experience.

> The general principle of empiricism depends upon the doctrine that there is a principle of concretion which is not discoverable by abstract reason. What further can be known about God must be sought in the region of particular experiences, and therefore rests on an empirical basis (Whitehead 1925, 178).

I find myself unconvinced that this argument does much to secure even a logical space within which theists can construct doctrines more to their liking. Certainly the use of personal language for this Principle is simply based on old tradition. The fact that Aristotle used "θεος" in connection with his Prime Mover (in the "entirely dispassionate" way approved by Whitehead) might account for the use of "god" for this Principle as a matter of rhetoric. It does point up the analogy. But the honorific capital, turning "God" into a proper name, roots in Christendom's baptism of Plato and Aristotle (Ferré 1996, 75–98) and is close to out-of-bounds, while the use of "His" in this context is a clear foul. Further, besides the use of tendentious language to which the argument earns no right, Whitehead's logic wobbles between "entity" and "principle." The introduction of Aristotle's Prime Mover suggests an entity, and Whitehead starts by explicitly endorsing this suggestion:

For nothing, within any limited type of experience, can give intelligence to shape our ideas of any entity at the base of all actual things, unless the general character of things requires that there be such an entity (Whitehead 1925, 173–74).

But then he announces that his analogue to Aristotle's Mover will be just a Principle, explicitly disclaiming actuality for this Principle, which nonetheless he describes in personal, causal language as "imposing" "His" nature. A final puzzle defeated even Whitehead himself, since he changed his mind about it: how can a Principle *do* anything if it is not "concrete actuality"? When it came time for rethinking, he pronounced his "ontological principle": "The ontological principle can be summarized as: no actual entity, then no reason" (Whitehead 1978, 19). This effectively rules out the suggestion that somehow god can be a reason for the actuality of the world while remaining other than concrete actuality. Appealing to a Principle bakes no bread.

In *Religion in the Making* (Whitehead 1926), based on the second set of Lowell Lectures, Whitehead turns from the analogue of the Causal argument to an analogue of the Design argument. The argument here is considerably more developed, involving elements of his quasi Causal argument as well as anticipating themes from *Process and Reality*, already in gestation. Whitehead's thought about God had come far in the year between lectures. Most important, he had dropped the indefensible view that God is not actual but still an explanatory influence. Several times in *Religion in the Making* he plainly states the opposite: "God is that non-temporal actuality," he writes, "which has to be taken account of in every creative phase" (Whitehead 1926, 91). Why so? Because (in an argument echoing the previous lecture):

> The boundless wealth of possibility in the realm of abstract form would leave each creative phase still indeterminate, unable to synthesize under determinate conditions the creatures from which it springs. The definite determination which imposes ordered balance on the world requires an actual entity imposing its own unchanged consistency of character of every phase (Whitehead 1926, 92).

Now the argument has subtly shifted. The "imposing" is done not by a Principle but by an actual entity, and what is imposed is not simply "limitation" but, far more significant, "ordered balance." And the actual entity providing this balance from *beyond* the world (in one phase of the process) is also *immanent* in the world (in another phase), actively implementing purpose. "The purpose of God is the attainment of value in the temporal world" (Whitehead 1926, 97). The harmony in God's nature, constituted by God's perfectly envisioning all abstract possibilities in their mutual relationships, provides a consistent, unchanging loom on which the finite threads of the world can weave themselves, not without conflict but with underlying stability. If there were no God to provide this "ordered balance," there would be no world at all. "There would be no creatures, since, apart from harmonious order, the perceptive fusion would be a confusion, neutralizing achieved feeling" (Whitehead 1926, 100). Whitehead insists that the primal order is a necessary condition for, not a product of, any world.

> It is not the case that there is an actual world which accidentally happens to exhibit an order of nature. There is an actual world because there is an order in nature. If there were no order, there would be no world. Also since there is a world, we know that there is an order. The ordering entity is a necessary element in the metaphysical situation presented by the ac tual world (Whitehead 1926, 101).

Here, as we recognized in connection with the family of Design arguments in general, we may have doubts. Must we judge that orderliness is not an intrinsic capacity of the fundamental events that constitute nature? Whitehead writes with confidence that primal orderliness must be externally "imposed," but arguments at this deep level of metaphysical intuition are awkward, and assertion tends to be met less by counterargument than by simple counterassertion. Further, we can quickly agree with Whitehead that "since there is a world, we know that there is an order," but we may balk at the gap between this and his next sentence where he takes for granted that this acknowledged order entails an "ordering entity." The situation, as we saw, is not so simple a matter of inference. Apprehensional premises and value judgments are required to bridge these two sentences. Certainly many reasonable minds will be led to cross from "there is an order" to "there is an ordering entity" (Whitehead's powerful intellect being one example), but as an argument this is less than compelling.

Whitehead lists three "formative elements" as metaphysically necessary for the world of finite events. These are the boundless energy of becoming that he calls Creativity, the realm of pure possibilities that he calls the Eternal Objects, and God. He holds that the first two alone are not sufficient since "this creativity and these forms are together impotent to achieve actuality apart from the completed ideal harmony, which is God" (Whitehead 1926, 115). I doubt that Whitehead has yet made a convincing case for absolutely requiring a "completed ideal harmony" before finite harmonies can begin to be woven by creativity on possibility, but we have not yet examined *Process and Reality* to see what further considerations he may offer.

Before leaving *Religion in the Making*, I should note, but not pursue, a variation on the Moral argument offered by Whitehead as a defense for having "complicated" his metaphysics by adding a God over and above the world. His reason is that the alternative would lock evil into the ultimate nature of things. He acknowledges that it would be easier to make do with the first two formative elements, creativity and possibility, and then to say, "Thus creative indetermination attains its measure of determination. A simpler metaphysic would result if we could stop at this conclusion" (Whitehead 1926, 92). But destruction of achieved harmonies, ugliness, lesser levels of beauty in place of higher—all of these are copiously found in our experience of the world. If this empirical world exhausted all that is, such evils would end the story, and loss would become ultimate. All that stops the slow slide into lesser and lesser levels of complex harmony, the slide into evil, is the steady, nontemporal presence of a good God, purposefully helping to nurture innovation and the retention of achieved beauty.

> Every event on its finer side introduces God into the world. Through it his ideal vision is given a base in actual fact to which He provides the ideal consequent, as a factor saving the world from the self-destruction of evil. The power by which God sustains the world is the power of himself as the ideal. He adds himself to the actual ground from which every creative act takes its rise. The world lives by its incarnation of God in itself (Whitehead 1926, 149).

This is a profound argument, defending against the possibility that our moral intuitions can ultimately be frustrated. It rests on basic values. What needs simply to be recognized here is that the Moral family of arguments, even more obviously than the others, reflects and relies on our deepest intuitions into what is ultimately right or wrong, fitting or absurd, decent or unacceptable. Whitehead articulates eloquently the intuitions of many when he chooses the word "good" to characterize the kind of limitation that God, according to his theory, imposes on the world. Any kind of limitation, as long as it is self-consistent, would serve the metaphysical function Whitehead earlier proposed. But quite literally this is not *good* enough for him at the end of this book. He writes:

> The limitation of God is his goodness. He gains his depth of actuality by his harmony of valuation. It is not true that God is in all respects infinite. If He were, He would be evil as well as good (Whitehead 1926, 147).

For Whitehead, who was not conventionally religious, this constitutes a personal faith commitment of the deepest sort. The fact of order in our world is empirically indisputable; the assertion that this order proves that God must exist as its explanation is metaphysically problematic, but the affirmation that

God's own conceptual order and divine purpose excludes evil is religiously powerful. Many will resonate to this. We shall return to these themes in the next section on pluralism as well as in the following chapter on evil.

Process and Reality was Whitehead's master work. It is as difficult as it is rewarding, but in it Whitehead worked out important additions to his ideas about the importance of a god for his metaphysical system as well as the religious attractiveness of God. I hope in the following paragraphs to lay out the essential points without indulging in excessive Whiteheadian scholasticism.

I shall present this in terms of three functions Whitehead proposes in *Process and Reality* for his fully ripened concept of God. The first two I consider principally metaphysical in motivation; the third I find primarily religious.

By the time of *Process and Reality*, in which the ontological principle, which I cited earlier, was fully formulated, Whitehead was fully content with the idea of God as an actual entity. God was to be offered as a reason for things, and "no actual entity, then no reason" (Whitehead 1978, 19). Moreover, "God is not to be treated as an exception to all metaphysical principles, invoked to save their collapse. He is their chief exemplification" (Whitehead 1978, 343). Therefore, God would share the bipolar character of all actual entities, consisting in a mental pole and a physical pole. The one thing God would not share with the finite actual entities is their "epochal" character, coming to an end and perishing. God is the one nontemporal actual entity, a divine permanency invoked for reasons we have seen above, to provide a constant background of perfectly harmonious ideal limitation to make it possible for finite entities to actualize themselves in intelligible social relationships. This key difference between God and all other actual entities (which Whitehead did not see as an "exception" to his metaphysical principles) is expressed by calling finite, temporal events "actual *occasions*" while God is described as the one actual entity which is not an occasion but a permanent feature (coeval with creativity and the eternal objects) with which the world of finite occasions is in constant mutual interaction.

Acknowledging the bipolarity of God, with both mental and physical poles, gave Whitehead a systematically coherent way of "locating" the realm of pure possibilities in the context of the ontological principle. Without God, the embarrassing question might arise: "But what to do with the eternal objects? They are offered as 'reasons' but they are not actual. Have you not violated your own ontological principle?" Whitehead's reply was to place them, as Abelard had done with the Forms (Ferré 1998, 76), in the mind of God. The mental pole of God, which Whitehead called God's "Primordial Nature," grasps all possibilities in all their abstract relatedness. They are eternal and so is the envisagement. But this abstract realm, though invoked in systematic explanations, does not violate the ontological principle, since the mental pole of God is only one pole of a fully actual entity. The other, the physical pole, which Whitehead called God's "Consequent Nature," serves another function, to which I shall return in due course.

Whitehead has here made a reasonable use of his doctrine of God to avoid the unintelligibility of a free-floating realm of abstractions. Unlike Plato, Whitehead conceived of pure possibilities as abstractions, not as mysteriously powerful Forms, real and effective in themselves. If abstractions are going to have a status in reality at all, it seems they need a mind in which to exist as ideas. God, once introduced into a system (for whatever reasons) neatly serves the purpose of providing a cosmic mind to contemplate the universal realm of pure possibilities.

But is this the only possible solution? Full-throated Platonism would decry the need, denying the characterization of eternal objects as mere "possibilities" or "abstractions," and offering instead a Realm of Forms invested with a reality superior to any mere actualities struggling to embody them in space-time (Ferré 1996, 46–55). Or we could compromise, acknowledging with Aristotle the importance of the formal aspect of things, insisting (in keeping with the ontological principle) that they can exist only in actual substances, but (parting company from Aristotle and Whitehead) proposing that all actual entities are finite and "epochal." That is, we might hold even more strongly than Whitehead to his rejection of "exceptions" to the metaphysical principles and argue that all actual entities are actual *occasions*. This would retain the benefit of a "locus" for ideal possibilities, in the mental poles of the finite entities making up the world, while avoiding serious puzzles introduced by the notion of a "nontemporal" entity. Such an entity would by definition be a contemporary to all occasions, but Whitehead strongly rejects causal relations between contemporaries. How could a nontemporal entity interact with temporal occasions? God's mental pole seems eternally occupied with unchanging contemplation and incapable of temporal activity, but God's physical pole, if lacking the "epochal" grasping that could place it in some "given actual world" (Whitehead 1978, 66), is temporally coextensive with a world made up of an endless sequence of contemporary occasions and so excluded from causal influence.

Being rid of these puzzles would be a significant advantage, but the disadvantage of losing a central mind, devoted to timeless contemplation of the eternal objects in their primordial togetherness, is that all pure possibilities might never be thought together at once in this way. In a universe made up entirely of finite entities, nothing would guarantee it. Would this be a serious loss? Whitehead was sure that it would be, as we have seen. He was afraid that without a harmonious background of contemplated possibilities there could never be a world at all. Metaphysical intuitions may differ on this. If finite entities, no matter how minimal their mental capacities, are capable of prehending one another, including the real possibilities incorporated in their immediate "given world," and if more highly evolved entities with powerful mental poles are fit to entertain alternatives to physically presented possibilities, especially when aided by sophisticated linguistic symbols, does there really need to be a central envisioning at all? The possibilities would be the same, whether centrally envisioned or not. Whitehead does not suggest that God's contemplation alters them in any way. Perhaps the loss of this function for God would not be devastating, after all.

But at this point Whitehead adds further functions, related to the last but not quite identical. These I plan to treat together. They are the functions of God in launching and luring every actual event toward the actuality it becomes. (1) *Launching*. Whitehead holds that every actual occasion begins with a "subjective aim," an ideal for what it might become. This ideal is present from the very beginning of concrescence, guiding what will be excluded from the immediate environment through negative prehensions as well as offering a goal of harmony for those prehensions that are positively included in the rising of an occasion out of its predecessor world (Whitehead 1978, 224). Whitehead attributes this primordial aim to the good purpose of God to maximize the quality of each concrescent individual entity. But, according to Whitehead, God does not leave it at that. (2) *Luring*. In every entity there comes a phase within the concrescent moment in which the given physical environment is compared to what might be but is not. This is the phase of "conceptual reversion" in which relevant alternative possibilities are entertained by the actualizing event. Here, too, God is at work as a lure, offering from the bottomless store of pure possibilities the relevant ones that might make for a richer outcome. At first Whitehead describes this as something that just happens, making novelty possible in a world that would otherwise merely repeat what it finds. But later he adds, "In conformity with the ontological principle, this [process] can be [explained] only by reference to some actual entity" (Whitehead 1978, 250).

> Every eternal object has entered into the conceptual feelings of God. Thus, a more fundamental account must ascribe the reverted conceptual feeling in a temporal subject to its conceptual feeling derived . . . from the hybrid physical feeling of the relevancies conceptually ordered in God's experience. In this way, by the recognition of God's characterization of the creative act, a more complete rational explanation is attained. The Category of Reversion is then abolished; and Hume's principle of the derivation of conceptual experience from physical experience remains without any exception (Whitehead 1978, 250).

Whitehead is pleased to be able to side for once with Hume, and also to achieve a still tighter system by tying conceptual reversion to God's activity. But neither of these motives are strictly compelling. Hume's authority is not absolute, but even if we accept his strict principle here, Hume never denied that ideas can lead to other ideas. The phase of conceptual reversion could be understood as "relations of ideas," one idea suggesting its opposite, or some complex new idea not created *ex nihilo* but mentally constructed out of available materials (Ferré 1998, 146–56). Furthermore, the ontological principle only calls for explanation in terms of actual entities. But there is already an actual entity present: the concrescing event itself. Calling in God is not necessitated by the principle. If God is available in the system anyway, then this is a possible use. It tidies up loose ends and ties otherwise unrelated matters more closely together, legitimate aims of all theorizing. But these functions of launching and luring by themselves are hardly enough to require that God be introduced in the first place. The rising of a subjective aim in a new entity is no more mysterious than the rising of a new entity out of creativity's relentless drive. Perhaps, in a phrase from *Religion in the Making*, this could be understood as "creativity with a purpose" (Whitehead 1926, 114), the "purpose," tendency, or vector always being toward maximal achievement of harmony in complexity. Subjective aim need not be externally imposed for each new moment of creativity. It might instead be implicit in the meaning of creativity itself. Similarly, conceptual reversion need not be accounted for by divine spoon-feeding from outside the mental pole. It might simply be the sort of thing that minds do, namely, entertain ideal alternatives to what is given. The "relevance" of these alternatives could be provided by context, both physical and (in high orders of mentality) symbolic. The syntax of language, as anyone who loves to read dictionaries knows, can lead far into the realms of the purely possible. Entities lacking language must remain closer to "home," the physically given.

One final function for Whitehead's God in *Process and Reality* relates, appropriately, to "last things," understood in several senses. In one sense it refers to the final phase of an actual occasion's concrescence. This has the theoretical advantage of rounding out a role for God at every stage of concrescence. At the *launching* (opening) phase, God provides the entity's subjective aim. At the *luring* (developing) phase, God offers ideal richness for possible novel harmonies. And now at the *leaving* (objectifying) phase, God offers special divine preservation for whatever positive the occasion manages to achieve. Actual occasions, as we have seen, are moments of subjectivity. They "perish" as subjectivity as soon as they achieve full objective actuality. As Whitehead puts it, "In the organic philosophy an actual entity has 'perished' when it is complete" (Whitehead 1978, 81–82). But this perishing is only as something for itself. Once it perishes as a *subject*, weaving incompatible possibilities into a self-consistent actuality, it becomes available as an *object* with definite achieved characteristics on which future occasions can build. If its novel achievements are prehended by successive moments and incorporated into a sequence of satisfactions, perhaps even further enhanced, this reiteration of the initial occasion constitutes its pragmatic usefulness and its "objective immortality." As Whitehead says, "The pragmatic use of the actual entity, constituting its static life, lies in the future. The creature perishes *and* is immortal. The actual entities beyond it can say, 'It is mine'" (Whitehead 1978, 82).

In contrast to its dynamic life as *sub*jective, the occasion ends by becoming statically "*super*jective," giving itself to the future; but *as subjective*—as a value for itself—it is no more. The inevitable fact of futurity (not as actual, of course, but as the inescapable indefinite domain of creativity yet to occur) is vaguely felt in every present as a vector, assuring that present achievements mean more than simply present enjoyment. For some this could be enough: to enjoy the intrinsic values of achieving while they are subjective and also to anticipate the instrumental value of these achievements when they will have become objective. Whether this is "enough" or not, however, is a matter of judgment. On the negative side, if "objective immortality" is all we can expect, then there can be no guarantees that one's hard-won achievements will prevail in the self-determining future. Successor occasions may ignore or lose or distort what for them will be data to be processed in their own coming to actuality. Then, the subjective values having perished, the pragmatic values unutilized, there would be nothing left of those bright moments of novelty once woven with creative excitement on the loom of possibilities.

To guard against this sad demise of the "last things" bequeathed by actual entities to an uncertain future, Whitehead argues that God can and does take up these last things into the divine Self and make them lasting. This is the function of the "Consequent Nature" of God introduced earlier. God, in keeping with the pattern of all actual entities, is bipolar, with both mental and physical functions. While the analogue of our mental pole, expressed in God's Primordial Nature, forever envisions the eternal objects in all their intricacies of relatedness, God's analogue of our physical pole feels the world's many concrescing entities, takes all their achievements into the Consequent Nature, and makes an indescribably rich harmony from them all, making of the Many, One. Then this pattern of cosmic achievement is reflected back again to the world in its myriad moments of individual creativity in which the One reverts to Many in a never-ending conversation between God and the world. In one phase the world is "many" in its subjective, self-determining moments; in the next phase the world is "one" in God's benevolent patterning, which always weaves the best out of the superjective heritage bequeathed by the many. This guarantees that the heedless future will not say the last word about last things. Every genuinely positive achievement of finite entities will persist, somehow, in the Consequent Nature of God, not only adding intrinsically to the beauty of the divine experience, but also becoming pragmatically available again within God's lure to the temporal world when circumstances once more are right.

This vision of beauty is itself a beautiful vision. Perhaps its sublime scale and endless rhythmic balance are enough to justify it aesthetically. Perhaps the encouragement toward the good it offers concerning our individual "last things," where everything worthy lasts, is enough to justify it morally. Perhaps the reassurance it offers regarding a cosmos in which there are no "last," or final, things, but always fresh resurgences of creativity grounded in endless permanent possibility and good purpose is enough to justify it religiously. I personally admire the vision, but I find no compelling reason to affirm it, even in a basically Whiteheadian worldview.

If we are not to make God a metaphysical exception, it is extremely difficult to see how God's Consequent Nature can prehend the finite entities that make up the "many" of the world. Physical prehension is normally of the objective world in one's immediate past. But God, as the alleged nontemporal actual entity, is prior to every finite moment of concrescent energy. Nothing is supposed actual prior to God. Moreover, contemporaries are simply out of causal relationship to one another. God is contemporary with all temporal entities. Therefore God is simply out of causal relationship to the "many" that make up the world. God's prehension of the world cannot be by physical feelings. It is worse than incoherent, it is contradictory to take the normal metaphysical principles and apply them without making God an exception.

Other solutions have been attempted. Some abandon the concept of God as a single, nontemporal entity, making God, too, a train of "epochal" occasions, thus allowing one or another phase of the "many" to be in the past of one or another of God's concrescent moments. Others rely on the concept of hybrid physical prehension as God's method of feeling the contemporary world, implying that God feels the "many" by a sort of mental telepathy in which the physical drops out of sight. This requires a good bit of creative theoretical extension of a concept, though epistemologically important, that was barely mentioned by Whitehead himself (Whitehead 1978, 308; Ferré 1998, 281–84). Given a religious commitment to a theistic religious world model, these and other tactics may help to diminish the cognitive dissonances implicit in Whitehead's own doctrine of God. Other friendly critics have much worthwhile to add to the conversation (Neville 1995). My point does not depend, however, on detailed assessment of such theoretical rescue operations. My point is that for all their acknowledged beauty, and for all the plausibility that further creative speculation may bring, these proposed metaphysical functions for God are not theoretically compelling, even within a generally ecological worldview inspired by Whitehead.

Although Whitehead made several references to God in his later writings, no additional metaphysical functions were proposed. Still, before we move on, it is worthwhile reflecting on a passage in *The Function of Reason*, originally lectures given in March 1929 at Princeton University, just three months after the completion of *Process and Reality*. In these lectures Whitehead deploys his metaphysical categories in an argument from physical cosmology that resonates today with discussions of the anthropic principle mentioned earlier in this chapter. Whitehead lived before the day of Big Bang cosmology and did not couch his remarks in terms of "fine tuning" of physical constants without which there could have been no stable universe, no solar system, no planet Earth, and no intelligent species reflecting on the remarkable coincidences that made such reflection possible. But Whitehead's general wonder at the evolutionary career of the physical order, leading to greater complexity despite the pressures of entropy, is of the same sort. It leads, in the same way, to a rejection of explanation by coincidence alone. In this variant within the Design argument family, Whitehead writes:

> The material universe has contained in itself, and perhaps still contains, some mysterious impulse for its energy to run upwards. This impulse is veiled from our observation, so far as concerns its general operation. But there must have been some epoch in which the dominant trend was the formation of protons, electrons, molecules, the stars (Whitehead 1929, 24).

It is tempting for doctrinaire materialists (whom Whitehead here calls "the physiologists") to ignore or deny the problem of accounting for the physical universe's trend toward complexity, life, and mind. But this is bad theorizing.

> The universe, as construed solely in terms of the efficient causation of purely physical interconnections, presents a sheer, insoluble contradiction. The orthodox doctrine of the physiologists demands that the operations of living bodies be explained solely in terms of the physical system of physical categories. This system within its own province, when confronted with the empirical facts, fails to include these facts apart from an act of logical suicide. The moral to be drawn from the general survey of the physical universe with its operations viewed in terms of purely physical laws, and neglected so far as they are inexpressible in such terms, is that we have omitted some general counter-agency (Whitehead 1929, 25).

Whitehead's analogy is organic. As mentality is to living systems, so some "general counter-agency" is to the physical universe. Something more than is known about physical categories needs to be added to account for the "appetition towards the upward trend" (Whitehead 1929, 24). Appeals to the "physical constants" will not suffice, since these are exactly what need to be explained. That they are "fine tuned" to such an astonishing degree, Whitehead did not know; but he would not have been surprised. At Princeton he did not mention the word, "God," but the cosmic actual entity who launches and lures each new moment of creative self-actualization toward its maximum potential for complex harmony was clearly implicit in what he said next:

> This counter-agency in its operation throughout the physical universe is too vast and diffusive for our direct observation. We may acquire such power as the result of some advance. But at present, as we survey the physical cosmos, there is no direct intuition of the counter-agency to which it owes its possibility of existence as a wasting finite organism (Whitehead 1929, 25–26).

The cosmos is a "wasting finite organism," for Whitehead, but full of a hard-to-detect agency pressing constantly upward against the downward trend to dissolution. What is most remarkable is that this "counter-agency" has been winning! The universe has not gone out with a whimper into its entropic death. Instead there has been more and more structure, complexity, novelty. Most complex of all, so far as we now know, is the human organism, capable of reflective symbolic thinking. And perhaps some day—Whitehead seems to hold out this hope—our species may acquire the power (by some technological advance) to place this "counter-agency," God, under "direct observation."

I cannot claim to know what Whitehead had in mind at this point. It is hard to imagine what sort of instruments would be capable of observing even the quasi-physical Consequent Nature, but much less the deficiently actual Primordial Nature, through which God, on this theory, works to launch and lure the world's "many" toward increased complexity in the rhythmic embrace described in *Process and Reality*. But it is quite possible to imagine some observations that might tend to confirm that the world contains a pressure toward life and mind. Astronomers are hard at work on them as I write. Planets with liquid water would enhance the likelihood of life elsewhere in the universe. Explorations of Mars could confirm that life once appeared on that planet. If so, this would reduce the chances that the appearance of life on Earth was sheer accident, despite being completely unpredictable from what we know about electrons, protons, molecules, and even crystals (Rolston 1999, 348–70). Radio telescopes are being trained on distant stars to listen for signals of intelligent life. If observations of this sort should succeed in finding intelligence elsewhere in the universe, then both the anthropic principle (broadened appropriately) and Whitehead's postulated counter-agency would be greatly strengthened in credibility. It seems likely that in one hundred years, at the start of the twenty-second century, the human race will have quite a good sense of whether or not life and intelligence are widely supported in the universe. If they are, as I personally hope, the ecological worldview of creative, relational, beauty-generating energy will be all the more adequate to the facts. If they are not, it may be necessary to think more deeply about what it means to live on a uniquely kalogenic planet, bright with value against a dark background.

These are questions for the future to decide. Humanity has already begun to spend significant resources on answering them. If we find that Earth is not alone in nurturing life or even intelligence, nothing since Copernicus, Galileo, and Newton will have had an equivalent impact on our worldview. But even if this happens, it will not count, quite, as an empirical confirmation of God. God is a possible explanation. Whitehead, though he did not name names at Princeton, clearly believed that the best explanation of the impulse for the world's "energy to run upwards" is God, omnipresent, nontemporal, functioning as appetition and lure. But, as we have seen in the previous discussion of this point, that is not the only possible explanation. Given *creativity*, the energy of making new actuality, and given *possibilities*, entities themselves in the world's character as "many" could embody the thrust to novelty. The physical categories would need to be radically revised, on this hypothesis, to include the subjective aim toward ever greater complexity and value that is currently omitted from physicists' accounts of fundamental entities. But kalogenesis, even the anthropic principle, does not need to rely on a centralized, coordinating "counter-agency." Even Whitehead was ready to call the needed agency "diffusive" as well as "vast." God is an answer, but not the only answer, to the improbabilities surrounding the evolution of life and mind.

Reasons why this conclusion could be a good thing both for postmodern world religion and for wider ethics grounded in personalistic organicism will be offered in the following section.

QUESTION OF PLURALISM

The point of the preceding wrestle with Whitehead was not to discredit his views on God, but simply to show that they are not theoretically coercive, any more than are the other, more familiar arguments from the various families of theistic "proofs" examined earlier. When wrestling with so powerful a thinker, one hopes at best for a draw. If this was achieved, then new vistas open toward a postmodern pluralism of religious traditions—not lazy relativism, not cynical agnosticism, not dogmatism, either theistic or atheistic, but respectful openness to alternative RWMs from within a positive framework that can support mutual respect and ethical cooperation in an otherwise fractured world.

I am, in other words, hoping for a new, much wider ecumenical movement. This would build on the achievements of twentieth-century discussions among Christians within the World Council of Churches and beyond it. It would lay the basis for serious rapprochement not just among Christians, Eastern and Western, Catholic and Protestant, but also among theists, Christian, Jewish, Muslim, and other. Not just among theists of various stripes, but also between theists and polytheists (as Native American, African tribal, and some popular modes of Hindu religion present themselves), and between theists and religious atheists (as classical Buddhism, Taoism, and Confucianism may be understood). Not just among acknowledged religions, but also between these and the functioning religions of naturalists and humanists—all could come to the table, as could dedicated socialists and communists intensely committed to social and economic justice. Wiccans, too, embracing the divinity of the Earth, could join the dialogue, as could environmental romantics who worship Gaia.

This sounds fanciful, and in part it is. New possibilities are always introduced to the world by fancy, the power of mentality (*a*) to take account of what is not embodied in the immediate environment, (*b*) to value these possibilities "up," (*c*) to entertain them repeatedly, elaborating and improving them, and (*d*) eventually to arrange the actual world so that room is made for such fancies in actual conversations, in actual efforts to realize them, and in actual institutions created to preserve such achievements and amplify them. There were dreamers behind the creation of the World Council of Churches, the United Church of Christ, the United Methodist Church. Before institutions materialize out of dreams powered by purpose, all such ideas seem fanciful.

In this case, what is needed to support the dream of wider postmodern ecumenism is a fundamental, independently defensible worldview (1) capable of being firm enough to support strong, life-nurturing, cooperative ethics, both social and environmental, while (2) capable of being flexible enough, at the same time, to permit alternative specific modelings by quite different traditions and imagery. This is not a wholly new conception. William James wrote seminally of the religious "over-beliefs" that outgrow their theoretical foundations (James 1902, 503–9). Every religion, as far as pure theory is concerned, goes too far. But this "too far" need not be the everlasting source of conflict. It can instead be the occasion for celebrations of specific historical traditions and the stimulus to wider consciousness among all participants.

I once urged that the fortunate underdetermination of RWMs by underlying metaphysical theory be noticed and embraced in a limited pluralism I called "Polymythic Organicism" (Ferré 1976, 109–21). My mother tried to dissuade me, not from the concept itself, but from the jaw-breaking terminology. She shrewdly suggested that I use the acronym "PMO" instead. I rejected this at the time, on grounds that it sounded too much like a toothpaste additive.

(Mother's riposte: "Good! Then it might sell!") Mother knew best, as usual, at least on the unsalability of the full phrase. I have heard, among other near-misses, my view labeled "Polymorphous Perversity" (à la Freud), but hardly ever what I intended. Therefore I now gracefully retreat. Let my wider ecumenical dream be known as "PMO," then,—or, better, "PMPO" (Polymythic Personalistic Organicism) to embrace more than "organicism" alone but, more specifically, the personalistic organicism I have been attempting in more recent decades, and especially in these last three books, to define.

Volumes could—and should—be written, detailing the ways in which various major RWMs can, and cannot, be articulated in the spirit of PMPO. In the next few paragraphs I shall make just a few sweeping gestures in that direction.

The most advanced work on this program, showing the capacity of Whitehead's philosophy of organism to interpret living imagery of current religious faith, is to be found in the writings and conferences of those generally known as "process theologians." These comprise an extraordinarily able group of thinkers, broad in interests, irenic in temperament, committed to Christianity, mainly liberal Protestants, nimble theorizers well-versed in Whiteheadian literature. Many are associated with the Center for Process Studies located at Claremont Divinity School in California. There is also a respected scholarly journal, *Process Studies*. A substantial number of these men and women, clergy and lay, inside and outside academia, can be found in far-flung locations in America, Europe, and Asia. (A "Note on the Center for Process Studies" can be found at the end of this book.)

Process theologians, for the most part, value Whitehead's thoughtful weaving of the concept of God into his philosophical vision. There are in-house disagreements over the question of how strictly to hew to Whitehead's original texts about God. The pioneer work of Charles Hartshorne (1962), deeply Whiteheadian in spirit and a creative philosopher in his own right, should not be classed with the "process theologians" at all, except perhaps as a lodestone attracting many capable theological followers. But he was indeed enormously influential among the process theologians. Hartshorne was the first to address seriously the weighty theoretical problems, described in the previous section, posed by the lack in Whitehead's God of "epochal" moments by which the world could in principle be prehended. Hartshorne solved these to his satisfaction by making a major change in the doctrine of God: in keeping with the metaphysical principles for all other entities, God's personal identity would be carried by a sequence of occasions. God's infinity would be expressed only in the Primordial Nature (which is deficiently actual); God's Consequent Nature would be actual but finite.

Hartshorne wrote as a philosopher, mainly concerned for theoretical consistency and coherence. John B. Cobb, Jr., although highly gifted philosophically, wrote instead as a theologian deeply versed in Whitehead and Hartshorne, above all concerned to find an adequate vehicle for Christian thinking and ultimately for Christian faith grounded in mental integrity. His *A Christian Natural Theology* (Cobb 1965) represents a milestone in synthesis. It remains the classic locus for interpreting a Christian doctrine of God in terms of Whiteheadian philosophy of organism. Beyond this, addressing the still more specific centrality of Jesus Christ in Christian faith, Cobb's *The Structure of Christian Existence* (Cobb 1967) provides a basis for thinking about the Incarnation and the Holy Spirit.

From the perspective of PMPO, Cobb's enterprise and the flood of works within the literature of process theology remain highly interesting and legitimate. The conceptual apparatus for interpreting the Christian RWM is clearly supported by personalistic organicism. It is possible to make a strong case for God from this perspective, as both Whitehead and Hartshorne chose to do. I believe, moreover, that the case is stronger when the models of Christian theism are articulated by Whiteheadian theory than when they are interpreted through other theoretical vehicles, such as Platonism, Aristotelianism, or Heideggerianism. There is a closer, more natural relationship to our scientific understanding of the evolving universe when the philosophy of organism is allowed to provide the underlying interpretation. If a concept of God can be plausibly shown to play a key anchoring and stimulating role vis-à-vis our universe and the flux of our own living experience, so much the better for Christianity. Here are abundant resources for faith seeking understanding. In any wider ecumenical conversations carried on in the spirit of PMPO, Christian process theologians, their friends, sympathizers, and critics (Neville 1991) will have a prominent part, too.

Judaism and Islam are in principle open to similar interpretation, but in practice the dialogue has not moved strongly in this direction. Both are strongly monotheistic traditions, for which the single God of Whitehead, in endless, detailed dialogue with the world, would make a good theoretical substrate. But there are many historical particularities in both religions that would require internal reflection and in some cases painful modifications. God as "Jehovah" is sharply criticized in Whiteheadian theory, for example, but in the Jewish tradition it is also held that God's "still small voice" can come as a whisper rather than a roar (I Kings 19: 11–12). Jewish thinking is multifaceted and highly sophisticated. Perhaps Jews will come willingly to the ecumenical table. For Muslims, it will be still more difficult, since the doctrines of God's absolute power and inscrutable will have long been central to most varieties of Islam. A "Whiteheadian Muslim" sounds at the moment like an oxymoron. But there is virtue in clarifying deep differences as well as in finding points of accord. From outside the tradition it is difficult to assess the amount of flexibility of interpretation that might exist now, or later. History shows that these matters can be fluid. One thing we need to remember is that, as we saw above, the "appropriateness" of the interpretation of a model by a theory is something that can only be judged by the worshipping community itself. Meanwhile, dialogue, especially where deep differences emerge, becomes more focused, intense, and potentially useful.

Most of the world's dominant religions are forms of monotheism, but polytheisms are also widespread. The spirit of PMPO will have no trouble inviting these modes of spirituality, as well, to the wider ecumenical table. In our own culture the polytheistic gods and goddesses of ancient Greece and Rome have vanished, but David L. Miller finds much contemporary polytheism to celebrate in his *The New Polytheism: Rebirth of the Gods and Goddesses* (1974). As we saw in the previous section, monotheism is a possible but not a compelling aspect of Whiteheadian organicism. Perhaps the universe is not centrally organized, after all. Perhaps there are entities, with minds and purposes, who have evolved beyond individual human minds. This would require some theoretical work to show how this could be conceived, but the notion is not entirely outlandish. Samuel Alexander (1859–1938), a distinguished British philosopher, insisted that we keep our minds open to the strong likelihood that the "nisus" toward complexity and higher orders of emergent traits may result in beings who would be as gods to us (Ferré 1996, 249–58). The idea is speculative, of course, but that is what is called for in any postmodern ecumenical movement. Let the "Reason of Plato" (Whitehead 1929, 10) soar! Huge numbers of religious persons, especially those often overlooked in Africa, have a characteristically profound sense of temporality for which the philosophy of organism could serve as clarifying articulator (Booth 1977). The opposite is the case for Hindu polytheists. Here is another case where ecumenical dialogue, if attempted, will reveal essential differences. South Asia's characteristic denial of the reality of time will challenge every "process" interpretation of Hindu RWMs that hang on the illusory status of history. It is not clear whether this divide can be bridged at all. Certainly organicism of any sort depends on taking time seriously. There is no such thing as a "timeless organism." The vision of the universe itself is relational and pulsational. Much will depend on whether Hindus themselves come to understand their many treasured stories set in narrative time as more precious and authoritative than their also revered theories about time as *maya*, mere tricky illusion. Postmodern ecumenical dialogue may merely serve to clarify insurmountable differences at this point. But this, too, might be healthful for all concerned.

"Religious atheism" sounds odd to Western ears accustomed to the monopoly of monotheisms in our, and immediately neighboring cultures. But for classical Buddhists it is not odd at all. Buddhism in its oldest form (and in Theravada, Zen, and other expressions) has no conceptual place for God or gods, Some forms of Buddhism are functionally polytheistic, and would be seated at that part of the ecumenical table, but the purest forms are atheistic. In the spirit of PMPO, they also would be welcome. One of the fortunate aspects of our finding that theism is not theoretically necessary in personalistic organicism is the special welcome this gives to Buddhist spirituality. Theism is a plausible path to take, as we saw; but the judgment of atheism is also fully to be honored. Again, Cobb has been a leader in Christian-Buddhist dialogue. There is much to talk about between Buddhists, convinced that there is no substantial, enduring Self, and Whiteheadians, agreed that the Self is best understood as a series of perishing moments. The ground is well-prepared for interpretation of the Buddhist ontology of self by the philosophy of organism. Buddhist "decentralized," nontheistic spirituality is also plausibly articulated within personalistic organicism. Other admirable work on ecumenical outreach, complementing the pioneering done by Cobb in *Beyond Dialogue: Toward a Mutual Transformation of Christianity and Buddhism* (Cobb 1982) and by Masao Abe in *Zen and Western Thought* (Abe 1985), has been done by Jay B. McDaniel, whose biography combines service under a Zen master with academic instruction from Cobb. McDaniel reports that at first he hoped that Buddhist Emptiness could be equated, somehow, with God, but: "The more I have talked with Zen Buddhists, the more it has seemed the truths to which they have awakened are different from those which enliven Christian faith" (McDaniel 1989, 93). A truly broadened ecumenical movement will not attempt to translate everything valuable into God-talk. The possibility of a rich atheistic spirituality is enhanced by the open texture of personalistic organicism, as ready to respect the absence as the presence of God.

Not all forms of atheism are recognizably religious, as Buddhism is. But on my understanding of "religious," discussed in the previous chapter, it is none the less true that some apparently secular atheists are in fact expressing their own mode of spirituality and therefore deserve a place at the ecumenical table. I take this to be the case particularly for dedicated reformers in quest of political or economic justice for the oppressed. As it happened, the Civil Rights movement for the liberation of African-Americans was led by theists. But socialist or communist reformers may burn with a similar intensity without a God to meet in prayer. Here the personalism of personalistic organicism takes special prominence, accentuating the unique value of persons, rich or poor, male or female. In a postmodern ecumenical movement, the spirituality that cares widely and deeply for justice will deserve a place among other modes. Personalistic organicism stresses the underlying relatedness of morally significant beings to one another and, within the relatedness, the intense importance of the special kinds of experience of which human persons are capable. Those whose religion is to see and honor caring, empathy, and justice will legitimately participate in the dialogue, with or without God or gods, with or without temples, gongs, or rituals. I am proud to acknowledge my father's risky pioneering in this ecumenical direction through a chapter, "Light for Communists and Other Pagans," in his delightfully controversial book, *The Sun and the Umbrella* (Ferré 1953, 127–56).

There are others whose most intense and comprehensive values are found not so much in the relationships between people, through social forms of justice, as in the relationships among people and the natural entities that make up the environment. That mode of spirituality needs to be drawn to the ecumenical table, too, and in the spirit of PMPO will have an honored place. Personalistic organicism offers a theoretical foundation for the strong sense of intrinsic value in nature that fuels religious naturalism, such as that of Ursula Goodenough (Goodenough 1998). The standard worldview of modernity has drained value from nature, reserving all worth for human valuers while creating dilemmas for understanding the place in nature even for that restricted domain of human mentality (Ferré 1996, 107–82). In legitimate reaction against this dessication of the springs of value, romantic spiritualities regarding nature rise to counter this terrible dryness. Personalistic organicism can well interpret the RWMs of such religious naturalism. The feast is set. Let those who hunger approach!

But not everyone is welcome. Even PMPO, though widely pluralistic, is not infinitely hospitable. Personalistic organicism, if it stands *for* something, must also stand *against* something. Only in this way will it demonstrate its difference from sheer relativism. Who, then, will *not* be welcome at the ecumenical table? First, quite obviously, fanatics will exclude themselves. Ecumenical dialogue is not a proper context for single vision, for claims to exclusive truth. By the same token, but at the opposite extreme, radical skeptics will not come. They exclude themselves from the start by discounting or scorning the quest itself, for which the dialogue is set. To be totally sure of the answers, and to be totally sure that there are no answers, both guarantee missing the feast.

Other positions will be excluded because of their content. Satanism, for example, if understood as the worship of evil and ugliness, will not allow interpretation by a worldview in which kalogenesis, the creating of beauty, is the universal and highest aim. Spiritualities of egoism, likewise, will not find any intelligible interpretation in a relational, ecological ontology where all things are to some extent part of each other, and where sympathy and empathy are the experiential roots for growing the special beauties of moral society. Likewise turned away will be all religions resting on exploitation, whether of other human beings (as in slavery) or of the natural environment. Exploitation and oppression are indivisible. Personalistic organicism will speak for the oppressed, but not the oppressor, for the exploited, not the exploiter. Therefore, there is no weak "anything goes" permissiveness in the pluralism of PMPO.

Ugliness and evil occur. In a spirit of "mutual affirmation and admonition" (Nickle and Lull 1993, 66), the ecumenism grounded in personalistic organism will face this fact with sorrow and determination. Each participant at the generous table of postmodern ecumenism will vow—each with a characteristic vow, and each to a characteristic ultimate—that ugliness and evil will not be allowed to have the last word.

7

UGLINESS AND EVIL

Ugliness and evil are by definition unpleasant subjects, but (alas) they are so pervasive in experience that a book like this, on ethical life in its ultimate context, needs to look at them without flinching. What are they, at bottom? What are their relations to one another? What are their general types? How should personalistic organicism interpret their ubiquitous presence in human society? In nature? What do they imply about the character of the cosmos? More practically, what do they require of us in daily living, in feeling and in action?

These are not easy questions for me, in particular, to ask. My position makes beauty central. I celebrate this universe as "kalogenic." Metaphysically, I locate the ultimate self-justification of existence in the processes that generate experienced beauty (Ferré 1996; 339–70). Epistemologically, I ground the beauty of knowing in the knowing of beauty (Ferré 1998, 366–73). Ethically, in the first part of this volume, I point to actualizations of beauty—complex harmonies of subjective satisfactions in varying degrees—as the primary intrinsic goods for the furtherance of which all duties and obligations spring. But where there are ethical rights, there are also wrongs, and while beauty abounds, so does ugliness. How does my kalogenic evolutionary naturalism handle these glaring realities?

Shallow optimism would wither in this glare, but my kalogenic version of personalistic organicism, though unrepentantly upbeat, has never been simply optimistic. Optimism is sure that good will prevail. I am not. But in the face of evil and ugliness, personalistic organicism offers real grounds for hope. Creative opportunities for actualizing better possibilities rise with every new moment. Sometimes, regrettably, the opportunity is missed; sometimes, tragically, achieved beauty is destroyed and replaced with something worse. But the arrow of time does not slope merely downward. There are stubborn counterpressures upward as well. Happy outcomes, though not *guaranteed* (as the optimist thinks) are not *ruled out*, either. But I realize that supporting this modestly hopeful thesis will require some clarification and argument.

EVIL AS UGLINESS

First, what are the domestic relations between evil and ugliness? The "ugly" is normally an aesthetic category; "evil" suggests the ethical. There are exceptions, especially one-way leakages from the aesthetic to the ethical. One can say, without straining language, that the boss is in an "ugly temper," and this generally conveys a negative ethical judgment, for example, that the boss is making unfair criticisms, is flailing out at employees in hurtful ways, and so forth. Other aesthetic words, such as "grotesque" or "distorted," can refer to acts or motives carrying obvious ethical freight. More positively, speaking of a "beautiful" act or life sometimes (depending on context) can confer ethical praise. It is less frequent to find "evil" or its cognates used in aesthetic contexts. At this writing, "bad" is used in some circles as a term of aesthetic praise for rock bands and rap singers, but as a word of general approval it is so loosely applied that it hardly counts one way or the other. And thus we get the hint from popular usage that aesthetic categories are wider than ethical ones. Aesthetic terms can perform ethical jobs in addition to their own, while ethical terms are more closely confined to whatever it is that distinguishes their domain.

Just what does distinguish "ugliness" from "evil"? Both are evaluative terms indicating the failure of a positive norm. First consider the ugly. "Beauty" provides the norm for which "ugliness" is the antonym. Just as we find degrees of beauty as we slide along the slopes of the normal curve plotting acceptable uses of the term, so also we find degrees of ugliness. Equally important, there are different types of both, and a vocabulary to match. "Plain" resides somewhere in the valley between these normal curves, an aesthetic category suggesting neither much beauty nor much ugliness. "Sublime" is on the opposite side of the "beauty" curve, far from the ugly, while "grotesque" and "horrifying," and their like, convey analogously extreme degrees of ugliness, on the far side from "plain." Along the "ugly" curve one may encounter the abhorrent, bizarre, deformed, distorted, drab, frightful, ghastly, hideous, homely, macabre, monstrous, repulsive, unattractive—and much more. Finding the *mot juste* in the domain of ugliness can be a delicate matter.

Interestingly, most of these terms can be imported into ethical discourse with the implicit or explicit addition of the adverb, "morally," before the adjective. A sight may be *visually* abhorrent, hideous, or repulsive to us if it seriously violates our norms of visual satisfaction, whether in jarring composition, clashing color, or unpleasant subject matter. An action, similarly, can be *morally* abhorrent, hideous, or repulsive if it seriously jars our norms of ethical behavior. The key in both cases is recognition of a state of affairs disturbingly outside the norm that we have accepted to govern in what we believe are the circumstances.

Again we need to ask: just what is added by the adverb, "morally," when it is attached to an adjective of more general appraisal? It will not suffice to answer that in the case of "morally hideous" actions we are dealing with "moral" norms, rather than aesthetic ones. This is true, but uninformative. Such circularity gets nowhere. To escape from it, we need to identify what is distinctive about moral norms. It cannot simply be that moral norms seize us more tightly, make demands on us more imperiously. This may not in all cases even be true. Sometimes it would seem that aesthetic norms command at least as strongly. In the lives of some great artists, the aesthetic imperative seems to drown out the moral. *All* norms become obligatory upon acceptance; in real life norms constantly trump one another, but not always in the same way. Some would hold that moral norms *should* always trump all other norms, and perhaps they are right, but if so, why? What is it about moral norms that makes them so important? Why should evil be held worse than ugliness?

I reject the implicit dichotomy. Moral evil, in my view, is a special kind of ugliness. It reflects distortion of norms when suffering, frustration, and harm to centers of subjectivity are at stake. As I argued in the previous part of this book, rich subjective satisfaction of entities in relationship—maximum coordinated beauty—is the goal of goals in a kalogenic worldview. Frustrating or destroying this goal of experienced beauty is the essence of moral evil. Causing or condoning the ugliness of suffering is prima facie evil.

Although all evil is ugly, not all ugliness is evil. There is even more ugliness in the world than there is evil, since the latter is a subclass of the former. The problem of ugliness is broader than the problem of evil. Both can and should be handled together, as I trust the remaining sections of this chapter will show.

TYPES OF UGLINESS

It is conceptually clarifying to distinguish between the two great types of ugliness (and, by subsumption, of evil). There is ugliness that rises from the failure to seize opportunities to enhance *possible* beauty, and there is ugliness that results from active destruction of *actual* beauty. These two distinct types deserve a name. I call the first source of ugliness Philistinism, the second Vandalism (Ferré 1996, 360). Put in more traditional language (Frankena 1973, 45–48; Ferré 1995, 79–80), the former represents a violation of the principle of beneficence (Do good!); the second reflects a breakdown of the principle of nonmaleficence (Do no harm!).

Philistinism has long been a term of aesthetic reproach against those who simply do not care about higher or finer things. As *The Oxford English Dictionary* puts it, a "Philistine," in this context, is "a person deficient in liberal culture and enlightenment, whose interests are chiefly bounded by material and commonplace things" (*OED* 1992; "Philistine," 4). And from such philistine attitudes we should not expect creative advances toward new achievements in subjective satisfactions, delicately harmonized from rich complexity. Philistinism is to beauty as obscurantism is to theory: both reject the importance of advance from achieved levels of satisfaction. Both recoil from the dangers of the better when it threatens to replace the "good enough." Therefore, both let possible opportunities go unexplored and unrealized. Without refreshment from the new, however, "the law of fatigue is inexorable" (Whitehead 1929; 18), resulting in a gradual loss of quality, even in what was meant to be saved.

Philistinism is *sub*-normative. It embraces the status quo too tightly. It may do so in the name of protecting its own sort of beauty, but compared to what it prevents, its beauty is relatively ugly. Such grosser beauty stands in the way of finer beauty, something "better," either morally or nonmorally understood.

Vandalism, in contrast, is *anti*-normative. It rejects the achieved beauty of the status quo by actively destroying and degrading it. If philistinism got its name from the crass culture that mocked Samson in Palestine, vandalism recalls the willful, ruthless destruction that a Germanic tribe, the Vandals, was remembered for wreaking (in A.D. 455) on Rome. Whether they were really that bad is debated by historians, but the word, "vandalism," legacy of their activities of the fourth and fifth centuries, has come to stand for objectless, malevolent destruction. Fifteen centuries later the referential status of this word does not depend on a verdict from ancient historians. We are far too well aware of this phenomenon as a raging reality in the present world.

These two types of ugliness seem exhaustive. One fails to build, the other tears down. One shrinks from creativity, the other destroys what has been created. Both appear in human culture; both seem to appear also in nature. It is time to look at each more closely.

Cultural Ugliness

Human culture is the usual place to begin thinking about most normative questions, but as we do, we should remember how unusual human culture is relative to the world as a whole. It is the one place, as far as we now know, where ideal imaginings, remote from current circumstances, can steer activities—often complex, subtle, and sustained—toward distant goals. Culture, in other words, is the realm of *purpose*. Likewise, it is the one place where alternative possibilities vie for approval, the one setting in which attraction by the ideal shares an effective role with compulsion by the actual. Culture, in other words, is the domain of *freedom*. Consequently, it is the one place where norms of all sorts—technical, aesthetic, ethical, religious—guide actions of all sorts by internalized felt obligation. Culture, in other words, is the locus of *responsibility*.

Responsibility to satisfy an accepted norm may be real but also may be shirked. This is the enormous difference between persons in culture and objects in nature. A falling body has no responsibility to satisfy the law of gravitation. Such a law is descriptive of how the physical world works. But norms, though describing an ideal, are prescriptive for entities that can entertain them conceptually. Once accepted, they generate their own sense of obligation, since every norm carries an "ought" with it. Once a student pilot understands and accepts that an airplane "should" be turned with coordinated use of ailerons and rudder, then this pilot recognizes the obligation to turn in that way, *not* to skid the plane around with rudder alone or yank it against opposing yaw with just the ailerons. This is in the first instance a technical norm. If you want to turn the plane most efficiently, without dislodging unsecured cargo, and so forth, follow this prescription. Since it is normative, not coercive, it need not be followed—and it is constantly violated. Beginning pilots, despite keenly feeling the obligation to produce a coordinated turn, may simply not know how to combine hand and foot pressures in such a way as to succeed. There are so many different angles of bank, so many power settings, so many sensations to sort through, so many muscles to control! Such a well-intentioned pilot recognizes the obligation, feels the responsibility, but simply cannot live up to the ideal. Explanation helps: ground school understanding of the forces involved and clear inculcation of the conceptual ideal. Demonstration helps: instructor-provided cockpit experience of what a coordinated turn should look and feel like through direct acquaintance with the actualized ideal. But only practice, repeated attempts to guide personal action by the accepted norm, will make perfect. Meanwhile, sloppy, uncoordinated turns generate felt pilot shame and instructor patience. If this seem a problem, just wait until we get to practicing landings!

I took my first examples of violable norms from aviation, because it illustrates how even a technical norm can generate strong felt obligation and sometimes severe self-criticism when an ideal is failed. An uncoordinated turn is ugly. This broad aesthetic term applies wherever an ideal is disappointed. Conversely, when a pilot succeeds in accomplishing a graceful coordinated maneuver, with mind and muscles and machine all harmonized, the pilot knows the intrinsic satisfaction that is beauty. True, there are other values attained as well. The successful application of the norm has minimized wasteful drag and kept fuel consumption efficient; it has also kept unsecured cargo from sliding around in possibly hazardous ways, but in addition to all those technical rewards there is unmistakable aesthetic reward. We need not stop here. Achieving such a technical norm may also satisfy an ethical obligation, to the extent that the harm or help of passengers is concerned. The ugliness of uncoordinated turns can lead to the ugliness of airsickness, or at least to discomfort, for those who have entrusted themselves to a pilot's skills. This becomes even more obvious when we use the norms of landing as our example. A pilot has a moral obligation to treat passengers with consideration, at a minimum to return them to the terminal in one piece! This seepage between the categories helps us see that there is no absolute "line" between technical, aesthetic, or ethical norms. Such designations are applied relative to what we are considering: Fuel efficiency? Complex harmonies of subjective satisfaction? Creating or preventing suffering for others?

I have thus far assumed that the agent has accepted the norm by which degrees of ugliness are to be judged. But this is not necessarily the case. If not, may such judgments still be made? Yes, they may still be made by observers who accept the norm as they assess performance. A student pilot who rejects the ideals of coordinated turns and smooth landings, stubbornly persisting in rough cross-controlling and rejoicing in jerky behavior, is publicly an ugly flyer. The norms of aviation are community norms. And since technical norms expose one to more immediate and obvious consequences than do many subtler measures of ugliness, it is likely that pilots who resist them too long will find their careers in the air not only ugly but short.

Cultural ugliness encompasses a huge domain, from ugly drivers on the highways to ugly auto salvage yards on the byways. In the ugliness of strip malls we are confronted with the ugliness of lives consumed by consumption. Philistinism lives here.

The ugliness (and evil) permitted by philistinism is endemic and ubiquitous. All that is required for its increase is to let the tragedy of the universe work unhindered. This "tragedy of the universe," as I call it, is the fact of constant loss. Physicists encounter it as entropy, described either (in thermodynamics) as the inevitable reduction of available energy in closed thermal systems or (in statistical mechanics) as the increase of random disorder. Without some balancing input from new energy or fresh source of order, unchecked growth in entropy would result in what Bertrand Russell, in "A Free Man's Worship," eloquently described as the Heat Death of the Universe (Russell 1951). But we need not look for tragedy on such a grand scale. It is the same principle that accounts for my desk always getting messy without my help or intent, requiring an extra expenditure of energy to get it back in shape. Machines break down; they do not fix themselves. Batteries and champagne go flat on their own. Skills deteriorate. Bodies grow flabby. Living organisms die.

Philistinism in culture is an accomplice to entropy. This is because refusal to invest in something better leaves the status quo vulnerable to decay. A minor sort of ugliness of this sort can be illustrated by a lazy violinist. Playing the violin takes the buildup of technical skills, without which one could not be called a violinist at all. But let us consider a violinist turned philistine. The imperatives implicit in the technical norms of bowing, fingering, and so forth, are accepted as relevant, but practice is a bore. Why work to maintain or improve presently acquired skills? The relative ugliness of a scratchy bowing technique is "good enough," this violinist decides. But with that decision about a technical norm come direct aesthetic consequences. The technical norms of string playing support aesthetic norms of musical enjoyment. Some degree of musical beauty may come from such playing, but it could have been much better (and at one time probably was), if only fresh energy had been invested in maintaining or improving skills.

Perhaps our philistine violinist plays in a small orchestra. If so, the aesthetic consequences of deteriorating musical norms are amplified by the richer complexities of sounds that can be attempted by an aggregation of players. What could have been a delightful concerto in the experience of all the players and the audience turns aesthetically disappointing. One member of the group has not cared enough, and the achievement of the whole is less than it could have been. Like a householder who lets the lawn and shrubs grow weedy in a neighborhood where everyone else works hard to keep ahead of entropy, our philistine violinist has permitted aesthetic blight. But such ugliness is more than aesthetic if we assume that the other members of the orchestra and the audience were to some extent harmed. Aesthetic suffering is real suffering. Listening to a bow scratching on an ill-tuned violin can be torture. Evil has been done.

I do not mean to exaggerate the weight of this little example. But we should notice minor evils as well as great ones. Small ones of this kind can give us a clue to the structure of one major type (the philistine type) of ugliness in culture, against many examples of which we may well rage. I have in mind such philistine outrages as the smug failure, even in currently wealthy American culture, to address urgently the ugliness of wasted minds through unreformed schools that fail to challenge and inspire, of widespread suffering through unreformed health care systems that leave millions without adequate treatment, and of millions more held by careless chains of race or class or gender below their possible levels of personal fulfillment.

Most of these are conservative failures in a nation grown increasingly too enamored of the status quo to let imagination play with ideal large-scale alternatives, or to allow room for empathy with the sufferings of the less fortunate. Some citizens may remain open to inspiration by the creative possibilities of a better future, but the raw stuff of imagination, the imagery on which imagination feeds, is so grossly distorted by the media of popular culture toward self-regarding consumption that it is difficult under present circumstances to predict a noble future. Some ideas for change toward a more beautiful culture will be provided in the last part of this book. But how to get beyond philistinism in practice is a deeper question. It requires grappling with the tragedy of the universe.

The sources of this first type of ugliness and evil are relatively easy to understand. They are sloth, dullness of imagination, weak powers of empathy, timidity before the new, exaggerated focus on the self, defensiveness of past achievements—all natural features of evolving society. There are even good reasons to defend the practical importance of what may look like philistinism to those inclined toward impatience or utopianism. Without healthy conservatism, without a major effort to perpetuate a stable status quo, neither biological species nor human cultures could establish themselves, nor could they perpetuate themselves against pervasive disintegration in a universe of constant perishing. Practical reason, with its slogan, "If it ain't broke, don't fix it," has a powerful role to play, fending off harebrained schemes of radicals, most of which would only make things worse. Likewise, within culture, the discovery of the self—of personal value in the first person singular—remains a magnificent achievement in the story of the universe. Sloth itself is simply an expression of finite energy where every actuality is finite. For personalistic organicism, there is no "problem" in understanding the origins of philistine evil and ugliness in a world where creativity needs constraint if actual value is to be achieved and passed on.

But what of the ugliness and evil from vandalism? This second type is not one of inaction, where opportunities for betterment are passively lost, where concern for others is merely missing. It is, rather, one of action, of defacing achieved value, of seizing opportunities for worsening the status quo, of delighting in the negative reaction of others.

We are surrounded in our culture with evidences of such ugliness. Graffiti sprout on our most beautiful public buildings and monuments, ear-shattering noises pour from sidewalk boom boxes and cruising cars. Knives slash great paintings; hammer blows defile even the *Pietà*. Arson fires ruin synagogues and churches; the daily news is full of drive-by shootings, rapes, and tortures.

Active ugliness offers so many examples that it is hard to choose. Shall we consider genocides? Then which ones? Those of the ancient Vandals or Huns? Those of European settlers against the indigenous North American peoples? Those of Hitler and Eichmann and their many accomplices? Those of the Hutus? Those of the Serbs? Or shall we reflect on terrorist acts? Shall these be political, such as the attack on Israeli athletes at the Munich Olympic games, Pan American Flight 103 at Lockerbie, or the World Trade Center bombing?

Or shall they be public outrages exploding from private outrage, like the indiscriminate bombings of the Oklahoma City Federal Building, Atlanta's Olympic Park, abortion clinics, and gay clubs? Or should we focus on the carefully aimed shootings of doctors daring to provide women with abortion services, or the meticulously planned destructiveness of the Unabomber's hand-carved mail bombs?

Do we need examples at all? This is an ugly side of life which, when merely touched on, spews so many concrete instances, not just large and public, but even more small and private, that we are in danger of drowning in bile. Luckily, my point in making these allusions hardly depends on details. I simply want to deal with the question where such things fit, how they are understandable, in a kalogenic worldview of naturalistic, evolutionary, personalistic organicism.

I believe there are two principal categories under which to interpret the ugliness and evil of vandalism, broadly understood. They are both distortions, but they are distortions of fundamental urgencies of life. Put in the ethical terms offered in first part of this book, some reflect the dark side of the Principles of Beneficence (Do good!); others the Principle of Justice (Be fair!); a few combine in a twisted way to reflect them both.

As Whitehead pointed out, the urge to live, live well, and live better is deep in all life, including life in culture (Whitehead 1929, 8). The Principle of Beneficence is a way of channeling life's aggressive desire to survive and prosper. It certifies the legitimacy of creating good, a least as a first step to a rich and whole life. Survival is prima facie good; survival with satisfactions is prima facie better; survival with complex, harmonized satisfactions is better still. In this both the magistrate and the carjacker can agree. To obtain a good life, the former has used social resources (especially education), has deferred gratification, has adapted within wider social relationships and institutions; the latter has followed the urge to live and live well in an aggressive, antisocial, shortsighted way. What was only a prima facie good, possessing the car, was taken by the carjacker as a genuine good under the circumstances, which it was not. The carjacker's temporary, shortsighted, pain-producing "good" may have been colored, as well, by a twisted sense of righting the unfairness of life, in which "they" have so much more of what it takes to live well. In this the Principle of Justice plays a distorted role, as it often does, disguised as vengeance.

Vengeance for perceived wrongs, not just for individuals like the carjacker but for classes, tribes, and nations, plays a huge role in generating the ugliness of vandalism. Rapists may feel nature's urge to live and reproduce in the lust of their bodies, but even more important to their disgustingly evil crime may be the hunger of their minds to balance the books against women or to take revenge upon some particular woman. In such ways the mirror image of justice is distorted into giving justification, and the cycles of abuse are extended. Writ large, this same analysis can be applied to ethnic and religious groups who maintain old hatreds by cherishing memories of injustices done, flogging their own imaginations bloody to warrant unspeakable acts of torture and terrorism against the ancient foe. The "memories" may be largely manufactured, unbalanced distortions of truth, but revenge is sweeter than accuracy. Further, when hatred fills the heart, there is no room for historical scholarship, nor for the subtle bonds of empathy on which moral relations must be founded. When the imperatives of a distorted Principle of Justice are powerful, it is easy to listen to expansionist leaders who claim "Lebensraum" in the name of both Justice and Beneficence, the creation of *our* good, so that *we* (who so richly "deserve" it) may live, live well, and live better.

Great hatreds need to be nurtured and fed, on the conceptual side, by mental imagery of past wrongs and present grievance, and, on the affective side, by prohibition of cooperative human relations with the foe, lest natural bonds of sympathy be formed. Any cure, however gradual, would need to reverse both these conditions. I shall return to this thought in the final chapter of this book. Right away, though, I should disclaim any expectation that vandalism, aesthetic or moral, will ever be fully "cured." Nastiness, I fear, will be an inescapable part of the human condition.

Take as a final cultural example the pure meanness of those highly educated, culturally advantaged persons who malevolently create computer viruses to infect the work and destroy the achievements of other persons around the world. What could motivate such disinterested infliction of ugliness and pain? My hunch is that one dimension of the act is affirmation of the virus maker's technical superiority, making something "beautiful" in its way—as "beautiful" as a terrible weapon can be lovely to its makers. J. Robert Oppenheimer, who with his brilliant colleagues opened the atomic era on July 16, 1945, by testing the first nuclear device at Alamogordo, New Mexico, named in clear aesthetic terms one compelling motive for doing so, despite the immanent end of World War II. It was "technically sweet." Donald Hornig, another participating scientist, said, "It was one of the most esthetically beautiful things I have ever seen" (Lamont 1965, 299). The clever virus is similarly "technically sweet" to its hidden maker. It is something done well, then done better. In its twisted way, it manifests creativity even in the interests of malevolence. It may also represent the revenge of an unhappy mind, but here in the absence of psychological data required for each case, I merely speculate. What is not so speculative, on my view, is that cultural ugliness of this sort will be with us for a long time. In a kalogenic universe, given free agencies capable of distorting both the urge to live and the felt imperative for fairness, we must expect human culture to contain much that is evil and more that is ugly.

Natural Ugliness

It is generally granted that there is abundant ugliness in culture, but nature presents a different case. Can nature be ugly? Can nature cause ugliness? There is a strand of romanticism that sees beauty and only beauty in everything natural. There is indeed so much beauty in nature, at every scale, from every angle, that one might well feel a certain discomfort in even raising the question of ugliness, much less evil, in this connection—a context that seems to invite philosophical category mistakes.

There are indeed ticklish issues involved, especially from the kalogenic perspective of personalistic organicism. One of these is raised by the necessary involvement of subjectivity in ugliness. Without some center of aesthetic appreciation, the root experience of beauty in any of its degrees would have no locus. The same must be true for ugliness. Without an experiencer to be offended, what status could be given to the aesthetically "offensive"? Just as the prime locus of beauty is rooted in the complex satisfactions of experience, so the prime locus of ugliness must lie in the revulsion of some subjective center. This does not mean that ugliness (or beauty) is entirely subjective. The objective conditions of experience supply the other half of the story. Both beauty and ugliness are subjective outcomes dependent in large part on what is given. Subjectivity, however, remains a necessary condition.

Thus, some may well ask: If the topic is *natural* ugliness, does this subjectivity requirement not make much of the issue irrelevant? Can it matter to a rock whether it is set in an aesthetic stink hole or on the edge of a grand vista? Is the question of ugliness in nature (and consequently, even more obviously, of evil) not simply out of order?

My answer to this motion to dismiss the question in general is to distinguish various questions in particular. I agree that rocks as rocks cannot be aesthetically offended. They, and many other natural objects that may be grouped as "aggregate entities" (Ferré 1996, 324–27), have no sense organs, cannot perceive anything, have no center of awareness or preference, are not even analogously "selves," and for these reasons cannot know ugliness or beauty. In connection with such natural objects, categories like these, presupposing some unitary experience, are misapplied. But rocks and mountains, lakes and clouds, stars and galaxies, though prominent features of nature, do not exhaust what is important in nature. Many other entities outside culture do warrant these categories. Earth overflows with sensate life in quest of various satisfactions, capable of repulsions and frustrations. Much evolutionary energy has been expended in many species on beautification for competitive advantage, in mating, for example, showing that seeking beauty need not be disinterested, simply for itself alone. Other species have developed various sorts of ugliness as repellants against predators. Some plants use repulsive odors to ward off enemies; some fish display horrible appearances that, with luck, preserve life, at least for a while. Our living world is filled with aesthetic attractions and repulsions. And where beauty can be a competitive advantage, lesser degrees of beauty, unfortunately for the less attractive, can be a handicap. Issues of beauty and ugliness in nature (now taking "nature" to refer to what is apart from human culture) are certainly a legitimate topic for discussion.

First, does it make sense, in the context of nature, to speak of philistine ugliness? Of course there is good sense to be made when we refer to human neglect of nature, where finer or richer values could have been realized but were not. But that will be grist for another discussion, to follow in the next chapter where environmental ethics will take center stage. At the moment I am interested in what it might mean to speak of nature "missing opportunities" for higher orders of beauty quite outside the context of human moral agents.

There may be many examples, but none more poignant for an ecological worldview than the manifest contrast between our planet, Earth, and our two closest neighbors in the solar system. Earth, seen from space, is a shimmering jewel of liquid water, swirling cloud, and varicolored land masses. Earth burgeons with life. Innumerable centers of preference—balancing, competing, creating—fill every nook and niche. A chorus swells from land and sea and air with Earth's vibrant song of life. But neither Venus nor Mars can join that outpouring of value. Why not? It seems that both our neighboring planets just missed what was necessary for Earth's unparalleled achievement. Venus is Earth's twin sister, with approximately the same mass, density, and rock composition. It has mountains and valleys; its year is not very different from ours at approximately 225 Earth days. But somehow the atmospheres of the two planets began to diverge. Carbon dioxide, which on Earth has come to be bound up in the liquid water of our oceans and in rocks like limestone, is free in the atmosphere of Venus, where it makes up 98 percent of the atmosphere. The heavy blanket of this largely CO_2 atmosphere both presses hard (with eighty-eight times the pressure of Earth's surface pressure) and intensely heats Venus, through its greenhouse effect in trapping incoming radiation from the Sun. Venus' surface temperature, 900° F (480° C), is far too hot for liquid water or for life to exist under current conditions, though analysis of the atmosphere suggests that at one time water might have been present, before the temperature started to rise. "If only" matters had gone differently, the surface of Venus might today be rich with value-seeking centers of subjective satisfaction—so at least we may speculate. But such beauty was not to be. The chance, if ever there was a chance, was lost in the sulfuric clouds that boil around that world.

Mars, Earth's smaller neighbor planet on the other side from Venus, is only half Earth's size and has only one-tenth the mass of our planet. It does not suffer from the oppressive atmosphere of Venus. This is part of the problem for

Mars, since despite the many common characteristics shared with Earth (seasons, a similar length of day, a magnetic field, similar rock composition), the relatively weak gravitational pull of this less massive planet has apparently allowed much of its atmosphere to escape into space. Lost, too, were the relatively warmer temperatures that allowed liquid water to flow and—possibly— that nurtured the appearance of primitive life forms, now probably extinct. Whether life ever existed on Mars, or even still exists in some form, the abundance of living beauty that "might have been" is missing. Cold and relatively still today, Mars can hardly compete with the incomparable beauty of the Earth. If a god is responsible for designing the Sun's system of planets, this is a philistine deity who could have done much more to stock the universe with subjective satisfaction.

Switching scales abruptly from planets to molecules, a different sort of comparative ugliness in nature can be found in the field of genetics. Genetically caused birth defects are one example of philistine ugliness. Here is no tearing down of achieved order, but rather, due to a misread or absent or mutated sequence in the DNA that guides normal organic development, health and organic function that might have been is missed. A harmony goes sour. Possible fulfillment is transposed into the key of frustration and pain. Whether it be the heartbreak of early death from macrocephalic deformity, or the slow torture of Lou Gehrig's disease, or one of a large array of genetic disorders, nature has failed to achieve the best. This need not mean complete failure of all sorts of beauty, as the cosmologist Stephen Hawking has proven by his heroic fight against Lou Gehrig's disease, but it is doubtful that the beauty of the universe was enhanced by Hawking's need to engage in that terrible struggle with the remorseless advance of amyotrophic lateral sclerosis in his crippled body. Multiple sclerosis, sickle cell anemia, muscular dystrophy, cystic fibrosis—these and a host of other failures at the chromosomal level add to the loss, the sense of what might have been. Here in organic failure and pain are evidences of the omnipresent entropic pull in the universe toward disorder. In such places, where "might have been" speaks volumes about good and beauty not realized, we encounter again in its most baleful form the tragedy of the universe.

The tragic loss of possible beauty is what I have called Philistinism; the tragedy of destruction, tearing down what is already actual beauty, I have named Vandalism. Just as we have seen that nature misses opportunities, producing ugliness of the first sort, so we must realize that nature destroys what nature has first built up, resulting in ugliness of the second sort as well. There is no shortage of obvious examples. Here is where traditional theologians wrestle with what is often called "the problem of natural evil." Voltaire made much of one instance, the great Lisbon earthquake of 1755, which occurred on a Sunday during High Mass, when the Lisbon cathedral was full of worshippers. The beautiful cathedral was destroyed, and with it the lives of almost all trapped within. How could such senseless slaughter, worthy of the Vandals in full cry, be part of a "best of all possible worlds" (Voltaire 1992)?

Such a dramatic example is only one from a nearly infinite supply. A great meteorite, striking Earth near the Yucatán Peninsula of Mexico at the end of the Cretaceous Period, most likely caused a great worldwide extinction, not only of the dinosaurs, but also of ammonites and many sea creatures as well. From its enormous Chicxulub impact crater rose debris, darkening skies long enough to bring drastic changes to the planet and to devastate millions of years of patient evolutionary differentiation and increased complexity. Some researchers prefer a volcanic theory of the great Cretaceous extinctions, but the philosophical and religious point remains the same. Volcanos are huge phenomena, but much simpler than the entities they heedlessly destroy. Every living blade of grass in a meadowland turned to cinders by an eruption of ash and lava is more complex, more intrinsically valuable, than any great pool of overheated magma. Lest I be misunderstood, I am not saying that volcanos are unimportant, or without enormous instrumental value in the story of planet making. But the people of Pompeii, at the mercy of Mount Vesuvius about to blow, though powerless before the force of the eruption, were—each one—more valuable in and to themselves than were the giant forces that consumed them. One cannot call the destruction of Pompeii an act of vandalism, since it was not an "act" at all, but an event. Still, in the language of this chapter it was an event of vandalism, the imposition of greater ugliness on greater beauty.

These horrific events happen all the time, some caused by nonliving entities, such as shown in my previous examples (plus hurricanes, earthquakes, tidal waves, tornados, floods, lightning, wildfires), but many others are caused by living organisms. In nature it is not always the more noble, the more beautiful, that win the struggle to live. It is easier for humans to watch aardvarks lick out ant hills than to witness a wounded gazelle be devoured, still living, by scavenger birds and vermin. But nature vandalizes everywhere. A beautiful, intelligent cheetah can fall prey to a crocodile; a ravening school of piranha will show no mercy to the personal promise embodied in an unlucky human child. We should not forget the microorganisms, as well, the parasites and bacteria that invade and destroy domains of complexity and value which are orders of magnitude beyond their own. An extreme example of vandalism in nature is the effect of quasi-living AIDS viruses on a creative artist, who is gradually destroyed by them. Can anyone compare these values without a shudder of grief at their incommensurability, at the tragedy of the universe?

HANDLING UGLINESS

There are various ways of "handling" grief at the ugliness and evil of the world, cultural and natural, in which we live. We are thinking beings who need to handle disappointments theoretically. We are feeling beings who need to handle negative matters attitudinally. And we are active beings who need to handle frustrations practically. I shall end this "unpleasant" chapter with reflections and recommendations on all three dimensions.

The theoretical problem is greatest for theists whose RWM focuses on a perfect God: omnipotent, omniscient, and utterly good. How, they may be asked, can this kind of world be theoretically squared with that kind of God? If God can do anything and know everything and is motivated by complete benevolence, then should we not expect a world, both cultural and natural, very different from the one we actually find? Either God *wants* a world less full of ugliness and evil and is *unable* to figure out or implement such an outcome (in which case God is not perfectly competent), or God is *able* to plan and accomplish a less ugly world but really does not *care* to make it better (in which case God is not perfectly benevolent).

This classic dilemma for the traditional theist has been met at the level of cultural ugliness and evil by a "free-will defense" that can go far toward resolving that part of the problem. A perfect God, the argument begins, would not prefer android puppets over morally mature persons. But moral maturity requires moral agency, genuine freedom to respect or disrespect norms of action, both moral and aesthetic. This means that a perfectly good God might well prefer a cultural world in which it is *possible* for humans to engage in philistinism and in vandalism—if in such a world free agents can discover in practice what it means to become genuinely responsible, actual persons. The ugliness and evil of human culture, from highway littering to the Holocaust, can be understood, the argument concludes, as motivated by perfect wisdom and benevolence by an all-powerful God whose aim for human life on Earth is not to prefabricate a comfortable harmony for androids but to nurture the free growth of creative persons.

Confronted with the terrible unresolved suffering often caused by "man's inhumanity to man," defenders of the free-will defense may draw on auxiliary hypotheses about God's ability and readiness to comfort and recompense victims in another life beyond this world. Given such a life beyond—in principle an endless opportunity for growth or learning—even the worst vandals from this life can freely learn for themselves (though perhaps under different learning conditions) God's better way of personhood. Then the raw cognitive dissonance between a loving, fully empowered God and the grisly facts of human life can be overcome in a theory that allows hope that eventually this world's

ugliness can be justified in a Kingdom of God in which all women and men
will have freely learned how best to live with each other and with their Maker.

My father shared this fervent hope, in pursuit of which (despite, or perhaps because of, constant arthritic pain) he developed his own version of the
free-will defense (Ferré 1947). He believed that it was adequate to deflect cognitive dissonances set up by cultural ugliness. He was not daunted by the auxiliary theories of postmortem existence involved—he welcomed them. But he
came to the conclusion, after much pondering, that this theory alone is not
enough to deal with the problem of natural ugliness. Animal suffering is such
a vast reality that it cannot in good conscience be dismissed as merely part of
the stage setting for our human drama. And yet there is no moral lesson to be
gleaned by animals themselves from their own pain. The free-will defense
does not apply (Ferré 1986b, 23–34). For this reason, consistent with the theoretical motive that animates the argument as applied to human beings, it may
be necessary to add yet another auxiliary hypothesis, promoting the postmortem development of *every* life, not just human lives, up to the level of personhood. This was in fact my father's answer.

> If pain is real, God must have a purpose with it or the highest claim of re-
> ligion is palpably false. That purpose, too, must apply to every individ-
> ual that experiences the pain. We can accept no less a solution. It seems
> less and less possible to us to explain animal pain on the basis of life in
> general. Even though the individual animal may not know that it has
> experienced pain, it nevertheless has. Nor can we be certain that each
> animal has so much more pleasure than pain that animal pain can be jus-
> tified in that way. Pain often ends its experience and rounds off other
> experiences of suffering and fear. We have, for these reasons, come to
> feel that there is an evolution of each individual soul up to the level of
> self-consciousness, or at least human existence (Ferré 1947, 62).

Such answers are admirable for their theoretical consistency and their
depth of sympathy with the suffering of others—*all* others. They are not subject to easy refutation. Neither, despite Voltaire, is the properly articulated
view that this is the "best of all *possible* worlds." When Leibniz put this in its
classical form (Ferré 1996, 190), he was simply drawing an obvious conclusion from combining premises generally accepted by traditional theism: (1)
that God wills the best, and (2) that God can do whatever is logically possible.
But not everything that can be imagined is logically possible when thought
with something else, as in having one's cake and eating it too. These two
desiderata are not logically *com*possible. God's omnipotence does not extend
to doing the absurd. Therefore whatever God chose to happen must have been
the best *under all the compossible circumstances*. We should not expect to

know what all these circumstances were. We are not omniscient. But if the Lisbon earthquake occurred in a world chosen by a God who always chooses the best compossible outcomes, we can be assured (with deductive certainty) that nothing better could possibly have happened. It was certainly not the best imaginable, but it was the best possible.

This is the fundamental logic of theodicy in classical theism, even when the hard deductive edges of Leibniz' mathematical style are softened. The free-will defense argues that responsible personhood is not compossible with absence of free agency, and that free agency is not compossible with absence of ugliness. Therefore human permitted and human produced ugliness is "for the best," assuming an afterlife for compensation and education. If natural disasters are interpreted as God's method of educating persons, then natural shortcomings from the apparent best and destructions of the actual good can also be seen as for the "larger best." Predictability is a fundamental good, since without a predictable world, general norms of action would not be compossible. If nature's lawfulness results in destruction, therefore, this must in the long run be interpreted as for some larger best, though we may not be able to imagine exactly what it is. As long as religious commitments require that unlimited benevolence be inseparably joined to unlimited power in God, the general logic of Leibniz' "compossible best" is inescapable in religiously motivated theories handling ugliness and evil.

Although everything, no matter how apparently horrible or depraved, must turn out to have been "for the best" in classical (absolute) forms of monotheism, where God is unrivaled and perfect in every respect, this is not so for every type of theism. In polytheism there is a place for conflict among the deities, even if one of the gods, like Zeus, is ostensibly in charge. Things can go awry in such a universe. Even though Zeus can throw his thunderbolts and take his revenge, he cannot always have his way. His wife, Hera, among others, sees to that. The gods can be foolish, vain, distracted. If polymythic personalistic organicism (PMPO) should be modeled by such RWMs, the problem of ugliness and evil does not bite very hard. What, after all, can one expect in a world where the ruling powers themselves are sometimes philistine in their neglect, sometimes vandalistic in their malice? Unfortunately, the problem of evil in such RWMs is replaced by the problem of disunity. For many, the urge to find some central focus in the universe is too strong to settle for the loose amphictyony of cosmic powers represented in polytheism. If the cosmos is to be represented as a "decent order," something more like classical theism is desired.

Two forms of limited monotheism have been proposed in recent years that might satisfy this religious and intellectual thirst for unity but escape the intractable problems of classical theism. One is associated with the Personalist philosopher, Edgar S. Brightman; the other is derived from the Philosophy of

Organism of Whitehead and his successors. Either one might be proposed to serve PMPO in its ecumenical mission of interpreting varied religious world models as they struggle to deal with the issues of ugliness and evil.

For Brightman (1884–1953) and his followers, most notably Peter A. Bertocci (1910–1989), the absolutely perfect God of Christian tradition cannot be squared with the abundance of ugliness and evil we find in the world. Admittedly, many evils can be accounted for in ways compatible with a deity unlimited in benevolence and power. The free-will defense goes a long way to exculpate the Creator of persons capable of moral responsibility from having to take direct blame for the ugliness and evil that they permit or do. But even here there seems to be just too much horror to explain as "for the best." Such explaining, especially when it starts to deal with historical black holes of hatred, torture, and destruction, feels more like explaining away than explaining. There may be no "line" where theorizing ends and explaining away begins, but it happens, and judgments of this sort must be made. Brightman borrowed a term from mathematics, "surd," to refer to whatever defies attempted rationalization, as in the "irrational" numbers, roots, and the like. He called the evils left over, when all the rest had been handled by the best theories available, to be the "surd evils." In his own words: "A surd in mathematics is a quantity not expressible in rational numbers; so a surd in the realm of value experience is an evil that is not expressible in terms of good, no matter what operations are performed on it" (Brightman 1940, 245, n. 6). Even beyond human wickedness, the natural destructions of positive value caused by storms, earthquakes, diseases, and the like are impossible to handle theoretically, consistent with classical absolute theism, Brightman argues, and therefore demand to be recognized as surd evils.

If they really are "surd," or "nondisciplinary," evils, as Bertocci preferred to put it (Bertocci 1951, 396–99), then they will never be "explained" by theory, both Brightman and Bertocci acknowledge, but they can at least be located on the theological map, if we are willing to give up the presumption of universal absolutes for God's nature. In this way these evils can be handled theoretically, though not really explained. The problem of ugliness and evil in the first place is caused by the tension between the presumed unlimited benevolence and the presumed unlimited power of God. Perfect goodness in God's nature is too precious to question, but unlimited power is not. Since Personalism lends itself to endorsing analogies between finite human persons and the divine Person, Brightman finds no obstacle to hypothesizing that the irrational subconscious, recently uncovered in humans, may have a corresponding place in God. God's conscious will is wholly good, but even God must struggle with an irrational Given that is not always subject to divine control. Nothing *outside* God can threaten the cosmic unity provided by monotheism, but *within* God there are rages echoed in raging storms and furies expressed in explosive volcanos or cataclysmic meteorites. Brightman writes of the Given in God:

> God's will is eternally seeking new forms of embodiment of the good. God may be compared to a creative artist eternally painting new pictures, composing new dramas and new symphonies. In this process, God, finding The Given as an inevitable ingredient, seeks to impose ever new combinations of given rational form on the given nonrational content. Thus The Given is, on the one hand, God's instrument for the expression of his aesthetic and moral purposes, and, on the other, an obstacle to their complete and perfect expression. God's control of The Given means that he never allows The Given to run wild, that he always subjects it to law and uses it, as far as possible, as an instrument for realizing the ideal good. Yet the divine control does not mean complete determination; for in some situations The Given, with its purposeless processes, constitutes so great an obstacle to divine willing that the utmost endeavors of God lead to a blind alley and temporary defeat. At this point, God's control means that no defeat or frustration is final; that the will of God, partially thwarted by obstacles in the chaotic Given, finds new avenues of advance, and forever moves on in the cosmic creation of new values (Brightman 1940, 338).

Surd evil remains surd, irrational, but for Brightman and his followers the evil and ugly are always in a context of benevolent intention and attempted control that refuses to give them the last word.

Brightman's and Bertocci's way of handling the problem of evil has prompted much debate, both religious and philosophical. Religious objections, first, rise from the image of God as not fully sovereign. Is a God who is finite in this way—unable always to control irrational urges that sometimes overwhelm good intentions—really a fit object of worship? Put succinctly: Is a limited God worthy of unlimited adoration? Philosophical objections, second, may demand stronger grounds for dismissing the possibility that God is limited in benevolence rather than power. The evidence of surd evil would accord equally well with a fully empowered deity who simply does not care infinitely about the suffering or frustration of finite subjective centers. Is there a ground, independent of religious revulsion from such a thought, for rejecting this alternative hypothesis? Answers have been given, and these answers in turn parried, in the debates. This is exactly appropriate for the ongoing ecumenical discussion encouraged by personalistic organicism. Let the conversations continue!

The other limited monotheism with a well-developed stance on evil and ugliness is inspired by Whitehead. The fullest statement of this position, by

David Ray Griffin, draws out the logical implications of what it means, at depth, to be a persuasive rather than a coercive God (Griffin 1976). It means that if the finite world is to be the domain of causality, where physical prehensions weave a framework of stability in nature while mental acts of reversion inject genuine novelty within this framework, then God's role is not causal. God is the ever-available lure toward better relevant possibilities, first encouraging subjective aims toward richer harmonies of actual achievement, then taking up these achievements to preserve and extend them, but God is not, in the end, causally responsible for the outcome. God can be and often is disappointed by finite entities that reject the lure and settle for less than could have been achieved. God can be and often is anguished by finite entities that tear down actualized values of their predecessors. If God were a causal agent in the world, tinkering with the trajectory of bullets or adjusting the height of waves, overseeing the grinding of tectonic plates or stirring up convective currents in the atmosphere, then God would be responsible for not sparing the victims of gunshot wounds, not saving sailors capsized by high seas, not preventing the destruction of villages by volcanos and of coastlines by hurricanes. But that is not God's role in the world. God's role is to offer attractive possibilities to the finite agents that do make up the coercive powers in the universe, and to encourage their positive subjective reception of these possibilities. More is metaphysically impossible. Blaming God for cultural or natural ugliness and evil rests on a category mistake.

Traditional theodicy, justifying God's actions or inactions, is not to the point in a Whiteheadian worldview, since God is simply not an agent among other agents. This is not easy doctrine for traditional theologians to hear, but after absorbing fifteen years of pounding and misunderstanding, Griffin effectively defended his position against all comers (Griffin 1991). The key is to abandon the image of God as artisan, central to many theistic RWMs, and thus allow the finite events that constitute the world to rise into their role of self-constructing, dynamic, and causally effective entities. Those rare entities which have the powers of conscious awareness and purposive self-direction (human beings, at least) are morally as well as causally responsible for what they do. Ugliness and evil are not God's doing or God's responsibility. God's persuasion cannot in principle force its own acceptance. "Passing the buck" for ugliness and evil stops here, in the finite world, with the indifference and destructive self-centeredness of free moral agents, and with the recalcitrance of gradually evolved structures making up the physical world.

The wider ecumenical dialogue called for in the previous chapter has room for many voices—traditional absolute monotheisms, finite monotheisms, polytheisms—in speaking to the painful questions of ugliness and evil. It also has room for decentralized naturalism (some would call this atheism), a short step intellectually (though perhaps wider affectively) from the process theodicy offered by Griffin. Atheism comes in many flavors. If it arrives pouring scorn on the idea of intrinsic value in the universe, on the importance of beauty and its creators, on the possibility of limited but genuine freedom, on the stubborn nisus toward growth in complexity and quality in nature—then it is not compatible with personalistic organicism and, as an RWM, cannot appropriately model this worldview. But as we saw in earlier discussion, this is not atheism's only face. Much modern atheism has been influenced by, even confused with, mechanistic reductionisms of various sorts. But a fully relational kalogenic universe can be conceived without a central divine entity. Such a universe can be evolutionary, not once-for-all created, dynamic, significantly free and open to possibilities, shot through with mentality and value, ecological in its networks of mutual support. This is a nontheism that leaves cynicism behind. It is not embarrassed by cosmic vision and even cosmic hope. It deserves a place at the ecumenical table, offering fresh spirituality and creative energy.

But what does it say to the realities of ugliness and evil? It acknowledges the myriad tragedies of missed opportunity and destruction. It does not rail at the universe as though someone should be blamed for the perpetual perishing of beauty. It understands such perishing as the inevitable correlative of actual achievement, highlighting the tenderness, the poignancy, of every new creative moment. It understands ugliness and evil as parasitical, recognized only through norms of beauty and goodness sadly unfulfilled, and it redirects attention and energy to those positive defining norms. In these ways a nontheistic interpretation of personalistic organicism would try to handle ugliness and evil intellectually, with neither dogma nor denial.

Handling the realities of frustration and pain, loss and missed opportunities—and especially the wanton destruction of irreplaceable value—is at least equally difficult emotionally. The intellectual problem can be deep and elusive, but sometimes philosophers and others who enjoy theory may be tempted to shield themselves from the real anguish of ugliness and evil by using ideas as a way of keeping the suffering of the world at arm's length. Abstraction transforms the painful problem into just an interesting puzzle: a very different matter. Taken to excess, an overintellectual approach to ugliness and evil can be a way of denying their existential force. Emotional rejection of evil is especially tempting among the comfortable. This is a deeply human response and is a widely recognized early response to grief (Kübler-Ross 1969). Practically everyone experiences it, at least briefly, when faced with loss of one kind or another. "No! It can't be!" But emotional denial is an unstable tactic. Like thin ice, it can give way without notice. As the denial cracks, under the pressure of implacable experience, peace of mind shatters, too. Then the question "Why? Why? Why?" comes back with a new force. To deal with such crises my father was sometimes called in to the homes of friends in times of tragedy to talk to suffering family members. He dreaded but in a way also welcomed these intimate conversations about the inscrutable problem of evil, far removed from classroom abstractions and the possibility of glib "solutions." Although he was a devoted Christian theist, he never tried to comfort by invoking "God's will." One incident that moved him deeply was the death of a wonderfully promising young man by a lightning strike. The parents, also religious, would not deny the facts but could not understand them. This, he thought, was right. "Understanding" too quickly can itself be a form of denial of the full depth of loss. But for emotions to regain balance, the mind needs something to cling to, and this, he thought, is the larger picture of nature's precariousness and nature's predictability, life's slow advance amid many defeats, the rise of consciousness and the human capacity to affirm meaning even in circumstances of destructive injustice, as in the deaths of Socrates or Jesus. For many Christians, specifically, there is the hope of life beyond this life and the presence of a loving God in times of pain.

But many do not share in these "over-beliefs" (to recall William James' expression) that come with the Christian RWM. They cannot take comfort in the Holy Spirit or in the hope of Heaven. After emotional denial fails for them, they are left with anger. Rage is one way of handling ugliness and evil. The universe is wrong to permit such features. Condemn it, then, and find emotional footing by fighting back! Indeed, anger of this sort has the strong recommendation of remaining true to perceived norms of beauty and goodness. To forgive the universe too easily for terrible events may be a kind of collusion. To say that we fail to understand a wrong but that somehow in the larger picture it must be right—a common emotional defense—is to undermine our sense of standards, to anaesthetize our conscience, to sleep with the enemy.

Unfortunately, anger of this sort, for all its clarifying purity, can lead to despair. But to give up on the universe, however well motivated, is self-defeating. As ways of handling emotions stirred by ugliness and evil, rage and despair may provide a kind of painful comfort—when one is armored against hope, the future can hardly disappoint—but these strongly felt negative attitudes are almost guaranteed to be self-fulfilling over the long run. If the universe is rigged to cheat, then why play to win? Why play at all? Defensive, suspicious lives, fueled by anger at the universe, are not likely to look for new possibilities, much less take risks for higher beauties and wider goods.

Handling ugliness and evil emotionally is not easy, at best, but the ecological worldview of personalistic organicism offers some guidelines and supports that may help. The first guideline is to accept what experience teaches: to acknowledge ugliness as a part of the deep structure of the universe. Dodging this truth leads nowhere. There is a tragic streak in the universe. Automatically, without expenditure of effort, order is replaced by messiness. Harmonies once achieved start at once to disintegrate. Every satisfaction perishes. But the corresponding support is the reminder that ugliness is parasitic: it could not exist without prior norms from which it falls short. Ugliness and evil are not, as Augustine held (Ferré 1996, 85), metaphysically "privative," in the sense that somehow "finitude," or "lack of being" are literally ingredient in them. For personalistic organicism, there are richer and poorer degrees of complexity in beings but no degrees of being. Still, ugliness and evil are strictly speaking *defective*. Philistine ugliness and evil are possible only against a field of better possibilities left unachieved. Vandalism requires first something higher to tear down. From this, personalistic organicism offers the supportive reminder that kalogenesis is not only real but primary. This is a universe constantly creating beauty. Against the very real forces of decay and destruction are aligned equally real counterforces of novelty and growth. Acknowledging the reality of loss does not require loss of hope.

A second guideline from personalistic organicism is to encourage sympathy: to nurture natural capacities for empathic relations with other centers of suffering and joy. This is the path to community and from community to moral concern. Seeing the world through the eyes of another subject of a life is the way out of solipsism and egoism. It is the way toward voluntary cooperation in quest of large goals, the way to amplify achievements of high beauty and great good, beyond the reach of individuals alone. It is the way to focus the world's counterentropic nisus toward higher complexity in ways that challenge the philistine and refuse to be discouraged by the vandal. In support of this guideline, personalistic organicism insists on the real internal relations binding subjective centers of this essentially social universe. Empathy is as basic as prehension. We feel into each other at the most basic levels of perception (Ferré 1998, 276–84). There is nothing "spooky" in infra- and extrasensory experience (Ferré 1998, 279). Empathy can be nurtured; sympathy can be taught. The suffering ones of the Earth, both human and nonhuman, can be embraced with fellow feeling, whether or not there is anything immediate we can do to lessen the ugliness or temper the evil. Our gain, even at the cost of accepting much pain, is enlargement of awareness, a fuller solidarity with the cosmos.

A third guideline from personalistic organicism on handling ugliness and evil emotionally is to focus anger where it counts: to discriminate between losses caused by unconscious processes and those caused by morally responsible agents. There is no point, as we recently saw, to blaming the universe for the pervasiveness of suffering and disorder we wish were not the case. That way lies despair. But there is much point to bringing principled anger to bear against personal agents who fail their minimal responsibilities or, even worse, tear at the fabric of values they encounter. The deliberate evils of this world are a subclass, but an important subclass in the inventory of pain and loss. It is right to feel the emotions of anger and indignation against wrong. These are attitudes that give rise to dispositions for behavior. Behavior is not always possible or appropriate, as in cases of past wrongs where remedies are out of reach, but our emotional repertoire still needs to be rehearsed, since moral dispositions sometimes will need the motivating fire of principled anger when circumstances allow. In support, personalistic organicism emphasizes that persons are genuine agents, capable of initiating causal changes in the physical world by making mental judgments guided by ideal norms. Felt indignation, coupled with the mental capacity to recognize a mugging in progress and to anticipate an unfair blow aimed at a victim, can lead to a physical intervention, warding off the blow. Persons are moral observers by virtue of their mental poles; they are moral agents by virtue of their embodiment as physical organisms. Moral indignation can sometimes directly change physical circumstances for the better because we are made of meat. This does not mean that we should always intervene physically. Sometimes moral appeals through language alone are called for instead. Perhaps we are too quick to resort to force, even in defense of beauty and good. But personalistic organicism reminds us that in a world of aggressors against value, pacifist preachment is not the only option available for expressing our principled moral feelings.

In the last paragraph I have started to discuss the third way of handling ugliness and evil. Beyond handling these theoretically and even emotionally, there is the question of handling them actively. This will be the focus of the remainder of this book. Active engagement against ugliness and evil is the point of living. From the kalogenic perspective, actualizing (not just thinking or feeling about) creative harmony is the final satisfaction, the goal of goals. But while this is true, it might be misleading to say this apart from the first two topics, which need to be taken together with action if action is to be genuinely kalogenic. *Thinking* well and clearly about ugliness, its nature, types, origins, is a restraint against wild striking out. Thoughtless activity is not true action. Likewise, *feeling* well and strongly, in focused ways, is preparation for sustained, effective action. Bland insensibility writes no major symphonies, rights no major wrongs. This said, I now can again affirm that action—implemented choice—is the bottom line of ethics. And in the interests of handling action ethically, personalistic organicism offers four simple maxims, as follows:

First, *do no harm*. Our behavior must not be permitted to add to the sum of ugliness and evil in the world.

Second, *protect existing good*. Where we see beauty in jeopardy, or centers of intrinsic value threatened, our intervention is called for to side against the ever-present forces of destruction, to limit the constant gnawing at fineness of achievement that is the tragedy of the universe.

Third, *create new good*. This way lies personal fulfillment, in the intrinsic satisfaction that every achievement of new beauty brings, and, when generalized, social fulfillment as well.

Fourth, *be fair*. Both the amount of good and its equitable distribution are vital considerations. Distributing crumbs, however equally, while everyone hungers calls for redress in the quantity of goods. Justice alone, without something to distribute, is a bare category. Justice needs good to be applicable. But heaps of cake for some, while relevantly similar others starve, calls for redress in the quality of social good. Good needs justice to be right.

These maxims, by themselves, are not enough. They can conflict. For example, perhaps the creation of new value requires the removal of old achievement that blocks the better with the merely good. What then? The maxims also leave many issues of application unresolved. For example, is intervention always required, every time evil or ugliness is threatened? If so, how could we possibly have time to create new good? Let this rough texture be admitted freely. Still, out of such maxims, forged to stand against the realities of ugliness and evil, a fuller ethic can be developed—applying, ranking, modifying, balancing the maxims—while bringing to greater concreteness what a constructive postmodern age will require to maximize beauty and goodness.

PART THREE

Ethics and Society

8

NATURAL VALUES

By "natural values" I mean not just the values that human beings direct toward nature but also the values that natural entities possess in and for themselves. This double reference does not involve a major change of subject, as orthodox modern thinking supposes, but reflects a continuous spectrum—a rich spectrum of valuing on which any coherent, adequate environmental ethics must be based.

This continuity between human and natural values animates these last three chapters. The present chapter moves inward from the vast expanses of outer space to planet Earth, then from inorganic to organic realms of terrestrial nature, and finally to human nature. Chapter 9 explores what human nature, playing out its role as *Homo faber*, toolmaker and tool user, can and should contribute to a just and sustainable postmodern Earth. Chapter 10 examines norms for possible postmodern human social institutions and ends with reflections on private personal life.

The notion that nature is full of entities with qualities valued in and for themselves is still highly controversial. Despite its mortal wounds, the modern worldview, tending to reduce all values to valuing by human valuers, remains powerful. But if there is any single theme that rises from the trilogy of books of which this is the concluding volume, it is that modern thinking was profoundly wrong to discount the pervasiveness of values and valuers independent of human preferences. Postmodern thought needs to break with its modern past in this respect above all. And although we should not entirely abandon the modern adage that values are subjective (as in "beauty is in the eye of the beholder"), we should at least overhaul and greatly expand the notion of subjectivity in nature. In such an expansion, subjectivity will grow so wide as to ground an objective view of natural values.

"Nature" itself is a difficult word. Before going any deeper, it would be well to clarify its various uses. Important to my discussion are three meanings—all legitimate and important—that are prone to confusion and must carefully be kept disentangled. An example of potential conceptual traps for ethics, when these meanings are scrambled, appeared in the opening chapter of this book, where deploying the phrase, "unnatural acts," in two different senses ("It doesn't happen in nature" versus "It violates our nature") led to contradiction in the evaluation of homosexuality. This confusion is especially dangerous because "natural" and "nature" are words carrying important valuational baggage. It is normal in our culture for positive attitudes to be associated with "natural," and often fiercely negative ones to be associated with "unnatural." Advertisers of "all natural" products, as well as polemicists against various allegedly "unnatural" practices, regularly make effective use of these associations.

Perhaps the most frequent use of "nature" is to distinguish between what is the result of human arts (artificial) and what is not. The "natural" in this first sense is whatever is not artificial, whatever is not brought about by human planning, intelligence, or craftsmanship. Let us distinguish this sense of "nature" and "natural" with a subscript. When context might leave the meaning ambiguous, I shall use "nature$_1$" for that which is *untouched* and *uninfluenced by artificiality*. This is a common meaning, distinguishing nature$_1$ essentially in contrast to human culture. As such (for better or for worse) this use is thoroughly anthropocentric.

Not at all anthropocentric is another common meaning of "nature," referring to the entire physical universe—"all that is," except for the supernatural, if such there be. With the latter exception, this use of the word is entirely inclusive, not discriminating between stars or trees or shopping plazas. When context requires, I shall supply a distinguishing subscript to instances of this use: "nature$_2$." *All that we can see and touch*—more, everything visible or invisible that is covered by *natural law*—is part of *nature$_2$*. This means that many things which do not belong to nature$_1$, like shopping plazas, are fully at home in nature$_2$. The two cognate adjectives made from these nouns have analogous properties; that is, a shopping plaza is not at all natural$_1$ but is fully natural$_2$. Is this confusing? Think how much more confusing such talk is, in ordinary discourse, without guidance from subscripts!

Ordinary discourse gets even more confusing, offering a third key use for "natural" and "nature" distinct from the first two. This is the oldest of the three uses in English, derived from medieval French, itself drawn from the Latin *natura*, "birth." The original English equivalent for this third sense of nature is "kind" (still reflected in the German *Kind* for child). I shall distinguish this additional use, meaning *essential character*, or what a thing was *born to be*, or what *it would be* if nothing prevented it, with another subscript, nature$_3$. When someone refuses to believe an accusation, saying, "It just goes against my friend's nature$_3$ to do such a thing," the normative force of this use is apparent. The norms need not always be positive. Someone may be thought to have a wicked nature$_3$ and consequently to be unable to engage in kindly acts, but this is still a "norm" in the sense that an abstract pattern or character is envisaged for that person—he or she was just born bad. But most of the norms indicated by nature$_3$ tend to be positive. Perhaps the rediscovery of Aristotelian thought (at about the same time that "nature" entered the French language) encouraged the popular sense that the essential birth character of something—its *telos*, form, or final cause—ought, all other things being equal, to flourish (Ferré 1996, 55–63). At any rate, a strongly positive evaluative link to the natural$_3$ has been forged in popular culture. The perfect apple would come from allowing an unblemished apple seed to germinate and grow into a perfect tree, unharmed by drought or blight, bearing perfect fruit, unmolested by worms or birds. This is an unreachable ideal, of course, in this world of conflicting natures$_3$, but it is a powerful one.

There are interesting relationships between the various uses of "nature." Not all conflict. For example, the adage: "Nature knows best," combines the senses of nature$_1$ (contrasting the natural against human arts) and nature$_3$ (assuming unhindered development of native traits), and could be written: "Nature$_{1,3}$ knows best." However, many do conflict. For example, if it is a person's nature$_3$ to crave "getting back to nature$_1$," this is not likely to be done in a city square, although the materials of the pavement are all perfectly natural$_2$.

Finally, after making these distinctions, it is important not to absolutize them. The natural$_1$ comes in degrees. Even outer space, obviously in the vicinity of Earth but now beyond the solar system, has been to some extent altered and influenced by human purposes and artifacts. If we take "untouched and uninfluenced" rigorously, it may be that nowhere on Earth can one still find absolutely pure nature$_1$ (McKibben 1989). Wilderness by now is largely an artifact of human definition and protection, but even such protection is at best partial and ineffective, since anthropogenic changes in the climate, ozone levels, acidity of rain and snow, and the like, are pervasive around the globe. There is a good use of the comparative when it comes to "natural$_1$," since things can be "more natural$_1$," and "less natural$_1$." The criterion dividing artificial things from natural$_1$ things is the extent of the ingredience of human purpose, craft, and intelligence in the origins of the things concerned. An apple orchard is somewhat artificial, somewhat natural$_1$. The ancestors of today's apple trees evolved ages ago without human intervention, qualifying them as fully natural$_1$ at least at the start. But goal-oriented horticulture and sophisticated agriculture have long since entered the causal history of today's orchards, making them *less* natural$_1$ than primeval forests but *more* natural$_1$ than completely paved city squares.

I will explore values from the "outside in," beginning where nature$_2$ is most unambiguously natural$_1$, in outer space. "Empty" space is where we find the heat of nuclear furnaces blasting into the chill of near absolute zero temperatures in near vacuum conditions. What could such nice things as values be doing in a place like this?

EXTRATERRESTRIAL VALUES

As we start this reflection, we should remember, and keep remembering throughout, that despite brilliant advances in astronomy and cosmology during the twentieth century, the human race remains profoundly ignorant about the vast universe in which we find ourselves. Most—some estimate up to 90 percent—of what makes up nature$_2$ is dark: invisible and undetectable, completely a topic for speculation. In the final decades of the twentieth century, new technologies made possible amazing discoveries about the detectable portion of the universe, discoveries that have narrowed old uncertainties and raised new paradoxes. We do not know many things, and—worse—we do not even know *what* we do not know! We are in a most exciting period when a deluge of new information is pouring in, more than we can readily absorb or make sense of. What I have to say, therefore, is based on educated guesswork, recognizing that the whole field is being revolutionized even as we ponder it.

Continuing in this spirit of appropriate epistemic modesty, perhaps I may suggest in what follows a possible Whiteheadian speculation on the missing mass of the universe. Whatever scientists eventually call the "entities" that make up the presently undetectable bulk of nature$_2$ (at this writing, exotic names such as "axions," "neutralinos," or "photinos" are being proposed under the generic term WIMP for "weakly interacting massive particles"), personalistic organicism will return to the concept of *actual occasions*. For this worldview, these fundamental entities constitute the theoretical "lowest level" (Ferré 1996, 340–56). Imagined as not clumped into atomic structures, hardly "structured" at all, but fleetingly concrescing in the unimaginably simple patterns prehended from (and superjectively bequeathed to) their unimaginably simple environment, these entities occupy and collectively constitute the "empty space" of what Whitehead called the "extensive continuum." This is the actual universe considered geometrically. But, on this worldview, the geometry of space is not made from nothing. On the Ontological Principle, it is what it is because of actual occasions of creativity, pulsations of relationships claiming momentary definiteness before perishing, giving way to successive moments of energy which, like them, wrestle actuality out of possibility.

The missing mass of the universe, whatever it may turn out to be experimentally (high speed neutrinos somehow, despite current theory, generating mass?), can be understood on a Whiteheadian view as the collective "weight" of actuality, achieved by "pre-clumped" energetic occasions. These occasions would then be seen as the energetic basis for the self-formation of elementary particles into the more complex social structures that make up, say, quarks, and eventually electrons, protons, neutrons, and the makings of atoms of all sorts. On this view, all the bright matter we now see would have evolved by the emergence and retention of novel complexities out of the dark, dynamic matter we now must merely speculate about. But if this, or something like this, is so, then value—the value of achieving actuality, of squeezing out the last bit of indeterminacy, of becoming a definite entity—would be present "all the way down," even in the missing mass of space-time itself. Each actual occasion, each puff of achievement, would have value both for itself and for its successors. Admittedly, the intrinsic quality of these "unclumped" occasions, the sentinels of empty space, would be extremely low. The "feelings" represented by their physical prehensions would be unconscious to the highest possible degree. But however "blind," and however "negligible" (Whitehead's words), the interiority of these lowest orders of actual occasions would contain some minuscule triumph of achievement for itself, some remote analogy to the experience of beauty. The kalogenic universe would then run upward from a background level of reality (currently undetectable but meaningfully postulated by current cosmological science) that is already kalogenic.

In this sense, natural$_2$ value is objectively there, in the universe, quite apart from human appreciations or aversions, and it has been objectively there since long before the solar system formed itself out of the debris of exploded stars. Like all value, it depends on subjective centers of appreciation, but these centers are literally everywhere in space-time. They constitute the actuality of space-time. Without them there would be no space-time. And without their self-formative energy, their capacity for introducing and sustaining novelties of significant form, there would be no elementary particles, no atoms or molecules, no suns or planets. Subjective value so pervasive and so essential loses its operational distinction from objective value. Are we confronted with natural$_2$ structures (like stars) comprised of natural$_2$ structures (like atoms) themselves formed from subatomic energies and possibilities of relation? If so, then we are confronted by the intricate residue of values achieved over untold eons of energetic self-organization, destruction, and reordering.

There is not much that ethical theory can recommend to "do" when confronted by a star. Nothing we do will affect that great nuclear furnace in any substantial way or in any foreseeable future. But, as I have remarked before, ethical theory often comes legitimately into play even when there is nothing anyone can do. The past is as much out of reach of our influence as is the farthest star (whose appearance to our eyes or instruments is also the past effective in our present), but we still appropriately make ethical judgments about past events. Likewise, judgments about the values embedded in outer space are quite in order. What might they be?

The first step toward adequate environmental ethics is recognition and appreciation of value, wherever it may be. By this I do not mean simply our aesthetic appreciation of something that kindles the experience of beauty in our own subjectivity. A star may strike us as beautiful, which is relevant, even important, in the full context of all that the star may be good for. But as long as the impression remains "our" experience of beauty (or even the sort of beauty we can anticipate other human beings will gain), the aesthetics of the star will not be the main point. If we were a sightless race or if Earth had a permanently overcast sky, this would not automatically make the star valueless, though it would eliminate for us its visible beauty. Instead, we should look first for more objective values. For Whiteheadians, in the background will always be the energetic pulsations of the countless occasions which together make up the systematic entity that is the star. But these individual occasions, too, can be ignored in the present context, since at their levels of complexity there is not much intrinsic value to admire, nor much uniqueness. One electron is very much like any other, inside or outside a solar furnace.

But the star itself, as a systematic entity, is more than the sum of its atomic parts. It started as merely an aggregate entity, a great cloud of gas, with no clear boundaries or identity, mostly made up of vast swarms of the simplest atomic society, hydrogen, a single electron pulsing with harmonious equilibrium in a long repetitive dance with its single proton partner. But, as these hydrogen atoms attract one another, then are unimaginably squeezed by gravitational compression, a new reaction begins, nuclear fusion; and what was an aggregate entity as a gas cloud starts to earn an identity it could not have claimed if it had been (say) half its size. It becomes a system organized around a reaction, an integral thing capable of sustained doing, radiating heat and light into its surroundings and, even more exciting, cooking new heavy elements deep in its interior. These heavy elements, made up of more and more complex societies of electrons and nuclei, could not have been formed outside the high-pressure synthesizing furnace. They are the elements that are spewed out into the geometry of space-time when the cycles sustaining the star's nuclear reaction run out of fuel and the furnace explodes. These are the elements, carbon, oxygen, iron, and so forth, that are swept up, clumped, smashed, reclumped, and stabilized in the planet-forming process, when younger stars cruise through, and warp, geometries containing such debris. These heavy elements, once synthesized in stars now long exhausted, are now what make up the bodies and the instruments of those living, human organisms on Earth who contemplate some other, newer star in full labor elsewhere in space-time. As we do so, we are in fact contemplating the womb of new possible planets, new possible organisms—stellar furnaces steadily generating greater complexity out of lesser, higher potential value out of lower. This is something to admire. This is something to approve, and if there were anything to do about it (as there is not), this would be something to protect. "Do no harm," in this context, means that if one could destroy a star, pregnant with complexity for the future of the universe, one should refrain, all other things being equal.

This first maxim and our second, "protect existing good," may have more footing for active application if we draw the focus of attention closer to our home star, the Sun, and its solar system. Here the human race recently has begun to have extensive dealings, and in the coming centuries it seems all but certain that extraterrestrial ethical issues will gain in urgency. We had better be ready in concept for what seems sure to become fact.

What might count as "existing good" in the environment of our solar system? One such good, at this writing, is the good we often find in wilderness: the other planets, our Moon, and the space-time geometry within which they rotate, are still nearly untouched nature$_1$. They have the alien majesty, the unmanipulated integrity, the pristine innocence for which many men and women thirst. It is not entirely clear whether this reflects something deep and essential in human nature$_3$, but it certainly is important enough in a cross-cultural way to have led to legislation in many nations, designation of wilderness areas on Earth, and large investment in means of protecting precious wilderness sites for future generations. Is this purely from anthropocentric motives? It could be, if human enjoyment—or, deeper, spiritual renewal—is the only consideration. It may not be, on Earth, at least, if consideration is also given to the intrinsic value of the many forms of wildlife that make their home in most wilderness areas.

The wilderness dimension of outer space is prevented from adding the latter consideration if we assume, as I do, that there are no living forms in our solar system outside the Earth. Are there then still considerations of intrinsic value, in addition to anthropocentric restorative value, in the nonliving structures making up the planetary environment of the Sun? We can set aside one sort of intrinsic value that on this worldview is pervasively present. The kalogenic concrescences of the actual occasions of empty space are, as Whitehead himself concedes, metaphysically significant but ethically negligible. Also negligible in this context are the low-order intrinsic values of such actual occasions as pulse within the silicon atoms that make up the desert surfaces of Mars. Such occasions are not only near the extreme end of the "blindness" spectrum, but also would be barely affected by their rearrangement into crystals or by the crystal's destruction. What, though, of the crystal itself? Here issues become more complex, in keeping with the complexity of the entities under discussion. Surely there must come a point where the sheer attainment of unique, identifiable, internally coherent structure is worthy of respect for itself. This does not mean that *the entity* respects itself. By hypothesis, it is not a living organism, has no "self" in the sense of a central occasion to which information flows from the related parts, has no "interests," even in the way that a living plant, though lacking a nervous system and central coordination or awareness, still has organic interests (e.g., in water or sunlight) that can be satisfied or frustrated. Neither a delicate stalactite in a dark cave on Earth nor a complex mineral formation on the Moon (both products of millions of years of patient natural$_1$ processes) cares whether it is idly smashed by a passing boot. But should we care, on its behalf? I suspect that we should, not just for the sake of potential enjoyment by humans or other sensate beings but out of respect for nature$_1$'s sheer achievement of unique complexity. This is not a mode of complexity that could give rise to a living thing. We are not discussing pregnancy here, but integrity of significant form. Is this a value without a valuer, earlier ruled out as no more possible than love without a lover? No, we are the valuers in this case, this is *our* value judgment, but we are judging achieved complexity: something that should be respected for itself, not for its utility or even for its capacity to contribute to beautiful experience. As Holmes Rolston, in a sensitive discussion of this topic, proposes that one way of telling whether an entity qualifies for this kind of respect is whether we consider it qualifying for a proper name. This is not a universal criterion. Not everything we name may be deserving of such consideration, since often names are given simply for human convenience, he points out. "But by the time we are drawn to attach a proper name to a place, there is enough particularity, differentiation and integration of locus, enough provincial identity to call for protection" (Rolston 1986, 173).

The maxim, to "protect existing good," may also help warn against polluting space and nearby heavenly bodies with heedless litter or contamination. The problem of space junk, left over from human feats of rocketry in long-term orbits around Earth, is considerable at this writing and will only become worse if centuries of technological advance are allowed to leave their detritus behind. National governments are aware of this obligation, and efforts are continuing at tracking hulks of old satellites, rocket casings, worn out experiments, and even tiny fragments. Environmental ethics will reinforce the ethical importance of these prudent policies. Similarly, an ethics inclusive of extraterrestrial values will strongly support efforts to eliminate nuclear explosions from space and to preserve the Moon and outer space "exclusively for peaceful purposes," as mandated by Article IV of the Treaty on Principles Governing the Activities of States in the Exploration and Use of Outer Space, including the Moon and Other Celestial Bodies (*Treaty* 1967).

"Do no harm" and "protect existing good" are defensive maxims, barriers against vandal ugliness and evil, whether perpetrated by ourselves or others.

But the torpor and gradual decay of philistinism is still a threat unless we invoke the third maxim, "create new good." What might that mean in the context of extraterrestrial values? Certainly the first possibility is for creating new orders of appreciation—aesthetic and cognitive—for the greater universe of which we are a part. This is something that can occupy us here on Earth, with a minimum of invasiveness, simply by looking and thinking. It is an old practice, engaged in from the dawn of recorded history, and doubtless long before. Different cultures have had different ways of thinking and, in consequence, of seeing the heavens. In ancient Babylonia the arts of observation and theorizing, including predicting, were taken to amazing heights of proficiency (Neugebauer 1969, 97–144). Egypt, Greece, Medieval Europe—all have looked and theorized in characteristic ways. Galileo opened a new chapter in human appreciation when he turned his telescope to the skies (Ferré 1996, 124–28), and since this beginning of modern astronomy our Earth-based instrumentation has multiplied exponentially in power and variety. Now we can "look" in many ranges of the electromagnetic continuum, in one of the most glorious expressions of human mentality in the history of the world. Motivated by restless speculative curiosity, disciplined by carefully noticing and naming perceived regularities, crowned by synthesizing new theories tested by abstract logic and concrete data—this is the "Reason of Plato" at its best, one of the luminous growing edges of the cosmos at work understanding itself.

But in the latter decades of the twentieth century, human mentality added greatly to its instrumentation from space-based vantage points. With such technological marvels as the now retired Compton Gamma-Ray Observatory and the still active Hubble Space Telescope in sublunar orbits, gathering huge amounts of data not accessible under the protective blanket of Earth's atmosphere, and with X-ray and infrared platforms, and many others planned, the scope of human thought will be vastly extended. In this the beauties of cognition, appreciative as well as explanatory, will be multiplied. This is a creative good not only for the astronomers themselves, whose passionate energies are engaged as never before, but also for the throngs of those who listen, learn, and wonder. Unavoidable here is, admittedly, some invasion of the wilderness of pure space. The region around the Earth's atmosphere is no longer so natural$_1$ as it once was. Probably it will never be so again, even with the most conscientious cleaning up of human space debris. There is a definite conflict here between protecting the goods of untamed space with the imperative to create new goods of knowledge and appreciation. Judgment is required to balance the maxims.

My judgment is that the creative goods of extremely high quality mental satisfactions, through delicate symbolic constructions of great power and comprehensiveness, contributing to the illumination of our whole species on our

setting within the grand physical scheme of things, far outweighs the disturbance to the wilderness aspect of space. Space, after all, remains a wilderness,
hostile and dangerous, despite these tiny specks of human instrumentation in
one little corner of the universe. By sending out these emissaries of human intelligence, we have not domesticated the universe. The proviso, "all other
things being equal," which needs to be added, explicitly or implicitly, to virtually all imperatives, here shows its importance. Yes, we should not harm
(should preserve the good of) the pristine qualities of space, all other things
being equal; however, when dramatically expanding the intrinsic beauties of
knowing is a real possibility, in return for minor disturbances, all other things
are not equal. Personalistic organicism will enthusiastically support the blos-
soming of mentality represented by orbiting observatories and space probes as
peaceful, legitimate extensions of human intelligence into the cosmos.

Human visitations to the Moon and Mars, and perhaps to other astronomical bodies where this might prove feasible, would also fall into this zone of
ethical approval, assuming that great pains are taken to minimize harms like
pollution and contamination. The intellectual and sheer emotional rewards of
such human adventures into extraterrestrial environments are hard to overstate, and surely are worth footprints and other minimal traces left behind.
But "creating new good" of this sort needs always to be balanced against
"protecting existing good," where it is found, and attempting to "do no harm"
in the process. One harm against which all interventions into extraterrestrial
environments need defense is biological contamination. Strenuous efforts
have been taken, and presumably will continue, against the remote possibility
of germs carried from Earth causing a plague in the heavens. The space environment is so hostile to life forms as we know them that it is only on the surfaces of potentially life-supporting planets or their moons that this is a practical concern, but it is and should continue to be a concern. It would be a harm
beyond imagining if our efforts to create new good were to result inadver-
tently in the destruction of a native biological form without $natural_3$ defenses.
The unspeakable tragedy that befell Native American peoples, who died in
droves from "childhood" diseases on first encounter with European explorers,
should be a warning.

This memory of European colonization of the New World draws our attention to the possibility of extraterrestrial settlement. What guidance do our maxims give? The imperative to "create new good" suggests that space colonization
might be a highly approved activity, since it brings more complex entities, capable of achieving richer harmonies of satisfaction, into domains hitherto dominated with relatively simpler orders of complexity and structure. In orbiting
space stations, devoted to increasing the cognitive dominion of humankind,
new discoveries about $nature_2$ (definitely including human $nature_3$ in intense,
confined conditions) could be harvested for the benefit of all. True, and all other

things being equal, such interventions would be hardly more problematic than orbiting observatories in the sublunar environment. What, though, of permanent stations on the Moon or on Mars? Again, the maxim to create new good must be heard, but always tempered by the warning maxims against intended or unintended vandalism in the name of some ideal that may glitter but turn out less than gold. One of the strong motives behind space colonization, beyond pure cognitive enlargement and the excitement of adventure, is exploitation of resources to keep Earth's ravenous appetites sated. Personalistic organicism is not against the satisfying of appetites, but in this context one must ask, "Which appetites?" and "At what costs?" Extractive and transport costs will be immense, of course, but we must assume that the total cost-benefit balance will be favorable in the marketplace, or the enterprise would not be launched or sustained. Added to these costs will be the deep environmental costs to the places mined. Pristine surfaces, undisturbed for perhaps billions of years, would be excavated, distinctive natural$_1$ structures would be destroyed, for the sake of . . . what? It would make an ethical difference whether the ravaging of extraterrestrial landscapes were to be done as an absolute last resort, to sustain life on an Earth so depleted of essentials that the alternative would be ecocide. But if not, if these extraterrestrial resources were to be "needed" to keep the engines of commerce feeding the exotic tastes of the wealthy who command the marketplace, then "all other things" would not be equal to the justification of such crass colonization. Earth *in extremis* may perhaps be allowed to raid the heavens, but environmental ethics should warn that the Moon is not just a resource pit to feed the ordinary hungers of manufacturing and commerce.

Colonizing hostile heavenly bodies, even exploitative colonization, represents a minor intrusion compared to dreams of "terraforming" planets to prepare them for massive transfusions of earthly life. The distinguished ecologist, Frank Golley, defines terraforming as "wholesale rearrangement of a planet's environment by modifications of its energy balance or its material composition so that the planet can be made habitable to life" (Golley 1986, 219). Despite his personal opposition (citing Carl Sagan), he suggests methods that might work. If algae were seeded into the carbon dioxide atmosphere of Venus, for example, and if these algae were able to convert this carbon dioxide into carbon and oxygen, then the freed oxygen might combine with the crust of Venus, thus greatly decreasing the enormous atmospheric pressure noted in the previous chapter. At the same time, the current greenhouse effect might be greatly reduced, and the immensely high surface temperature of our sister planet might be correspondingly lowered (Sagan 1973, 151–53). Golley expresses some technical doubts, but finally concludes:

> As a biologist, it would seem to me that terraforming might be best accomplished by contamination of appropriate planets or moons with

lower forms of life such as bacteria, algae, or protozoa. If the conditions were favorable for life, these organisms would survive, grow, and begin the evolutionary process that transformed this planet into a habitable one. If contamination was successful, possibly we could guide the process into directions congenial to human goals and also speed the process. Whatever the method, terraforming provides an alternative to direct space-colony design (Golley 1986, 220).

Golley's expressed concerns are with the technical means. Let us assume that some such means could give birth to new conditions on planets like Venus and Mars, which could then bloom with the wonderful beauties of living, even thinking organisms, as we know these on Earth. Would this not be a great advance in values over the present state of these planets, which I offered earlier as prime examples of comparative natural$_2$ ugliness? Yes, all other things being equal, personalistic organicism could not help rejoicing over such an enlargement of the domain of quality, complexity, and creativity. Multiplying the now unique beauties of Earth would be a noble ideal, a cosmic challenge worthy of organisms, like humans, capable of being aware of their own altruistic impulses. It would be as close as can be imagined to a God-like act, not quite of "creation from nothing," but of creativity for the sake of sharing our own good.

Pure altruism is hard to find, of course, and some consider terraforming an answer to our species' population crisis, a way of preparing other worlds into which the huddled masses of our distant future may escape. This, too, is (all things being equal) not an unworthy dream. But as an escape it tends to deflect full attention from the need to avert the extreme population crisis on which the dream is predicated. What would be the costs, in addition to losing the uniqueness of Venus and Mars in their natural$_1$ states and thus to losing diversity from the solar system, of transforming other planets to be like Earth? The costs of such an enormous project must be assumed to be proportionally enormous. Who will be required to go without goods that are spent on such an Earth-devouring project? Who will bear the burdens? Who will reap the eventual rewards? Is there any degree of equity in this moral equation?

Terraforming and space colonization are in themselves legitimate goals, aimed at creating new good. But our fourth maxim, "be fair," must give us pause. Can we afford these goods? Will suffering on Earth go unaddressed, will environmental resources be savaged, for the sake of dubiously attainable dreams? When we think of reproducing Earth, should we not first make sure that Earth itself is as full of good and fairness as it can be? Theologian John Cobb cites scripture wisely in this connection: "In Paul's language, all things are permitted, but not all things are helpful. Diverting attention from the pressing problems of a sick and suffering biosphere to the conquest of space is not helpful" (Cobb 1986, 310). This discussion of extraterrestrial values has not, in my view, been a "diversion," but assuredly it must be followed by a focus on Earth. This is the home planet. It is where nature$_2$ has spontaneously flowered with moral concerns. It now demands our focus.

EARTHLING VALUES

From the time of its original formation, out of the heavy elements left from explosions of earlier stars, or from materials torn from their stellar wombs during a near collision between the Sun and another star, Earth has been—and still is—an enormously dynamic entity. It is internally as well as externally heated, both by its own geothermal energies (from radioactive decay and compression) and by incoming radiation from our local star. Earth's internal heat, though amounting to only a few thousandths of a percent of the heat received from the Sun, is enough to have kept our planet churning during its entire history of constant self-organizing change.

This history is generally agreed to have begun about 4,600 million years ago. The date is inferred from the age of oldest Moon rocks and meteorites, thought to be about the same age, but the Earth was so active in its first 500 million years that no original rock remains. Our oldest samples come from 4,100 million years ago, by which time water and atmosphere had already been squeezed through volcanic vents out of the mantle (nearly 2,000 miles thick). This mantle is a dense, primitive structure separating two others that precipitated out of it: above it, a thin granitic crust, and, below it, a liquid core made up of molten iron and nickel. Rotation of the upper part of this liquid core, slightly out of phase with the rotation of the Earth as a whole, produces the Earth's constantly migrating magnetic field. Plates of the relatively light granite crust, cool and thus rigid, came to float on denser, partially melted layers of the mantle where shearing can occur, permitting these plates to drift. These processes took much time to get organized—perhaps up to half the history of the Earth to date—but by 2,000 million years ago they were under way. Since then, continents have repeatedly smashed together and torn apart, great mountain ranges have many times risen up and been worn away. One major period of mountain building (orogeny) occurred 1,100 million years ago, another about 600 million years ago; meanwhile, major periods of glaciation further changed the Earth's face 2,300 million, 875 million, 740 million, and 610 million years ago. All this while, huge chunks of extraterrestrial matter were hitting the Earth, leaving large craters. This occurred primarily during Earth's first 1,000 million years but continued with fair frequency throughout this long first epoch, known as the Precambrian, which ended 543 million years ago. One of these late hits, as we shall see, was fraught with importance for the story of planetary life.

Remarkably, evidence of life is found in some of the oldest rocks to have survived intact, unmelted, unmetamorphosed, to the present. Perhaps by 3,800 million but surely by 3,500 million years ago, simple prokaryotic organisms, bacteria and algae, asexually reproducing cells with no internal organelles, membranes, or nucleus, had already appeared in primeval ponds and oceans. These and their modified descendants became further agents of change reacting back on the dynamic Earth. As our discussion on terraforming Venus already foreshadowed, algae were responsible for radically altering Earth's atmosphere. Photosynthetic blue-green algae, appearing as early as 3,000 million years ago, were able to absorb carbon dioxide and release free oxygen, replacing the mainly water vapor, methane, ammonia, and nitrogen atmosphere that had originally been vented from below the Earth's crust, with enormous consequences for the possibility of fueling more complex, oxygen-powered life forms to follow. Life even left its mark in the kinds of rocks that girdle the planet. Sedimentary pressure formed limestone from the carbonaceous mud produced by the bodies of tiny organisms. Hundreds of millions of years before the end of the Precambrian period, complex life forms, including soft-bodied animals floating or crawling in shallow waters, some growing up to three-feet long (the Ediacaran fauna), were flourishing in the seas of the dynamic Earth (Monastersky 1996).

My point in these reflections on the Precambrian era is not merely to give honor due to a period that constitutes more than 88 percent of Earth's entire story to date, but more to celebrate the constant, roiling self-creating character of our home planet from its earliest days. Bombarded with energy and material from beyond itself, powered by its own internal boilers, and offering a synergistic interface for major mutual organic-inorganic transformations, the early Earth is a kaleidoscope in the original sense of that invented word: a "way of seeing" (*skopein*) of "beautiful" (*kalós*) "forms" (*eídos*) as they fall together in constantly new ways. We who live in recent times of change should realize that we have the honor of participating in a long tradition. But more on that later.

Sometime within the Precambrian time, during which life was active as early as our extant geological evidence can penetrate, and during which not only prokaryotic algae and bacteria but also eukaryotic organisms (having specialized internal nuclei and organelles), both unicellular and multicellular, plant and animal, developed in the early oceans. Eukaryotes have now been identified as early as 2,700 million years ago (*New York Times*, 13 August 1999: A 10). And with complex nuclei came another enormously significant innovation: meiosis and sex. The earliest forms of life, the prokaryotes, were asexual in reproduction. With their single chromosome of tightly coiled DNA, they cloned themselves, multiplying their genetic information over and over again. This was in itself an amazing achievement in self-organization. The very idea of "information" is an astonishing leap, an entirely new plateau in ways of organizing order. As Holmes Rolston puts it, "there is no cumulation of information in the hydrological, climatological, orogenic cycles, but there is in the birth, life, death, genetic cycles" (Rolston 1999, 23). Asexual division is an efficient way of producing progeny, of filling the Earth with one's own kind. It is so efficient, indeed, that it puzzles some that asexual reproduction ever made room for sex. Now the vast majority of forms of life, plant as well as animal, are eukaryote and sexual (Raven 1976, 123 ff.). Even some asexual organisms switch to sexual reproduction under stress. But, for theorists with strong commitment to the popular axiom that genes are necessarily "selfish," always arranging evolutionary outcomes for the utmost maximization of their own unique DNA coding, sex represents a paradox, even a contradiction, to received orthodoxy. In sexual reproduction, half of an organism's genetic information is frittered away. In the next generation, even that precious half is cut in half, and so it goes, in a process of rapid dilution down to the point where individual genetic identity is negligible. How can this be? Did life make a terrible mistake 1,000 million years ago?

No. The beauty of sex (evolutionarily speaking)—its deeper joy—is in its kaleidoscopic character. The stable, predictable efficiencies of asexual ways of "filling the Earth" are unable to cope with urgent needs to innovate, while the Earth, at every period, makes sure that such needs recur. Asexual reproduction plods; sexual reproduction dances. Its dance is full of chance steps, forward and back and sideways. When the dance floor is blocked in one direction, sex can quickly find another way. When a tricky step is rewarding, it can be incorporated into the regular repertoire. In other words, the "dilution" of an organism's own traits with another's allows for greater diversity and flexibility of genetic information for the good of the species as a whole. New combinations can be tried out. Those that succeed can be quickly reproduced and the rest discarded. On the face of the dynamic Earth—a rocking, rolling dance floor— life's best bet for carrying on its vector toward novelty, complexity, creativity, is through the sacrifice of individual "selfishness" in the sexual embrace. This should not be overinterpreted. Individuals still count. It is only individual organisms, not species, that can be successful, or not, on the actual dance floor of life. Only individual organisms find mates and leave progeny.

The joys and pains of sex are only directly experienced at the retail level. But on the wholesale level, where trading on futures is the name of the game, the justifications of sex are adaptive flexibility, innovation, retention of successful methods, and opportunistic openness to hitherto untried ways of proliferating the satisfactions of being alive.

All this was in place before the end of the first great era, and fortunately so, since about 610 million years ago, toward the end of the Precambrian era, came the first of the great extinctions that punctuate the history of the Earth. Up to 70 percent of living organisms died, probably from sharp cooling and shrinking of the seas as enormous sheets of ice formed at the poles. This was to be the first of seven mass extinctions marked in the geological record during the 12 percent of time remaining in Earth's story between the start of the Cambrian era and our own age.

What is most remarkable about these mass extinctions is their sequels. In every case, life rebounds from despeciation with equally massive respeciation. Each time the Earth is scrubbed partially or even largely clean of the species of the previous age, new species of even greater complexity and flexibility swarm into the inviting vacancy. By the end of the Precambrian, vast numbers of algae and bacteria had been removed, and in their place during the Cambrian period (beginning about 543 million years ago) many new families of marine invertebrates developed, including trilobites. Most of these, in turn, were wiped out roughly 515 million years ago, but in the Ordovician period that followed, more invertebrates (including brachiopods) took their place, and primitive fish developed, the first of the vertebrates. Many of these were in their turn extinguished 435 million years ago, but in the following 65 million years, comprising the Silurian and Devonian ages, new organisms replaced them and even began to invade the dry land for the first time. During the Devonian period, ferns and primitive evergreen trees, spiders and mites, appeared on the land, as did four-legged, air breathing amphibians. About 363 million years ago, the end of the Devonian era was marked by another mass extinction, the first to affect land organisms, but then came the rich Carboniferous and Permian ages. During the Carboniferous, sometimes called "the age of cockroaches" because of the hundreds of species that then appeared, huge developments of ferns and many swamp trees occurred, now known to us as coal beds. No extinction separated this age from the Permian, but during the Permian there were great extinctions due to climate change and dramatic continental drifting. The supercontinent Pangea, a fusion of all continents into one great land mass, formed at this time, about 225 million years ago, eliminating many coastal areas and, with the destruction of these habitats, many species. This was the greatest of all the mass extinctions, with 90 percent of species lost. It marks the end of the Paleozoic Era. However, new species and whole new families of species burgeoned, in place of those which disappeared. During the Triassic period, which followed, amphibians and reptiles flourished and the first of the dinosaurs appeared along with flying reptiles and a group of mammal-like reptiles, the terapsids. Ferns and conifers, as well as ginkgo trees, spread over the land. But by the late Triassic, around 190 million years ago, another large extinction is recorded in the relative dearth of fossil remains from this time. This vacancy, again, is more than made up for in the Jurassic period which followed, when new reptiles ruled and there came to be an abundance of life of all sorts, flora and fauna, on land and sea. The first true birds took to the skies in this period, and true mammals also appeared. This abundance continued without a break into the Cretaceous period, during which the continents and oceans began to resemble their present shape, and in which the dinosaurs, including the famous tyrannosaurs, dominated the landscape. Tiny mammals, including early insect-eating marsupials, did what they could to survive in a reptile world.

That world came to its abrupt end 65 million years ago in the last of the great extinctions, probably the only extinction to have been caused not by Earth-powered climate changes or continental drift but by an extraterrestrial invasion, that is, by a large meteor which struck off the Yucatán Peninsula of Mexico, near the present town of Chicxulub, with catastrophic effects on the atmosphere. Around the globe, skies were filled with dirt from the huge impact crater, darkening the sun, and the climate suddenly became much colder, less hospitable to the mighty reptiles, more supportive of warm-blooded, adaptable, multifunctional, relatively clever organisms like mammals. Once again, life did not hesitate to start filling the vacancy.

But it was different life. As in other cases of extinction, room created was room to be filled. Here I must enter an important caveat, for fear of misunderstanding. No responsible scientific opinion at this time favors the model of smooth "upward" progress toward any particular "goal" by which to recount the story of life on the dynamic Earth. At no time has such a model been appropriate, since there are as many sidesteps in the dance of life as forward steps. There are backsteps, too, whatever be chosen as the measure of "forward" and "back." Complexity does not always increase; neither cleverness nor speed nor armor, nor whatever the parameter, can guarantee survival. But the curious fact is that over the grand sweep of time, punctuated by the great extinctions that have at least partially cleared the floor of the dominant dancers, organic complexity has tended to increase. And with complexity has come a trend in animals (not universally, or necessarily, but visibly overall), toward greater sensitivity to happenings on the surrounding dance floor, a greater capacity for swift and effective dealing with shifting patterns in the dance, a defter, more centralized self-control of the steps, the whirling and dipping, to be engaged in by the organism as a whole. This is true not only for the period since the last great extinction but throughout the story of life. In the Precambrian waters, amoebae or paramecia were far better equipped to pursue nourishment than blue-green algae, fish than trilobites. Later forms, especially after an explosion of novelty is made possible after a significant extinction, tend to exhibit new powers, or if familiar, then powers with remarkably improved competencies.

The disappearance of the dinosaurs marked the beginning of the Cenozoic Era, our era, divided into two unequal parts, the Tertiary (lasting 63 million years) and the Quaternary Period (lasting 2 million). The Cenozoic as a whole represents only 1.5 percent of the story of the Earth, but it represents the time in which much that is most familiar to us came into being. The plants we most love and need developed during the Tertiary period. These are the angiosperms, including wildflowers, the flowering trees, shrubs, vines, and all the essential grasses, including the ancestors of modern corn, wheat, and rice. With the spread of grasses, the mammals, especially the grazing mammals, could extend their range and size and diversity. The Tertiary period, indeed, is the age of mammals of all sorts, which were able to spread into the niches previously filled by reptiles, great and small. It is also the age of birds. At about 50 million years ago, the land route connecting Europe and North America was closed and separate evolutionary careers were required on both sides of the Atlantic Ocean. Toward the end of the Tertiary period, the mountain ranges known to us as the Alps, Andes, Rockies, Himalayas, Cascades, and Olympics rose.

The Quaternary period, our own, is divided (extremely unequally, in a ratio of 200 to 1) into the Pleistocene and Recent eras. The nearly 2 million years of the Pleistocene's duration is marked by even more than the dynamic Earth's normal rate of changes, especially in climate. The Pleistocene is a time of glaciers, whose comparatively rapid advances and retreats made a huge difference to the living organisms of the Earth, especially of the Northern Hemisphere. At one time it was thought that there were only five of these great glaciations, occurring at 1.6 million, 900,000, 600,000, 200,000, and 75,000 years ago, respectively. But sea bed research has revealed that the Pleistocene was disturbed by perhaps as many as thirty cycles of advancing and retreating ice, with relatively brief (10,000 to 15,000 year) interludes of warmer weather between the cycles. The ice fronts reached as far south as today's Berlin, New York City, and Wichita, and with their advance and retreat, climate zones in the interglacial periods were shifted as much as 20 to 30 degrees of latitude. The plants and animals under such pressure were naturally[1,2] selected, under these conditions, for mobility and adaptability, awareness and responsiveness. Mammals and birds were especially well suited for such circumstances, and about 10,000 years ago, by the end of the last ice age in North America, large fauna roamed, including mammoths, camels, saber-toothed cats, ground sloths, mastodons, horses, and lions. Strangely, however, all these species disappeared from this continent early in the current Recent era (which is perhaps simply the latest of the Pleistocene's interglacial remissions), the era that then succeeded the Pleistocene. These species died out even though climatic conditions became ever more benign as the ice withdrew northward and sea levels rose. Some speculate that hunting and other deliberate activities of human beings, not climate alone, may account for this new round of extinctions.

HUMAN VALUES

If this mention of human activity seems startlingly sudden, it reflects reality, given the geological scale on which the story of Earth values developed. Our species practically popped into existence, geologically speaking, over a period taking only 3 percent of the time since the disappearance of the dinosaurs. Assuredly, there was a more gradual evolution of the primate line of mammals that might have been included in the previous section, as leading to Homo sapiens, but I preferred to omit that detail altogether rather than indulge in even a hint of anthropocentric breath holding. I hope, instead, that between the previous section and this one, the story of Earth values and human values will be seen as woven out of a single cloth. Human values do add something extremely important that is not found among the Earth values except through our species, but this human addition is completely natural$_{2,3}$ and therefore fully at home in this chapter.

The uniquely human addition is, of course, ethical values, the red thread running through this book as a whole, now emerging again in connection with a search for a coherent, adequate, and applicable environmental ethics. Ethical values are not to be found anywhere in nature$_{1,2}$ prior to the entrance of language-using, symbolically free, imaginative, deliberative, responsible organisms—persons—in the story of Earth's development. But other values, nevertheless, are found in plenty. Organic values abounded, and still abound, in nature$_1$ before and beyond the human realm. Organisms fight to survive ("to live," as Whitehead put it) and to thrive ("to live well"). Long before the arrival of sentient species, the preference of living organisms for growing, proliferating, flourishing, changing form, entering new niches, is written in fossil records from the Precambrian swamps. I do not intend the word "preference" in any conscious sense, but if anything should be clear from the Earth's long adventure with life, it should be obvious that there is a tendency, a bent, a vector, a nisus, a trend, a pressure—choose whatever word you will—toward organic surviving and thriving, adapting and changing, defending and invading. If we look at the big picture, not through the reductionist lens of modernism but with fresh eyes wide with wonder, we may see a *telos* toward creativity. And if we are willing to sit loose on popular dogmas, we may also see a similar vector (less clearly, since it has no means to store information for itself or learn from its success and failure, as organisms can) in the preorganic Earth. There, too, we found the dynamics of self-organization, the rise of complexity out of simplicity, and the invention of the rudiments of system. From the clumping of heavy stuff cooked in star systems, to the organization of atmospheric-oceanic cycles, to the nurturing in its waters of far more complex molecules capable first of self-replication and then of mutating, spreading, growing in quantity and quality, the Earth's history has revealed a tendency toward complexity, sensitivity, and beauty. "But what of the great convulsions?" someone may ask. "The dramatic episodes of extinction?" Even these were always followed by explosions of creativity, as we have seen, and followed regularly by the coming into being of dramatically more complex and more sensitive entities whose various beauties warrant respect and often even admiration. Even our prime example of natural$_2$ vandalism, in the previous chapter, the Chicxulub meteor that destroyed the established good of the dinosaur kingdom 65 million years ago in the last of the great extinctions, was the painful event that forced open the Earth to the rapid development of mammals and birds, and to the special sort of mammals represented by the primates.

It is possible to speak meaningfully about "primate values," as distinguished from organic or mammalian values in general. Since human beings are primates, we should not be surprised to find a number of values we still recognize in ourselves. Primates, from very early on (from about 53 million to 37 million years ago), are characterized by special interests in seeing and handling. The primates' favored niche at the outset was arboreal. Living in trees focused special value on accuracy of sight, and accordingly the faces and brains of primates changed (at the expense of the sense of smell) as natural$_{1,2}$ processes selected for good eyesight, enhanced by binocular vision through eyes set side by side (giving needed depth perception). Likewise, since grasping was more valuable in the trees than tearing, claws were replaced in primates by nails (leading to more sensitive fingertip perceptions) and thumbs became opposable to help grip tree limbs. Feeding with one hand, with the other otherwise occupied, then became possible and so did closely inspecting things, taking an interest in what could be held and turned by the hands before the eyes. These aids to curiosity and manipulation became even more prominent as the true apes appeared between 23 million and 5 million years ago in Africa, Asia, and Europe but not in North America (separate evolution having long been required in the Western Hemisphere, with the closing of the land bridge 50 million years ago). In South America, some forms of New World monkeys evolved from primate ancestors that predated the isolation of the continent, but the main center of evolutionary creativity was in the Old World, especially in Africa.

It was in Africa as early as 4 million years ago that the first prehuman species began to walk upright while not in the trees. *Australopithecus* lived in mixed environments of woods and grasslands, not in the deep forests. Hands and eyes again were featured in value. Finding and picking berries, carrying provisions, self-defense, and so forth, were all greatly enhanced, and these useful traits were of selective advantage. Whether *Australopithecus* is in the direct ancestry of our species or not, it is clear that important changes were afoot, and by 2 million years ago, perhaps earlier, true humans (*Homo habilis* and *Homo rudolfensis*, the first to bear our genus' name) were chipping and flaking stone tools and weapons. Social cooperation of unprecedented complexity as well as manipulation of unprecedented quality are represented by tools and by the hunting and butchering they made possible. Energy from meat, supplementing foraged fruits and berries, allowed the growth of a large, energy-hungry brain, which in turn stimulated successful innovations in many directions. Another human species (*Homo erectus*) invented the finely chipped, versatile hand ax and spread widely through Africa, Asia, and Europe. This early human species also discovered the use of fire, perhaps as early as 1.5 million years ago. Skills in manipulation, curiosity, intelligence were being rewarded. Indeed, intelligence warranting the "sapiens" qualifier was manifested by *Homo sapiens neanderthalensis* by 180,000 years ago. Fully human, these Neanderthal men and women built dwelling places, scraped and tanned hides for clothing, engaged in art, and buried their dead. Since some of these dead were elderly or handicapped, the social order sustained by Neanderthal humans must have been generous even to nonproductive members. And since the burials show signs of ritual, it seems likely that Neanderthal culture involved symbolism and perhaps religion.

Homo sapiens sapiens, our own species, appeared about 100,000 years ago, first living in Africa, then expanding across the Old World continents. Modern humans must have migrated to Asia and Australia by 60,000 years ago, when a land route to the Australian continent was still open. They moved into Europe by 40,000 years ago, where Neanderthalers continued to dwell until roughly 25,000 years ago (perhaps victims of competition with our ancestors), and some crossed the land bridge from Siberia at least 12,000 years ago, while sea levels were still lowered by glaciers, and entered North America. There they found large herds of the Pleistocene mammals mentioned earlier, and there they learned the elaborate social organization needed to kill these herds. By the time the ice fronts had retreated north and the land bridge was flooded by rising seas, warmer weather allowed forests to replace the windy grasslands where mammoths and camels could be hunted en mass. Thus, at the beginning of our Recent period, new technologies had to be invented, including the bow and its blade-tipped arrow, to hunt the more solitary deer, moose, and elk hiding in the woods.

By this time, a mere 10,000 years ago, a time when simultaneously in the Old World the initiation of agriculture was laying the foundation for cities and civilizations, kings, priests, and armies, there can be little doubt that human values were abroad on the Earth. The human species, in common with all living forms, is like other species in certain respects and is unique in others. It is important to retain both aspects of this universal interplay of like and unlike if we are to avoid both the old temptations of human chauvinism and the newer confusions of well-meaning egalitarianism.

Humans share organic values with all organisms, including the plants, whenever we take a positive interest in food and drink, respiration, and reproduction. There is nothing surprising in the human quest "to live, to live well, to live better." We share that quest even with bacteria. Since we have these values in common with all living things, in principle we should be able to sympathize with all forms of life, to that extent, even though we may need to resist their values when they are directed against us. We may, that is, defend our cupboard against a family of mice, but we should, as the saying goes, at least "know where they are coming from." This is easier in the case of mice, fellow mammals, than it is in the case of mosquitos, though the principle is the same. Mosquitos, mice, and men are all hungering organisms with needs, with satisfactions and frustrations, and with characteristic methods of obtaining the former and avoiding the latter. We are often in competition with other living things, but humans, on reflection, should be able to understand that the competition itself is an expression of a common origin and a common organic existence.

Besides the most general organic values of survival, nourishment, and reproduction, we share sexual values with all species, plant and animal, that reproduce by meiosis; we share vertebrate values with a smaller but still huge class of animal organisms with interior skeletons and the tendency to develop nervous system focusing on a skull and brain; we share mammalian values with other sexually differentiated vertebrates which give milk to their young; and, of course, we share primate values with curious, manipulative, vision-oriented mammals like us. We are wholly immersed in the world of life, "plain citizens," as Aldo Leopold put it, of the biotic community (Leopold 1966, 262). But we alone are empowered to *know* this!

Yes, we can know all this. We know that we can, and sometimes do, sympathize even with the mouse, "wee, sleekit, cowrin tim'rous beastie," (Burns 1900, 38), against whose fellows we actively defend our stores. This makes us different in a particular, species-defining respect, from the other "citizens" of the biotic community in which we live. It is not objectionably "speciesist" to acknowledge, as fact, this distinguishing trait. What would be objectionable, rather, would be a chauvinist use of this fact to belittle or disdain the other forms of life merely because they have species-defining traits different from our own. Speed, strength, grace, tenacity, olfactory sensitivity, visual acuity, soaring flight, deep-sea diving—all these and countless more are kalogenic capacities achieved by the creative struggles of living entities toward their own modes of beauty. Human chauvinist disparagement of these wonderful achievements and the creatures who exercise them would be entirely out of place in environmental ethics, or ethics generally. The idea that humans are innately "better"—tout court—simply because in one respect we have a capacity that no other species on Earth can equal, is absurd.

But it would be no less absurd to deny, or be embarrassed by, the plain fact that over the ages of primate evolution, several species carried the tendency toward upright bipedal locomotion, manual manipulation, curiosity, brain-size enlargement, social cooperation, communication, tool use, and inventiveness to unprecedented levels. The fact is that language, which probably first emerged as a powerful aid in large hunts and other such socially useful contexts, developed into a symbolic vehicle for taking account of possibilities, both present and absent (Ferré 1998, 284–340). The surviving hominid species of which we are members is called "*sapiens*" just because of this conceptual capacity to deal with abstract symbols. Considering absent possibilities, such as future states of affairs, gives *Homo sapiens* an important edge in designing tools suited to accomplishing future goals. A log is not a canoe, but hollowed and shaped it can become a canoe; a future hollow state can be helped by fire and scraping; a sharp rock will advance the process of scraping and shaping. Similarly, alternative future states of affairs can be considered, given the powers of conceptual freedom from the present sensory environment. Which of several not-yet-present possibilities—a sharpened stone, a hollowed log, a successful hunt—should be brought into actuality? Which is most important? Might one be a helpful means to achieving another? Thus, once *Homo sapiens* learns conceptual freedoms, such as planning alternative futures, comparing importances, and judging preferences, the road is cleared for ethical deliberation as well.

We saw that the ethical process, discussed in more detail in the first part of this book, depends on the development and acceptance of norms and the exercise of sympathetic imagination. These capacities are possible for human beings once they have learned the freedoms of language and have felt the pressures of social expectation. These capacities, as such, do not make human beings "better" than other life forms, but they introduce a new dimension, the normative dimension, into adult human behavior that is not found in other species. It is only in this dimension that judgments of "better" and "worse" occur. Unfortunately, it may reveal human behavior as much "worse" than the behavior of any other species. Having a conscience is nothing to brag about. It often is a burden. For the first time in the history of the Earth, morally obligatory self-restraint becomes an issue. There is no point in preaching self-restraint to the forces of tectonic drift or orogenic upthrust, no way to persuade a predator to have pity on its prey. If human beings were "plain citizens" of the biotic community in the sense of being in no way importantly different from all the other entities in nature$_2$, then arguing over environmental policies would be beside the point. Then humans could not foresee the long-term consequences of their behavior, would be under no obligation to show restraint, or even to cultivate "enlightened self-interest." Ours is the only species capable of fretting under the constraints of environmental ethics. To put it bluntly, ours is the only species capable of acting irresponsibly toward other species and the Earth. Like it or not, this comes with the territory, with being a fully socialized adult human, with being (in other words) a personal organism free to consider alternatives under the aspect of norms, and decide consciously, deliberately, what to do.

The only animal so far evolved with the necessary equipment, physical and cultural, to weigh alternatives and decide about different possible ways of treating other animals is *Homo sapiens*. This fact makes moral reciprocity between our species and the others an impossible dream (even for those who have thoroughly enjoyed the story of the human who talks to animals in the *Dr. Dolittle* books [Lofting 1948]). We humans can (if we will) think normatively about our duties to the other species; they cannot even start to conceive deliberating about their "duties" to us. We have significant obligations, as I shall shortly discuss, to flora and fauna; flora and fauna can have no duties to us. What does this imply for the question of animal "rights"?

The answer is somewhat subtle. "Rights" normally correlate with "duties." That is, if I have a "right" to bodily integrity, then you have a corresponding "duty" to leave my body in one piece. This could be generalized: wherever there is a "right holder" there is a "duty bearer." If your claim for a right to vote is valid, then I (and all others) have a duty not to prevent you from voting. Reciprocally, if I have a duty not to bear false witness against anyone, then you (and everyone else) have a right to my truth-telling. Whether these norms are legal or moral makes no difference. They are norms. Humans operate all the time within them; animals and plants, so far as we know, do not. The degree of generality appropriate to rights and duties is important. Some rights are narrow. If you have contracted with me to deliver a load of wood, then I have a right to the delivery of that wood. My neighbor, not involved in the contract, has no such right to the delivery of my wood. Your obligation under this contract is to me, not to the neighbor. Still, the neighbor has a general interest that contracts be honored. On a yet more general level, it might be argued that the neighbor has a right to the protections of a legal system and that we all bear corresponding obligations to honor contracts and uphold civil society. Even more fundamental rights might include such rights as those to life, liberty, and the pursuit of happiness, normally claimed against all comers. Anyone who has such fundamental rights implies, reciprocally, that *everyone* is under obligation to respect them.

It is on this more general level that most discussion of "animal rights" occurs. If one claims that animals have the "right to life," for example, this is so basic that on its face it seems to put everyone under obligation not to kill whatever has this right, certainly not without due process of law. But who is "everyone"? Does a deer in the wilderness have a "right to life" against the wolf that is stalking it? This would be the case only if the wolf has a reciprocal obligation to respect the life of the deer. But a wolf is not the kind of organism capable of obligations, legal or moral. Moreover, since the wolf is carnivorous by nature$_3$, it might well be credited by those who speak of "rights" with having a "right" to eat the deer in the furtherance of its own "right to life." Despite this, the deer, lacking any language of norms, is under no obligation to respect the wolf's "right" to devour it, any more than the wolf is under obligation to respect the deer's "right" not to be devoured.

Something is radically wrong with this picture! The language of "rights" and "obligations" is out of place in the context of animal-to-animal interactions; it is out of place in the context of animal-to-vegetable, or vegetable-to-vegetable, interactions; it is out of place in the context of organic-to-inorganic interactions. It is appropriate *only* in the context of human beings and their various interactions. That is, if we have an obligation to avoid cruelty to animals, then in this limited context animals can be said to have a "right" not to be treated cruelly *by humans*. Perhaps rhetorically it is persuasive, even important, to use the language of rights in a society deluged with claims to rights of all sorts: civil rights, women's rights, gay rights, and so forth. Our culture is so accustomed to arguing ethics in terms of "rights" that I might be misunderstood if I were to deny that animals *have* rights. In the universe of discourse defined by "rights" talk, this might be misinterpreted by some as asserting that humans have no obligations toward animals. But such a view would be the exact opposite from mine. I believe that animals have value and that moral agents have obligations toward value of whatever sort, wherever found. The logical fact remains, however, that animals, trees, and lakes can be said to *have* rights, if they have rights at all, only in a derivative way, based on human duties toward them and applying only to human behavior in their connection. If there were no moral agents in the world, there would be no duties. If there were no duties, there could be no rights. It makes no sense to speak of "having" a right that no one is obliged to respect.

We must be careful here. It makes good sense to speak of having rights that no one actually does respect. My wood supplier *should* have fulfilled the contract but *did* not. I had a right that was violated in the breach. In this case the wood supplier was genuinely obliged but failed the obligation. If, however, in some context there is literally no obligation for *anyone* to do or refrain from doing *anything*—a very different matter—then it makes no sense, in that context, to claim a right to anything. The "right" would have no referent.

As long as Robinson Crusoe was alone on his island (Defoe 1936), he had no rights there. Is this shocking? It should not be. As a moral agent, he had moral *obligations*, for example, not to do unjustified harm to the flora and fauna around him. But since there were no other moral agents present, his claiming rights would have been without meaning. He had no rights against the sea, no rights against the rain or wind, no rights against the palm trees or the wild pigs. "Rights" are an artifact of human culture. In the absence of culture there are no rights.

Animal rights questions are therefore complex from the start. They presuppose entities with value, toward which humans ought to direct moral consideration, and they presuppose human culture. I welcome the recent development of "animal law" in some leading law schools (*New York Times*, 18 August 1999: 1, 16; and 22 August 1999, Sec. 4: 1, 4). From the perspective of personalistic organicism, the new emphasis, taking nonhuman animal members of the human environment seriously for their intrinsic importance, is overdue. What would be problematic, but what may be happening at this writing, would be casting the issues excessively in terms of "rights." Here I am willing to compromise, however, in a good cause. If it is practically important to speak loudly of the genuine but derivative anthropogenic "rights" reflected back from animals in the light of human moral obligations, such speaking is surely a worthy use of rhetoric in the fight against massive human unconcern. Such unconcern may not always have been the dominant human attitude, but it seems to have characterized modern civilization, in which most humans have been insulated from regular contact with wild animals (Midgley 1984). Still, the short-term usefulness of rhetoric aside, in good logic it would be better, when founding animal law, to emphasize instead the real *values* of animals (and of plants and even of inorganic entities) and the powerful *obligations* human beings have toward these. A legal and ethical framework, to be secure against the many foreseeable storms that will inevitably howl against it, should be well-anchored to the ground. That ground is not "rights" but real value and human obligation.

A powerful voice urgently calling on the human race to seek such a ground was Aldo Leopold (1886–1948), a professional forester and pioneer environmental ethicist. In his essay, "The Land Ethic," a key chapter in his *A Sand County Almanac* (Leopold 1966), Leopold noted that ethics is an evolving phenomenon, gradually becoming more inclusive of what deserves to be taken seriously, what possesses significant value, and what therefore has proper ethical standing in human deliberations. Odysseus thought nothing of hanging "all on one rope a dozen slave-girls of his household whom he suspected of misbehavior during his absence" (Leopold 1966, 237). He regarded his slaves as mere property, to be treated without ethical constraints. But in the intervening millennia, the range of recipients of human moral concern has slowly but steadily widened. Virtually all mature codes of ethics now include other ethnic and language groups, prisoners of war, people of color, and women, within their range. The next step, Leopold urged, is to stop considering the Earth mere real estate but instead embrace the fertile land, including the animals and plants that live on it, as also morally significant. In his words, "The extension of ethics to this . . . element in human environments is, if I read the evidence correctly, an evolutionary possibility and an ecological necessity" (Leopold 1966, 239). I heartily agree, adding only that from the viewpoint of personalistic organicism it is also a welcome *metaphysical* possibility (Ferré 1996, 305–70).

In the same famous essay, Leopold states how such a "land ethic" will then define "right" and "wrong": "A thing is right when it tends to preserve the integrity, stability, and beauty of the biotic community. It is wrong when it tends otherwise" (Leopold 1966, 262). This I believe is a profound formulation and well worth some meditation. In the end I do not believe it is quite adequate for a full ethical framework, but as a stimulus for environmental ethics it has proven enormously rich (Callicott 1987; also 1989).

In the following paragraphs, I will reflect from my own perspective on the three key elements of Leopold's land ethic: biotic *integrity*, *stability*, and *beauty*. I do not limit myself to explicating Leopold's own interpretations in what follows. These will be my mediations, from the perspective of personalistic organicism combined with the ethical principles reached earlier. But they will be thoughts stimulated by Leopold's insightful guidance in this new domain. For this leadership I, and many besides me, are deeply in his debt.

First, Leopold asserts that human actions are right that tend to preserve the *integrity* of the biotic community. What does integrity mean in this context? To me, integrity at bottom refers to wholeness, to unity, completeness. It comes from the same stem as "integer" in mathematics, a whole number, not a fraction. Preserving integrity is fundamental. Just as one's bodily integrity is basic to organic survival, integrity of the biosphere and its various subcommunities constituting our environment is the first necessary obligation that humans must recognize as normative. "Do no harm." Breaking up the relevant environment is vandalism. From a Whiteheadian point of view, the immediate environment is the precondition to richness in prehension. Beware! Fragment this physical environment at peril, since its many achievements are the inheritance of each new concrescent occasion. If this heritage is allowed to be broken, process will continue, but with diminished resources for kalogenic achievement.

I take this to be a warning not to break up habitat. The habitat of any biotic community is partly living, partly nonliving. Atoms of oxygen are nonliving but essential; molecules of water are nonliving but crucial for everything alive. Polluting air or draining water are ways in which humans destroy the integrity of habitat. These nonliving entities are not themselves in much danger. Their dim subjectivities will continue to perpetuate their molecular forms with or without our nurture. But as providing habitat for living organisms (subjects of lives of their own), such material molecules have great instrumental value although their intrinsic value is small. They perform their instrumental goods not just as molecules, of course, but in structures, "societies" of living and nonliving things tangled together. Breaking up the tangles, Leopold reminds us, is prima facie wrong. Perhaps there can be justified disturbances of habitat. If not, human beings could hardly live on Earth, since everything we do impacts some habitat or other. But such disturbance needs to be recognized as posing an important *ethical* question, whether or not the justification is strong enough to make it moral to harm the integrity of the biotic community. This, in sum, is what Leopold says to me on his first point: preserving the wholeness or unity of the natural$_1$ environment, all other things being equal, is the right thing to do. "First do no harm."

Leopold's second great watchword, "stability," is a process term. It may not immediately sound like one, since "process" is usually associated with "change." But, no less than change, stability takes time to take place. It is in fact essentially a dynamic notion, like equilibrium. And, like equilibrium, it requires constant adjustment to be maintained. What specifically contributes to the self-restoring of biotic communities is an empirical matter, currently much debated. Though empirical questions of this sort are not a philosopher's job to settle, certain general observations are in order.

As the history of our dynamic Earth reminds us, absolute stability is no realistic goal. Let us grant that Leopold knew this perfectly well and was not recommending an impossible ideal. All stabilities are finite and provisional. The stability of my body's metabolism had a beginning and will have an end. Likewise, the stability of species, ecosystems, and landscapes are not forever. Further, nature$_2$ knows no absolutely normative state. Stabilities are always relative to a background and to the players active in the foreground. Extinctions and radiations of species, mutations, invasions—all the dynamics we have recently noted—define new stabilities even as they displace old stabilities. Yet within all this finitude and relativity, stability remains profoundly important. Even though the stability of my body's metabolism is finite, I value it dearly. It is the precious background equilibrium that makes the realization of all my other values possible, from moment to moment and over the long-term. Without active systems for attaining and prolonging homeostasis, maintaining my body temperature within a normal range, keeping my blood pressure and heartbeat within a stable compass, suppressing antibodies that would hijack my life, and much more, my existence across time as a personal organism would not be possible, and the achievements I most value in past or prospect would be ruled out. Therefore dynamic stability, however finite, provisional, relative, is indispensable.

What makes this wonderful equilibrium possible in my body, and in the biotic community, is systematic complexity. Built-in redundancy, "fail-safe" mechanisms, make airplane and space vehicle systems stable in performance and greatly contribute to their success. In similar ways, biological organisms and communities benefit from complexity. In a simple ecosystem depending on only one predator, for example, the likelihood of wild gyrations in population, extreme instability, is magnified. If some misfortune befalls the lonely predator, the prey will multiply unchecked until food supplies or other environmental constraints force a crash. But if many predators compete in a more complex system, the likelihood of dynamic equilibrium between predators and prey is hugely increased. If one predator is disabled, the others will fill in to retain the balance. The point could be expanded indefinitely. Biological diversity, in consequence, becomes a corollary imperative for the assurance of stability in the biotic community. (For those versed in his language, a Whiteheadian interpretation of this ethical demand in terms of the phases of concrescence would recognize it as paralleling the phase of complexity—reversion and comparative physical feeling—when maintaining maximal complexity is of the essence.) Without diversity, and the encouragement of diversity, no stability can long endure. Stability must forever fight against entropic decay. Just holding on is not good enough. To maintain the values even of provisional and finite stabilities takes investment in diversity, novelty, adventure. "Protect existing good" is not an imperative to passivity. Nature$_2$ has worked hard to bring about the complexities of existing good, and lazy philistinism toward the environment is no appropriate response. Without the active intervention of human legislation, without public and private protective policies, endangered species will perish, the biotic community will be steadily diminished, and stability will suffer. As I hear Leopold on stability, in sum, he is saying: whatever we can do to preserve the diversity and dynamic equilibrium of the biotic community, all other things being equal, is the right thing to do.

Leopold called, third, for human ethical attention to the "beauty" of the biotic community. What does this mean? I cannot believe that Leopold, whose whole effort was to push his readers away from anthropocentric thinking, could have referred merely to the beauty that human beings enjoy in contemplating the biotic community. He was a person much aware of the beauties in nature$_1$ to be enjoyed by humanity. He wrote feelingly about, and sketched skillfully scenes from his natural$_1$ environment. But visual beauty does not reside in human eyes alone. Bees, butterflies, and birds are drawn to, and enjoy, the beauties of blossoms tossing in the breeze. Flowers have become beautiful because there is selective advantage in good looks. The beauty of the biotic community is defined primarily by the aesthetic satisfactions of its own membership, of which we are one, the appreciative species which alone can verbalize about its appreciations. But we are only one, with our own species-dependent appreciation equipment. Millions of other species have vision, smell, taste, but not exactly like ours. Ours may be sharper and more intense in some ways, due to the powers of consciousness, memory, and anticipation, but others may exceed ours in other ways. Richness, complexity, and depth of appreciation may not be perfectly correlated with numbers of neurons. We simply do not know how rich the subjectivities of other organisms may be. Still, we have no reason to judge dogmatically that other organisms do not appreciate at all. The evidence is all on the other side. Even microorganisms are attracted to bits of food. The full beauties of dining by candlelight and chamber music may be denied other species, but the satisfactions of digestion are not. Nature$_2$ abounds in beauties appreciated on every scale of time and space.

On this third dimension of Leopold's imperatives, we finally come to recognize the proper place of the unique individual. "Integrity" refers primarily to habitats, "stability" to species and ecosystems; but "beauty" has its primary locus in individual subjectivities, simple or complex. Without appreciators there are no appreciations, and beauty cannot exist without appreciation. Its being is in its being appreciated. There can be beauti*ful* things, existing quite objectively, provisionally apart from appreciations, things such as paintings locked away in closets, but what we mean by "beauti*ful*" in such cases is that these paintings can be relied upon, under appropriate circumstances (lighting, etc.), to stimulate aesthetic appreciations in relevant appreciators. The idea of an appreciator must always be in the background of any talk about beauty or the beautiful. Individual organisms count, then, in the ethical perspective recommended by the Leopold's land ethic. They are the loci as well as the exemplars of beauty.

From a kalogenic Whiteheadian perspective, the basic reason for beauty anywhere is in the satisfactions achieved everywhere by actual occasions of creative energy. These individual occasions are always in relation, as we have seen (Ferré 1996, 316–24)—they are in large part constituted by their relations—but their value is their own. The ethical application (many societies of occasions and orders of complexity later) is that an individual deer, though perhaps one of too many for the good of the species or even of the habitat, also has a good of its own apart from its species or its habitat. All other things being equal, it is for that unique good, for the sake of the specific beauty of its individual existence, that the habitat or the species is important. If its beauty must be sacrificed for the larger good of the habitat or the health of its species, what is finally meant by these "larger" goods is the actualization of many more unique goods over the long run. All other things are not always, or even usually, equal. The values of some individual organisms may not trump the values of many more diverse sorts of organisms for indefinite ages to come. But those individual values are none the less real, within the collective beauty of the biotic community. They are in an important sense fundamental, not to be dismissed (even when sometimes they must be sacrificed) for the "good of the whole." Preserving and enhancing the beauty of the biotic community is a matter calling for constant balances, repeated judgments between individual and group goods, between short-term and long-term needs.

The preservation of a species depends on constant multiplication of individual members, and in this minimal sense even *preserving* calls for *creating*. Insofar as each new exemplar of a species has a good for itself, Leopold's imperative to "preserve" beauty already hints at our third maxim: "create new good." But I would prefer to think that Leopold would not, on reflection, resist a friendly amendment to his overall statement of his land ethic by the addition of the words "and enhance" to his emphasis on preservation. He wrote, "A thing is right when it tends to preserve the integrity, stability, and beauty of the biotic community." I think it would not violate the spirit of this ethic to say, "A thing is right when it tends to preserve and *enhance* the integrity, stability, and beauty of the biotic community." With this amendment, environmental ethics can more easily take cognizance of the realities of Earth's dynamic history and probable future. Preservation is not our only duty. Even the preservation of integrity, stability, and beauty, as we have seen, is not a static matter. Enhancement is needed to stave off decay. Enhancement, moreover, seems good in itself. It is the enlargement, widening, improvement of what is already good or beautiful. True, human beings should not be excessively confident that they are clever enough or powerful enough or pure enough in motive to launch major projects for enhancing the natural$_1$ environment. Our record over recent years has been dismal. But, in principle, anthropogenic interventions need not always be destructive of beauty, diversity, or the capacity of nature$_2$ to thrive in directions of complex richness. *Homo sapiens*, with an enhanced moral perspective and more mature attitudes, may cautiously try to be more a gardener than a forager through the ever-changing universe. If there is a persuasive "counter-agency" working against the forces of decay in the universe (whether centralized or decentralized is not now the issue), then we, as a species in a postmodern context with postmodern attitudes, might find ourselves cooperating in a great cosmic project. Or, better, perhaps we might say that our species could be a local expression of the cosmic project toward enhanced beauty and deepened awareness in the universe as a whole. "Create new good," done wisely enough, could lead to a new epoch on the ever-freshened Earth.

I find these meditations on Leopold's seminal declaration inspiring, but not enough. He omitted the important processes of thinning and cultivating that every healthy garden needs. Without benefit of a hoe, thoughtfully employed, seedlings run wild and choke each other. What is missing in Leopold's definition of the land ethic is a principle of distribution, normative control of the important goods he calls for. What we need to add, in other words, is the imperative: "Be fair." Justice needs to oversee the balance among the claimants of the biotic community, including human claims. The hardest part of postmodern environmental ethics will be attaining ecojustice in a world of fiercely competing centers of value.

All the species of the world can be fierce, unprincipled, ruthless in their strategies of growth—except for *Homo sapiens*. Or should I put it differently? Humanity *can* be fierce, unprincipled, ruthless, as we have amply proven in action, but only humanity *could* be mild, thoughtful, or merciful, through policies forged in sympathy, conceptualized by norms, and freely implemented. The special beauty of justice, the harmony of harmonies that blends and resolves the clash of many worthy toots, whistles, and roars, is humanity's alone to conceive, approach, and—to the extent it is achieved—enjoy. Justice is a norm which, like all norms, can be (and regularly is) ignored or rejected, but it is nonetheless a mighty ideal. In our unique role of purposeful caretaker of the Earth, we can, if we choose, apply this standard to policies that have bearing on the distribution of vital good among other species. And this ideal can, if we choose, also be applied to policies that have bearing on the distribution of vital good between other species and the human race, in our common role of fellow life form on the Earth—just one more needy species, but one whose conscience adds a special moral need.

Let us start by considering fairness in our unique role of purposeful caretaker, where human interests are not directly challenged. Some might ask, do we even have a right to such a role? Alas, if we can understand the question, it is too late to ask it. Since we are by nature$_3$ intelligent animals, equipped through language with concepts freeing us from being concerned only about the immediate environment, since we take account of alternative future outcomes, acting or refraining from acting in ways that have foreseeable consequences, and since among our concepts are those of behavioral norms (like "having a right" to a role), *we cannot escape* the morally responsible position of purposeful caretaker, even if we would. As soon as we understand that weeds will choke our garden if we neglect to use the hoe, we share responsibility for the outcome whether we choose to defend our radishes and lettuce or not. Since our anticipated crops have value to us, greater value than the invading weeds, we normally consider it warranted to distribute the space in our garden, and with it access to soil, water, and sunlight, in favor of our seedlings. Between weeds and radishes, our clear interests tilt the scales of justice toward favoring the radishes.

But now, acknowledging the inescapability of our responsible role in a world of competing organisms, a world in which either actions or inactions will have predictable consequences, what does "being fair" mean when human interests are negligible, or evenly balanced? This is a most general question, and we had better be warned not to overdetermine any answer. It would be a foolish environmental ethics that presumed to lay down specific recommendations in the absence of specific circumstances. Defeasible guidelines, rules of thumb for dealing with concrete issues, not recipes for every occasion, are called for at such a level of generality. (Here something like W. D. Ross' "prima facie duties," commended in the opening chapter of this book, might be most in order.)

Two rough prima facie duties are not out of reach, given the previous discussion. A primary rule of thumb in reaching distributive justice among competing interests, for example, is conservative: make no interventions, avoid "adjusting" the scales, without adequate cause. "Do no harm" to the existing distribution, that is, unless a greater harm can be anticipated from inaction. This familiar warning, now at the level of distributing existing good rather than simply defending it, respects the processes of nature$_{1,2}$ as first resort. "Benign neglect," where intervention is not clearly called for, is a rule of wisdom. Responsible restraint is not always easy for our species, but as our ecological understanding increases, perhaps we will improve our skills in holding back, trusting nature$_{1,2}$ to balance its own books in its own time.

The second obvious prima facie duty is more interventionist in thrust, an inverse of the first. Where greater harm to the quality of distribution of goods can be anticipated from inaction, then action to prevent such harm is fair. "Defend existing good" holds for the good of equitable distribution of goods as well as for raw goods themselves. Here judgments of quality and quantity are unavoidable. If, for example, a species of microorganism were to threaten, by unchecked increase, to destroy all the grasses in a rich, diverse prairie ecosystem, the continuation of the richer good could justify preventative intervention by humans able to limit the microorganism and save the prairie. This would, by hypothesis, be an intervention not for the sake of human interests (let us assume that none were involved), but out of respect for the myriad interests and rich biocentric beauties of the grassland ecosystem itself. But note. There is a metaphysical assumption here (one that personalistic organicism is happy to make) that there are (or would be) *more real values* in a diverse, highly evolved prairie ecosystem than in a nearly empty desert filled with microorganisms perishing from lack of a host. Environmental ethics, if it is to deal with ecojustice, must be able to speak of more value and less value. For any who are squeamish in principle about ever making such judgments, the very notion of "fair distribution" can gain no traction. This example, pitting the values represented by my hypothetical microorganisms against the values represented by my thriving prairie ecosystem, including the grasses, herbivores, insects, birds, and predators, should be a test. Can it be admitted without embarrassment or resort to quotation marks that the latter situation would hold *more values* than the former? If so, the road to a postmodern environmental ethics remains open. If not, no more talk about ecojustice should be indulged.

I find the road open, even inviting. Therefore it is time to confront the hardest question of all: how can humans, as one life form, a product of the pitiless struggle for survival, uniquely responsible to norms of conscience without hope of reciprocity, do justice to *other* life forms lacking speech or conscience when urgencies of real values conflict?

Any easy, optimistic answer would be fatuous. Most humans actually deal with their environments as needy organisms more than as normative persons. Personalistic organicism must recognize how fragile the personalist webs of moral restraint become when our organic needs—even minor wants—are in question. But as a species we have come a relatively long way in (geologically speaking) a relatively short time. Aldo Leopold was right to point out that there has been a significant evolution in ethics. Not all have participated. It is a cultural rather than a biological evolution, not secured by changes in genetic codes. Nothing guarantees its advance, even its retention. Still, at least a few of our species have managed and do manage to control their actions by norms, even when by doing so they relinquish maximizing personal or species benefits. Moral norms do count within the repertoire of a significant fraction of our fellow humans, even when self-renunciation is required. There is no reason in principle to despair of this fraction becoming larger if human knowledge and sympathy enlarges in the postmodern era.

Not all ecojustice even requires renunciation of human interests. Sometimes it is fair to insist, while respecting values of every kind wherever found, that human values legitimately outweigh those of rival species. Defending a personal life against the onslaught of microorganisms is not unjust. Even millions of barely aware microbial value centers, hungering for reproduction, cannot come close to matching the qualities of beauty open to creation by a single conscious human self. "Preserve existing good" is as valid for saving persons as for saving prairies. There is at this writing a visceral reluctance in some circles to acknowledging that sometimes human values do legitimately trump others. Well-intentioned resistance to human chauvinism occasionally swings too far in the opposite direction.

I have frequently asked my classes in ethics to consider what they would do if, driving down a country road, they were suddenly confronted with a chicken running into the road from the right and a child from the left. Which way would they swerve? Years ago virtually all my students, without much hesitation, would choose to save the child's life over the chicken's, with due commiseration for the innocent bird. But more recently, this little example has become seriously problematic to a significant number of conscientious believers in "biocentric egalitarianism." I understand their impatience with widespread reflex assumptions of blanket human superiority, leading to heedless policies of anthropocentric favoritism in all cases. But "blanket" thinking of all sorts is just the problem, including the reflex view that human values are always suspect, no more worthy than or perhaps usually inferior to any other claims. Personalistic organicism, as I have already tried to make clear, supports no blanket claims and certainly opposes human chauvinism, but it seems to me strange dogma to find nothing to choose, quite aside from the legal consequences of killing the child, between the potential intrinsic values represented by a child and a chicken. Our species, while guarding against blind self-congratulation, needs to acknowledge appropriate self-regard. Sometimes the verdict of distributive justice comes down on the side of human interests. If it never did, the judge would have to be considered biased.

These are not the problem areas, however. Sometimes the verdict of distributive justice must come down on the other side, less pleasant for humans. Personal norms of justice will then clash with organic desires. When might this be? How might resulting conflicts be resolved? It is again impossible and inappropriate to offer detailed answers to ethical questions in the absence of specific circumstances, but three domains of prima facie duties to fair distribution may at least suggest what would be involved in making real decisions.

First, a basic clash between human interests and the needs of other organisms may appear at the great shared interface with habitat. Habitat, as we saw earlier, is the organic-inorganic precondition for what Leopold called the "integrity" of the biotic community. To destroy habitat is an immensely serious issue for the ethical treatment of the Earth, because with habitat go unnumbered forms of life dependent upon it. How shall finite habitat be distributed if we are to be fair both to our own values as a species and, as appropriate, to the myriad other species whose destiny our decisions control? One issue, if we are to be fair, revolves around the intensity and comprehensiveness of the values involved. Would disturbing this habitat have the foreseeable consequence of bringing about the extinction of a species dependent on it? That would be a matter for great intensity of concern, since extinctions are forever. Extinction, that is, is not simply a matter of inconveniencing individual products of nature$_2$'s artistry, forcing them to move or regroup elsewhere, but it is a vandalizing of irreplaceable formal achievements of complexity and beauty. The Endangered Species Act in the United States, and similar legislation elsewhere, codifies the moral gulf between killing and extinction, transforming moral duty into legal obligation to protect habitat on which life forms, recognized as in danger of extinction, depend.

Inevitably such legislation becomes controversial when human interests are frustrated by such protections. These human interests are not negligible. Livelihoods may be lost, for example, by loggers and lumber mill workers in the northwestern United States if such duties to nonhuman species are maintained and enforced. These are serious matters, with the well-being of human families, neighborhoods, and even regions threatened, not to mention the wealth of stockholders and corporate officials. But extinction is forever; lumbering is not. Since adjustments can be made, and, given human good will and inventiveness, new means of economic support can be developed, the balance of fairness calls for humans to adjust. Still, equally in fairness, not all the burden should fall on the local people alone. If the ethical concern leading to the legislation is national, then resources to assist in the adjustments should be national as well.

Another ethical consideration is the quality of the needs or wants that are in conflict, when conflict arises. This could be illustrated at every level, including but not only at the level of habitat. Just how urgent are the urgencies involved? Are humans exaggerating their problems and clinging inappropriately to the comforts of the status quo? These are morally relevant issues to raise when weighing judgments of fairness. They come up vividly, on a second general level, in connection with ethical questions about the diversity of the biotic community, what (in honor of Leopold) we called the "imperative of stability." The reintroduction of wolves into some areas of the western United States has been well supported by arguments from the "ecological good." The biotic community needs its larger predators for optimum stability, let us grant. But is this fair to the ranchers whose grazing animals may become prey? Again, human interests are asked to give way to the claims of nonhuman good. How strong are the interests against letting wolves once more range in their previous haunts? At this writing they have not been demonstrated to be intense or comprehensive enough to convince government agencies that injustice is being done by this human intervention on behalf of biotic diversity. It is important to note that it is conceivable that a convincing case might be made. If a genuine act of ethical deliberation is to be done, under norms, the outcome must be responsive to the detailed factual context in concrete circumstances, and circumstances can change, as can our understanding of these circumstances.

It is hard to imagine, however, circumstances that would justify as fair the suffering of individual rabbits and other experimental animals in the interest of, for example, cosmetic development and testing. This is a third dimension, where individuals are involved directly in the weighing of ecojustice. Species go extinct, but only individuals suffer. Both these truths count in weighing human policy toward nonhuman nature$_1$ on the scales of a comprehensive ethical framework. Here the quality of the human need is critical. Realistic environmental ethics must acknowledge the reality and the inevitability of animal suffering. Beauty and pain energize the world. But when human beings deliberately cause animal suffering, the demands of ecojustice require that at a minimum it be in service of a cause urgent enough to justify it. Medical research, properly controlled by ethical norms, may qualify under the standards of fairness as justifying the pain inflicted on experimental animals. Perhaps the suffering of these individuals may contribute to the greater health of their own species, if veterinary medicine is at issue. Perhaps this suffering will be for the sake of basic understanding that will enhance organic health in many species, including the human. Even if human health alone is the goal, under specified circumstances this may be justified, though always with the proviso that painful animal experimentation be used only as a last resort, that needless or redundant experimentation be forbidden, that every possible means be taken to minimize pain, and the like. Frivolous ends, in contrast, do not weigh heavily in the scales of justice, not against concrete frustration and suffering. Finding exotic new cosmetics for evening wear does not count as an organic urgency that warrants dripping corrosive liquids into immobilized animal eyes in the Draize Eye Irritancy Test, a standard modern practice (Fox 1990; Roszak 1969, 276–78; Midgley 1984, 37–39). "Be fair!" must at some point draw lines even when human desires, backed by enormous economic forces, clamor for what is wrong.

A similar argument is pursued by ethical vegetarians, who consider the exploitation of animals for meat (some add animal products in general) to be an equally flagrant misuse of human power. Personalistic organicism will listen respectfully to these concerns, and will be sympathetic at many points, especially regarding unfair infliction of animal suffering, but in the end I do not believe our position requires abstinence from the full banquet set by nature$_2$ to delight our natures$_3$. I would like, therefore, to add a short reflection on the ethics of eating, as a coda to this chapter on natural$_{1,2,3}$ values.

It is well to begin with a reminder that "life is robbery," as Whitehead succinctly put it. "The living society may, or may not, be a higher type of organism than the food which it disintegrates. But whether or no it be for the general good, life is robbery. It is at this point that with life morals become acute. The robber requires justification" (Whitehead 1976, 105). With the exception of the primary producers (that is, the green plants that long ago "learned" to synthesize organic compounds from inorganic materials by using energy from the Sun), all living organisms depend for their nutrition on other already living sources. The herbivores "rob" the green plants; the carnivores "rob" the herbivores; the decomposers "rob" all of the above. Thus, for humans to live at all, we must exploit living things. We have no other choice, short of species suicide. Vegetarians cannot properly assert that "exploitation is indivisible," or the like, as though we were dealing with absolutes rather than with carefully nuanced choices and thoughtfully considered means. Even regarding the vegetable kingdom, the maxim "do no harm" is a prima facie obligation that should warn humans against vandalizing created value. Casual smashing of plants or despoliation of trees is wrong. Elephants in the wild walk heavily on their vegetative environments, but humans should not. Ours is the species with a conscience.

We need not eat our berries and grains with a bad conscience, however, if we are careful to minimize harms and keep them proportional to legitimate needs. Especially when we have followed the maxim to "create new good" by ecologically thoughtful agricultural practices that vastly increase the supply of fruits and vegetables, grasses and grains, we are entitled to rejoice in the bounty we have coaxed from nature$_2$ as we ingest the nutrients necessary for our lives and delicious to our senses.

Once the principle is established that "taking life" for human survival and enjoyment is allowed, the question still remains, "what kinds of life?" Vegetarians are not unanimous in their answers. Some allow "exploitation" of animal products, such as milk, eggs, or leather, and some do not. Some allow the eating of fish, ruling out only land animals, while some eschew eating or using any living thing, aquatic or terrestrial, or any products of living things, except primary producers and fungi. For the purposes of this brief reflection, I shall focus on the one sort of eating that all vegetarians forbid, namely, beef, lamb, pork, chicken, or turkey, the favored meats of the modern world. Is it licit to "take life" from sentient creatures, mammals or birds, for the sake of our human nourishment and pleasure?

We should begin by probing the reasons thoughtful people give for answering "no" to this question. Let us assume (an actually disputed point) that eating meat is not necessary for human health, that it is a wholly optional matter. Then, if freely chosen practices of breeding, raising, and slaughtering animals should bring about a net amount of suffering in the world, these practices, no matter how entrenched in traditions and institutions, would be wrong. I agree that if the world's net value, in quality and quantity, is actually reduced by eating meat, we should not participate in such eating and should work, despite obstacles, to end the practice as soon as possible.

But is it the case? Here personalistic organicism will insist on examining the facts in context, as all thoughtful ethical deliberation requires. And in such examination, personalistic organicism must certainly be affected by horror stories of confinement and cruelty, when they are reliably told. Whenever economic motives in late-modern-agribusiness are allowed to override consideration for the welfare of sentient creatures dependent on human care, a serious wrong is done. Chickens, kept all their lives in tiny cages in which their wings cannot be spread, calves, confined to stalls in which they cannot move, will rightly stir to indignation any humans who consider animal frustration morally relevant and, when possible, stir them also to appropriate action. Selective refusal, as in declining to eat veal produced in cruel ways, or selective shopping, as in deciding to buy more expensive eggs from free-ranging chickens in support of economic alternatives to battery cage monopolies, will be ethically appropriate actions, when available. When such means are not available, perhaps wider boycotts and more strident political actions are called for.

Still, political and economic campaigns to remedy discovered wrongs are different in scale and aim from the wholesale rejection of meat implied by vegetarianism. Let us agree that in the current situation, where humane practices in animal husbandry are arguably more notable for their absence than their presence, some may find it symbolically needful to reject meat entirely. This is an option, I believe, that should be respected, especially if it is accompanied by efforts to regulate and enforce modern institutions of animal care and slaughter so as to minimize animal frustration and pain. Taken in this light, such a decision for vegetarianism could represent the sacrifice of an historically important good in human life for the sake of raising general awareness and, if possible, changing the history of human-animal relations for the better.

In my view, however, such a decision, though approvable, is not morally obligatory for all, even for those who care about, and work against animal abuse in the meat industry. Despite the currently shamefully imperfect ethical state of meat production, there are strong reasons for humans to continue participating fully in the food chain, including the moderate eating of meat (Ferré 1986a, 391–406). If we were somehow to find that the net experience of life is negative for a majority of the untold millions of animals bred into existence simply because of the human demand for meat, then my answer might be different. Such a finding, I believe, would tilt the ethical scale against eating meat as long as such a condition persisted. But this condition is not prima facie suggested by the mainly contented behavior of cattle, sheep, and pigs observed around the world. Whether it is the case for poultry is an open question, deserving of debate.

Sometimes we are in danger of anthropomorphic sentimentalism when we deliberate on animal experience. We think of ourselves being fattened on ample daily rations, treated to good health care, and the like, but with the constant dread awareness hanging heavily over us of our inevitable doom in the slaughterhouse. It would be terrifying! We might wish that we had never been born. All our experiences, no matter how physically comfortable in the present, would be ruined in every moment by the horror and resentment of our knowing that the future of our personal selves is to be degraded to the status of meat alone—that our very existence was motivated by nothing but being used in this way. This would be a strong argument, if we needed one, against the morality of cannibalism, but it does not apply to creatures whose natures$_3$ do not include the conceptual capacity to worry about their long-term futures. The present and the short-term future are what count for these sentient but conceptually limited organisms. If humans take care that these morally relevant experiences are satisfying, and that the unanticipated end to all experience is swift and painless, the balance of lives so lived will be positive additions to the values of the world. Human meat-eating in such conditions would contribute, under the maxim "create new good," to the rich texture of the living world.

Humans, moreover, are natural$_3$ meat-eaters. The extra energy stored in meat once gave our evolutionary ancestors an edge over the eaters of roots and berries alone. Our species may not be required to eat meat, as lions are, but we can choose to nourish ourselves in this way, and we have done so gladly, as a species, from the earliest days.

Strong symbolism rises here, too, if humans use the occasion of eating meat to affirm their place in the full ecological cycle, both historical and nutritional. We need not live in shame of our historical heritage. There has been a gradual awakening of conscience and a gradual expansion of ethical consideration over the course of time. Rather than regret our past, we can nurture the continued growth of this moral tendency with ecological knowledge and ethological insight. If human beings have been heedless and cruel in the past (and we have been), this can be mitigated and corrected for the future without drastically isolating ourselves from our ancestors and from the natural$_2$ cycles of the food chain. Eating and being eaten is a large part of the story of life on Earth. Earthling values, full of the urgencies of change, fecundity, death, and renewal, become incarnate in the intimacy of eating.

Since we are by nature$_3$ thinking animals, we need not eat unthinkingly. Mealtime thoughts on a postmodern diet might include long historic memories of organic existence, satisfactions too deep for words, and gratitude for lives shared. In this varied world of organisms, values of many kinds are supported, including feasting on meat. And among our mealtime thoughts, from time to time, could be included the ecological acknowledgement that we, too, were destined by nature$_2$ to be eaten! Sometimes we resist this destiny with the wiles of culture. We try to slow the process by arranging for our remains to be embalmed with materials designed to resist natural$_2$ decay. Over geological time, we may realize, this aim is futile, but, despite this, some go to great lengths to insulate their remains from decomposition. Sometimes, instead, we opt to be artificially devoured, outflanking our biological decomposers through the ancient human artifice of fire. But the destiny of decomposition is still served. One way or another, we cannot in the end escape being "eaten." Finally, our remains return their elemental qualities to the Earth from which they came. These old materials, once synthesized in the wombs of stars, now living in us, will be made available by being decomposed—rapidly or slowly makes no difference—and readied for new adventures.

As we feast thinkingly, we may further reflect that if we were to let nature$_2$ take its course, our biological decomposers would be astonishingly similar to the bacteria that were among the earliest organisms to make Earth a living planet. We, among the latest to arrive, find that our individual returns to stardust would in that case be processed by the earliest to arrive. There is no horror in eating and being eaten. We are fed by, and in turn feed into, the natural$_2$ values of our cosmos.

9

TECHNOLOGICAL VALUES

A most striking characteristic of human mentality is its expression in artifacts. Technology is the embodiment of the purposes, values, and knowledge of those who invent and apply it. Since the word, "technology," is often used in confusing ways, it will be useful to begin with a brief explanation of how I intend to use this language.

Standard dictionaries tend to stress the importance of the "-logy" ending of "technology," in parallel with "biology" or "anthropology." This has the effect of identifying "technology" as above all a species of study and knowing, and in particular of scientific knowing. *The American Heritage Dictionary*, for example, gives as the word's first definition, "The application of science, especially to industrial or commercial objectives" (*American Heritage Dictionary*, 3rd ed., 1992). Great institutions of higher learning, using "Technology" in their names, reinforce this recognized use. I agree that knowing is essential to technology, and further agree that scientific knowing has made a huge transformation in what we now understand as technology, but I would not stop at this level of abstraction.

Another widespread use of "technology" goes beyond the domain of knowledge alone to the realm of things, and goes before the time of modern science to the era of crafts and folk techniques. The "technology of an age" on this broader use would include reference to the period's practical knowledge, but would also include its artifacts, tools, utensils, weapons, and devices. Should the age be prescientific, then such artifacts would be products not of scientific theory but of practical intelligence and memory (Ferré 1995, 30–40).

Clashing definitions, as I have argued earlier (Ferré 1998, 325–34), are fundamentally contests between rules for the governance of language. As rules, not descriptions, they should be evaluated as "useful or ineffectual" in advancing the relevant purposes of language, not as "true or false." I believe that adequate philosophical thought is better served by the more inclusive language of "technology" as designating implements as well as ideas, folk crafts as well as science-based devices. I support this wider definition because it is easier to introduce distinctions within a single domain than to show vital linkages between concepts that have been initially set up as essentially different. Obviously, science-led techniques and hardware contrast greatly with the ancient crafts that first led our species out of barbarism to civilization, but it is useful to be able to see commonalities as well. If we should adopt a linguistic rule that eliminated prescientific crafts from being seen as "technologies" at all, it would be doubly difficult to appreciate the continuities that provide the background against which the later differences make sense (Ferré 1995, 41–53).

In the interests of adequate philosophical generality, I propose that "technologies" be understood as *practical implementations of intelligence* (Ferré 1995, 26). "Technology" is then the general noun under which technologies are grouped.

The proviso that technologies be "practical" rules out implementations of intelligence that are done for no motive beyond themselves, sheerly for their own sakes. The fine arts certainly implement human intelligence, often to a high degree, but they would not count, on this recommended use of language, as "technology." There may be overlap, as in the case of beautifully designed bowls or cutlery, but this definition would help to sort out which are the technological features (the practical) and which are the purely aesthetic.

Further, the proviso that technologies involve "implementation" distinguishes technological exercises of human intelligence from purely "in the head" calculations that are never embodied in artifacts. Not every invention is technological. The Arabic invention of the zero in mathematics, for example, has been embodied in countless technologies but was in itself not technological.

The emphasis on implements will also allow something important for any word to be genuinely useful: a null case. That is, there should be situations in which technology is clearly *absent* as well as situations in which it is *present*. Here I would disagree with Lewis Mumford, who asserts that the human "mind-activated body" is the "primary all-purpose tool" (Mumford 1972, 78). A naked person, bereft of tools, alone in the wilderness, on my understanding would constitute the paradigm case of a nontechnological situation. Picking up a rock with a practical purpose in mind would change the situation at once. Guided by intelligence with a practical objective, the rock becomes an implement and "technology" is at hand.

This approach can include the dictionary definition, but clearly includes more. It refrains from limiting technology to applied science. Technology should refer to much more than this. Practical as well as theoretical intelligence can drive technologies. Only recently, since the rise of modern science, has theoretical intelligence taken the driver's seat. Even then, the key dictionary term, "objectives," must not be overlooked. Technology is not driven by knowledge alone but also by appetition. The different types of knowing can contribute their own distinctive character to the implements they suggest or shape.

In parallel with knowledge, which allows the implementation of technologies, is purpose, which stimulates knowledge and guides its application. A better image than a car with a single driver would be an airplane with dual controls and two pilots coordinating the flight. One pilot is concerned with the destination, where to go; the other determines how (and whether it is possible) to get there. For the greater part of human history, the pilot in command was Values. Human hungers, fears, taboos (e.g., religious bans against eating certain otherwise nourishing foods) directed the course of early practical implementations of intelligence. The copilot's seat was left to Knowledge. To the extent made possible by collective memories of fortunate methods, Knowledge, wearing the hat of practical know-how, allowed humanity to follow the lead of Values. In those days, when Knowledge tried to wear the hat of theory, attempting to explain why successful methods worked, these explanations were usually farfetched, ad hoc, and auxiliary. But, since the rise of modern science, the pilots have had a change of status. Knowledge and Values still jointly direct the flight, but Knowledge has won seniority.

Sometimes (e.g., radio and television, the atomic bomb) objectives are actually not able to be conceived until preceded by theory, which then suggests what might be possible to desire. The possibility of conceiving and desiring wireless communication depended on the equations, published in 1873, of James Clerk Maxwell (1831–1879) and the theoretical demonstration in 1887 of radio waves by Heinrich Rudolph Hertz (1857–1894). The possibility of conceiving, fearing, and seeking the implementation of nuclear energy, including the bomb, depended on the prior theoretical work of Albert Einstein (1879–1955). Old taboos, too, are challenged by scientific theories; new fears take their place. The very character of Knowledge, once easygoing, practical, qualitative, general, and vague, changed to insatiable, theoretical, quantifying, specialized, and precise. Values, now flying as copilot, has therefore had to change as well. Technologies of precision, maximization, reduction, and the implacable extension of human power have increasingly replaced less efficient, prescientific folk methods of relating to nature and other humans. Our implements, too, have taken on the changed personalities of the pilots, and many passengers fear a crash ahead.

This image of these two pilots will not, I hope, mislead readers who have followed my argument in this volume and especially the volume preceding it

(Ferré 1998) into supposing that I imagine knowing and valuing to be as separate as the metaphor of two persons might suggest. Quite the contrary, knowing and valuing are indissolubly intertwined at every point. Even the most austere and objective modes of knowing are valued for their austerity. Each way of knowing is propelled by values and promotes its own set of values. But as cognitive methods and background beliefs change, values can also undergo a sea change. This occurred with the triumph of modern scientific ways of knowing, and the changes are found in the implementations of our practical intelligence for every aspect of life. If there is to be hope for a postmodern way of living on Earth that is more in accord with the natural$_2$ values and environmental ethics we explored in the previous chapter, we are in need of fresh thinking about the technosphere in which we live and move and have our being.

The obvious fact that modern humans are swathed deep in layers of technology means that no mere chapter can hope to be more than suggestive of directions that might be taken in line with the postmodern ethical aspirations of personalistic organicism. (I have already written one introductory book just on the topic of technology [Ferré 1995], and many more would be needed for anything like adequate coverage.) But if technology is the practical implementation of intelligent purposes, and if practical purposes can be naturally classified in general terms, then perhaps even a short survey can give a sense of perspective. From such a perspective, detail can be worked out to whatever extent is needed.

Technologies address wants or needs. Some of these our humanity shares with all living things, including plants; some we share with all animals; some are specially directed to our species' defining traits. In what follows, I divide all practical purposes, for which technologies are the implementations, into two great "kingdoms," the first being *organic* and the second *personal* objectives. Personalistic organicism will recognize—insist—that, for human beings, organic objectives cannot be absolutely quarantined from personal ones, since human organic needs are simultaneously the needs of persons. The further fact that these technologies are the fruit of intelligent purposes suffuses them with personal qualities and normative considerations. But if our classification is based on the character of the needs themselves, it still can be useful. As Aristotle pointed out (Aristotle 1951b, 125–32), there are certain basic functions shared by all living things, namely, *nutrition* and *reproduction*. Animals are then distinguished from the kingdom of plants by the additional functions of *locomotion* and *sensation*. These four together can constitute for us the kingdom of organic objectives. Human animals, Aristotle went on, have all four of these basic organic functions, plus the capacities of *calculation* and *reflection*. These latter two will stand for the kingdom of personal objectives. Let us then deploy these six subdivisions to take a general look at possibilities for technologies of a postmodern future, keeping in mind our overarching objective that we should subject all our practical purposes to the norms of an adequate and coherent Earth ethic.

TECHNOLOGIES OF THE ORGANIC

NUTRITIONAL OBJECTIVES

All living things need to develop what biologists sometimes call a "strategy" for nourishment. The demands of metabolism are inexorable. Find nourishment or die. Included in this imperative from nature$_2$ is also the demand for respiration and water. Even the green plants need oxygen to release the energy that fuels their cells, though plants (while exposed to light) produce more oxygen through photosynthesis of carbon dioxide than they require for their own respiration. Human beings share these needs for food and water and the oxygen that provides the energy to keep organic processes functioning and removing their wastes. Even the basic sorts of food we need—carbohydrates, lipids, proteins, vitamins, and minerals—are characteristic needs of life forms from the simplest to the most complex plants and animals.

In the earliest days of our species, as we noted in the previous chapter, the human strategy to meet these universal needs was foraging and hunting. The human diet depended on such items as seeds, roots, berries, fruits, nuts, ants, locusts, snakes, lizards, fish, and rodents (mice, rabbits, etc.), supplemented by occasional kills of larger animals, such as deer. Roughly 12,000 years ago, flint sickles began to reap wild grains, a useful preagricultural food technology. But approximately 10,000 years ago, in the Near East, the real revolution in strategy occurred: grain seeds were spread around, and people waited for a harvest. Sheep, goats, and some cattle were domesticated in the waiting areas where permanent villages could be founded. Instead of searching for a food supply, humans began to cultivate reliable food supplies at home. Thus began the story of cities, of civilization (from the Latin *civus*, city), the growth of populations, and eventually the modern world.

The postmodern world, unless a completely unexpected population crash is caused by some catastrophe, will be extremely full of people, all hungering with basic organic needs for food, air, and water. In a full treatment, "green" technologies, both for defending the atmosphere against pollution and for purifying water for its life-giving functions, would need to be discussed. There is an enormous volume of material on these vital matters, befiting their importance. But since this must be a highly selective, illustrative treatment, and in view of the meditation on eating with which the previous chapter ended, I shall almost completely ignore these huge areas, instead focusing on two technological revolutions now under way in food technology. They should be seen as exemplary, giving a sense of how the ecological worldview of personalistic organicism might approach the many other technologies of what Aristotle called the "nutritive soul."

For one example, let us consider the possibilities of a revolution in obtaining food comparable to the agricultural revolution itself. In that first great technological change from hunting and gathering to domesticating plants and animals, the land was seen and treated differently, not as territory for foraging but as constant source for nourishment through human care and attention. The consequences of those changes on the land, from the invention of the stone hoe and eventually the plow, to our own day of Global Positioning System (GPS) tractor technologies, have been explosive. Agriculture allowed great growth in human population; it brought forth cities, kings, priests, codes of ethics, commercial enterprises, leisure classes engaged in learning and discovery; it nourished writing, libraries, theology, philosophy, science, and science-led technology.

Now, 10,000 years later, an analogous revolution may be occurring in the 71 percent of the Earth's surface not taken up by land, in the great salt oceans. Aquaculture is not absolutely new. China has used this technology extensively for centuries. Freshwater aquaculture, fish farming, is already a major technology contributing virtually all the trout and catfish consumed at American tables. But for most of the world, including the modern developed world, fishing in the oceans has remained at the hunter-gatherer level. Even the sophisticated fishing fleets of the late modern era, equipped with sonar, GPS, and other means of giving human predators great advantages over their prey, are still hunters on the trail.

It is hard to imagine the full consequences of a major change from seeing and treating the seas as a place to roam in quest of food to a place where food can be reliably raised with the help of human care and attention. A case in point involves salmon, an excellent fish, varieties of which can breed and flourish in pens in the colder waters of the North Atlantic. At this writing there are intense struggles occurring between advocates of this new way of obtaining nourishment for humans and those who support the older ways of hunting and gathering (*New York Times* 28, August 1999: A1, A8). The ethical maxims supported by personalistic organicism may shed some light on all this heat.

"Do no harm" is the most fundamental maxim of them all. What are the main ethically relevant harms that should be considered as we deliberate on what to approve? One harm is the obvious possibility of reducing the charm of the seaside areas where salmon aquaculture might be planned. The aesthetics of plastic pens versus relatively more natural$_1$ inlets, bays, and beaches is no trifling matter on a kalogenic worldview. This granted, one must also consider the antiaesthetic harms of hunter fishing, especially as practiced in modern massive processing fleets or by means of miles long drag nets, indiscriminately scooping up unwanted fish, sea turtles, or marine mammals. These are ugly things to contemplate. And the harms to the experiences of those relatively more complex life forms dragged and drowned are not trifling matters, either. In the case of sea turtles, there is in addition the potential permanent harm of causing the preventable extinction of an ancient evolutionary work of art. Aquaculture should not be expected to eliminate hunter fishing, even if greatly expanded, any more than agriculture eliminated all hunting on land. But if it could significantly reduce dependence on hunter fishing, making it more feasible to regulate hunter fisher practices to protect, for example, dolphins and sea turtles from casual, unnecessary destruction, then the aesthetic harms of plastic pens might be justified, on balance, weighed against the harms they might mitigate.

There are in addition significant environmental harms that might follow large-scale aquaculture. Oxygen is a necessary condition, as we noted, for life processes, yet a large number of salmon in a relatively small volume of water could deplete the oxygen supply in that area, endangering both the salmon themselves, and the many other living things dependent on that volume of water. The feces from the fish, together with bits of unconsumed feed, could make fertile ground for dangerous bacterial mats. Contagious disease in such confined areas might threaten not only the crop fish themselves, but also wild salmon swimming nearby, or those infected by contact with escapee salmon.

There is no gainsaying such highly possible harms from aquaculture. Except for the last, they are the direct analogues of familiar harms we have learned to expect from agriculture. Damage from nutrient-depleted soil, from land fouled with fecal waste, from infectious diseases, from the runoff of pesticides and fertilizers, from lowered water levels, desertification, and poisoned aquifers, from eroded topsoil—all are familiar (and serious) complaints against farming the land. It is not surprising that similar serious problems may weigh against farming the oceans. The question remains whether any or all of these allow mitigation sufficient to warrant, on balance, the technologies themselves.

Billions of human lives, worldwide, depend on the productivity of agriculture, for better or for worse. There is no easy turning back. Instead, great efforts are expended in the prevention or mitigation of these bad consequences on land. Perhaps aquaculture can learn from the history of agriculture enough to plan its implementation with proactive strategies. Avoiding areas of sluggish currents would help in several respects: it would diminish the likelihood of oxygen depletion, it would scrub the sea bottom of wastes and prevent bacterial mats, and it might diminish the probability of infectious disease spread in sluggish waters. Since increased difficulty and cost would doubtless correlate with increased rapidity of currents, this precaution might at first be resisted by aquaculturalists, but ethical obligation and suitable regulation could prevent long-term regrets.

"Create new good" is an important imperative in this context. It is hard to imagine the speed with which human population is increasing at the start of the twenty-first century. At this point on our exponential curve, unprecedented burdens on the food supply (as well as air and water) are inevitable. The majority of the Earth's human population now in existence have not yet had their children. This world population passed the six billion mark during the writing of the previous chapter. During my grandchildren's expected lifetime, four billion more humans will probably be added. Unless adequate nourishment can be provided by new and better technologies, this demonstration of human fecundity will be nothing to celebrate. Assuming that creating new human persons, all other things being equal, is something good in itself, it becomes urgent that "other things" be indeed equalized. Clearly the exponential curve of population growth needs to be controlled (something soon to be discussed), but as these efforts are made, the innocent children born into the world in the interim need decent nutrition if their potential human good is to be realized. This consideration must weigh heavily for those deliberating the ethics of a postmodern aquacultural revolution.

"Be fair" remains to be considered. Where lie the issues of justice among humans and between humans and other subjects of moral consideration? Property owners of seafront tracts reasonably fear losses in real estate values, as well as aesthetic values, from construction of salmon pens, installation of feeding machines, and so forth, in unspoiled coves and estuaries. In contrast, workers anticipate the creation of many new well-paying jobs in a nascent industry with enormous promise for the future. But what of other interests? The lobster or shrimp grounds that may disappear are of importance both to established fishing interests and to the lobster and shrimp themselves. How shall fairness be expressed? There is no point in pretending to solve such conflicts in the abstract. What is vital is to assure a voice to all concerned, including the natural$_1$ values of nonhuman species through some recognized spokesperson and to make judgments that respect the particular circumstances in each case. If wild salmon, for example, already perilously stressed, are found to be seriously endangered by the placement of a particular salmon farm, this would be a weighty matter and could outbalance human calculations of profit or convenience. But when all responsible precautions are taken to defend endangered species from extinction and local habitats from needless damage or disease, and when efforts are made to minimize aesthetic insults as well as to compensate those burdened with private harms borne for public benefits, there should be a presumption favoring the increase in nutritional good that this new technology offers a hungry world.

There will be mistakes, as there have been also in agriculture over the millennia. Still, creation of new good has never been cost free. The eventual beauties rising from the aquacultural revolution will be a complex harmonization including and resolving many dissonances. In due course, one may well imagine that even the aesthetic satisfactions now associated with verdant farmers' fields, the "amber waves of grain," could be felt also in the contemplation of acres of silver fish leaping in well-husbanded waters. For humans, aesthetic pleasures are not static.

Similar dynamics are present also in the genetic alteration of foods of all kinds. The human race has deliberately manipulated the genetic structure of our foodstuffs for thousands of years. Until recently this has been done without genetic theory, by trial and error in the craft tradition, by selective breeding of desirable plants and animals. Now Knowledge has taken over the pilot's seat in this area, too, and direct genetic engineering opens radical new possibilities to tempt our desires. As in the case of all temptations, ethical norms hover in the background. What might an ethic based on personalistic organicism contribute to the deliberations—today often conducted in loud voices—concerning genetically engineered food?

For the most part, the raised voices heard in arguments over genetically altered food are concerned about the profoundly important maxim: "Do no harm." Many people, notably European at this writing, are deeply suspicious of foods that have been changed in their basic genetic structure by purposive scientific interventions. They remember, with good reason, that human good intentions are not proof against terrible mistakes. "Human error" is the sad (or maddening) refrain too often for this possibility to be ignored. What angers many even further is that regulators have typically acted to prevent even the labeling of genetically altered foodstuffs, so that consumers who would choose to avoid ingesting artificially manipulated items are deprived of the information that might allow it. Regulators, at least in the United States at the time of this writing, justify their policy by (a) citing scientific research showing that artificially altered crops, milk, and livestock are indistinguishable (in all respects affecting health) from unchanged specimens; and (b) that large investments in genetic engineering would be put at risk if panicky rejection should spread in the marketplace. European regulators are sharply criticized for their "overprotective" policies, and heavy pressures currently are being applied to force open European markets to scientifically modified meat, soybeans, corn, and other products. I mention these current events because they are exemplary. As specific issues are resolved, others are bound to replace them in this area of deep suspicions, huge financial stakes, and intimate concern for what persons take into their bodies to become part of their organic selves.

Personalistic organicism accepts a falliblist epistemology, even in respect to best attested scientific findings (Ferré 1998, 341–73). Therefore "Do no harm!" echoes strongly within this ethical framework, in which even thoroughly tested theories are in principle capable of being overthrown. Especially problematic is the deliberate imposition of ignorance on consumers who would strongly prefer to make an informed decision on what they buy and eat. Preventing personal autonomy of this sort is itself a clear harm. It is a limitation on responsible freedom of action in a matter of intense interest. Even if there is nothing to fear, inflicting fear is a palpable disvalue. Therefore, on ethical grounds, personalistic organicism would strongly urge that accurate labeling information be provided for genetically altered foodstuffs, wherever it is marketed.

As to the practice itself, there are balancing considerations to be observed. First, we need to remember that "natural" and "artificial" are not all-or-nothing terms. There are many degrees of "artificiality." It simply means, as we noted earlier, that to a significant degree intelligent purpose has made a difference in the coming to be of whatever is called "artificial." In that sense, practically everything moderns touch and eat is artificial. Over the years, deliberate breeding practices in horticulture as well as animal breeding, have changed everything on our table. For the most part, these have been changes welcomed by generations of beneficiaries of much intelligence and hard work. This is not universally the case. The contemporary blueberry, and (even worse) the current thick-skinned, tasteless tomato, have suffered in qualitative respects for the convenience of the industries that pick, pack, and ship them (Hightower 1973). This warns us to be on our guard, selectively approving and disapproving the technological efforts of those who "improve" our foods.

And exactly such selective judgment needs to be made in connection with foods that are "improved" by direct alteration of DNA strands rather than by selective breeding. Blanket approval or condemnation would be abdication of thoughtful judgment. Some changes made by genetic engineering may be greatly beneficial for humankind. If some crops (e.g., corn) now heavily dependent on artificial fertilizers (e.g., nitrogen), can be genetically altered to fix their own nitrogen from the soil, this would significantly reduce major burdens not only of costs to the farmer, but also to the land itself and to precious water supplies now poisoned by runoff. Unfortunately, potential harms must be weighed, as well, since modified strains may be more vulnerable to diseases, and catastrophic losses from inadequate diversity may be experienced as blights sweep through nearly identical plant forms over thousands upon thousands of acres. Harms to human health from genetic engineering are of great concern, but after taking all conceivable precautions, the creative good possible from plentiful new strains of plant and animal nutrients may well warrant a positive verdict. Still, this would be so only if adequate information is made available to the consuming public. Allergic reactions are a constant risk. Organic health is not the only possible harm; more personal norms should also be respected by postmodern food policies. This is especially important when transgenic engineering, in which the genetic material of different species are transplanted, creates new artificial life forms containing elements of species prohibited under religious norms. If the genes of peanuts should be laced with pork, for example, this should be made known to Jews and Muslims. A constructive postmodern age will rejoice in and honor diversity with ample information.

Although Aristotle did not explicitly deal with it in discussing the "nutritive soul," respiration is an organic need we humans share with all living things. Postmodern technologies assuring good air to breathe will be as necessary as food technologies. One brief example should show the sort of approach personalistic organicists will be seeking. It also illustrates the "win-win" goal that should motivate all such planning.

The Rodale Institute experimental farm in Kutztown, Pennsylvania, has for over fifteen years, at this writing, been working toward an ecologically wise answer to the pollution of the Earth's atmosphere caused by carbon emitted from the modern world's factories, cars, and trucks. A combination of old farming techniques spurred by new purpose and scientific intelligence is showing how we can turn farmland into carbon "sinks." Reducing use of chemical fertilizers and systematically rotating corn with legume crops that fix nitrogen in the ground, manuring, and occasionally plowing early crops under the surface greatly increase ground carbon levels, thanks to carbon dioxide retained by the soil. Responsibly reported in *Nature* (Drinkwater and Sarrantonic 1998), the application of these simple techniques could reduce our civilization's net carbon dioxide burden on the atmosphere by several percent. In addition, if trees are preserved along streams, if plowing is minimized (something made increasingly possible by "low-till" technologies), and if cover crops are planted to hold the soil during the winter months, such agricultural techniques may make a highly significant contribution to the respirability of the air and at the same time reduce the greenhouse effect and its influence on global warming (Lal 1995). The Rodale experimental farm is showing that this can be done without sacrificing crop yield, and that the reduction of chemical fertilizers saves farmers a significant expense while preventing water pollution caused by runoff.

Small-scale techniques are sometimes difficult to apply to huge agribusiness operations, but much of the difficulty is not technical. It is posed by counterpressure from the economic and political status quo. Know-how and constructive purposes are sometimes blocked by institutional conservatism, both economic and political. The latter topics must be deferred until the final chapter. It is worthwhile noting here, however, that even "light" technologies often carry heavy political and economic baggage. Where human values of all sorts are embodied, that finding should not be in the least surprising.

REPRODUCTIVE OBJECTIVES

Nowhere are ideological waters more roiled than by the subject of human reproduction and techniques for its deliberate control. I shall try to steer a course through the heavy weather guided more by the principles of personalistic organicism than by any political landmarks, but political and religious implications will be obvious.

Reproduction, like nutrition, is another human function that is common to all life forms. What makes it distinctly human is not its organic but its personal aspects. Just as all life takes nourishment (while only humans dine by candlelight), likewise all life reproduces (while only humans poeticize their lovemaking). Still, in this discussion I am interested in the "kingdom" of organic objectives, in this case those linked with the universal drive to perpetuate species existence. If we confine our selected examples to the technologies of human organic reproduction, what values do we encounter?

Let us begin with cloning. The irony is that biotechnology's recent bombshell, the cloning of an adult mammal, is in fact a sophisticated redeployment of nature$_2$'s earliest method of reproduction, by asexual replication. This method has the advantages and drawbacks we noted in the previous chapter. Perfect or near perfect copies of organisms can be made retaining full genetic information from the duplicated individual; but the species-supporting diversity gained from constant mixing in the sexual lottery is lost. We may safely assume that the old-fashioned method of human reproduction will not be abandoned simply because an asexual means might become available. Our species enjoys sex too much for it to become dominantly asexual even if this were to become an easy alternative. Therefore, the values and disvalues of cloning, assuming that this becomes a technical possibility, need to be assessed less in terms of the health of our species in general than on narrower grounds.

The maxim urging us to "create new good" is key to understanding why anyone might wish to reproduce by cloning at all. The most innocent answers might make reference to childless couples (or individuals) eager for offspring but prevented by some disability. Or perhaps someone might clone tissue from a child, mortally wounded in some accident, to give those special genes another chance. As in any ethical deliberation, these ends need to be subjected to normative scrutiny. Today, when cloning is not a practical possibility, we might counsel adoption (or a growing range of fertility enhancements) to childless people, and acceptance to grieving parents. Grief therapy is the best we can do, confronted with a dying child. But if the practical possibility of an alternative is available, should we continue to counsel restraint and "letting go"? Would this be morally analogous to refraining from other technological interventions such as inoculations against disease? If this is "different," how so? I shall return to this question in a moment.

Other objectives in "creating new good" with cloning might be more suspect. Worst would be creating new human beings for mere use: for "spare parts" as involuntary donor banks for persons in need of organs that will not be rejected, or as cannon fodder in vast armies of identical offspring from magnificent specimens of fighting men or women. Somewhere between on the moral scale would be the objective to create new people with known talents (tall basketball players, brainy theoreticians, beautiful fashion models, popular entertainers).

What, for personalistic organicism, justifies these ethical rankings into "worst," "middling," and "best"? The answer is that these cloned individuals will by hypothesis be human persons, entitled to the full dignity of personal choices and the fulfillments made possible by human brains and cognitive capacities. The worst violation of personality, as we saw in our discussion of eating, is to consider a person merely as meat, valuable only for consumption by others. Fantasies of persons confined in organ farms are horrifying because they consider only the organic side of what it is to be human. They ignore or deny the intrinsic value of each personal organism, seeing each only under the filter of "spare parts." Similar extreme reductions would be committed by treating cloned persons only as cannon fodder. Far less extreme, but still objectionable, would be treating persons as born only to fulfill a predetermined function, whether it be playing basketball, singing, or constructing theories.

First, there is the question, Who will be able to order the cloning? Will it be only for the wealthy, the powerful, the fashionable? It will be extremely difficult to follow the maxim to "be fair," under such circumstances. Second, what standards of "desirability" will be reflected in the cloning into flesh of norms like beauty, strength, intelligence, or the like? Subtle strands of racism and other provincial values are likely to be woven into these judgments, tilting the human genetic pool in questionable directions. Third and most important, clones as fully human will need to be allowed their own preferences. Perhaps the clone of a basketball star would prefer to go into medicine, or the clone of a great scientist to become a concert violinist. Personalistic organicism insists on the freedom of persons to create themselves in deep ways, not simply to repeat choices made by earlier persons whose DNA they share. Clones will be identical twins genetically with the individual they replicate, but they will not share experiences in the same womb or experiences of the same environment. Some tendencies or physical abilities will be shared as in the case of any identical twins, but each will be self-determining persons within this organic framework. It would be unfair to hold a clone to a predetermined career. But in the case of cloning a dying child, it can safely be presumed that this objectionable feature is not at all in prospect. Just as the dying child was loved for itself, so the new exemplar of his or her genetic material (we can reasonably hope) will be valued for unique, intrinsic qualities and nurtured to responsible adulthood, just as a sibling, more particularly a twin born at a different time into different circumstances, should be.

Technologies of reproduction by cloning are not properly subject to "blanket" condemnation. But we were assuming too much when we assumed that these technologies can be taken as reliably in place. They are not. The maxim reminding us to "do no harm" is at this writing highly relevant to the question of biotechnological tinkering with human tissues. "Failures" are inevitable in any complex, new technological effort, and the problems of disposing of or caring for human monstrosities, resulting from premature application of cloning methods, would be morally horrific. Personalistic organicism would counsel great caution in entering this potential quagmire.

I should note that all the above discussion has been limited to "straight" cloning, the duplication of *whole* organisms from *unaltered* genetic information. Different ethical issues rise from changing either of these conditions. What might be our assessment, for example, of a technology capable of reproducing organs alone, not as part of whole organisms but simply as living complexities of specialized cells, incapable of life on their own but available for transplantation into organisms in need? More specifically, how should we assess a technology that might be able to grow and indefinitely sustain human hearts, lungs, livers, kidneys, or the like? Stem cells retrieved from embryos in the first days after fertilization are still undifferentiated, thus capable of being guided, given proper DNA information, into becoming any kind of human tissues.

At this writing, privately funded research is proceeding which might lead to the creation of such technologies, and publicly funded research is being debated. The National Bioethics Advisory Committee in the United States has strongly recommended public support (*New York Times*, 15 September, 1999: A 18). The debate is mainly focused on the "retrieval" of stem cells which inevitably destroys the embryo concerned. Does this violate the maxim to "do no harm"? Prima facie it does. A tiny blastula—a hollow ball of undifferentiated cells—is certainly harmed. This cell structure, given nurture, could eventually develop into a human person. Mitigating this harm is the fact that these in vitro embryos could not all be provided nurture, implanted in wombs, born, and raised. They are living cell structures but far from human persons. They have not yet attained the status of a fetus, much less a child. Personalistic organicism would acknowledge the presence of some faint subjectivity in the component cells, and these would be satisfactions lost. But the tiny ball as a whole, lacking any internal neural structure, would not be capable of centralized subjectivity; it can be nothing for itself. The blastula, otherwise to be discarded, would instead contribute one or more of its stem cells to an effort that might result in an enormous medical advance for the benefit of organisms who are unambiguously human persons. For personalistic organicism this would weigh heavily in balancing the harms and goods involved. There is neither unfairness done, under the circumstances, nor are the unavoidable harms sufficiently grave to overbalance the potentially huge goods that might be created.

The first alternative, engineering organs for medical benefits, seems something on the whole desirable for a postmodern world; far more problematic would be the other alternative, reproducing (either by cloning or by in vitro manipulation of sexually produced embryos) whole, breeding human organisms, genetically engineered for "improved" characteristics. There is every reason to applaud genetic interventions to remedy disabling conditions in unfortunate individuals who have inherited diseases, such as sickle cell anemia or Tay-Sachs disease. Few would object to a biotechnological campaign to eradicate these conditions if possible and with them such scourges as multiple sclerosis, cystic fibrosis, hemophilia, Down's syndrome, and the other examples of natural, Philistinism and Vandalism we discussed in chapter 7. There is much reason to be wary. The human tendency to "create new good" has a sorry history of blundering into unforeseen harms. If genetic engineers, serving their clients (governments, wealthy private interests?) in less well-considered ways, were to "improve" the human germline in irreversible ways, significantly altering the gene pool by trying to heighten intelligence (which kind of intelligence?) or physical attractiveness (whose ideal of attractiveness?) or the like, there would be grounds for grave apprehension (Shinn 1996). Cultural prejudices, conscious or unconscious racism, ephemeral fashions could make their way into flesh as permanent distortions of the genetic history of our species. Personalistic organicism therefore holds up an urgent caution sign to any such applications of genetic technology, lest the postmodern be allowed to resemble the "brave new" world (Huxley 1946).

To escape the crowded, stratified, regimented, engineered world of Aldous Huxley's nightmare, the people in the new century will need to devote themselves earnestly to limiting human reproductive rates. This will be a distinctively human expression of personal intelligence over organic instinct. Some other species have strategies for reproductive limitation such as stress reaction, territoriality, or monogamy; most populations simply rise and fall opportunistically with environmental circumstances; only the human species can foresee distant population problems and plan deliberate methods to avoid them.

Postmodern methods should avoid modern mistakes. Abortion, particularly forced abortions required by governments, is a terrible method. All abortions are tragic from the perspective of personalistic organicism since every abortion prevents the potential good of human personhood from coming to be. Some abortions are necessary to "preserve existing good" or to avoid greater harms, but if human fulfillments at their best constitute the highest qualitative goods, the prevention of concretely possible human persons always poses a serious ethical crisis. Compounding the crisis is the radical invasion of responsible personal agency when a state intervenes to force termination of a pregnancy. There must be no place for the invocation of the "whole" against the "part" in a postmodern world shaped by the ideals of personalistic organicism. This theme will be amplified in the last chapter.

Other modern mistakes have included a reliance on mechanical methods of birth control. I am not now disparaging the technologies of latex or the biotechnologies behind the advent of the Pill. These are benign and needed technologies in the context of voluntary, responsible planning. I refer instead to the gimmicks and regulations attempted in some developing countries to control birth rates manipulatively rather than rationally. On a trip to India some years ago, I witnessed the ubiquitous billboards and radio spots plugging smaller families and learned of the incentives offered for vasectomies. I also learned of the countermanipulations to which superficial techniques lend themselves. In this campaign, a certificate of vasectomy could be exchanged for a small portable radio; therefore, some men submitted themselves to multiple operations and sold the radios they won to other men who then felt free to propagate large broods of children. In other cases, boys nine or ten years of age would turn up for vasectomies. Resentments were created; the birth rate did not fall. Mechanical remote controls of this sort have no place in a postmodern society.

Instead, the personal should be cultivated to take voluntary control of the organic processes of reproduction. Particularly apt for developing nations, where exploding populations and perpetual poverty are especially alarming, are emphases on education—for girls as well as boys—and social security. First, education for all opens new awareness of hitherto undreamt of possibilities for fulfilled lives with fewer children. More, education breaks the iron grip of sheer tradition, subjecting familiar methods to speculative critique, allowing human minds to explore ways of "living well and living better." In particular, allowing women to extend their education permits a delay in the start of their childbearing years if they choose this as a desirable pattern. The learning itself, intrinsically valuable for the enlargement of mental satisfactions, can additionally include practical knowledge of voluntary methods for both spouses, including condoms, and so forth, for spacing childbirth without sacrificing conjugal joys.

But without a reliable social technology for old age support, some trustworthy system of social security, it may not be in a family's rational self-interest to limit their offspring. They may well calculate that their children will be necessary to support them in old age. If infant mortality rates can be demonstrably lowered, and if old age security can be believably promised, then the calculation changes. Well being for the family will be enhanced by fewer mouths to feed and backs to clothe. The family's small inheritance will fare better if not divided among so many children. It is probably no coincidence that where the dream of prosperity takes realistic hold, the size of families tends to drop. This "demographic transition" has already occurred among the wealthier nations. In the postmodern world that I envision, the effort would be to press hard for education, security, and prosperity everywhere, to make obsolete current hopelessness, poverty, and desperate reproduction.

LOCOMOTIVE OBJECTIVES

To this point we have been considering technologies that address human functions—nutrition and reproduction—shared with all living things. Aristotle identified these as functions of the "vegetative soul" since the plant kingdom is characterized by these great functions alone. The animal kingdom retains these functions but adds two more, Aristotle said. The added functions are of locomotion and sensation. That is, animals move around in ways not shared with plants, and animals take account of their surroundings in special ways, by sight, hearing, and so forth, that further distinguish them from vegetation. Since Aristotle identified the "soul" with the functioning of the body in its characteristic ways, he spoke of the locomotive soul and the sensate soul. In this section, I consider what our "locomotive soul" might mean for human technologies in a postmodern society.

First, we should note that human locomotion poses severe environmental problems on a modern landscape burdened with parking lots, strip malls, and paved highways and on an atmosphere poisoned by fumes from aircraft engines and automobile exhaust pipes. Smog, a threat not just to human health but equally to other life forms all in need of respiration, is mainly produced by cars. The noise of jets adds stress to life near airports, and the stress of travel by every means—herded into public transport or fighting traffic on the crowded highways—detracts beauty from human experience. Should a postmodern world simply ban all locomotion?

No. Personalistic organicism recognizes these and many other problems with the modern expression of human ways of getting around, but the "locomotive soul" is a deep part of the organic, animal side of our species. It is a function in need of expression, but its expression is in need of reform by taking thought about the values embodied in our various means of transportation.

Ideally, a constructive postmodern world should begin by eliminating much needless or ugly moving around. Commuting to and from work in private, petrochemically powered, internal combustion machines, for example, ought someday to be remembered sadly as a modern aberration, ugly for the experience of the millions of persons participating in it and highly destructive of the environment. This practice will be remembered as profligate of nonrenewable products produced from green plants under the unrepeatable conditions of the Carbonaceous era, precious products needed by our descendants for much more delicate objectives—medicines, and so forth—than for mere burning. It will be remembered as requiring the paving of soils that could have been put much more fruitfully to work. It will be remembered as polluting the air, threatening health (not only of the human species), and resulting in greenhouse warming of the Earth. It will be recalled as a huge economic drain on individuals and society, and as a practice regularly resulting in injury or death for many thousands of persons per year.

Similarly, the redundant shipping of goods, whether by highway, rail, sea, or air needs to be rethought for a postmodern world. E. F. Schumacher was right to criticize the absurdity of producing cookies in California to ship to Maine, while in Maine almost identical cookies are being produced and shipped to California. Somewhere in midcontinent, soot-belching tractor trailers meet, roaring in opposite directions on their unnecessary missions (Schumacher 1973). Commerce itself is not necessarily an evil, but long-distance trade should be restricted to items not found or easily producible in the local region. Commercial networks should increasingly feature the uniqueness of local products. This would provide the twin benefits of enhanced aesthetic diversity between regions and of minimized locomotive stress on society and the environment.

But locomotion, though inevitably extracting a cost, can be gladly celebrated in a kalogenic world. No matter how much change can be made in the conditions of work by teleconferencing and virtual workplaces, some people will need to move bodily to locations where their presence is needed to "create new good." Other legitimate objectives for constructive postmodern travel will inevitably include such age-old satisfactions as paying visits to family and friends. Virtual contacts will never replace a good hug. There is also the soul-refreshing locomotion involved in just "getting away" to different places for a change of view. Rural dwellers may long to visit a big city; urban people may feel the need for a wilderness region. And even more distant trips to other lands may deepen awareness of cultural diversities and enrich aesthetic delight in scenic diversities. Tourism when done right enhances intrinsic value. It, too, will be welcome in a rethought future.

It should be clear what deep changes are needed in modern technologies of locomotion. Currently popular sports utility vehicles (SUVs), for example, are diametrically opposed to what the postmodern world needs. These moving mountains on our highways (and in our parking places) are the apotheosis of hypermodern aggressive individualism as embodied in steel, glass, and rubber. These "urban assault vehicles" are murderous in collisions with normal-sized automobiles and murderous also in their effects on the environment, both as to the quantities of precious hydrocarbons they consume and as to the volume of poisons they emit. Personalistic organicism would do well to look in the exactly opposite direction from the SUVs for technologies that might implement the human "locomotive soul" in more constructive ways.

Instead of aggressive individualism, we need to rethink transportation technologies that integrate cooperative community orientation with personal satisfaction. Instead of environmental vandalism, we need "green" transportation technologies with minimal destructive effects. Instead of seeking personal safety in increased weight and armor, we need "smart" technologies to keep us comfortably separated.

Modern "public" transportation as commonly understood is a start, but not good enough. Characteristically, public vehicles are uncomfortable, polluting, and inconvenient in their schedules. We must do better. Some philosophies of organicism alone might be content with moving many bodies around in efficient ways for the good of the whole society, but personalistic organicism will care also about convenience, comfort, and individualized preferences of persons in the framework of community cooperation. "Community" here is key to the proposals I am about to suggest. Since the total community has a large interest in nurturing kalogenic technologies of locomotion for its members, recognizing both their diversity and their common needs, the total community must be prepared to make large investments from common funds to implement the necessary means. Without such community spirit, the values of the SUV will rule.

Consider this thought experiment. Society, let us suppose, has found ways to minimize the pressures of ugly or unnecessary transportation and has reached a broad consensus that human locomotion should be primarily for the fulfillment of personal satisfactions, for the creation of experiential beauty. With this consensus comes the determination to impose the lightest possible burdens on the environment and to protect the safety of human life and limb to the bargain. This is recognized as a good for each and a good for all, worth spending major common resources to achieve. Since the members of this society realize that they individually contribute these common funds, but also that they stand to save on the enormous private expenditures they once in the "old modern days" lavished on cars, insurance, repairs, and so forth, they are ready to embody their values in alternative technologies. Perhaps they will decide to make local transportation a free resource. Going from home to church or club or sports stadium, or to the nearby woods for a quiet nature walk, could be done by small electric vehicle (modeled on a battery powered golf cart, perhaps) that could be picked up near one's home and left at one's destination. Like shopping carts at a supermarket, they could be used and abandoned at will. They would be community property, provided and maintained for the common good. They would need to be so plentiful that no one would need to do without or feel possessive. If this sounds too anarchical, perhaps a technique used in Europe with shopping carts could be adopted to help assure responsible use: a coin or token could be required to disconnect a personal electric vehicle from its charging outlet, the coin being released again when the vehicle is reconnected to another charging outlet.

Local pathways for these vehicles could curve through sweet-smelling hedges. Many conveniently located multistory underground dropoff and pickup terminals, brightly lit and air conditioned, could replace acres of asphalt surrounding shopping malls, schools, and churches. Churches with a conscience would be relieved that they no longer were required to cover large tracts of potentially fruitful land with dead pavement just so that tons of private metal and rubber could occupy the space for roughly one hour a week.

Another free resource such a postmodern society might decide to offer could be simple bicycles, again to be picked up and dropped as needed. Many members of the community might prefer a bit of exercise on a pleasant day. The organisms that we are would benefit. If the weather should turn foul, they could always grab an electric vehicle for the return trip. Cycling itself would gain new favor when cyclists no longer needed to compete for the road with exhaust-spewing, road-hogging cars and trucks.

What of the trucks and of the need to carry supplies to the shops and factories? This community might well have decided to use subway systems with electric transports bringing supplies to underground terminals where shipments could be directly unloaded to basement loading docks of merchants and manufacturers. Such tunnel making would be a great expense, but the very shape of towns could be compacted, making subterranean deliveries more efficient once the pressures for large parking lots and multilane highways were lifted.

Long-distance transportation services would have been greatly enhanced in speed, comfort, and convenience. Magnetically levitated high speed passenger trains would more than rival air transportation for medium hauls. Frequent departures, city center to city center convenience, free personal electric vehicles at either end—all these combine to make coming home for family reunions or visiting friends or seeing new sights a pleasure, not a grind.

The need for air transportation would not disappear in such a society. Longer hauls, especially for travel across oceans, would require flight. But the postmodern experience of flight should be more beautiful than what is typically the case in the late modern era. A society that cares enough about the personal satisfactions of its flying public will do something about the long lines through which passengers are impersonally herded and do something about the ever-shrinking seat accommodations and services to which passengers, when finally boarded and strapped in, are treated. One constructive factor facilitating such postmodern reforms would be the near elimination of business air travel. This should be possible as teleconferencing and virtual handshakes become perfected and more widely used instead. In order to create their important instrumental goods, businessmen do not need hugs from those whom they visit, as family and friends do, and therefore should not occupy the seats of those who travel in search of more intrinsic values.

Aviation, as perceptive readers of these volumes will have noticed, is something of personal importance to me. I invested several decades in learning how to fly and in introducing others to the beauties of flight. As an instrument flight instructor for single engine aircraft, I have had intimate acquaintance with the system that separates aircraft, large and small, in conditions of restricted visibility, and keeps pilots and passengers safe. Some such system is clearly necessary, and I confess that I have found that working smoothly in it is for me a source of joy and beauty. The combination of personal choice with precise cooperation required by interpreting the instruments while flying in the air traffic system is a constant test of knowledge, experience, and physical skills where stakes are high and rewards flow as freely as adrenalin in moment after intense moment (Ferré 1984b, 53–59).

Is there a place for private flying in a postmodern world? My answer needs to be qualified. Flying is not like driving. After years of giving flight instruction, I have concluded that personal flight will never become as democratized as cycling or learning to maneuver a small electric vehicle on land. Too much focused attention, physical coordination, visual acuity, weather knowledge, understanding aerodynamics, remembering rules, and good judgment are required to expect everyone to succeed in the pilot's seat. The skies are not (despite the popular impression) too "crowded" to allow general aviation to flourish in a postmodern society. Reforms will doubtless be necessary. Inexpensive proximity warning devices are technologies much needed in every aircraft. In their absence, the day of being free to fly cross country without radios or radar transponders, even in inviting weather, could be drawing to a close. Midair collisions are fortunately extremely few, but social responsibility requires that they be kept that way. Despite my personal enjoyment of instrument flying, it would be a shame to force everyone to fly on instruments all the time within the traffic control system. Such a move would quickly lead either to the outlawing of personal flying or to the collapse of an already overworked system, or both.

Still, we can imagine postmodern technologies, perhaps drawing on satellite information, that can perform the normative safety function of warning pilots (in three dimensions and in real time) about other aircraft in their vicinity. Given such technologies, we can foresee the indefinite continuation of wonder-filled personal experiences, liberated from the bonds that have held our species so long to the surface of the Earth. Not everyone can be expected to master the arts and sciences of flight, but we should not expect everyone to excel at everything. I hope value-guided technologies will arise for a postmodern world in which genuinely diverse satisfactions, including indescribable joys of personal flying, will remain real possibilities for the many who will be both interested and qualified, long into the indefinite future.

SENSORY OBJECTIVES

Locomotion is one of the two characteristic ways animals have of distinguishing themselves from plants, as Aristotle noted. The other is sensation. This last of the "kingdom" of organic objectives borders on the personal, at least in humans, and it certainly is transformed in humans (as are the other three we have discussed) by the powers that come with personhood. But it is something our personal organisms fully share with the other animals, simple and complex. The various species of animals have a great range of sensory capacities and acuities, many of them far beyond the powers of humans. Bats, hawks, and whales are famous for their special sensory abilities. Other species still keep us guessing: how do migrating butterflies, sea turtles, geese, find their ways so precisely to their destinations and home again? What do our dogs really smell with their potent olfactory equipment? But for all their powers, the other animals need to make do with their evolved sensory equipment. Only *Homo sapiens* is capable of amplifying the effectiveness of our "sensory souls" by the use of artifice.

Aristotle noted the direct rewards we get from fulfilling the natural$_3$ functions of perception, remarking on

> the joy we take in our perceptions, which we cherish for their own sakes, quite apart from any benefits they may yield us. This is especially true of sight, which we tend to prefer to all the other senses even when it points to no action, and even indeed when no action is in prospect; a preference explained by the greater degree to which sight promotes knowledge by revealing so many differences among things (Aristotle 1951a, 67).

Here it is easy to follow Aristotle. We still find satisfaction in just looking at things and noticing them, discriminating their changes, their subtle differences and similarities. There are joys too in listening—the sheer perceptual act of hearing sounds—and of tasting flavors, smelling odors, and feeling textures. All this, as Aristotle would have recognized, with the naked senses.

But we should consider how our species has managed to extend the reach of our sensory functions since Aristotle's day. Then there was nothing to do about myopia or astigmatism (much less cataracts). The Romans invented a pinhole device which, held before an eye, could somewhat clarify vision. But it was the invention of eyeglasses in the Middle Ages (doubtless before the time of their nominal inventor, Roger Bacon [c.1220–1292]) that effectively magnified the joys of visual discrimination for countless humans.

The lens-making craft created to produce eyeglasses figured powerfully in the birth of modern science, since it was through lenses placed in a "viewing tube," purposefully constructed by Galileo and turned on the Moon and

Jupiter, that the counterintuitive speculations of Copernicus were finally confirmed—through technologically extended powers of the "sensitive soul." Many an amateur astronomer can confirm Aristotle's report of the "joy" that comes from sheer looking at the stars and the special joys that come from seeing through telescopes what cannot be seen with the naked eye.

It is hard to resist imagining the sheer pleasure that Aristotle himself might have taken in the technological extensions of vision provided by the telescope and soon afterward the microscope. Just to look and notice and compare and learn! What would the genius of Aristotle have done, coupled to the microscope's ability, for example, to watch Paramecia use their coordinated cilia to "row" after food, then sexually and asexually reproduce themselves from time to time?

The ecstasy that Aristotle might have felt with a simple telescope or microscope is available to us manyfold in virtually all sensory directions. Scientists, doctors, policemen, and soldiers can "see" in infrared and X-ray electromagnetic spectra that Aristotle never even dreamt of. Ordinary persons can "hear" friends and loved ones—as well as those by whom we would rather not be contacted—through telephone lines connected to nearly every home and through radios in nearly every room or car. Everyone can both "see" and "hear" events, trivial and momentous, through television screens that have become nearly ubiquitous in modern civilization. The Internet is exploding exponentially with means of "connecting" its users across all barriers and potentially in additional sensory ways through virtual reality equipment, gloves, helmets, and full body suits that can stimulate senses of smell and touch (Wexelblat 1993; Heim 1993; Harrison and Jaques 1966; Zhai 1998).

Why, then, is there so little ecstasy, given the intrinsic joys of perception and the huge amplification of our natural$_3$ sensory powers? I suspect the reason is that modern norms for the daily use of these magnificent extensions are inadequate and need to be rethought for a postmodern world. One of the key modern preferences has been for quantity over quality (Ferré 1996, 120–82; Ferré 1998, 170–87). Here, in the domain of modern technology's extension of our senses, quantity indeed rules. To take the telephone as an easy example, it is quite clear that there is no shortage in the numbers of those we can "reach out and touch"; but more alarmingly there seems to be no limit on the numbers of those who can quite effortlessly "reach out and touch" us. The maxim to "create new good" has been swamped in its application. We have through our telephone technologies made ourselves vulnerable in our homes, offices, and increasingly in our cars or even on the streets, in parks, restaurants, and concerts, to calls from others. Often these are intrusions. Sometimes they amount only to disturbances of personal peace, violations of the maxim, "preserve existing good." Sometimes they are genuine harms, as when an author's complicated chain of thought is shattered by a solicitation for unwanted investment advice.

Television is another technological domain in which the urge to "create new good" has choked on modern measurement by quantity and mistrust of quality. The genuinely wonderful capacities of television to expand horizons of awareness, enlarge sympathies, encourage community feeling, were proven in the United States during the latter half of the twentieth century in various major televised events; for example, the grief over the funeral of President John F. Kennedy, the agony of the Vietnam War, the horror of the *Challenger* explosion. Television technology will have a place of honor in a postmodern world for what it can do well. If the standards of personalistic organicism apply in which norms of quality are no embarrassment and quantity is not king, the institutional dependence on large audiences will not carry over their baleful leveling effects. Community support for a wide range of programing will replace commercial sponsorship of the lowest common denominator. The magnificent educational potential of this powerful medium will be more fully realized, drawing the public into wider contexts for understanding in vivid, immediate ways. Entertainment as well will be celebrated and enjoyed in a kalogenic society. As Aristotle said, we all enjoy watching for its own sake. Viewing should be fun. Creating beauty of all sorts is just the sort of function that could be helped by reformed norms of television's objectives. This, if genuinely motivating the making of television programs, would put the ugliness and evil of violence in a new perspective. Depictions of evil and ugliness have their place in art. No world, postmodern or otherwise, will be exempt from dealing with these pervasive realities of life. But gratuitous sensationalism has no place. It does not effectively deal with the ugliness of the world, it adds to it.

Unlike the telephone or the Internet, television is not interactive and poses little threat to privacy. This is a positive feature for television in its current form, but technologies change and the possibilities for interactive television allied with the enormous electronic network now being woven around the globe raise a warning flag. What interest does personalistic organicism take in privacy questions? Should not privacy be classed as a "modern" value, a relic of the "billiard-ball individualism" organicists often make the object of their scorn? It is certainly true that personalistic organicism warmly welcomes the arrival and expansion of the World Wide Web. It is holistic and nonhierarchical, democratic, and potentially strongly mind opening, leaping across nearly every form of parochialism. It can sustain close friendships across thousands of miles of geographical separation. It can bring the vested knowledge of the world to the humblest computer terminal. By means of the Web, music and art of all sorts can be shared. We can see and hear far beyond our unassisted sensory boundaries. It is a glorious advance. But privacy matters, too. Adding "personalistic" to "organicism" means that there we must insist on a recognition of essential dignity for the unique center of value and self-concern whose intimate details should be shared voluntarily, if at all. This is not an outmoded norm even in a "wired" world where medical, financial, library, and other records are neatly digitized, ready for distribution. Neither Web "detective agencies," nor government snoops would be welcome in a world shaped by personalistic ideals and restraints. More on this in the final chapter.

In this discussion of the technologies of extended senses I have not made much of the most astonishing and most unalloyed advances of all: the gigantic leaps in scientific instrumentation that now allow members of species to see the extremely tiny structures, even at the molecular level, and to see and hear extremely grand domains of our space-time universe itself. I have deliberately held back from this not because the instruments themselves are so heavily dependent on theory (the same is true, to a large degree, for all the technologies, except perhaps for bicycles, that I have chosen for illustration in this chapter). Rather, I have held them until last, and then only to mention them, because they are extensions of our senses that are wholly in the service of understanding. The "line" between sensing, perceiving, and understanding is never sharp (Ferré 1998, 267–340). Here it is almost indistinguishable. Scientists do not see mere marks on a photographic plate or hear mere beeps from a loudspeaker. Their senses are tuned to the theory of their instruments, and the items they see and hear are immersed in a network of interlocking concepts. The instruments vastly extend the range of human senses, but they are expressions of and in the service of what Aristotle called our "rational soul."

TECHNOLOGIES OF THE PERSONAL

What we have seen so far are technologies, first, in the service of objectives that are shared with all living things (nutrition, reproduction) and, second, in the service of objectives shared with all other animals (locomotion, sensation). Now we turn to objectives that are distinctly human. This is not to claim that there is no trace of these objectives outside humankind, but rather to acknowledge that the rational functions are present in human beings in ways so prominent and comparatively outstanding as to define our species among the animals. Rationality is not an all-or-none quality. Like intelligence which is certainly found in animals far beyond the human race, it comes in many degrees, but rationality as I intend it here is not identical to intelligence. It is intelligence clothed in symbols (Ferré 1998, 314–34). Symbolic intelligence is what makes personhood possible. Having the freedom to take account, through symbols, of the physically absent as well as the physically present allows long-term planning, stimulates imagination, permits sympathy, generates ideal norms, urges obligations, sets the context for deliberation between courses of action, grounds moral responsibility—lets complex, intelligent organisms become persons. As Aristotle insisted, the rationality of human animals transforms the significance of all the other living functions and makes them distinctly human. Nutrition and reproduction are universal among forms of life including the plants, but when humans feed and engage in sex, these functions become morally relevant actions since they are being performed by rational agents, by persons. One can eat in ways that are right or wrong, too much, too little, justly, unjustly. One can copulate in accordance with moral norms or in violation of them. The organic functions remain, but are given new meaning because in humans the "vegetative soul" and the "locomotive soul" are blended into and become integral parts of the properly ruling "rational soul."

One does not need to be an Aristotelian in all respects (I am not) to appreciate the wisdom in these classifications. They are useful, they keep us thinking comprehensively, even when our selection of technological examples must be severely limited. All aspects of human life today are touched by technology. The underlying fact that technologies rise from what Aristotle called the "rational soul," in that they are embodied expressions of personal purpose, illustrates again how vastly important personal objectives have become for postmodern life.

One last bit of help from Aristotle divides this section into two parts. "Rationality" itself is illustrated by two functions—two obvious sorts of conceptual behavior—which we can consider separately. The first is our human capacity to calculate, to do arithmetic. With this I shall classify our general abilities to figure things out nonarithmetically, too. In daily life we can and do constantly calculate likely outcomes. In chess we try to think several moves ahead: "If this, then that," and so forth. We calculate in committee meetings, in the neighborhood, in the family. When we use our symbols, mathematical, linguistic, for such objectives, we are expressing rationality of the first sort.

There is another sort of rationality, as Aristotle reminds us. It is the rationality of deep reflection, of seeing things in relationship, of understanding, and ultimately of wisdom. A small example of this from chess would be the contemplation of the whole board, understanding the apparent strategies involved, seeing positions of strength and weakness. Another example is recognizing a face straight off without calculating from the various features to an inferred identity. Larger examples would include reflecting on the meaning of life, thinking about the context of contexts for our ethical norms, taking time to weigh worldviews with examined values and clarified life aims in full display.

CALCULATIONAL OBJECTIVES

Aristotle, though an undoubted genius, was not the mathematical whiz his teacher, Plato, sought for his successor at the Academy. What would Aristotle have done with a modern pocket calculator? Would the history of philosophy have been profoundly changed if calculational abilities had been downgraded or equalized in ancient Athens?

The abacus was known (though perhaps not yet in Aristotle's day) in ancient Greece as well as China. In Greece this calculational technology was implemented by combining grooves drawn in sand (or lines on a board, the *abax*) with pebbles; in China somewhat later its embodiment was in the more familiar beads on wire. The pebbles (or beads) symbolized numbers depending on their position. In one sandy groove or board column or wire, the pebble or bead would symbolize a single unit; in the next position it would symbolize ten, then one hundred, and so on. Calculations could be assisted by moving the pebbles or beads as a memory aid when large numbers were involved. The abacus does not do the calculation; the person remains the calculator, but it is a great help.

Early automatic counting devices were known as early as the first century, A.D., described then by Hero of Alexandria. A worm gear could be meshed with a ratcheted gear wheel to count the revolutions of a carriage wheel, translating these into units of distance travelled much as modern odometers work in cars. These ancient gear trains were used by Blaise Pascal (1623–1662) at the beginning of the modern era to invent the first true automatic calculator (1645) capable of adding sums without a mathematically knowledgeable human operating them. Because the wheels and gears of the machine were lined up in columns like an abacus and the columns connected, sums could be dialled in and results read off with no further mental effort. Gottfried Wilhelm von Leibniz (1646–1716) extended the powers of Pascal's machine to include multiplication based on repeated additions. Hand-cranked machines became familiar in the eighteenth and nineteenth centuries, aiding in clerical tasks. Electrical calculators arrived in the latter half of the twentieth, making the slide rules I grew up with obsolete.

Now we have computers of enormous calculational power and speed. My own computer beats me regularly at chess and Scrabble. It is docile. It will give me hints if I put my pride aside and request them, such that I can hold my own, sometimes. I am glad it is not my enemy. My "calculative soul" is extended (tried and tested, too!) through its powers in ways that Aristotle could never have imagined.

When human calculational rationality cannot keep up, shall we say that our machines are more intelligent than we, at least in this once-exclusive calculative domain? Given the important qualifier, the answer is yes. Intelligence is not exhausted by calculational ability, but if we focus just on this respect, we know we have built tools, amplifiers of our own skills, that surpass our unaided powers. This shocks and bothers some people who bridle at the very thought of "artificial intelligence." Even those who acknowledge intelligence outside the human sphere (an important stream of modern thought has been loath, following Descartes, to admit even as much as this), many would draw the line at natural, biologically evolved organic intelligence. But it is not clear why this should be so. "Strength," for example, is a quality of human muscles. There are various degrees of strength outside our species, some greater, some less, expressed in myriad ways. We admire the ant, whose strength allows it to lift burdens many times its own weight. This is natural$_{1,3}$ strength, unaided by the intervention of intelligent purpose. There is artificial strength, too. Our construction cranes are able to lift huge loads; the simple jacks with which we lift our cars to change flat tires are stronger than we are in that respect. These displays of strength are implementations of purposive intelligence. They are valuable instances of genuine strength—there is nothing illusory or fictional about them—but they are produced by art, are artificial. "Artificial" does not mean "unreal." Now that biotechnology is able to synthesize insulin, using DNA splicing techniques and bacteria rather than depending on extractions from the pancreases of animals, this does not result in "fake" insulin. It is real, useful artificial insulin, approved for use by diabetics.

Similarly, artificial intelligence, when we confront it, is real intelligence. Can it, of its sort, be greater than ours? Yes, in the same way that the strength of construction cranes can outdo our natural$_3$ strength. Our reason for designing strong cranes is to amplify our natural$_3$ muscular powers to achieve our practical purposes. Our reason for designing fast computers is to amplify our natural$_3$ calculational abilities to achieve our practical purposes. These are parallels that should not disturb us, and after a few generations they will doubtless cease bothering members of our species, who will then live more comfortably with their intelligent artifacts.

What are some of the ethical issues posed for a postmodern culture with extremely powerful calculators at their disposal? We can dismiss the science fiction concern that binary computers, even vastly more powerful ones, will "revolt" against their masters or require moral consideration as artificial persons deserving civil rights. Calculational intelligence of this sort is destined by its hardware not to be able to take a larger view of its situation or reflect on "itself." It does not have a self or the makings thereof. Its processes are all sequential, though extremely fast, and all discrete. A binary computer can only do one thing at a time, accurately but routinely opening or closing an electrical circuit: on or off, yes or no, zero or one. It can also magnetically retain huge quantities of data in what we quite properly call its memory. Given the right commands, bits of these memorized data can be retrieved and made active. But here a dash of metaphysics from Whitehead is clarifying. Digital electronics does not provide the ontology from which consciousness, self-awareness, or self-motivation arises. That ontology, as I described it earlier (Ferré 1998, 267–334), involves simultaneous prehension by a "regnant occasion" located within an enormously complex organic field from many affectively rich sources of information about actualities and possibilities relevant to the concrescent moment and its likely future. As long as we restrict the issue to calculative intelligence only, and as long as the hardware used depends on "counting out" solutions as binary computers are required to do, we may admire the calculative skills of our intelligent machines without also attributing to them personal dignity.

What might personalistic organicism say about the possibility of other types of computers, advanced analog designs based on "wetware" or artificial organic processes? This would be a different story. The question is, of course, highly speculative—orbiting at an even higher altitude than this happy speculator normally flies—but consider the following conditions: (1) if postmodern engineering were to be capable of developing holistic models in which computers could give centralized attention simultaneously to multiple streams of information (paralleling the nervous system and brain in vertebrates), and (2) if such (probably cyborg) entities somehow were empowered with preferences and aversions, and (3) if these intelligent machines were able to choose their symbols with some degree of apparent freedom, under recognizable norms, then it might in principle be possible to have a discussion with them on their duties and their rights as well as their choice of words. The idea of an artificial person is highly improbable at this writing, hard to imagine, but not a theoretical impossibility.

We are principally dealing with calculational objectives, however, and in such terms the previous paragraph was a digression. Other ethical questions for a postmodern society equipped with powerful binary calculators remain. One is the extent of human responsibility when computers calculate faster than humans and when circumstances are extremely urgent. Should humans always accept recommendations for action proffered by their intelligent machines? If machines, "expert systems" used in medical diagnosis, call for an emergency procedure that a doctor might otherwise consider irrelevant or wrong for the circumstances, should the doctor subordinate human diagnostic judgment to the computer? Or, analogously, if computers designed to calculate "war games" call for immediate launching of nuclear missiles long before humans can see any need for this, should a political leader risk national destruction by refusing the preemptive strike? For personalistic organicism, the "paradox of expertise" with which we began has returned with a vengeance. What is crucial to remember is that whether we choose to follow the advice of another (human or machine makes no difference here) or whether we choose not to, we stand responsible. The machine is not responsible for our action or inaction. It gives its input as it was designed to do. With regard to moral deliberations, there are no "expert systems" that can take humans off the hook.

Another serious ethical question for a postmodern world living with powerful calculational technologies is that of personal privacy. The memories of countless computers will be stocked with every kind of information about our lives. What books do we check out from the library, what films do we rent from the corner video shop, what grocery items do we present for scanning together with our credit card, what are our destinations and tastes in travel, what run-ins have we had with the law, how favorably are we evaluated at work, how much tax do we pay, what sorts of deductions do we claim, how long do we wait before we pay our bills, do we pay our child support, what sorts of insurance do we purchase, what illnesses have we suffered, what probable genetic fate does our DNA indicate that we have in store? These are just some of the items that can be stored in the faithful (but sometimes misinformed) magnetic memories of giant calculating machines. The political implications for control implicit in all this information can be set aside until the next chapter. The ethical issue of harms to persons for whom the protections of private dignity are potentially stripped away by the misuse of all this ocean of information is pressing. Will wisdom, including the capacity for voluntary renunciation of technological powers, rule calculation in the postmodern setting?

WISDOM OBJECTIVES

The concept of "wisdom," perhaps reflecting its less precisely calculational character, tends to evade crisp definitions. It is easy to recognize that wisdom goes beyond possessing information, even beyond knowledge. One may amass much information, know many things, and yet not be wise. Having wisdom somehow involves gaining perspective, seeing relationships among the (many or few) things that one knows, being aware of how much one does not know, having good judgment about the relative importances of things. Wisdom involves openness, synthesis, relatedness, integrity, acknowledgment of limits. The goal of this section is to reflect on how postmodern technologies might serve such objectives.

It might be clarifying to start with a negative example, what would *not* help in the implementation of the goal of wisdom. Out of innumerable examples, let us consider controlled nuclear fusion energy, which many consider the key to final human liberation from energy shortages of any kind.

The technical pursuit of this source has been intense, especially in the United States, Japan, South Korea, and the former Soviet Union. The difficulties are huge since in essence the goal is to create and capture a miniature star, a self-sustaining reaction in which lighter nuclei (of hydrogen) combine under intense pressure and heat to form heavier nuclei (of helium). Essentially, enormous thermal energy (over ten million degrees Kelvin) under enclosed conditions overcomes the electrostatic repulsion between the protons concerned, and energy is released. In principle, even more energy is released from the process than is needed to maintain it (just as sunlight streams from the Sun even as its own internal fusion furnace continues to produce more radiant energy), and a potentially inexhaustible fountain of power awaits human exploitation.

The fuel for such fusion reactors, isotopes of hydrogen found plentifully in water, would be ample for millions, perhaps billions, of years of use by technological civilizations unleashed from any need to conserve energy. Best of all from the environmental perspective, the residue from the reaction is benign: harmless helium. The problem of disposal for lingering radioactivity as in nuclear fission reactors would be completely avoided. So, too, would be the harmful carbon dioxide that comes from every form of burning.

But would this technology be in the interest of wisdom? Calculational rationality is thrilled by the prospect of literally limitless energy. In principle, there would be no need to hold back. Every energy-hungry project could be fully supported. How wonderful! The Promethean dream of inextinguishable fire would be realized. But wisdom takes a different view. The very fact that no hard choices would need to be made, no priorities set, no judgments of comparative importance debated, would worry any reflective rationality grounded in concern for the optimum rather than the maximum, the best rather than the most. Such Promethean technologies forget—or try to deny—what in Chapter 7 I called "the tragedy of the universe": that ugliness, at least in the sense of shortcoming, is ultimately beauty's unavoidable shadow partner. Judging by current and historic levels of human maturity, unleashing all projects from the need to consider energy limits would spell disaster. Even without the fear of radioactivity or carbon dioxide as consequences of energy production, the environment could be put at extreme risk by humans armed with limitless energy supplies. As a physicist colleague once warned: with fusion power "we would be able to pave over America—and might just do it!" Personalistic organicism will view efforts to tame the thermonuclear reaction with intellectual respect but great ethical caution. Fusion advocates are on a mission whose single-minded maxim is "Create new good!" But wisdom must remind the enthusiasts of fusion power to consider also the prior imperative, "Do no harm!" Ironically, sometimes we need to be grateful that we live in a world of limits. It forces us to make choices, to consider what is more and less important, to see situations in relation, to appreciate what is costly, to accept what is necessary and to look for fulfillments that remain possible within the framework of a finite planet.

For a positive example of technologies in the service of wisdom objectives, I have chosen a new building project which is being dedicated at the time of this writing at Oberlin College in northern Ohio. The building is a singular example, but one that is by its own intention exemplary, its designers and builders hoping to encourage many others by its success. It is the Adam Joseph Lewis Center for Environmental Studies, inspired by the creative ecological spirit of David Orr, Director of the Center. True to Orr's spirit, this building is far from a solo project. It began in 1992–93 in a class involving twenty-five students and twelve architects. The class, true to wisdom's starting point, asked "why?"—is this an important objective to try? Could renovating an older building do equally well? If not, what should a new building at the dawn of a new century try to teach by its materials, layout, treatment of energy, water, and the like? Orr describes the initial outcome:

The basic program that emerged from the year-long class called for an approximately 14,000-square-foot building that

- discharged no wastewater, i.e., drinking water in, drinking water out;
- generated more electricity than it used;
- used no materials known to be carcinogenic, mutagenic, or endocrine disrupters;
- used energy and materials with great efficiency;
- promoted competence with environmental technologies;
- used products and materials grown or manufactured sustainably;
- was landscaped to promote biological diversity;
- promoted analytical skill in assessing full costs over the lifetime of the building;
- promoted ecological competence and mindfulness of place;
- became in its design and operations, genuinely pedagogical; and
- met rigorous requirements for full-cost accounting (Orr 1997, 597–98).

These are tremendously ambitious goals: integrative, prioritized for importance, sensitive to near and long-term relationships, accepting of finite limits, yet profoundly affirmative. The conceptual ideal of the building settled on by the class dared to dream greatly and at the same time insisted on tough cost accounting. It played freely with possibilities but demanded that these possibilities be realizable.

Now, after the involvement of some two hundred and fifty students, faculty, and community participants with whose help goals were refined further in 1995, and with the engagement of many skilled professionals (including Amory Lovins from the Rocky Mountain Institute, and NASA's Lewis Space Center for meeting electrical objectives; John Todd and Michael Shaw in meeting water discharge objectives; Andropogon, Inc., for landscape objectives; the structural and mechanical engineering firm Lev Zetlin, Inc., for materials and efficiency objectives), and weekly conferences between architects, engineers, and college officials, the possibilities have been realized. Since the technologies incorporated in the building are constantly changing, they were designed to be replaced as needed, leased rather than purchased. As Orr puts it, "Typically, buildings are a kind of snapshot of the state of technology at a given time. In this case, however, we intended for the building to remain technologically dynamic over a long period of time. In effect we proposed that the building adapt or learn as the state of technology changed and as our understanding of design became more sophisticated" (Orr 1997, 598).

In this new building, the wastewater plant (named the "Living Machine") is composed of diverse organisms including both plants and microorganisms and replicates the cleansing and filtering processes of wetlands. Grey water is recycled in the building's toilets. Even water from nearby roads and parking lots will be treated in the building's Living Machine and will return to the watershed cleansed of nonpoint pollution that collects on the pavement.

The building is a net energy producer. Relying entirely on energy income from the Sun, its active and passive solar collectors keep the building lighted and comfortable all year, despite its northern location, and are able to export excess electricity to the general community. Its landscape design including an earth berm and a grove of trees gives thermal protection at all seasons and integrates the building into its locality.

The materials used have been selected to avoid ecological or social exploitation. The chain of custody of the wood and other substances incorporated into the building was carefully scrutinized to make sure that neither injustice nor destructive practice would be embodied. "We intended to use materials that did not compromise the dignity or health of people somewhere else. We also wanted to use materials that had as little embodied fossil energy as possible, hence giving preference to those locally manufactured or grown" (Orr 1997, 598).

The complex, integrated technologies of this project teach in practice what is being taught in the classes and other programs of the Center. Instead of disconnection or even contradiction between the content of environmental thought and the physical enclosures provided by typical classrooms built unmindful of biological cycles and social obligations, this building offers coherence. Instead of abstraction from the richness of objectives that make for meaningful life, this building offers adequacy.

The teaching task intended for this building is broader than its classrooms or auditorium can attempt. It is meant to teach modern society how to become constructively postmodern. Orr hopes it will not remain an "island" on the Oberlin College campus, but that it will serve as a model to administrators for new construction and renovation. Yet more than campuses alone, the whole wasteful civilization can take a lesson from this case study in wisdom.

> By some estimates, humankind is preparing to build more in the next half century than it has built throughout all of recorded history. If we do this inefficiently and carelessly, we will cast a long ecological shadow on the human future. If we fail to pay the full environmental costs of development, the resulting ecological and human damage will be very large (Orr 1997, 599).

But if we think creatively and build sustainably, finding balance, acknowledging finitude, incorporating healthy relationships to humans and to nature,[2] in our building—in our warming, cooling, drinking, bathing, sheltering, working, entertaining—the future can be more beautiful.

> Do we now have or could we acquire the know-how to power civilization by current sunlight or to reduce the size of the "human footprint" or grow our food sustainably or prevent pollution or preserve biological diversity or restore degraded ecologies? In each case I believe the answer is "yes." Whether we possess the will and moral energy to do so while rethinking political and economic systems and the distribution of wealth within and between generations remains to be seen (Orr 1997, 600).

The goal of greater beauty is central to the objectives of the Lewis Center. Orr summarizes his basic intentions in the larger aesthetic language I also embrace for personalistic organicism. "We intend, in other words, a building that caused no ugliness, human or ecological, somewhere else or at some later time" (Orr 1997, 598). This could be wisdom's motto: No ugliness, now or later, human or ecological!

Technologies are rare that can even come close to meeting such a standard. In a literal or absolute sense, no technologies can intervene in any situation without making some disturbance. From the standpoint of the existing good, such disturbances will inevitably represent at least local and temporary ugliness. Making a simple meal on wild berries will deplete for a time the beauty of the bush. Playing a symphony in the park will drive out the cheerful cacophony of birds and crickets. The maxim, "Do no harm," followed absolutely would mandate complete passivity for human intelligence and purpose in all circumstances. It would be tantamount to "Do nothing." For these reasons, wisdom would understand the relevant imperatives as "Do no *unwarranted* harm," and "Create no ugliness, now or later, that is not *in the service of, and fairly integrated into*, some greater beauty."

Even this, calling for the mature weighing of relative beauties and a thoughtful judgment of fairness in their distribution is hard enough. It means that sometimes, even in stringent circumstances, available technologies may need to be renounced in the interest of wisdom. When to accept them, when to leave them alone, is potentially an agonizing problem. For example, advanced medical technologies, defying what once would have been all normal odds, are increasingly capable of keeping us or some loved one alive. Not long ago a person with failed heart, lungs, or liver would simply have needed to come to terms with death. Now, and foreseeably into the postmodern world, technological interventions with transplants or artificial devices can add useful, satisfying years to lives that would once have been given up as hopeless. If so, and assuming this can be done without unfairly denying health resources to others in need, this is a cause for unalloyed rejoicing. My younger sister who died in infancy as a "blue baby" with an improperly closing heart valve, might have had a life full of kalogenic achievements for herself and others if only open heart technologies now considered routine had been available at the time. Recently, a close friend in his middle years suffering from congestive heart failure was given still more years in which to create beauty by the implantation of a "space age ceramic" valve in his heart. All who know and love him cannot but cheer the medical technologies that have given this wonderful gift of his extended life.

An infant, a person in the full bloom of adult life, these two instances constitute one type of moral and medical situation; aged persons wracked with multiple infirmities constitute another. Increasingly, the costs of medical care are shifting toward sustaining those who approach terminal status, as complex means of heroic intervention become available to extend life marginally when human organisms show signs of wearing out. What course then serves the objectives of wisdom? Personalistic organicism would offer no "blanket" answer, but surely the option of voluntary renunciation needs to become a more frequent and more highly honored choice. Will elaborate medical technologies serve to enhance kalogenesis, or serve mere biological prolongation? If the latter, then wisdom might suggest renunciation and would suggest it strongly if the experiential state of the prolonged organism is likely on balance to be not merely unkalogenic but downright unsatisfying. Will expensive medical technologies serve to extend a mainly used up life at the cost of denying widespread attentions to more basic medical needs in society as a whole? If so, then wisdom would recoil at the implicit injustice of technologies and institutions that distribute good so badly. The right to renounce extraordinary medical technologies sometimes becomes a duty.

For an ecological postmodern world, the technologies of the hospice will become as important as those of the hospital. Palliative measures, tender attention to relief of pain, means for supporting personal dignity in extremis, can be less costly but more valuable in a world where finitude and mortality are accepted as part of the larger reality of the universe. Death must not be seen always as the enemy. Sometimes wisdom will decide to fight death; sometimes it will greet death as an inevitable friend.

To make this point more clearly I need to enlarge the scope of our discussion once more to include more cosmic questions. The issue of finitude has been with us through this trilogy and never more than here. Readers will perhaps have noticed that in this chapter I have normally preferred to discuss "technologies" rather than the more global "technology." Technologies, no matter how grand and exiting they may be, are always finite, with limited objectives. Technology, however, considered as the general disposition of humanity to control practical circumstances by implementing intelligent purpose, is in principle more unlimited and more problematic. Wisdom will recognize that sometimes trying to control circumstances is a legitimate objective; sometimes we should limit our urge to control, renounce "enframing" the world by our manipulative will (Heidegger 1977, 28).

Personalistic organicism is not "for" or "against" technology. There is no such single thing to be for or against. There is no "technology" to welcome or fear, be optimistic or pessimistic about. When we do strike these attitudes, we are in effect expressing a judgment about human values and human intelligence and our hopes or anxieties about them in a world where the best intentions often go wrong and where fullest information is often lacking crucial elements. Specific technologies do give us plenty of reasons to fear or rejoice, but "technology in general" is a different matter. If we say we place our hope in technology, this is shorthand for affirming confidence in the creative powers of human mentality, which are demonstrably real. And if we say we fear technology, this is another way of expressing deep awareness of a tendency in human mentality toward *hubris*, something else also demonstrably real. Speculative reason, as we have repeatedly noticed, can float free from the immediate actual and therefore initially knows no bounds. Internally, it needs to limit itself by its own invention of method (logic); externally, it needs to be slapped down by circumstances (Ferré 1998, 356).

Postmodern civilization will not live without its technologies. The crucial matter is to help shape the values of the coming society so that they will implement environmentally informed, humane, and just objectives without too much destructive slapping down. One of the deepest reforms in consciousness that will be needed if postmodern values are to limit the tendency toward human hubris (and the well-meaning catastrophes that overweening intelligence can wreak when powered by energies and techniques able to tear the Earth to pieces) is a renewed appreciation for finitude. Here again metaphysics helps. On the philosophy that has informed the ethics recommended here, all actuality is finite. The concrescing events that are finally the real elements in this complex universe of events are actual only as they eliminate contradictory possibilities and settle on their own created harmonies. In those harmonies, their created actualities, lie satisfaction, beauty, intrinsic value. Without actuality, no value. Without finitude, no actuality.

Acquiescing in finitude is a difficult balance in practice. It does not always mean acquiescing in the status quo. Sometimes—often—the existing situation deserves to be changed, improved, woven creatively upon in ways that increase the beauty of the experiencers concerned and the world as a whole. Then these technological values aimed to "create new good" are worthy. It would be unwise to renounce them without reason. Still, the objectives of wisdom are not always to be attained technologically. To find the fulcrum on which this balance hangs depends on human judgment, fallible though it is. We have nothing else. Therefore we seek wisdom.

10

POLITICAL VALUES

Here I intend to use the word, "political," in its broadest sense: having to do with how human beings organize societies, large and small, definitely including economic arrangements. The values underlying the *polis*, the city or town, and the members thereof, today extend upward to the nation-states that currently claim legal sovereignty over us, and outward to the global network of markets that influence our actual lives in untold ways. Human values linked to human know-how, through countless decisions of people great and small, known and anonymous, have gradually solidified into the institutions that form the practical context for virtually all our actions and reactions. We find our relationships with the natural₁ environment strongly influenced by social institutions shaped by our ancestors and sustained by our acquiescence. Similarly, we find the scope and character of the technologies we would invent, adopt, use, or reject profoundly shaped by embodied political values: legal, economic, customary—values as pervasive and substantial as the invisible air we breathe and soar upon.

It is time to bring this volume to a landing on the concrete realities of law and commerce. Two cautions should be noted on our checklist as we prepare for such a touchdown. First, we need to remember that the realities that now are so "concrete" took time to harden, and that they need not be forever as they are today. What human hopes and fears, knowledge and ignorance, have conspired to create will not sustain itself without continuous effort for renewal. Proud institutions can collapse unless continually reiterated by fresh affirmative acts. This is the "tragedy of the universe," the entropic wearing out that leads to philistine ugliness. But equally it represents opportunity to introduce

317

novelty into the actual world. For human beings guided by reflective consideration of alternative possibilities, ideal norms can shape history as well as be shaped by what has already become actual. To acknowledge this is not naive idealism. It is realistic reporting on the reciprocal influence between ideas and material conditions, purposes and stark necessities. Material conditions deeply circumscribe what is possible at any given time; they are the "concrete" on which every present moment gains traction. But equally, a clear, illuminating ideal of what should be, reiterated and sustained by many over time, can introduce changes that create conditions for its own realization, beginning in small enabling steps that open new real possibilities and ending—for a while—in its own fresh concreteness. Thus, the "concrete" we need to land on in this chapter is both hard as rock and malleable. Our reason for dealing with it here is to envision its remolding.

The second caution on our prelanding checklist is not to pursue too much detail. The vision of what could be—*should* be from the perspective of personalistic organicism—burns clearer when not filtered through the enormous dust clouds of contemporary discussion. In making a safe landing, it is important that the pilot keep focused well down the runway, not on the near pavement rushing by. What follows will aim for the long view, hoping to be suggestive of ideal goals, not reactive to current literature. As a result, this final chapter can serve as a summary and review on several levels, reprising not just this book, but also the general approach of personalistic organicism illustrated in this further application, and the trilogy of books as a whole through which my worldview has been presented.

This worldview, inspired by the ideals of healthy life (organicism) overlain with the ideals of fulfilled human existence (personalism), prompts us to look at the institutions of human life as expressions of social ecology. If personalistic organicism can suggest basic ecological norms of thriving shared by individual living organisms, populations, and persons, then our broad look toward healthy postmodern political values can be organized in terms of such norms.

CREATIVITY

Healthy life is creative. First, when viewed in general historical terms, the most distinctive thing about the story of life is its burgeoning, its lust for novelty. It spreads, modifies itself, diversifies, grows, evolves, fills every niche. Second, when viewed theoretically, to distinguish in principle the organic from the inorganic, the living from the nonliving (Ferré 1996, 269), we find no bright "line" between crystals (nonliving), viruses (partially living), and bacteria (fully living), but instead a discernible qualitative difference in the importance of self-induced novelty and spontaneous behavior, moving from less to more fully living entities. To be a living entity simply is to exhibit significant degrees of novelty. Third, when viewed from the sheerly biological perspective of an individual living organism, health depends on continuous growth to stay ahead of the tendencies of decay and disorganization. For complex, multicellular organisms, the young exhibit obvious net gains in growth; at all ages, however, healthy life depends on constant renewal, fresh creativity. When creativity wanes too much, life ends. Fourth, when viewed in terms of thriving populations, including entire species, there must be reproduction, the creation of new organisms to carry on the unique achievements embodied in the population's germ line. Fifth, when viewed in terms of thriving human communities, we find—besides the universal biological expressions of reproduction and nurture of the growing young —cultural forms of creativity enriching the experience of members. And we remember how much creative energy needs to be spent sustaining, reiterating, preserving, and extending against the "tragedy of the universe" cultural treasures inherited from past episodes of creativity. Sixth, when viewed in terms of a single thriving human person, someone physically healthy and positively supported within a community of other persons (Ferré 1998, 366–75), the opportunity for unique self-expression, for creative achievements in many possible directions, marks the zenith of qualitative satisfaction in the kalogenic universe.

Of all the economic arrangements aimed at the production of sheer masses of goods and services for feeding, housing, transporting, and entertaining human populations, the profit motive seems to have no close rival. For all its excesses, some version of capitalism seems by far the winner in the contest for material creativity. Indeed, capitalism revels in excess. More is literally merrier. The internal dynamic of profit demands constant growth: rising expectations, rising sales, rising investment for rising productivity to meet rising payrolls and to pay for ever-rising indebtedness. In the twentieth century, great experiments were attempted with alternatives to capitalism, but at the start of the twenty-first, none of these remain viable. Managed economies, it turns out, can put bread and salt on the table and weapons in the arsenal, but simply cannot compete in terms of creativity with the spirit of competition itself. Now the world's largest institution, the global marketplace, requires every political entity to conform to the economic rules of competition as they are embodied and enforced by the International Monetary Fund, the World Bank, and a skein of international agreements to keep markets open and profits growing.

Personalistic organicism needs to give capitalism its due. Creativity is a great value. Whatever economic arrangement we foresee for the postmodern world will need capitalism's powerful material productivity in some form or other. Huge numbers of yet unborn human persons will require creation of basic material necessities to avoid the ugliness and suffering of poverty in a crowded world, and all human persons should have the means for at least simple satisfactions beyond the bare necessities.

Yet two deeply troubling problems remain. First, capitalist free markets are oblivious to terrible injustices in distribution of the bountiful goods they create. Second, capitalism's creativity has no built-in control against over-growth, environmental destruction, and the culture of material crassness.

Injustice is built into unqualified capitalism, because the market alone has no way of distinguishing between demand and need. Demand is measured in terms of monetary units bidding for available goods; need is measured entirely otherwise. A starving person—the paradigm case of need—represents zero de-mand if that person has no money to bid for food. For the market, such a per-son does not exist. In America's Great Depression, while hunger was rampant, oranges were burned or plowed under the ground and milk was poured out be-cause prices were too low to warrant marketing. In an era of huge need there was a dearth of demand. Capitalism knows how to create goods better than any other system, but it fails the norms of distribution.

Overgrowth, as well, is built into unrestrained capitalism, because quality is systematically submerged by quantity and value is confused with price. The monetizing of value means that it is difficult or impossible to find an "optimal" level of sustainable production, since "more" is always defined as merrier. If a stand of old-growth forest, for example, is valued only by its price on the mar-ket, then it makes no economic sense to preserve it. Its price in present mone-tary units drops steadily—even faster when interest rates are high and rapidly diminish the future value of present prices. *Any* positive interest rate com-pounding over time will have the same effect in capitalist logic. The present value of getting anything in the future is always reducing with time. The Earth's limited treasures, renewable or not, become "resources" and workers become "hands." The products so created follow "demand" rather than need, and quality is unimportant as long as enough monetary units (often stimulated by advertizing) are bid. The bidding provides its own justification for products (no matter how shoddy, useless, or even harmful), since it shows what "people want" and what "the market can bear."

Turning to the question whether there is one outstanding system of human governance that best channels and nurtures the norm of creativity, the answer is less clear. At first glance, aristocracy may seem the leading contender for this role, in view of a historical record in which is found the magnificent blos-soming of all the arts—visual, architectural, musical, literary—under the pa-tronage of princes. If we also consider royal regimes, including empresses and emperors (as in China and Japan) and maharajas (as in India), together with theocratic systems, including popes, under the general head of "aristocracy," it seems quite likely that most of the great expressions of creative art could be traced back to one or another of these political systems.

The question remains whether rare excellence, manifestations of genius, are purchased in those systems at the price of lowered personal autonomy through society as a whole. Personalistic organicism rejoices in the creativity of a Mozart or a Michelangelo. "Mozartian moments," richly integrating a vast multiplicity of disparate elements into large harmonies of achievement, can even be used to symbolize what are "at or near the top of the known scale" of creative satisfaction (Ferré 1996, 355). But it would be hard to show that the aristocratic political system under which Mozart flourished (and suffered) was a necessary condition for such creativity. It would be still harder to demonstrate that the net intrinsic good of the whole society constituting Mozart's Vienna at the time of his death was best arranged to optimize the possibilities for personal creativity among all its members.

Some form of democracy has captured the imagination of much of the world at the start of the twenty-first century. Electoral majoritarian democracy, self-rule of the people by representation, in which representatives are chosen by popular majority vote and policies are subsequently adopted by majorities fashioned by these representatives, is the primary model at hand. Direct participatory democracy in which each person expresses (*a*) her or his preference (and the reasons for it), (*b*) earns thereby some influence, and (*c*) has a vote on the issue being decided, is relatively rare except in small groups, such as faculty meetings. Even in these cases, the majoritarian presumption, that half-plus-one of the participants should fully determine the outcome, is normally retained.

Majoritarian democracy is better designed than most of its alternatives to unleash the powers of agency and personal responsibility among peoples privileged to determine their common courses of action. Those with the power of choice, even though it may be limited to choice of a representative, enjoy a dignity not available to those ruled from above by persons without need for accountability to or endorsement from the populace. At the end of the twentieth century the world witnessed in South Africa, when the black majority were given at last an opportunity to express their political preferences, and in East Timor, when the populace was allowed to make a decision on independence, how dearly valued majoritarian democracy can be for those long deprived of its avenues for responsible personal expression. Enfranchisement provides the deeply satisfying recognition of the individual person as self-determining agent, partially (with others) shaping the future from ideals and hopes. Personalistic organicism treasures such ordinary but widespread satisfactions as well as the rare Mozartian moments of high creativity. Analyzed philosophically, the decision whether to vote and the deliberation over one's best representation constitute a process that plucks definite value out of a swirl of genuine but incompatible possibilities. These choices are not made all at once or once for all, but, rather, over a sequence of responsible moments of deliberation and decision, reiteration and refinement, moments which channel the importunate press of cosmic creativity—the advance of time—into political character, self-clarification, and personal dignity.

South Africa, at the end of apartheid, and East Timor, on the brink of independence, are not the rule, of course. The grubby reality of majoritarian democracies is less inspiring. In the United States, often cast as a world beacon of representational democracy, significantly fewer than half the qualified voters have recently bothered to cast their votes, even in major elections. A majority of the minority is usually sufficient to choose representatives who will decide—with much aid from lobbyists and heavily beholden to financial support by special interests—vital issues on behalf of "the people." Public cynicism is strong, and mistrust of a government once billed as "of . . . for . . . and by the people," is widespread among the people themselves, many of whom seem not to see it as "theirs" at all.

Since Plato, philosophers have pointed out the weaknesses of democracy. Rule by the "common people" (the *demos*) is by definition not rule by experts. "Commoners" will be subject to passions and lured by short-term hopes and fears. Representatives will be tempted by the "race to the bottom," appealing to the lowest common denominator.

Some of these warnings have turned out to be correct. Current representative democracies, electing temporary rulers for a relatively short period of years, do have a systematic bias toward the near term, both regarding the problems that are publicly noticed and the solutions that are offered. No elected official of the United States, for example, enjoys a term lasting more than six years into the future. These few "longest" term officials are the one hundred members of the Senate. American Presidents are elected for only four years, and members of the House of Representatives are granted only a two-year term. As a result, the next election is always looming soon, with huge sums of money to raise and records to build quickly, while the advantages of incumbency are in hand. Since an ecological worldview will stress, on the contrary, the importance of long-term processes in the environment and in social life, a postmodern polity will be rightly dissatisfied with such structural biases against the long view.

Personalistic organicism will take less alarm than Plato, however, from the fact that rule by common people will involve more passion and less reliance on experts than in his ideal Republic. This difference in politics reflects a key difference in epistemology. Plato, defining knowledge by the epistemic ideal of absolute certainty, held out hope for an exact science of morality (Ferré 1998, 28–40). If the epistemic ideal itself is out of order and if genuine knowing is always normatively immersed in values and judgments (Ferré 1998, 267–373), then "rule by experts" (alone) can be a dangerous delusion. Of course there must be experts, and they can be hired to perform their necessary functions as needs arise. But still more important is cultivating good judgment in hiring the right experts. On the political level we encounter here a vivid reminder of the "paradox of expertise" with which this book opened. Part of the dignity and burden of being an ethical agent is the inescapable need to take responsibility for the experts we would follow. A further ethical consequence of this paradox is recognizing our responsibility to take all needful steps to increase the quality of our judgments, filled with emotion and fallible though they inevitably are. How we might do this is what this book has been about. What is true for ethical individuals is also true for societies in which each member is allowed to wield a paint brush somewhere on the mural of history. Imposing "experts" to do all the painting, without the consent of the governed, is not just disenfranchising the "common people" politically, it is also excluding them morally from the full dignities of socially responsible personhood.

What postmodern polity needs, from this perspective, is far greater attention to methods of nurturing good judgment among ordinary people. The goal would include getting facts about circumstances into clearer focus, extending awareness of contexts (including wider temporal frameworks and more comprehensive philosophical and religious ones), deepening sympathies between diverse groups, clarifying basic priorities, and noting commonalities in fundamental preferences. This goal assumes and improves a society of responsible creative agents rather than shrinking from democracy itself.

Still, there remain dangers from unrestrained majoritarian democracy despite—or perhaps because of—its power to release the creative agency of ordinary people. Majority rule, expressed primarily through voting, sets the stage for bitter factionalism and for tyranny by the majority over unreconciled minorities. When majorities are narrow and minorities large, we tend to find the former; when majorities are overwhelming and minorities are tiny, we may find the latter.

In the first case, when there is a large minority, majoritarianism, rule by half-plus-one, assumes extraordinarily good sportsmanship from the half-less-one (or so) whose arguments are rejected and whose preferences are not followed after a vote. The system works, if it does, only when those who happen to fall into the minority approve so strongly of the overall system of governance that they are willing to swallow their disappointment in individual cases, accept the good faith of the majority not to inflict intolerable damage on their interests in any of these cases, and nurture realistic hopes of someday belonging to a responsible majority themselves. If these value-laden commitments falter, if suspicion and ill will among the representatives of the people replace basic trust and shared commitment to the common good, then there is ample ground for public disillusionment about such government. Perhaps under these circumstances, in which the moral foundations of politics are especially noteworthy by their weakness, less reliance should be placed on voting and more effort put into nurturing sympathy and consensus. Partisan politics, anger, revenge, discord, hatred, narrow vision, and foolish policy are the bitter fruits of majoritarian democracy stripped of such underlying social bonds as empathy, respect, and mutuality. Personalistic organicism will place less emphasis on parties and more on persons. Less on votes and more on vision.

In the second case, when a minority is small and weak, facing the creative juggernaut set up by majoritarian democracy, there is a different danger. The risk is of being crushed. This, too, requires a remedy. A solution to the overpowering force of creativity may not lie implicit in the great norm of creativity itself, but fortunately, healthy organisms do not live by creativity and growth alone. Creativity, in this and other cases, must invent its own constraints. Its need, and democracy's, is for homeostasis.

HOMEOSTASIS

Just as we saw in earlier chapters that the ethical maxim, "Create new good," needs to be balanced by the dual maxims, "Do no harm," and "Preserve existing good," so we find that for normative health in individuals and in populations, creativity requires limits. Unrestrained growth in populations leads to collapse; unrestrained growth in tissues—the tragedy of cancer—ends in death.

Restraints, fortunately, are everywhere built into healthy life. The pioneer physiologist, Claude Bernard (1813–1878), discovered in 1851 that when an organism is chilled, its nervous system sends messages to its blood vessels, constricting them with the effect of conserving body heat. Since then, many automatic systems have been discovered for preserving the stability of organic internal environments. When warm-blooded animals are too cold, shivering makes the muscles work and helps keep them warm. When such organisms are too warm, responses such as perspiring or panting come into play. Such living "mechanisms," named "homeostatic" by the twentieth-century physiologist Walter Cannon, work in all living things at every level of organization: in the molecule, the cell, and the whole organism. The chemical composition and physical properties of organic fluids such as blood are monitored and regulated for gases, hormones, nutrients, and the like. When too much supply of some ingredient threatens the chemical equilibrium, such excess local "creativity" is shut down in negative cybernetic feedback loops, maintaining internal constancy despite large fluctuations in external circumstances.

Homeostatic controls function even beyond the level of single organisms, regulating the stable relationships among populations in thriving ecosystems. In the absence of such stabilizing governors, as in the case of a lake suffering from an out-of-control algal bloom, other life is choked off, perhaps by depletion of oxygen supply, and we are left with rotting slime. Without homeostasis, the only "winners" are the decomposers. Then the drama of life needs somehow slowly to begin again. But with limits of one sort or another, such as territoriality, predator-prey oscillations, or (in the case of humans) deliberate policy decisions, creativity can continue to thrive without burial in its own excess.

Mention of human policy brings the discussion back again to political values. For personalistic organicism, an immensely important norm for any adequate political arrangement will be a well-tuned institutional means to limit the choking, juggernaut character of creativity. This will be by internal social "mechanisms" capable of sustaining equilibrium, providing the dynamic counterpressures against sheer creativity that creativity needs in order to maintain itself. These social arrangement will not be literally "automatic," since human policies lie in the sphere of conscious purpose, but they should be cybernetic restraints that are as close as possible to self-triggering.

A good example is found in the Constitution of the United States, which can be analyzed in terms of personalistic organicism as a masterful exercise of placing creativity deliberately under constraint by homeostatic mechanisms.

The genius of the framers of the Constitution was shown by the deftness with which they harnessed the vast creative energies of their new nation within a flexible web of institutional restraints we have come to call "the Separation of Powers." In the beginning there is creativity: individual persons bubble with new ideas and ambitions. Private institutions, formed by those individuals out of shared personal interests, amplify the effectiveness of those ideas and ambitions toward an endless variety of goals—wealth, knowledge, beauty, worshipping God in some specific way, taming the virgin land. To let this happen without total mayhem and mutual destruction there must be some kind of government. "To govern" comes from the Greek word, *kubernao*, "to steer" or "to pilot" (from which the word "cybernetic" also derives). But if there is to be a pilot or helmsman, there must be some mechanisms of unified control over private urges to pure creativity, which, in the political context, would mean pure anarchy. The need for government, seen within our framework, is thus the need of life for homeostatic restraints.

The framers had seen enough of government to know that such restraints, though necessary in general, can be intolerable if imposed by a too well-coordinated, heavy hand. The blood of the American Revolution against monarchy was still fresh when the shape of new government was being debated. Doubtless this accounts in large measure for the initial adoption of the easygoing Articles of Confederation that were so weak as to make the effective "steering" of those confederated sovereign states virtually impossible. The Constitution, in contrast, was drafted to allow greater effectiveness of piloting for those at the helm. In organismic language, the Constitution was designed to enhance the overall aims of political creativity by introducing multiple feedback mechanisms between the steerers and the steered and—most innovative of all—by deliberately setting up homeostatic countertendencies (with feedback loops carefully arranged between them, too) within the governing structures themselves.

To this end the framers of the Constitution used what they took to be one of the constants of human nature, the drive to defend one's person and one's interests, as a weapon to battle another no less constant tendency, namely, the urge to maximize power over others and extend turf. This brilliant juxtaposition of mutually resistant creative energies, expressed in quasi-independent parts of the governing structure that were designed to press against one another to produce dynamic homeostatic self-regulation and control, is written largest in the Separation of Powers between the Congress, the Supreme Court, and the Presidency. But also within the Congress, there are two Houses designed to be jealous of each other's prerogatives and to look after competing real interests between large and small states. Similarly, within the Supreme Court there are nine quasi-monarchs with life-tenure who must fashion and refashion fragile and shifting coalitions among themselves. Even within the Administration, which comes as near as the framers allowed to representing a single will, there are cabinet officers and the various other departments and offices fated to struggle between and among themselves.

Beyond this there are the even more visible homeostatic controls put upon the Administration by Congress's possession of the purse strings, the congressional right of confirmation, and the congressional powers of making law that the President is sworn faithfully to carry out.

In addition, important from the beginning, is the American Bill of Rights. Within the philosophical framework presented here, the ten initial Amendments stand out as crucial additional homeostatic controls, wisely added to provide internal restraints upon the more powerful, and therefore more potentially dangerous, central government that took effect under the new Constitution. They are all restraining mechanisms of one kind or another. The First Congress, at its opening session in New York, September 25, 1789, submitted these proposals to the states for additional controls in certain areas of special sensitivity. These were the areas of religion, speech, the press, and petition (the First Amendment); a citizen militia (the Second Amendment); private homes, persons, papers, and property (the Third and Fourth Amendments); legal due process (the Fifth and Sixth Amendments); trial by peers (the Seventh Amendment); punishments (the Eighth Amendment); and residual rights of individuals and of the states (the Ninth and Tenth Amendments). The original states, beginning with New Jersey on November 20, 1789, joined the ratification process; and when, on December 15, 1791, Virginia became the eleventh state to ratify, these first ten Amendments came into effect. They have performed their restraining functions, greatly ramified by judicial opinion but unmodified by Constitutional amendment, to this day.

To summarize, an organismic assessment of the American constitutional system will stress its many parallels with healthy organic life. Ideally, at least, there is ample scope within the system for expressions of citizen creativity; however, there are hierarchies of homeostatic controls that should, if they are well served by the network of communications channels that interconnect all levels of the system, function to restrain any dangerous excesses of various parts for the sake of the well-being of the whole. The first level of Federal government under the American Constitution is itself internally restrained by multiple levels of internal homeostatic controls created within the system, with the powers of government carefully separated and balanced in perpetual dynamic tension against one another. Then this complex self-regulated system is itself further restrained by the set of additional homeostatic devices now called the Bill of Rights.

Governing, "steering," society is essential for the possibility of joint creativity, the achievement of common aims. But we have learned from painful experience over the ages that government needs an automatic braking system, cybernetic controls, if individual creativity is not to be crushed. The Pharaohs of Egypt ruled over huge joint achievements with the building of the pyramids, organizing laborers by the tens of thousands in work projects as meticulously fitted together as were the great stone blocks between which no chinks of light could shine. Within this despotic system, lacking homeostatic controls to limit the will of the ruler, the personal dignity of laborers, mainly slaves, counted for nothing. Modern democratic societies have freed slaves and promoted ordinary people to the status of rulers, unleashing personal creativity for the many, but still there remains risk of despotism if no stubborn braking system is in place to slow down sheer majoritarian power over the nonconforming few.

The "mechanisms" for achieving such homeostatic controls may vary with circumstances and history. The American example cited is one way, still at work. The norms involved, rooted in the Enlightenment's discovery of the intrinsic dignity of the individual person, have been widely proclaimed. The American Declaration of Independence (1776) and the French Declaration of the Rights of Man and of the Citizen (1791), for two prime examples, represent historically influential statements on the need to codify restraints on governmental power.

The General Assembly of the United Nations adopted the Universal Declaration of Human Rights in 1948. Putting such declarations into practice, the European Court of Human Rights, based in Strasbourg, France, offers still another practical way. Founded after the Second World War and the Nuremberg Trials, this Court rules on issues brought under the European Convention on Human Rights and Fundamental Freedoms (1953), holding participating governments to account against their own private citizens. Under the Convention, specific positive rights for persons, including the right to privacy, the right to freedom of expression, and the right not to be tortured are officially recognized and enforceable.

In Britain, these rights are at this writing in the process of being incorporated into domestic law, to make it unnecessary for Britons to go to Strasbourg to plead their cases. This will be an impressive evolution. Even Britain, the land of the Magna Carta, which placed homeostatic constraints on monarchy (1215), and of the first modern Bill of Rights, which guaranteed parliamentary supremacy (1689), has until now offered no explicit, legally codified, guarantees of the rights of its citizens against the constant possibility of an oppressive parliamentary majority. Personalistic organicism will warmly welcome these additional protections for persons. In Britain, it seems, creative governing is still devising fresh ways of controlling creativity's own tendency to "govern" to excess. The modern notion of "state sovereignty," in which governments claim not to be accountable for the treatment of their people, requires just such reexamination and worldwide reform for a normative political future. Homeostatic controls at every level of organization, local, national, regional, and global, need to be invented and incorporated into the fabric of relations among persons in postmodern society.

Similarly, the material relations defined by free markets need careful rethinking and reform from the perspective of personalistic organicism. Private need and common good must be incorporated into the economic calculus. In principle, the common goods of breathable air, drinkable water, and unpolluted land must be priorities of any postmodern economic system. Likewise, in principle, persons must not be allowed to sink below a dignified threshold for nourishment, health, and protection from the elements. For reasons we noted earlier, market capitalism is not automatically responsive to either of these great principles. Left to itself, the pure market responds only to demand defined in terms of money and willingness to pay. The literally priceless is not valued. Therefore, the market requires added homeostatic controls, artificial "pricing" mechanisms, designed to hold back the great engine driven by creative personal enterprise from destroying itself through environmental collapse or the unsustainable vandalism of injustice.

MUTUALITY

Talk of injustice reminds us of our fourth ethical maxim, "Be fair," proposed to help guide in the struggle against ugliness and evil. The possibility of fairness, together with the whole ethical enterprise, rests on felt relations. It depends on the power of mentality to get beyond the urgencies of the ego and to recognize real values located elsewhere in a system of values, a system of which we are an intrinsically significant part and in which we find ourselves under obligations.

Personalistic organicism, honoring the norm of healthy life, grounds the obligation to be fair—indeed, the very possibility of ethics—in the intimate interconnectedness of living organisms both within and among themselves. Admittedly, this is not a fully adequate model for justice. Justice blossoms far beyond its organismic roots, only in the developed mentalities of persons living in norm-guided societies. Organic models alone are not enough (Ferré 1989, 231–41). True, but unless some buds of obligation grew first from organic mutuality, there would be nothing that could bloom eventually into fairness.

I trust that in the previous section I said enough to show that homeostasis is vital for healthy life. What makes homeostasis itself possible? The cybernetic controls that keep creativity in equilibrium are based on intricate networks of information and on repertoires of response to changes throughout the system. Organisms are governable only because they are functional wholes, in which the condition of some parts makes a difference to the responses of others. Populations, likewise, if they are to avoid extremes of overshoot and collapse, are stably governable only to the extent that they are functional wholes, sensitive to changes in conditions and actively responsive to them. This organic capacity for systematic interaction, information feedback, and guided coordination is sometimes named "holism," a term I admit to having used (Ferré 1989; 1991; 1993). The word has become so freighted, however, with special philosophical associations—technical baggage of no concern here—that I now prefer the cleaner term, "mutuality."

Mutuality in human society among persons, as in cybernetic mechanisms, plants, or simple animals, involves two main ingredients. There must be a free *flow of information*, and there must be a *disposition to respond* to information received. Without well-defined, reliable feedback channels for information about the condition of various significant parts, there could be no mutuality within the system, since there would be nothing to respond to; without readiness to recognize received information as the appropriate trigger for a response, no amount of information alone would result in an effective state of mutuality among the parts. At the level of a living cell, receipt of chemical information may trigger the increased production of some enzyme. At the level of a living animal, receipt of visual information may trigger a sudden hormonal release that aids in "fight or flight." At the personal level, where human society is organized, we can dub mutuality's necessary ingredients *knowing* and *caring*.

Any human political system aspiring to harness its creativity through homeostatic governance needs to establish reliable channels for the flow of information between its parts. If there is some entity or society (a government) responsible for providing effective unity by setting policy for the system as a whole, healthy functioning requires the flow of accurate information from every affected domain. A reciprocal outflow of information to every part of the society is no less imperative. Ideally, mutuality depends on everyone's knowing what is going on, what is hurting, what is satisfying, what is lacking, what is planned.

But knowing is not enough. Mutuality rests equally on caring. Caring is the trigger that motivates response. For personalistic organicism, the reality of caring is woven into the texture of the universe. Felt real relations are the stuff of all actuality. We can teach ourselves not to care, deflect our attention from the immediate prehensions of other significant centers of value, be so injured that spontaneous feelings of empathy are dulled or even destroyed. Emotions of hatred, fear, greed, or vengeance can be cultivated so as to overwhelm caring for selected others. But, from this philosophical viewpoint, the natural$_{2,3}$ bonds of intuited empathy and imaginatively enhanced sympathy are normally also present to be cultivated, if we will. We must do so, if we are to envision effective mutuality in human society. Given caring, information about the pain or frustration of others will trigger sympathetic responses. Specifically what these responses will be must depend on the actual context and the social levers of power available for remediation. A creative postmodern society designed for homeostasis and mutuality must therefore make thoughtful provisions for enhanced *knowing* and *caring*, and must also make practical provisions for *doing* what defends against harm, preserves existing good, creates more good, and is fair.

In keeping with my resolve to keep the focus of our discussion well "down the runway" as I bring this book to its landing, I will deal briefly with just two remaining topics under the present head of mutuality and fairness. Nonorganicists might want to distinguish these remaining topics as "social" and "personal" ethics, but personalistic organicism rejects such a bifurcation as wrongly implying the notion that the personal can be radically isolated from the social. Persons are always in relationship with other persons, if only in memory and imagination, language and norms. Were it not for social relations, a human individual could not become a person. Therefore, my own distinction between the two remaining topics will be between "macroethics" and "microethics." By macroethics, I mean to suggest norms applicable on the large scale, as in economic systems, national governance, and global polity, recognizing that even the greatest institutions are what they are because of the intelligence and purposes of socially empowered individuals. By microethics, I refer to norms applicable to the conduct of individual lives, recognizing that individual persons always achieve themselves in a social context.

This social context, when it is among persons rather than between persons and other things, permits the full language of "rights" that is awkward and misleading when applied to our ethical relations with animals or the nonliving environment. I have argued that human obligations to value, of whatever type, wherever found, are the basis for nonreciprocated duties. We have duties to respect the kalogenic potential of a rare species, the intrinsic satisfactions of living creatures, the achieved beauty of nonliving environmental features, but none of these has duties toward us or toward one another. They are not moral agents, nor do they have rights in nature$_1$ alone. The gazelle has no "right to life" against the hungry lion; the delicate stalactite formation has no "right to preservation" against the clumsy bear (or earthquake). To the extent we speak meaningfully of "rights" in these cases, we are bending the power of rhetoric to remind humans of their duties toward real values. Rights are a cultural artifact. Only persons can claim them.

But in the society of persons, rights can and should be claimed in the defense of those unique qualities of value achievable by thinking, planning, hoping centers of self-awareness, creativity, and beauty. The mutuality underlying human-to-human relations makes the language of rights reciprocal and literally appropriate. This is not in discontinuity with environmental ethics, in which duties are recognized toward real value; it is a refinement of it. In human society, duties are still based on respect for centers of real value, rights are still reflections of those duties, but in human society our duties are directed toward the special values inherent in moral agents capable of claiming their rights (drawing attention to our duties) and thus to persons under mutual obligation to us and one another. Beyond organicism, this is the personal significance of mutuality: each person in the network of persons, as conscious achievers of intense harmonies of experience, can rightly claim the same basic status that we enjoy.

Looking toward the larger economic picture, two significant "threshold" concepts are crucial for personalistic organicism. The first is "personhood" itself. The qualities and powers that define the personal are far from constant, even during a day's normal experience for a single individual, much less among persons with different levels of physical health or cultural advantage. And yet the qualities of the personal are so important ethically that in most developed cultures even infants who are not yet fully persons, and the ill or handicapped who are no longer (or perhaps were never) able to exercise moral responsibility, significant freedom, or even consciousness, are rightly granted the legal protection and general dignity due to persons. When this respect is extended, it indicates how intensely even potential persons, former persons, and quasi persons are honored by normal adult members of the one species in which, in the standard course of affairs, these personal qualities can be manifested.

Such honor is entirely appropriate. For personalistic organicism, persons represent no radical metaphysical exception but they are exceptionally empowered on the mental pole that functions to some extent in all reality. The attainment of consciousness, of symbolic freedom from the immediate here and now, of long-term anticipation, normative judgment, moral responsibility—these personal capacities thrust human beings, for better or worse, into unique roles in the known universe. As a species we can deliberate, worry, worship, create the highest beauties, and suffer the most intense agonies. As fellow performers in these roles, all normal human adults, and by extension all human beings, pass the threshold of fundamentally mutual moral consideration.

Turning this consideration onto the material needs of human beings, we encounter another threshold concept, that of "poverty." Below a certain level of material conditions, the human organism will survive, if at all, only in misery from hunger, thirst, exposure, fouled respiration, disease, or a mixture of these. This can be empirically defined. Scientists can specify ranges of calories required for good human health, ranges of temperatures that human organisms can tolerate, and so on. Doing this defines "species-based poverty." This is the poverty that concerns me here. Many other thresholds could be defined in other contexts, since "perceived poverty" is notoriously relative to cultural expectations and the economic status of others in the comparison class chosen. People can live richly kalogenic lives in great simplicity without feeling impoverished, though distant others might regard them as far below some culturally defined "poverty line." Perhaps the latter should be called instead the "envy line," to distinguish between fundamental species-based, organically defined, need-reflecting poverty and ever-changing levels of personal wants, in modern culture often generated by advertizing.

The macroethical combination of these two threshold concepts, of personhood with poverty, brings personalistic organicism to the judgment that no person (actual or honorary) should live in poverty unless all must. That is, the standard of fairness reckons each person equally undeserving of a life of misery. If there is an alternative, no human being should be done harm of this sort; if there is an alternative, no human being should be denied the new good of being assisted out of conditions of this sort.

We must be cautious here. The standard of fairness does not call for absolute mathematical equality among all persons. All are equally deserving of life without material misery. If material resources exist that can alleviate such misery, these resources should be distributed first to this end. If this requires the marginal reduction of the material wealth of others living far above species-based poverty, then this is appropriate. But there is no ethical imperative to erase all economic discrepancies on behalf of some homogeneous ideal of a world society shorn of significant differences.

Quite the contrary, personalistic organicism welcomes real cultural variety. There is more than a trace of cultural imperialism in the presumption that every human being requires similar material conditions in order to lead a fulfilled life. Kalogenesis is the goal, not a car in every garage. Joyful experience does not depend on a wealth of machines or even on much "wealth," as that is defined by modern developed nations of the Earth. Some rightly worry what would happen to the environment if all the inhabitants of India, China, Indonesia, and so forth, were to be provided with the same life-style as modern Americans or Europeans. It would place an impossible burden on nature$_2$ and is obviously an absurd goal. Fortunately, it is not an ethically appropriate goal. True, Americans in particular will need to learn much about living more lightly on the Earth; postmodern technology in every domain of life will need to become far wiser. But, for all this, modern hyperdeveloped civilization, even in a reformed mode, need not be taken as the norm. As much as its ecological impossibility, the odor of hegemony rising from the implicit supposition that the "high-tech life" should be the world's universal standard alerts us to its wrongness. The planet can and should support many different modes of life, each with its own beauties, joys, and satisfactions; each with its own sorts of ugliness and evil to combat.

Stepping down from the global scale to the politics of these diverse cultures, a few major ethical concerns will apply to all of them. For personalistic organicism, the maxim, "Be fair," and the norm of mutuality remain relevant, despite differences in cultural contexts. More concretely, this means that it is ethically imperative within cultures to establish and maintain free flowing, reliable information channels. Effective feedback loops make possible early homeostatic responses to destabilizing stresses within the system. People need to know who is in pain, why, and what is needed to restore social health. "Do no harm" and "Preserve existing good" both depend on having accurate and timely information. Put in currently fashionable economic language, every society needs "transparency," both for the good of frustrated individuals in an otherwise unresponsive system and for the good of the system as a whole.

Political homeostasis and mutuality are not ends in themselves. They both serve (and are shaped by) creativity. The point of urging many diverse cultures to bloom, each in its own way, is precisely that they bloom. A kalogenic worldview wants each society, large and small, "to "live, to live well, to live better" (Whitehead 1929, 8). This requires that each member, so far as possible, has the physical and cultural environment needed to support maximum fulfillment as a person in relations. The standard of minimal justice demands for every culture that no member of it live in species-based poverty (unless all must); but beyond this minimum, the norm of creativity urges that something better be achieved in every life. The lure toward relevant novelty is a fundamental factor in all healthy experience. Sometimes this lure may be felt across what I earlier called the "envy line," where discrepancies (always relative to a given cultural comparison-class) may become incentives. For personalistic organicism, personal striving to better oneself is not bad. Paths must be open (this is part of any society's obligation under the fairness maxim), but as long as paths are open they may legitimately be steep. It is not ethically required that everyone end at the same place.

Creativity, focusing on greater goods of kalogenic achievement; homeostasis, focusing on controls against harms of excess; mutuality, focusing on distributional fairness—all are ideals fit for a culturally plural postmodern world. Economic and governmental institutions need to be held to these standards, shaped or reformed accordingly. But what happens when ugliness and evil enter the picture, as personalistic organicism predicts they will? These, I argued, are permanent features of the cosmos, either as vandalism or as philistinism. What ethical measures are appropriate politically in dealing with the tragedy of the universe?

Resolutely focused, as I must be, on that rapidly approaching spot down the runway where I am soon to make a landing, I shall deal in broad ethical terms with this question under the heading of interventions, forceful and otherwise, at different orders of social organization. Ugliness—demanding an ethical response—rises at many levels, including global policies, national laws, local interactions, and family affairs. What are some of the main ethical considerations that personalistic organicism would urge on these remaining macroethical issues?

The question of ethically permissible, or even obligatory, interventions on a world scale barely registered on philosophical radar screens prior to the final years of the twentieth century. From now on, this issue is bound to be a hot one. Part of the reason for its newness is a consequence of the inhibiting effect of the modern doctrine of state sovereignty. As long as it was supposed that nation-states were absolute and unaccountable, especially for what were traditionally called "internal affairs," there could be no circumstances under which positive interventions would be licit. The only issues on the screen would concern the evils of aggression and the mitigation of conflict in "just wars." There are other more practical reasons as well for the new importance of this question. One of the most important is the technological advance toward international "transparency" provided by satellite sensors, telephones, facsimile machines, the Internet, and television. Details about distant disasters or cruelties are now capable of flooding into homes around the world, heightening awareness and kindling sympathy. Just as supposedly sovereign borders are unable to guard against environmental pollutants, climate changes, and the like, so such borders are increasingly less able to keep dirty secrets from being aired. At the same time another ethically significant change has been occurring: now it is possible to do something about catastrophes and atrocities as they unfold. When it was not possible, and whenever it remains impossible, the ethical imperative to intervene does not arise, since "ought" presupposes "can." Even in such cases, there remains the ethical need to make informed judgments. Perhaps such judgments may be institutionalized in ways that will allow them to be effective later, when the circumstances of "can" are changed.

Assuming the presence of solid information and the capacity to influence events, what are the primary ethical considerations before us? First, it is important to notice that we have not yet alluded to contexts in which the maxim, "Create new good," comes first to mind. Yet this is a type of international intervention we must not forget. Governments can be powerful forces for advancing the creative urge toward new satisfactions in the experience of many. Thoughtful technological transfers, cultural exchanges, and the like, are policies in general to be fostered. "Preserve existing good" can seem more dramatic, especially when the survival and well-being of persons threatened by sudden catastrophes, such as earthquake or flood, are what beg for preserving. Ethical interventions of both sorts will be needed in a postmodern world made aware of the many levels of real relatedness urged by personalistic organicism.

But what of helpless persons suffering atrocities against which their own governments are taking no preventive action, or are actively complicit? Advanced information technologies turn up the heat on public sympathies. Observers, outraged by witnessing violations of such basic ethical maxims as "Do no harm," and "Be fair," urge forceful intervention. What was once seen as "meddling in internal affairs" is seen instead by many as a duty to protect basic human rights. From the perspective of this book, this shift in ethical perception is welcome. But careful ethical thinking is still called for, before this prima facie "seen" duty to forceful intervention is determined to be a real one, on balance. Military force applied by states is a blunt instrument. Many unanticipated harms will be done inevitably when it is unleashed. If the suffering can be alleviated by other means (e.g., by diplomatic pressure or economic leverage), it should be. We are obliged to examine our own motives and the likely consequences of our proposed actions as minutely and suspiciously as we scrutinize those of others. Certainly we should refrain from military interventions to "Create new good." The harms we would commit would outweigh the new good we might accomplish. But as a last resort, and in the sober recognition that "Do no harm" is an impossible standard, even in the virtuous quest of preventing worse harms, states (or coalitions of states) may sometimes rightly take it upon themselves to redress grievous wrongs in other states where they are being perpetrated.

Much better, in a postmodern world, would be a standing international enforcement agency, preemptively legitimated by international consensus, trained in minimizing harms, recruited to reflect multicultural diversity, disinterested in particular national or regional ambitions, available for prompt deployment in response to reliable information, and powerful enough to be a credible deterrent to cruel rulers or hate-filled mobs. Personalistic organicism is skeptical of resort to military coercion, but is not a pacifist position. The world is physical as well as mental. Sometimes coercive ugliness and evil need to be met by physical countermeasures. Yet—for all this—these occasions should be as few as possible. Reaching for a weapon should always be done reluctantly, lest the means destroy the end.

Interventions, next, within the national or state level seem far more obviously appropriate, and indeed they are. Intervening to achieve common aims is what governing is all about. The mechanical governor on a simple steam engine intervenes when the machine runs too fast. The brain in vertebrates governs with innumerable interventions, coordinating behavior in response to huge flows of information. To the extent that a nation or state is a coordinated society, it will intervene in the lives of its members. The ethical problem is to judge the degree of such interventions, their aims, and their quality. For personalistic organicism it is not automatically the case that the government is best which "governs least." Rather, the best government will be the one that supports conditions conducive to optimum kalogenic achievement for the widest range of its members, while maintaining fairness, preserving existing good, and defending all against harms, internal and external. This implies, in accordance with Hobbes' view, that an obvious fundamental ethical obligation of government is to protect against the sorts of evils I have called Vandalism, both from foreign enemies and domestic criminals. Military and police forces are legitimated for these functions. But in addition, more positively, personalistic organicism implies that government is also obliged to intervene against Philistinism, making sure that the health and educational needs of its members are fully served. This does not necessarily mean that care of body and mind needs to be "provided" by government, but postmodern government operated on these principles will take care that in fairness no one is excluded from the basic advantages needed to combat the entropic decay represented by illness and ignorance. The tragedy of the universe will never be defeated, but it can and should be fought with the combined resources available to political institutions.

Beyond these fundamentals, personalistic organicism would support governmental assistance, perhaps through subsidies, for the organic and personal technologies. Defense of pure food, clean air, potable water, and decent housing; support for satisfying systems of transportation, and the like—these would be high on the agenda for legitimate governmental intervention. A mixture of creative personal incentives with benevolent regulatory oversight would best reflect personalistic organicism's model of healthy life. Creativity under constraint for the good of further creativity is a worthy goal in the context of mutuality and openness.

Always in the picture for personalistic organicism is the urgent need to arrange political institutions so that there will be homeostatic controls against interventions that are unfair or harmful, especially to minorities otherwise unprotected. "Bills of Rights" (or their equivalent) must be included to govern government, to control the controllers. Active government need not be feared as long as it is designed to assure that its own frailties, its tendencies to excess, are realistically countered.

Apart from official governments at different levels, there are local social situations in which intervention—whether to intervene or not, if so, how to intervene—may become an ethical problem. Neighborhoods and apartment complexes, departments and clubs, have their own political structures. Decisions that can help or harm others need constantly to be made in these nongovernmental political contexts.

Personalistic organicism could have much to say about such contexts, given specifics. Here a few general guidelines will suffice. A loosely knit neighborhood of private, single-family dwellings, for example, can provide an environment for many kalogenic satisfactions. There is the basis in adequate spatial separation for individual freedoms, but also the basis in shared streets, sidewalks, and public areas for friendly relationships according to choice. Ideally, even within a completely informal structure, communication loops can be maintained so that if one household is expecting to hold a large party, the other households potentially affected by noise or parking congestion will be informed in advance (in some cases given invitations) and will respond without rancor. Or perhaps, if a neighbor is disturbed by another neighbor's loud music, there will be good-natured ways of communicating this fact and obtaining voluntary relief. Sometimes neighborhoods form loose associations, electing officers and holding occasional meetings to discuss common concerns. Intervention then can become more structured, but still remain reliant on the neighborhood's own resources. A group of neighbors, for example, may call on a neighbor who is disturbing the community's peace; letters may be written on behalf of the neighborhood association to absentee landlords whose tenants are in violation of community standards. Given creative imaginations, sympathy, and good will, much can be done in neighborhoods before turning outside to governmental remedies such as "calling the police."

From the viewpoint of personalistic organicism, the principal ethical maxims in such informal neighborhood arrangements are "Preserve existing good," "Do no harm," and "Be fair." In some cases, no doubt, it is possible in addition to seek to "Create new good," perhaps by community tree planting, cleaning up, fixing up, and the like. But often these well-intentioned efforts to "improve" fall foul of resentments about intrusiveness and "going too far." The main ethical vulnerability of neighborhood associations is the temptation to encourage "do-gooders" in the pejorative sense we all recognize. The main ethical strength of such associations is defense against harms, unfairness, and the erosion of existing good. Especially when this is expressed through neighborhood "crime watch" activities, when people mutually look out for each other's well being, we see ethics in action. But I need not stress this dimension here, since this is one of the many points at which a smaller, "nested" society is intimately related to a larger society of laws and enforcement. When a crime is observed or suspected, intervention of this sort is no ethical problem; failure to intervene would be the real problem. Since all are aware that there have been shocking examples of such failures, community methods for encouraging mutual responsibility seem well worth a few inevitable cases of irritating busy-bodies.

Condominium living, when organized under a legal declaration or expressed through a corporation with directors and other officers, offers a somewhat different ethical profile. By binding themselves officially together, the owners (unlike the single-dwelling neighborhood) establish a stronger normative interest in positive interventions on behalf of advancing the common good. Defense of existing good and the avoidance of harms still remain strong ethical motives. But, in addition, creating new good may be corporately sought in imaginative projects aimed to increase the kalogenic potential of the condominium as a whole. One warning, however, needs to be voiced. Through all this, and ruling all this, rings the ethical maxim, "Be fair." Nothing erodes condominium satisfactions faster than injustice, using common resources to favor one party's private interest over another's or giving easements to some that could not be universalized to all.

The same need not be said, or need not be said in quite the same way, when we consider family life. For personalistic organicism, families should be based more on love than justice. Basic fairness is still relevant and important. Egregious favoritism that sparks resentment can be a sign of no love or unhealthy love. Love, if it is wise, will make sure that fairness is felt over the long run. It is also vital in family life to make sure that harms are not done and that existing good is preserved. On behalf of such goals, family interventions—by scolding, holding, correcting, protecting—practices intolerably intrusive in other social relationships, are routinely and properly practiced. But the special key to the ethics of family life is not so much protection as creativity. Sometimes this will take biological form, sometimes cultural. Here interventions to boost other family members' kalogenic capacities in ways that could not possibly be universalized are properly carried out. Perhaps everyone scrimps so that one of their own with special aptitudes can go to college. This could not be done for any of the others, much less for neighbor children. But concretely it is recognized as right, though not abstractly fair. Family life is the least "abstract" of the macroethical levels. That is, personalistic organicism sees family life as the closest of all multipersonal relationships to the organic, to the fully natural$_3$ human capacity for feeling preferences.

All family life is richly woven through with thought, since we are thinking animals, but (in Whiteheadian language) causal efficacy is more potent in family relations than in any others. The mental pole is active, as in all personal relations, but here it is most obviously entangled with prehensive feelings and devoted to superjective aims. Family relations, compared to all the societies set up by humans, are the least artificial.

For personalistic organicism it is ethically appropriate that I favor my children over the neighbor's, do things for my spouse or my life partner that I would never dream of doing for everyone in general. There is no need to universalize the maxim of our behavior in these cases.

It could be dangerous to say such things! I do not want to be misunderstood. Personalistic organicism would not want to stimulate or condone predatory instincts of family units toward each other. "Be fair" continues normative in dealings at the neighborhood level and certainly also under the laws of the state or nation. Moreover, families remain under basic ethical obligation to do their just share in preventing anyone's being forced to live in species-based poverty, even if this share requires genuine sacrifices. I also do not want to be interpreted as abandoning the need for qualitative fairness within the family itself. Sometimes a parent needs to say to a child, "But, dear, if I did it for you, I would have to do it for all the other children, and that's obviously impossible." This is often the way that our first sobering lessons in fairness are learned. Sometimes a parent's wise love for the other children can be best expressed in firmly requiring fairness for each. But although fairness counts, love counts even more. In sum: a parent is not a department head. Both are hard jobs. Both call for an appropriately different balance among the ethical maxims. Both depend, in the end, on vulnerable personal judgments.

We return at last where this book began, to the question of vulnerable personal judgments—thus raising once again the paradox of expertise. In ethics we cannot take refuge behind "experts." No one can absolve our ethical judgments of personal responsibility. Even if we put ourselves under some moral authority, we must finally take moral responsibility for that, too. Conscience is fallible. Yet conscience, representing the best ethical norms we know, is not lightly ignored or violated.

Conscience is highly personal, the intimate pull of internalized norms, yet its discussion is not out of place at the end of a chapter on political values. Persons would not be what they are apart from social relations. When we deal with personal ethics, we deal with the microethical, not the unpolitical. To have ethical concepts at all, whether general ones like "good" and "right," or more specific ones like "cowardly" and "generous," requires public language. Ethical concepts are learned along with all others in social interactions. We notice what words are used in which general sorts of recognizable situations, whether in the identification of colors or in the application of moral assessments. As we learn language, we become adept in the evaluative uses of the word "nosey" ("Don't be so nosey about your sister's affairs!") and in distinguishing that word from "selfish" ("It was selfish to take all the cookies!"), even as we discover that both classify as "bad." At the outset of personal life, our childish consciences are formed by internalizing such public concepts, learning the language of morals along with talk about table manners and the colors of our crayons. As long as we are children there is no paradox of expertise for us. There are plenty of experts—our parents, older children, teachers, clergy—all eager to set us straight. But while we are children we are not yet fully responsible persons. The politics of personhood changes as we become adult.

There is, as usual for personalistic organicism, no abrupt "line" to show when moral responsibility becomes a reality. For some it may come early, for some quite late, and for some morally handicapped individuals, sad to say, it may not come at all. But it happens for most humans, assuming normal social contexts, sometime near sexual maturity. From that point, unless advanced senility or some other condition returns us to a childish state, our ethical judgments are our inescapable responsibility. The buck stops with us. What causes we support, whether we worship and with whom, which technologies we employ, whether we vote and for whom we vote, how we relate to our neighbors and the environment, whether we have children and how we rear them—all are fraught with ethical implications and depend on our personal normative judgments. In all this, ethical integrity demands that we follow our best information and our examined conscience.

But we need not remain stuck with the conscience of our childhood or pubescent years. Conscience need not be static.

Between the opening of the first chapter and the ending of this one, this book has variously dealt with ways in which the internalized norms constituting conscience can be recognized as dynamic, open to enlargement and thoughtful correction. For some it is an important liberating thought that ethics has a history of change.

The aura of arbitrariness depends in large part on having fallen prey to an avoidable epistemology. Ethical skepticism is one of the less savory fruits of general modern nervousness about an epistemological gap between human knowing and reliable truth. Personalistic organicism offers a different understanding of the relationship between concepts and experience, experience and the world, in which there is no room for an epistemological gap (Ferré 1998). One ethically essential element of experience is empathy, the feelingful awareness that others are real and important. Empathy is a wholly natural$_3$ feature of human life and can be attended to, cultivated, and enlarged—if we care to. Our modern culture has not much supported such empathy-enlarging exercises in its characteristic institutions or its philosophical attitudes. It has instead tended to foster alienation, isolation, moral atomism. Fortunately, in my view, the dominance of the modern now shows signs of coming to an end. Whatever the postmodern world becomes (my hope is for an Age of Ecology), its first ethical need is to cultivate concrete, relational caring. Once this is done, newly amplified capacities for fellow feeling (physical pole) can be extended through thought and imagination (mental pole), thus nurturing broadened ranges of sympathy in a world parched for kindness.

Can our vision of the world reasonably support such hopes? Whether we can coherently believe that we are free moral agents at all, in a universe described by physics as made up of pulsing energy events, is crucial for the question whether personal norms of conduct can be enlarged by experience and disciplined by thought. Any answers to such questions must themselves rest on value-laden judgments, as we found. But these judgments need not be unthinking. They can be evaluated in a logic appropriate to ultimate questions that insists in principle on considering all the evidence and also on fitting this evidence into patterns that make sense as a whole (Ferré 1996). Such comprehensive and critical thinking is not fashionable among many late modern philosophers; many would argue that ethical thinking can be done without it. Perhaps. But if so, it will be limited ethical thinking, not self-critical about how ethics as a whole fits into the larger contexts of physical and biological science, anthropology, ethology, literature, art, and religion.

Finding the master context for understanding and criticizing our ethical norms, exploring the "context of contexts," required me to deal explicitly with religious world models (RWMs). RWMs help depict to those who hold them what matters most, within which all ethical judgments need to be made and evaluated. Maturing, responsible consciences can be clarified by confronting and being challenged by RWMs. Religion can prod norms that have not hitherto been consciously related to any widest picture. In their turn, RWMs are themselves subject to prodding by norms. Nothing escapes evaluation. I proposed, for this still higher level of assessment, the norms of adequacy, coherence, and effectiveness. But nothing escapes evaluation! Even these norms themselves need to be judged appropriate or not. There is no escaping normative judgment, but at least by the time we have reached such a level of scrutiny, the ultimate values at stake and their connections will have become clear. Taking personal responsibility for judgments by this point will be far from arbitrary, in the sense of "unthinking" or "merely wilful"; instead, these judgments will be the most important—and revealing—expressions that could possibly be exhibited by the finite living persons who make them.

Perhaps the most revealing personal judgment to be made in Western culture, steeped as it is in biblical imagery, is on the question of God. Is this enormous universe guided by a single, central purpose? Are personal categories, such as benevolence, wisdom, and moral perfection, applicable to a real entity responsible for the cosmos? Answering yes declares one's ultimate values and sets a comprehensive "context of contexts" for all one's ethical judgments. Inevitably one's answer, yes or no, must be a matter of judgment, since all the arguments for God themselves rest on basic valuations. The affirmative judgment is widely shared and honorable, one that I fully respect and once joined in myself. That I no longer affirm a single, central image of God does not mean that I cease to hold the personal qualities of benevolence, wisdom, morality, and purpose dear among my highest values. It is the centralization that makes me dubious. The universe contains competing trends. We find vectors toward disintegration, others toward complexity. Perhaps a centralized RWM is oversimple. Perhaps images from polytheism have a better claim to interpret in bold imagery what we find in experience. Or, were we not so firmly enculturated in the West, perhaps we would be drawn even more strongly toward nontheistic imagery from the Buddha or the Tao.

My main concern is that undergirding whatever specific judgments we make on the question of God or gods, the Path or the Way, there should be intelligible theory binding together whatever is healthiest in organic life with what is most excellent in personal existence. The values implicit in such theory do not encompass everything. Exploitation of the Earth or of fellow humans is excluded. Reductionism is incompatible with it. It rejects all-devouring totalitarianisms and alienating atomisms. But there will be a wide, welcoming ecumenism possible on the basis of this underlying worldview. Theists, polytheists, and nontheists of many specific varieties could join in discussing their specific differences and deeper commonalities with "mutual affirmation and admonition." I hope this will become the ecumenism of a much more intimately acquainted, multicultural, postmodern world.

There will be plenty of problems for such ecumenical allies to face. Ugliness and evil are, and will remain, realities to be understood and countered. Distinguishing the two faces of ugliness and evil is a first step. There are only two kinds, in general, but neither can be ignored. Vandalism is the more obvious kind, aggressive and maleficent. Not all vandalism need be "malevolent," strictly speaking, since malevolence (willing evil) suggests deliberate purpose, whereas there are forms of evil and ugliness in nature$_2$ that, although not consciously intended, are no less destructive of existing good. Philistinism, in contrast, may sneak below our notice and defenses. It is powerful, however, since it is allied with the "tragedy of the universe," the tendencies of the universe toward disintegration and disorder. It is as dangerous in the long run as vandalism.

If human beings, the only moral agents with whom we are yet acquainted in this surprising cosmos, are to deal positively with ugliness and evil, we need to band together. We need to bend the energies under our mental control toward swimming upstream against slow entropy and building fresh structures of beauty despite sudden tantrums of natural$_1$ or cultural destruction. We do this as persons in relationships. We create societies, governments, economic systems, technologies. We establish institutions for learning, preserving what we have learned and extending what we know. We expand our understanding of the universe and our planet so that our postmodern technologies can wisely implement the organic and personal values we have examined and found inclusively good. We show tenderness toward our physical environment, respect for our living environment, empathy for our fellow humans. We live according to an Earth ethics that includes cultural ethics as a seamless consequence, committed to showing due respect for real value, of whatever kind, wherever found. We live expansively to achieve new beauty for ourselves. We live restrainedly to be fair to other achievers of beauty, human and otherwise. We live as organisms with needs, but also as persons who can understand and prioritize such needs in relation to a common good.

We live hopefully, appreciating a universe throbbing with the creation of new value. We live thoughtfully, guided by knowledge that is grounded in value. We live mutually, nurturing an ever-expanding web of compassion.

WORKS CITED

Abe, Masao. 1985. *Zen and Western Thought*. Edited by William R. LaFleur. Honolulu: University of Hawaii Press.

Aquinas, Saint Thomas. 1948. *Summa Theologica*. In *Introduction to Saint Thomas Aquinas*. Translated and edited by Anton C. Pegis. New York: Random House.

Aristotle. 1946. *Nicomachean Ethics*. Translated by H. Rackham. Cambridge, Mass.: Harvard University Press.

———. 1951a. *Metaphysics*. Translated by Philip Wheelwright. New York: Odyssey Press.

———. 1951b. *Psychology*. Translated by Philip Wheelwright. New York: Odyssey Press.

Austin, J. L. 1962. *How to Do Things with Words*. Edited by J. O. Urmson. Cambridge, Mass.: Harvard University Press.

Ayer, Alfred Jules. 1946. *Language, Truth and Logic*. London: Victor Gollancz.

Baldwin, Peter A. 1997. *Four and Twenty Blackbirds: Personae Theory and the Understanding of Our Multiple Selves*. Las Vegas, Nev.: Bramble Books.

Bennett, Jonathan. 1974. The Conscience of Huckleberry Finn. In *Philosophy* 49.

Bertocci, Peter A. 1951. *Introduction to Philosophy of Religion*. New York: Prentice-Hall.

Booth, Newell S. Jr. 1977. *African Religions: A Symposium*. New York: NOK Publishers, International.

Brightman, Edgar Sheffield. 1940. *A Philosophy of Religion*. New York: Prentice-Hall.

Burnet, John. 1961. *Early Greek Philosophy*. 4th ed. (1st ed. 1892). Cleveland and New York: World Publishing.

Burns, Robert. 1900. To a Mouse, On Turning Her up in Her Nest, with the Plough, November, 1785. In *The Complete Poetical Works of Robert Burns: With Biographical Introduction, Notes and Glossary*. New York: Thomas Y. Crowell.

Callicott, J. Baird, ed. 1987. *Companion to A Sand County Almanac: Interpretive & Critical Essays*. Madison: University of Wisconsin Press.

———. 1989. *In Defense of the Land Ethic: Essays in Environmental Philosophy*. Albany: State University of New York Press.

Cobb, John B. Jr. 1965. *A Christian Natural Theology, based on the Thought of Alfred North Whitehead*. Philadelphia: Westminster Press.

———. 1967. *The Structure of Christian Existence*. Philadelphia: Westminster Press.

———. 1982. *Beyond Dialogue: Toward a Mutual Transformation of Christianity and Buddhism.* Philadelphia: Fortress Press.

———. 1986. Theology and Space. In *Beyond Spaceship Earth: Environmental Ethics and the Solar System.* Edited by Eugene Hargrove. San Francisco: Sierra Club Books.

Commoner, Barry. 1971. *The Closing Circle.* New York: Bantam Books.

Davies, P. C. W. 1982. *The Accidental Universe.* Cambridge: Cambridge University Press.

De Gennes, P. G. 1990. *Introduction to Polymer Dynamics.* Cambridge: Cambridge University Press.

De Gennes, P. G. and J. Prost. 1993. *The Physics of Liquid Crystals.* Oxford: Clarendon Press.

Defoe, Daniel. 1936. *Life and Adventures of Robinson Crusoe.* New York: Rand McNally.

Descartes, René. 1960. *Discourse on Method.* Translated by Laurence J. Lafleur. Indianapolis: Bobbs-Merrill.

Dickens, Charles. 1988. *A Christmas Carol.* Oxford and New York: Oxford University Press.

———. 1960. *A Tale of Two Cities.* Garden City, N. Y.: Doubleday.

Dostoevsky, Fyodor. 1976. *The Brothers Karamazov.* Translated by Constance Garnett. Edited by Ralph Matlaw. New York: W. W. Norton.

Drinkwater, L. E., P. Wagoner, and M. Sarrantonio. 1998. Legume-Based Cropping Systems Have Reduced Carbon and Nitrogen Losses. In *Nature* 396, Issue 6708 (November 19):262–65.

Du Noüy, Lecomte. 1947. *Human Destiny.* New York: Longmans, Green.

Elder, Frederick. 1970. *Crisis in Eden.* Nashville, TN: Abingdon Press.

Ferré, Frederick. 1961a. *Language, Logic, and God.* New York: Harper.

———. 1961b. The Use and Abuse of Theological Arguments. In *The Journal of Religion*, Vol. XLI, No. 3.

———. 1962. Coauthored with Kent Bendall. *Exploring the Logic of Faith.* New York: Associated Press.

———. 1967. *Basic Modern Philosophy of Religion.* New York: Charles Scribner's Sons.

———. 1970. Grünbaum vs. Dobbs: The Need for Physical Transiency. In *The British Journal for the Philosophy of Science* 21: 278–80.

———. 1972. Grünbaum on Temporal Becoming: A Critique. In *International Philosophical Quarterly* 12, No. 3: 426–45.

———. 1976. *Shaping the Future: Resources for the Post-Modern World.* New York: Harper and Row.

———. 1982. Religious World Modelling and Postmodern Science. In *Journal of Religion*, 62, 261–71.

———. 1983. Organizing Images and Scientific Ideals: Dual Sources for Contemporary Religious World Models. In *Metaphor and Religion: Theolinguistics 2.* Edited by J. P. van Noppen. Brussels: Free University of Brussels.

———. 1984a. In Praise of Anthropomorphism. In *International Journal for Philosophy of Religion* 16: 203–212.

———. 1984b. Urge to Fly. In *AOPA Pilot* 27, No. 9: 53–59.

———. 1986a. Moderation, Morals, and Meat. In *Inquiry* 29; No. 4: 391–406.

———. 1986b. Theodicy and the Status of Animals. In *American Philosophical Quarterly* 23, No. 1: 23–34.

———. 1989. Obstacles on the Path to Organismic Ethics: Some Second Thoughts. In *Environmental Ethics* 11, No. 3: 231–41.

———. 1991. Science, Technology, and Our Bill of Rights. In *The Bulletin of Science, Technology & Society*. Special Issue: *Technology and the Public Life* 11, No. 3: 125–33.

———. 1993 Persons in Nature: Toward an Applicable and Unified Environmental Ethics. In *Zygon: Journal of Religion and Science* 28, No. 4: 441–53.

———. 1995. *Philosophy of Technology*. Athens: The University of Georgia Press.

———. 1996. *Being and Value: Toward a Constructive Postmodern Metaphysics*. Albany: State University of New York Press.

———. 1998. *Knowing and Value: Toward a Constructive Postmodern Epistemology*. Albany: State University of New York Press.

Ferré, Nels F. S. 1947. *Evil and the Christian Faith*. New York: Harper and Brothers.

———. 1951. *The Christian Understanding of God*. New York: Harper and Brothers.

———. 1953. *The Sun and the Umbrella*. New York: Harper and Brothers.

Feuerbach, Ludwig. 1957. *The Essence of Christianity* Translated by George Eliot. New York: Harper and Row.

Fox, Michael W. 1990. *Inhumane Society: the American Way of Exploiting Animals*. New York: St. Martin's Press.

Frankena, William K. 1973. *Ethics*. 2nd ed. Englewood Cliffs, N.J.: Prentice-Hall.

Golley, Frank B. 1986. Environmental Ethics and Extraterrestrial Ecosystems. In *Beyond Spaceship Earth: Environmental Ethics and the Solar System*. Edited by Eugene Hargrove. San Francisco: Sierra Club Books.

Goodenough, Ursula. 1998. *The Sacred Depths of Nature*. New York: Oxford University Press.

Griffin, David Ray. 1976. *God, Power, and Evil: A Process Theodicy*. Philadelphia: Westminster Press.

———. 1991. *Evil Revisited: Responses and Reconsiderations*. Albany: State University of New York Press.

Hargrove, Eugene, ed. 1986. *Religion and Environmental Crisis*. Athens: The University of Georgia Press.

Harrison, David and Mark Jaques. 1966. *Experiments in Virtual Reality*. Oxford: Butterworth/Heinemann.

Hartshorne, Charles. 1962. *The Logic of Perfection, and other Essays in Neoclassical Metaphysics*. LaSalle: Open Court.

Heidegger, Martin. 1977. *The Question Concerning Technology and Other Essays*. Translated by William Lovitt. New York: Harper and Row.

Heim, Michael. 1993. *The Metaphysics of Virtual Reality*. New York: Oxford University Press.

Herskovits, Melville J. 1948. *Man and His Works: The Science of Cultural Anthropology*. New York: A. A. Knopf.

Hightower, Jim. 1973. *Hard Tomatoes, Hard Times: A Report of the Agribusiness Accountability Project on the Failure of America's Land Grant College Complex*. Cambridge, Mass: Schenkman Publishing.

Hobbes, Thomas. 1993. *Leviathan*. In *Morality and Moral Controversies*. Edited by John Arthur. Englewood Cliffs, N.J.: Prentice Hall.

Hume, David. 1955. *Treatise*. Edited by L. A. Selby-Bigge. Oxford: Clarendon Press.

Huxley, Aldous. 1946. *Brave New World*. New York: Harper and Brothers.

James, William. 1902. *The Varieties of Religious Experience*. New York: Modern Library.

———. 1948. The Sentiment of Rationality (1880). In *Essays in Pragmatism*. Edited by Alburey Castell. New York: Hafner.

Kant, Immanuel. 1929. *Critique of Pure Reason*. Translated by Max Müller. Edited by Theodore Meyer Greene. New York: Charles Scribner's Sons.

———. 1949. *Fundamental Principles of the Metaphysics of Morals*. Translated by Thomas K. Abbott. New York: Liberal Arts Press.

———. 1956. *Critique of Practical Reason*. Translated by Lewis White Beck. Indianapolis: Bobbs-Merrill.

———. 1963. *Lectures on Ethics*. Translated by Louis Infield. Indianapolis: Hackett.

Kierkegaard, Søren. 1954. *Fear and Trembling*. Translated by Walter Lowrie. Garden City, New York: Doubleday.

Kirk, G. S. & J. E. Raven. 1962. *The Presocratic Philosophers: A Critical History with a Selection of Texts*. Cambridge: Cambridge University Press. First printed 1957.

Kübler-Ross, Elizabeth. 1969. *On Death and Dying*. New York: Macmillan.

Kuhn, Thomas. 1970. *The Structure of Scientific Revolutions*. Chicago: University of Chicago Press.

Lal, Rattan, ed. 1995. *Soil Management and Greenhouse Effect*. Boca Raton, La.: Lewis Publishers.

Lamont, Lansing. 1965. *Day of Trinity*. New York: Atheneum.

Leopold, Aldo. 1966. *A Sand County Almanac: With Essays on Conservation from Round River*. New York: Ballentine Books.

Lofting, Hugh. 1948. *The Story of Dr. Dolittle, Being the History of His Peculiar Life at Home and Astonishing Adventures in Foreign Parts*. Illustrated by the author, with an introduction to the 10th printing by Hugh Walpole. Philadelphia: Lippincott.

Lovelock, J. E. 1979. *Gaia, a New Look at Life on Earth*. New York: Oxford University Press.

Maslow, Abraham. 1970. *Motivation and Personality*. New York: Harper and Row.

McDaniel, Jay B. 1989. *Of God and Pelicans: A Theology of Reverence for Life*. Louisville, Ky.: Westminster/John Knox Press.

McKibben, Bill. 1989. *The Death of Nature*. New York: Random House.

McNaughton, David A. 1988. *Moral Vision*. Oxford: Basil Blackwell.

Midgley, Mary. 1984. *Animals and Why they Matter*. Athens: The University of Georgia Press.

Mill, John Stuart. 1993. *Utilitarianism* (1861). In *Morality and Moral Controversies*. Edited by John Arthur. Englewood Cliffs, N.J.: Prentice-Hall.

Miller, David L. 1974. *The New Polytheism: Rebirth of the Gods and Goddesses*. New York: Harper and Row.

Monastersky, R. 1996. Living Large on the Precambrian Planet. In *Science News*, (May 18).

Moore, G. E. 1956. *Principia Ethica*. Cambridge: Cambridge University Press.

Mumford, Lewis. 1972. Technics and the Nature of Man. In *Philosophy and Technology*. Edited by Carl Mitcham and Lewis Mackey. New York: Free Press.

Murphy, Nancey and George F. R. Ellis. 1996. *On the Moral Nature of the Universe: Theology, Cosmology, and Ethics*. Minneapolis, Minn.: Fortress Press.

Nagel, Ernest. 1961. *The Structure of Science*. New York: Harcourt, Brace and World.

Neugebauer, O. 1969. *The Exact Sciences in Antiquity*. 2nd Ed. New York: Dover.

Neville, Robert C. 1991. *Behind the Masks of God: An Essay Toward Comparative Theology*. Albany: State University of New York Press.

———. 1995. *Creativity and God: A Challenge to Process Theology*. 2nd Ed. Albany: State University of New York Press.

Nickle, Keith F. and Timothy F. Lull. 1993. *A Common Calling: The Witness of Our Reformation Churches in North America Today*. Minneapolis, Minn.: Augsburg Fortress.

Nietzsche, Friedrich. 1954. The Gay Science. In *The Portable Nietzsche*. Edited and translated by Walter Kaufmann. New York: Viking Press.

Odum, Eugene. 1971. *Fundamentals of Ecology*. Philadelphia: Saunders.

Orr, David. 1997. Architecture as Pedagogy II. In *Conservation Biology* 11, No. 3: 597–99.

Paley, William. 1963. *Natural Theology: Selections*. Edited by Frederick Ferré. Indianapolis: Bobbs-Merrill. (Originally published 1802.)

Peacocke, Arthur. 1993. *Theology for a Scientific Age: Being and Becoming—Natural, Divine, and Human*. Minneapolis, Minn.: Fortress Press.

Plato. 1937a. *Apology*. In *The Dialogues of Plato*. Vol. 1. Translated by B. Jowett. New York: Random House.

———. 1937b. *Protagoras*. In *The Dialogues of Plato*. Vol. 1. Translated by B. Jowett. New York: Random House.

———. 1954. *The Republic of Plato*. Translated by Francis MacDonald Cornford. New York and London: Oxford University Press.

———. 1985a. *Crito*. Translated by R. E. Allen. In *Greek Philosophy: Thales to Aristotle*. Revised and expanded edition. Edited by R. E. Allen. New York and London: Free Press and Collier Macmillan Publishers.

———. 1985b. *Timaeus*. Translated by F. M. Cornford. Indianapolis: Bobbs-Merrill.

Polkinghorne, John. 1994. *The Faith of a Physicist: Reflections of a Bottom-Up Thinker*. Princeton: Princeton University Press.

Rasmussen, Larry L. 1996. *Earth Community, Earth Ethics*. Maryknoll, N. Y.: Orbis Books.

Raven, Peter H., Helena Curtis, and Ray F. Evert. 1976. *Biology of Plants*. 2nd Ed. New York: Worth Publishers.

Rolston, Holmes III. 1986. Preservation of Natural Value in the Solar System. In *Beyond Spaceship Earth: Environmental Ethics and the Solar System*. Edited by Eugene Hargrove. San Francisco: Sierra Club Books.

————. 1988. *Environmental Ethics: Duties to and Values in the Natural World*. Philadelphia: Temple University Press.

————. 1999. *Genes, Genesis and God: Values and Their Origins in Natural and Human History*. Cambridge: Cambridge University Press.

Ross, W. D. 1988. *The Right and the Good*. Indianapolis: Hackett. (Originally published 1930.)

Roszak, Theodore. 1969. *The Making of a Counter Culture*. Garden City, N.Y.: Doubleday Anchor Books.

————. 1973. *Where the Wasteland Ends: Politics and Transcendence in Postindustrial Society*. Garden City, N. Y.: Anchor Books.

Russell, Bertrand. 1951. A Free Man's Worship. In *Mysticism and Logic: And Other Essays*. London: George Allen and Unwin.

Sagan, Carl. 1973. *The Cosmic Connection*. Garden City, N. Y.: Anchor Press.

Schumacher, E. F. 1973. *Small is Beautiful: A Study of Economics as if People Mattered*. London: Bond and Briggs.

Shinn, Roger. 1996. *The New Genetics: Challenges for Science, Faith, and Politics*. Wakefield, R. I. and London: Moyer Bell.

Sinnott-Armstrong, Walter and Mark Timmons. 1996. *Moral Knowledge? New Readings in Moral Epistemology*. Oxford: Oxford University Press.

Toulmin, Stephen. 1961. *Foresight and Understanding*. Bloomington: Indiana University Press.

Treaty on Principles Governing the Activities of States in the Exploration and Use of Outer Space, Including the Moon and Other Celestial Bodies. 1967. 18 U.S.T. 2410, T.I.A.S. 6347, 610 U.N.T.S. 205, 27 January.

Truman Show, The. 1998. Directed by Peter Weir. Paramount Pictures.

Voltaire. 1992. *Candide*. Translated by Richard Aldington. New York: Modern Library.

Wexelblat, Alan, ed. 1993. *Virtual Reality: Applications and Explorations*. Boston: Academic Publishers Professional.

White, Lynn Jr. 1967. The Historical Roots of Our Ecologic Crisis. In *Science* 155, (10 March):1203–1207.

Whitehead, Alfred North. 1925. *Science and the Modern World*. New York: Macmillan.

————. 1926. *Religion in the Making*. New York: Macmillan.

————. 1929. *The Function of Reason*. Boston: Beacon Press.

————. 1938. *Modes of Thought*. New York: Macmillan.

————. 1978. *Process and Reality: An Essay in Cosmology*. Corrected Edition. Edited by David Ray Griffin and Donald W. Sherburne. New York: Free Press.

Wilson, E. O. 1998. *Consilience: The Unity of Knowledge*. New York: Knopf.

Zhai, Philip. 1998. *Get Real: A Philosophical Adventure in Virtual Reality*. Lanham, Md.: Rowman and Littlefield.

Note on Supporting Center

This series is published under the auspices of the Center for Process Studies, a research organization affiliated with the Claremont School of Theology and Claremont Graduate University. It was founded in 1973 by John B. Cobb, Jr., Founding Director, and David Ray Griffin, Executive Director; Marjorie Suchocki is now also a Co-director. It encourages research and reflection on the process philosophy of Alfred North Whitehead, Charles Hartshorne, and related thinkers, and on the application and testing of this viewpoint in all areas of thought and practice. The center sponsors conferences, welcomes visiting scholars to use its library, and publishes a scholarly journal, *Process Studies*, and a newsletter, *Process Perspectives*. Located at 1325 North College, Clarement, CA 917111, it gratefully accepts (tax-deductible) contributions to support its work.

Name Index

Abe, Masao, 210
Abelard, Pierre, 197
Abraham, 11, 12, 119, 149
Adam, 34
Aesop, 83
Alexander, Samuel, 209
Allan, George, xi
Anselm, Saint, 179
Aquinas, Saint Thomas, 35–37, 38,
   181, 183, 184
Aristotle, 27, 30–33, 35–36, 38, 171,
   188, 192, 193, 194, 198, 284, 286,
   291, 297, 302, 303, 304, 305–306,
   307
Augustine, 34–35, 235
Ayer, A. J., 54–57, 59, 68, 99, 101, 102

Bacon, Roger, 302
Bennett, Jonathan, 98
Bentham, Jeremy, 50–51
Bernard, Claude, 324
Bertocci, Peter A., 230–31
Brightman, Edgar S., 229–31
Bruno, Giordano, 153, 154
Butler, Bishop Joseph, 52

Cannon, Walter, 324
Cobb, John B. Jr., xi, 207–208, 210,
   252
Commoner, Barry, 156
Copernicus, Nicholas, 151–152, 153,
   154, 205, 303
Cromwell, Oliver, 42

Darwin, Charles, 183–84

de Gennes, Pierre-Gilles, 134
Democritus, 32, 153
Descartes, René, 39–42, 59, 102, 108,
   110, 179, 181, 307
Duns Scotus, John, 37–39, 42, 59

Eichmann, Adolf, 220
Einstein, Albert, 126, 157, 283
Epicurus, 40, 61
Eve, 34

Ferré, Nels F. S., 211, 228, 233–34
Feuerbach, Ludwig, 161
Freud, Sigmund, 207

Galileo, 40, 44, 151, 153, 154, 205,
   249, 302
Goodenough, Ursula, 211
Golley, Frank, xi, 251–52
Grange, Joseph, xi
Granrose, John, xii
Griffin, David Ray, xi, 232–33

Hamlet, 180
Hammurabi, Babylonian king, 26
Hartshorne, Charles, 179, 207–208
Hawking, Stephen, 225
Hegel, Georg, 171
Heidegger, Martin, 171
Hero of Alexandria, 307
Herskovits, Melville J., 74
Hertz, Heinrich Rudolph, 283
Hitler, Adolf, 10, 92, 220
Hobbes, Thomas, 40–42, 59, 63, 102,
   336

SUBJECT INDEX